THE GANGS OF
MANCHESTER

Reviews for *The Gangs of Manchester*

'With the skill of a novelist, Davies weaves together the fruits of meticulous research to recreate the Manchester of the late 19th century in all its appalling fascination. An absorbing read and a must for anyone who wants to understand life in the classic slum.'

Family History Monthly

'A vivid account of the scuttlers, local gangs of fighting youths who defended their honour and territory with fierce aggression. They terrorised Manchester and Salford for thirty years, up until the late 1890s, and Andrew Davies brings extraordinary detail to bear in his study. This is an absolutely fantastic achievement.'

Geoffrey Pearson, Emeritus Professor of Criminology, Goldsmiths College, University of London.

'Andrew Davies' lively, well-researched book demonstrates clearly that the knife-wielding teenage gangster is not a new phenomenon … Davies has done a masterly job in piecing together the lives of the scuttlers and the rise and fall of different gangs in different districts of Manchester.'

BBC History Magazine

'Exposes the ugly history of the city's unique brand of adolescent warfare … Fascinating.'

Salford Advertiser

'Well thought out, brilliantly told, historically accurate and definitive work about a phenomenon that swept the slums of Manchester during the Victorian times…If you don't know the streets of Manchester or Salford, it will not impair your enjoyment for a book that is simply the best of its kind.'

Mike Duff, author of *Low Life* and *The Hat Check Boy*

THE GANGS OF MANCHESTER

The Story of the Scuttlers
Britain's First Youth Cult

Andrew Davies

MILO BOOKS

First published in September 2008 by Milo Books

This edition published in May 2009

Copyright © 2008 Andrew Davies

ISBN 978 1 903854 85 3

Photographs reproduced with kind permission of
Staffordshire Record Office, Greater Manchester Police Museum,
Manchester Central Library and Salford Lads' Club.

Printed in Great Britain by
Cox & Wyman Ltd, Reading, Berkshire

MILO BOOKS LTD
The Old Weighbridge
Station Road
Wrea Green
Preston PR4 2PH
United Kingdom
www.milobooks.com

For Mike Duff

Andrew Davies is a senior lecturer in history at the University of Liverpool. He specialises in the history of crime in modern Britain, and has published widely on gangs, crime and policing. He lived for many years in Salford, Greater Manchester.

Contents

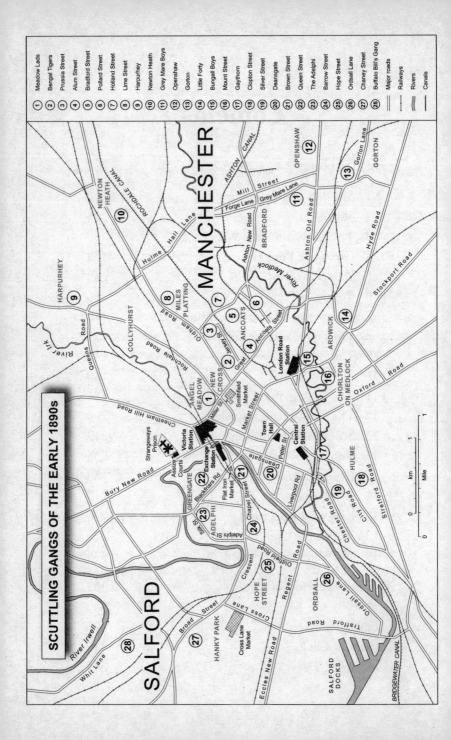

SCUTTLING GANGS OF THE EARLY 1890s

①	Meadow Lads
②	Bengal Tigers
③	Prussia Street
④	Alum Street
⑤	Bradford Street
⑥	Pollard Street
⑦	Holland Street
⑧	Lime Street
⑨	Harpurhey
⑩	Newton Heath
⑪	Grey Mare Boys
⑫	Openshaw
⑬	Gorton
⑭	Little Forty
⑮	Bungali Boys
⑯	Mount Street
⑰	Gaythorn
⑱	Clopton Street
⑲	Silver Street
⑳	Deansgate
㉑	Brown Street
㉒	Queen Street
㉓	The Adelphi
㉔	Barrow Street
㉕	Hope Street
㉖	Ordsall Lane
㉗	Chaney Street
㉘	Buffalo Bill's Gang

▬▬	Major roads
┼┼┼	Railways
≈≈≈	Rivers
- - -	Canals

CHAPTER 1

Scuttlers and Scuttling

AT A QUARTER to ten on the night of Sunday, 3 August 1890, a gang of youths from Harpurhey in north Manchester went to war. Armed with knives and heavy-buckled belts, they left their regular stamping ground and marched for a mile and a half towards the heart of the city's slums. Their path, Rochdale Road, a broad, cobbled thoroughfare scored by the metal tracks of the horse-drawn tramway, took them south through the district of Collyhurst. On they went, passing street after street of soot-blackened, two-up, two-down terraced cottages, their brass-tipped clogs clattering over the cobbles. Bystanders stared as the grimly determined, stunted figures swept past. Knots of youths gathered on the street corners melted into the shadows. A few shouted defiance. They were swiftly scattered, but the Harpurhey lads had not come to wreak random violence. Their enemy lay ahead.

The marchers quickened their step as they approached New Cross. This was a dismal neighbourhood, rank with foreboding. Thick, sulphurous smoke filled the air. In the shadow of the Rochdale Road gas works, tucked beneath a railway bridge, they found their quarry. A group of youths was waiting for them outside the Saracen's Head public house. The lads gathered around the pub door were members of the Bengal Tigers, the most notorious gang in Manchester. Hailing from Bengal Street in nearby Ancoats, they were seasoned street fighters. They had heard the oncoming band approach and were ready for the fray.

The Harpurhey lads were risking all, for Ancoats was Manchester's own 'Dark Continent'. Fields and woodland on the outskirts of the old town had given way to the greatest concentration of industry in the world. Cotton mills, many six storeys high, now dominated the skyline, their chimneys towering over narrow, cobbled streets in which rows of tiny, jerry-built terraced houses huddled under a permanent pall of smoke. Many of the houses had been built back-to-back, without windows on three sides or yards of any kind between them. Iron foundries, engineering works, dye-works, glass-works, timber-yards, brickyards and canal wharves had been crammed together to make Ancoats the heart of what journalist Angus Reach called 'smoky, dingy, sweltering and toiling Manchester'. Barges plied the filthy waters of the Rochdale and Ashton canals. In the maze of side streets and dilapidated courtyards, with their communal taps and privies, poverty had combined with drink and violence for three generations.[1] A well-heeled lady visitor, touring the district, was shocked to find the same grim conditions in street after street, court after court: 'dirt, squalor, and wickedness everywhere. Heavy-eyed men, half-dressed, lounge at the corners and favour you with a stare of surly curiosity as you pass; untidy women with bare arms and tousled heads sit on the dirty doorsteps, alternately gossiping and quarrelling. You glance in at the open doorways, and shiver at the filth and wretchedness.' Few outsiders dared to venture into Ancoats at night when the drink fiend was unloosed and broken shins and split heads were all too common.

The Harpurhey lads steeled themselves. Tom Penders stepped to the front of the mob and challenged one of the Bengal Tigers by the name of John Connor. Before Connor could reply, the Harpurhey mob charged, swinging the buckle ends of their heavy leather belts above their heads. Connor tried desperately to fight back. He wrestled a belt out of Penders' hands and lashed it at the heads of his assailants before he was overpowered by weight of numbers. Three of the Harpurhey lads closed in on him. Drawing their knives, they plunged them into his neck, shoulders and back. A companion of Connor's, Pat Maloney,

---

1 A privy was an outdoor lavatory without plumbing. The contents were emptied by 'night soil men'.

fared even worse. As the fight spilled into Lees Street he took a blow from a belt to his right eye, causing the eyeball to haemorrhage. Maloney had already lost the use of his left eye in a previous street fight. Suddenly blinded, he staggered about the cobbles in a daze as his gang were cut down around him. In all, around a dozen Bengal Tigers suffered knife wounds. Martin Jennings was stabbed in the arm and neck. Charlie Heery was stabbed in the cheek, shoulder and chest. Heery's thirty-year-old brother, Michael, went to his aid but was in turn stabbed in the face and body and left lying unconscious in the street. The wounds were carefully inflicted. The Harpurhey lads' intention was not to murder, but to maim and disfigure.

Their mission accomplished, the Harpurhey group split into twos and threes to render themselves as inconspicuous as possible as they made their way back up Rochdale Road. The most severely wounded of the Tigers were taken by their friends to Manchester Royal Infirmary, where their cuts and contusions were treated. Pat Maloney was immediately admitted as an in-patient. The police learned of the carnage only when they were notified by staff at the Infirmary. A sergeant and two constables were sent to make inquiries, but the injured youths refused to name their assailants. Instead the police questioned residents of Lees Street and began to piece together an account of the fighting. Tom Penders and John Dumphy were arrested before the night was out. Three of their associates – Bobby Hartley, Jimmy Barlow and John Ford – were taken into custody over the course of the following week, and the five Harpurhey youths stood trial together before the Recorder of Manchester, Henry Wyndham West, Q.C., at the Quarter Sessions on August 12, charged on five separate counts of inflicting grievous bodily harm.[2] The jury accepted an alibi on behalf of Ford, but found Penders, Dumphy, Hartley and Barlow guilty. The foreman told

---

2 The Quarter Sessions served as an intermediate court, hearing cases that were deemed too serious to be dealt with by magistrates with their limited powers but not serious enough to be tried before a judge at an Assize Court. The Recorder of Manchester acted as a part-time judge and presided over all trials held at the city's Quarter Sessions.

the court that his fellow jurors were appalled by the defendants' apparent disregard for the gravity of the offence. In the jury's view, the prisoners ought to be flogged.

Recorder Henry West agreed that flogging would be the 'most wholesome' punishment for such youths. However, he held no such powers under English law, which permitted flogging for robbery with violence but not for inflicting grievous bodily harm. Mr West called for a public debate on the utility of flogging in cases of scuttling. Meanwhile, he sentenced Dumphy and Barlow to five years' penal servitude, a combination of imprisonment and forced labour which had replaced the old system of transportation. Hartley was jailed for twelve months, Penders for six.

The convicted youths were all aged eighteen. They worked as labourers, hired purely for their stamina and strength. The work, whether on building sites, in warehouses and markets, or in the innumerable factories and workshops of Manchester's industrial districts, was monotonous and poorly paid, but they had few legitimate alternatives. The lads' criminal records were unremarkable. John Dumphy and Bobby Hartley had a shared history of petty lawlessness and brushes with the police. Dumphy had four previous convictions for assault; Hartley had two for assaulting the police and five for drunkenness. Jimmy Barlow had just one previous conviction, for obstructing the highway. Tom Penders had no criminal record. Leading the charge on the night of August 3 was more than likely Penders' way of proving his mettle in the eyes of his peers.

The Harpurhey lads were bound by allegiance to territory. In matters of religion and national identity, they were ecumenical: their ranks included Protestants and Catholics, Englishmen and Manchester-Irish. Dumphy, a Catholic, was a native of Wexford in Ireland. His family had moved to Manchester when he was a young child. His father worked as a hawker, eking out a living by selling foodstuffs from a barrow. As a schoolboy, Dumphy lived in a four-roomed, 'two-up, two-down' terraced house with his parents, three brothers and one sister. The house was shared with another family of recent migrants from Ireland comprising a labourer, his wife and their three young children. With four adults and eight children crammed into a house built for a single family, Dumphy effectively grew up on the grimy streets off Rochdale Road.

At eighteen, Dumphy was five feet, three inches tall. He was heavily scarred: prison officers noted two scars across his forehead and one on his chin, plus multiple wounds on his legs. His friend Jimmy Barlow was just five feet tall. A thick scar across the back of his head had been inflicted with the buckle end of a belt. Dumphy and Barlow were initially held at Strangeways Prison in Manchester. After four weeks they were moved to Stafford gaol, where they spent the next twenty-eight days in solitary confinement, picking oakum in their cells. Oakum consisted of pieces of old ship's rope, thick with tar, and prisoners were required to pull the strands apart until they were as fine as silk. This was an arduous task and the oakum was filthy, more like wire than flax. Failure to pick the required three pounds per day was punishable by a bread-and-water diet, leaving many convicts in a state of more or less constant hunger.

Their spells in 'solitary' over, the two scuttlers were introduced to the treadwheel. Once on the wheel, the convict had to lift his body up three feet at each step. Prisoners at Stafford were required to ascend 16,630 feet each day. It was not unknown for strong men to be led away crying after their first stint. A survey of the gaol in 1887 noted that the effects of the wheel were quickly seen in a prisoner's appearance. Within a fortnight, his friends 'would be horrified to see him, and he would scarcely recognise himself if he looked in a mirror'. The wheel could be dangerous, too: 'one man fell off from sheer exhaustion. The cry "a man down" was soon raised, and the mill was at once stopped, but not until he had been terribly crushed by it.' In May 1891, Dumphy and Barlow were transferred to Portsmouth Convict Prison to serve the remainder of their sentences. Here prisoners were divided into gangs of a very different sort: silent work parties, constantly watched over by the warders. At Portsmouth the work was much more arduous than at Stafford; stone-breaking was the very definition of 'hard labour'.

There was little to distinguish the Harpurhey lads from their victims, two of whom – John Connor and Charlie Heery – also worked as labourers. Martin Jennings was employed in an Ancoats dye-works, whilst Pat Maloney was a hawker. The Ancoats lads' surnames testified to their Irish-Catholic backgrounds, but they had not been targeted on account of their nationality. This was a territorial conflict. The purpose of the raid was simple: to etch the name of Harpurhey alongside Ancoats in the annals of the Manchester 'Rough'.

The affray on the night of August 3 was just one in a long series of outbreaks of gang violence in Manchester and the neighbouring county borough of Salford during the spring and summer of 1890. Indeed, the Manchester conurbation had witnessed an epidemic of gang-fighting over the previous twelve months as a number of long-running territorial feuds came to a head. Henry West's call for a debate on flogging led to a special meeting of the Manchester magistrates on August 28. A resolution in favour of the lash, the dreaded cat o' nine tails, was passed unanimously and plans were made to send a deputation from Manchester to petition the Home Secretary on the subject. The local press was aghast at the level of violence in the city's poorer districts, noting with horror that the rising generation of slum-dwellers appeared to be addicted to violence. These youthful desperadoes even had their own word for gang fighting: they called it 'scuttling'.

TO THE liberal, and predominantly middle-class, readers of the *Manchester Guardian*, scuttling was a puzzling as well as disturbing phenomenon. Ensconced in their villas in salubrious suburbs such as Withington, Didsbury and Higher Broughton, they knew little of the lives of young people in Manchester's impoverished factory districts and they understood less. Why on earth, they wanted to know, did these gangs of lads band together to wage war on each other? In response to a stream of letters from appalled readers, the *Guardian*'s editor, C. P. Scott, commissioned a lengthy feature article on 'Scuttlers and Scuttling' which he published on September 5. The article was written by Alexander Devine.

Outside the ranks of the scuttlers themselves, Devine was as well-qualified as anyone to comment. Then aged twenty-five, he was only a few years older than many of the lads whose lives he described. In terms of social standing, however, he came from a different universe. Devine's father owned the Cornbrook printing works and his family, plus servants, lived in a grand house in the middle-class enclave of Rusholme. In his youth, Alexander Devine was a popular Sunday school teacher and an aspiring journalist, establishing his own journal, the *Rusholme Magazine*, in his late teens. At nineteen he launched the highly successful *South Manchester Gazette*, only to find himself squeezed out of the editorship by one of his financial backers. He found alternative employment as a police court news reporter for the *Guardian*.

Devine's daily visits to the City Police Court in Minshull Street quickly familiarised him with the perils of scuttling. The Police and Sessions Courts had been completed in 1873 at a cost of £81,000. This handsome Venetian Gothic structure, with its impressive clock tower, had been carefully designed so that those seeking entry to the public galleries were unable to mingle with the judges, magistrates or jurors in any of its corridors. The cells were in the basement. Here Devine encountered a class of youths whose behaviour initially appeared almost to defy comprehension. Keen to discover the roots of the violence, Devine entered into a series of discussions with police officers and clergymen. He became convinced that the origins of scuttling lay in the neglect of the welfare of working-class lads between the ages of thirteen and seventeen.[3] As Devine saw it:

At that age they are rapidly losing the smattering of education they obtain in the Board Schools, and are receiving a very different one in the factory and the street. They go to work at twelve or thirteen years of age and during the day they are employed. But at night what becomes of them? They have no

---

3 'Board Schools', controlled by locally elected school boards, were established for pupils aged from five to twelve under the terms of the 1870 Education Act.

homes worthy of the name in which to spend their time; but are thrown on the streets or other less desirable places, exposed to all kinds of temptations, the victims for which crime and mischief of all kinds is hunting.

As a court reporter in the years 1884-5, Devine covered the trials of dozens of scuttlers. In January 1887, he established Manchester's first working lads' club in Hulme. Later that year, he secured the newly created post of Police Court Missionary to Lads, working with first-time offenders so that they might be spared the stigma of imprisonment. Devine devoted the next three years to voluntary work with youths in some of the city's worst slums. Feeling obliged to define the terms 'scuttler' and 'scuttling' for the benefit of readers with no direct knowledge of the gangs, he wrote:

> It is surprising how few people, outside of the police and those residing in the immediate neighbourhoods where the outrages occur, really know what 'scuttling' is. In the first place, the 'scuttler' is not a thief, nor does he aspire to be a highwayman; he does not 'scuttle' for any actually dishonest purpose.

WHAT IS A SCUTTLER?

A 'scuttler' is a lad, usually between the ages of 14 and 18, or even 19, and 'scuttling' consists of the fighting of two opposed bands of youths, who are armed with various weapons.

In Devine's account, Manchester's gang conflicts were borne of a sheer love of fighting.

Before attempting to probe more deeply into the causes of scuttling, Devine gave a detailed account of the spread of the gangs and the nature of their feuds. Bands of scuttlers were found throughout the poorer, working-class districts of the Manchester conurbation. Most took their names from the thoroughfares in which they congregated: the 'Grey Mare Boys' from Grey Mare Lane in Bradford; 'Holland Street' from Miles Platting; 'Alum

Street' from Ancoats; 'Ordsall Lane' and 'Hope Street' from Salford. Others, like the Bengal Tigers, adopted more exotic names: the 'Bungall Boys' from Fairfield Street off London Road; the 'Little Forty' from Hyde Road in Ardwick; the 'Buffalo Bill' gang from the colliery district of Whit Lane in Salford. Devine noted that scuttling gangs were highly organised. They frequently fought by appointment, with times and venues announced via chalked messages days ahead of the impending clash. Gang fights, or 'scuttles', took place on crofts, pieces of vacant ground in the otherwise densely-populated districts that ringed Manchester city centre, or in the streets, to the consternation of passers-by and local shopkeepers. Feuds between rival gangs extended over periods of twelve or even eighteen months in seemingly endless tit-for-tat raids. And scuttlers did not necessarily fight fairly. As Devine pointed out, 'Often a number of lads forming part of a certain set will attack, without any provocation, a lad who is known to belong to a rival gang; this is done for the purpose of terrorising and showing the superiority of one set over another.'

Devine was appalled and fascinated in equal measure by the array of weapons wielded in scuttles between rival gangs. He had built up a formidable collection himself through his duties as Police Court Missionary. His haul included knives, old cutlasses, pokers, sticks loaded with lead, pieces of leather strap with iron bolts fixed to the end, and specially made pieces of iron. The latter – 'very dangerous-looking' – had been used to Devine's knowledge on one occasion only: a furious battle in a street off Deansgate in Manchester city centre. The scuttler's favourite weapons, however, were stones and belts. Stones were hurled at the start of a scuttle before the hand-to-hand fighting commenced. A scuttler's belt was a truly terrifying weapon, as Devine pointed out:

> The most dangerous part of the belt is the buckle, and this is made of brass, and usually measures about three inches in diameter, though I have seen them both smaller and larger. These are used by the 'scuttler' fastening one end of the strap into the buckle end, and then, winding his hand round the strap from his wrist, he grasps the leather, leaving about eight

or ten inches of the belt to use as a weapon, the winding of it round his arm preventing it from being readily dragged from him in a fight.

Used in this way, a blow from the buckle end of a belt could easily fracture a man's skull.

Scuttlers were intensely style-conscious. The scuttler's belt was his most prized possession and was as much an item of display as a weapon. Devine told the readers of the *Guardian* how:

Many of these belts are very curious, bearing remarkable designs upon them. These are made by the insertion of a large number of pins, which are used to form a design the whole length of the belt. The pins are inserted into the leather, then broken off, and filed down to a level with the leather. These designs include figures of serpents, a heart pierced with an arrow (this appears to be a favourite design), Prince of Wales' feathers, clogs, animals, stars, and often either the name of the wearer of the belt or that of some woman.

The belt was part of a highly distinctive uniform, as was the scuttler's choice of footwear: narrow-toed, brass-tipped clogs. These too served both ornamental and offensive purposes.

Devine attributed scuttling to four causes. Firstly, he pointed to a lack of parental control over children and young people. Devine wondered whether the growth of welfare organisations during the previous decade had encouraged a weakening of parental responsibility. He was alluding to the work of the National Society for the Prevention of Cruelty to Children, which was active in Manchester and other major cities from the mid-1880s, prior to the establishment of the national organisation in 1889. In any event, he concluded that it was 'high time that parents should be taught their duty; at present they seem either regardless of this or utterly afraid of correcting their children'. Secondly, Devine identified a lack of discipline in schools. He noted that the Elementary Education Act of 1880, which made schooling compulsory between the ages of five and ten, appeared to have contributed to a diminution of other forms of crime but had failed to reform the manners of the rising generation of young roughs. Whereas boys from the 'higher grade of society' were routinely flogged with the birch rod at England's elite private boarding schools, their working-class counterparts were spared the rod. According to Devine, teachers in the state schools were 'not allowed to correct the boys properly, or to instil in their minds anything like respect for authority'.

Thirdly, he pointed to the pernicious effects of 'base literature'. The favourite reading matter among working-class lads was the 'penny dreadful'. Much bemoaned by educational reformers and youth workers, penny dreadfuls were sensational novels, published in weekly parts, whose characters – often highwaymen, pirates or brigands – were 'cheerfully amoral, openly defied authority and revelled in bloodshed'. In Devine's view, the penny dreadfuls engendered 'a morbid love of horrors and atrocities that may account to some extent for the many acts of violence committed by lads of this class'. Finally, he highlighted the sheer monotony of the day-to-day lives of lads in Manchester's poorer districts. Days of unremitting toil for those lucky enough to be in regular work were followed by evenings spent in 'listless idleness' in the streets. As Devine saw it, 'A street fight or a scuffle with the police affords a welcome relief to this dullness.'

What was to be done about scuttling? Devine advocated a two-pronged approach combining harsh repressive measures against the existing ranks of scuttlers with preventive work among the rising generation of boys in Manchester. As the pioneer of the local lads' club movement, Devine was proud of the record of Manchester's existing clubs, located in working-class districts such as Hulme, Ancoats and Openshaw. Yet as he acknowledged, the provision of recreational clubs for boys was too big a matter for private philanthropists alone: 'What we need is that our City Council and the sister Corporation [of Salford] should take up the matter, and form in every district gymnasia and clubs or playrooms for working lads.' In Devine's vision, these municipal facilities would provide a formidable counter-attraction to the streets. Their impact would be greatly enhanced, he suggested, if other men of the middle classes were to follow his example and devote a portion of their leisure time to voluntary work in the clubs. Through heart-to-heart relationships with such gentlemen, the character of Manchester's working lads might truly be lifted up and scuttling would soon be a thing of the past.

Turning to the immediate question of how to deal with the existing gangs, Devine was a passionate advocate of corporal punishment. His work with young offenders had taught him that 'imprisonment is no complete remedy, and never will be'. In Devine's experience, scuttlers tended to show little but disdain for the criminal justice system. Referring to the batch of Harpurhey lads charged with inflicting grievous bodily harm following the affray in Ancoats the previous month, Devine told how:

> Their conduct in the dock at the police court was most flippant and callous. On one side stood the witnesses, several of them bearing marks of severe stabs in various parts of the body, and in the dock the youths laughed and turned round to wink at friends in the gallery, and even down below in the cells they whistled and sang, and upon my entering into conversation with them, one replied, 'Oh, it will only be twelve months for me!'

Such disregard for the processes of the law was by no means unusual. Devine also referred to a batch of Grey Mare Boys, from the Bradford district (not to be confused with the better-known Yorkshire city of the same name), convicted at the Quarter Sessions. Here, Devine cited the *Guardian*'s report on the trial. After the sentences were announced, 'The prisoners put on an air of bravado as they left the dock, and made as much noise as they well could with their clogs as they passed to the cells.' The sound of brass-tipped clogs clattering against the walls of the courtroom was deafening and few of those present were left in any doubt of the scuttlers' contempt for the proceedings.

Drawing on his experiences as a police court missionary working with first-time offenders, Devine relayed further evidence of the apparent futility of imprisonment as a deterrent:

'A worker who daily stands at the gate of our city gaol in connection with the Prison Gate Mission tells me of the scenes that occur on the release of these young ruffians; how they are met by crowds of lads and girls, hailed as *heroes*, and treated as such. This any warder or policeman in the district of the gaol will corroborate.' He was left in no doubt that the only remedy for scuttling was flogging: 'I have had practical dealings with these lads, and know them well. They cannot endure pain. I am convinced that an experience of sound whipping applied in these cases would absolutely and completely prove the solution of the difficulty. As a repressive step, I know no more merciful and truly humane measure.' Devine claimed that the Manchester magistrates shared this view, as did most of the best-known philanthropists and educationalists of the day. He drew the line at floggings with the 'cat', since only the strongest of grown men could withstand this most gruesome punishment. For scuttlers, Devine recommended the canes deployed, in the hands of prison warders, on industrial training ships: 'I venture to think that a nautical "dozen" or "two dozen" would take all the "scuttling" out of the stoutest youth ever charged.' Flogging, Devine added, should be utilised as the only effective deterrent to scuttlers. Nonetheless, it should be secondary to the 'great preventive step' of establishing lads' clubs and gymnasia across Manchester and Salford.

SOME YEARS later, one of the *Guardian*'s regular columnists, a self-styled 'Wanderer in the Slums', managed to arrange a rare interview with four scuttlers from Ancoats. The lads told how districts such as Ancoats were effectively divided into distinct territories, each belonging to a different gang. Hostilities between opposing gangs within the same district were periodically eclipsed by wider antagonisms between scuttlers from different parts of the Manchester conurbation. Thus: 'All the scuttlers of Ancoats, for example, are the natural enemies of the scuttlers of Salford, and they might, under pressure, mingle their ranks against the common enemy.'

The Ancoats scuttlers wore pointed clogs and 'bells', or bell-bottomed trousers, measuring fourteen inches around the knee and twenty-one around the foot. The 'lids', or flaps, of their coat pockets were cut into little peaks and buttoned down and they wore 'flashy' silk scarves round their necks. Their hair was cut short at the back and sides, but they had grown long fringes which were worn in a parting and plastered down on the forehead over the left eye. 'Pigeon-board' peaked caps were also worn tilted to the left, and angled to display the fringe. To dress in this way was to signal that the scuttler was no ordinary, working-class lad; he was a street fighter.

Within their own districts, scuttlers wore their uniforms with pride. However, the *Guardian*'s columnist noted that they only warily left the safety of the immediate neighbourhood. Journeys into the city centre were usually made mob-handed, but even short distances were travelled, whenever possible, in threes and fours since it was dangerous for a scuttler to venture beyond the gang's recognised territory on his own. As the Wanderer in the Slums put it, 'The solitary scuttler who wanders, through reck-lessness or necessity, into foreign territory will inevitably be questioned, molested, or wounded by superior numbers.'

In such cases, the lad's friends were obliged to avenge the injury. There were two means of exacting revenge. The enemy territory might be invaded en masse, without warning, precipi-tating a full-scale scuttle if the offending mob were found. Alternatively, a challenge might be issued, 'Will your best lad fight our best lad?' If the challenge was accepted, it was generally understood that the fight between the two 'champions' should be a 'fair' one, with fists rather than weapons. If the challenge was refused, the two sides gathered their forces for a scuttle with bricks, knives, and belts 'by appointment'.

The Ancoats scuttlers were pressed to explain the consequences of venturing out wearing 'bells' and hair brushed into a scuttler's fringe. 'Suppose you went into a strange part of town,' the Wanderer inquired, 'you'd be like a red rag to a bull, wouldn't you?' One of the youths replied, 'Just like that. Suppose you want someone to fly at you, you just soap your hair down over your left eye and put on a pigeon-board cap. Then you go into Salford. Then-you-go-into-Salford.' His friends erupted in knowing laughter. The scuttlers cheerfully admitted that they knew that they would be stopped and questioned whenever they entered districts in which they were not known. Local youths would accost them, demanding to know, 'Who's this lad? Where's he come from?' Asked how they negotiated such potentially dangerous encounters, one replied, 'The best thing to do is to look as though you are going to hit someone.' Those who looked truly menacing were, as often as not, allowed to pass unmolested.

Asked to identify the causes of feuds between rival gangs, the lads were unanimous in their answer, 'Oh, it's the girls, they're much worse than us lads.' According to their account, girls stirred up trouble between bands of scuttlers, egging the lads on to acts of violence and even carrying bricks and bottles to be thrown at the start of an affray. The lads in turn were not shy of proclaiming their romantic conquests. 'One of the lads showed me the initials of his loves tattooed on his arm,' relayed the *Guardian*'s columnist. 'Generally a bracelet is tattooed round the wrist, and immediately above that begins the list of initials, extending often up to the elbow. This lad must have had a list of thirty. Picture the complaisance of the girl who comes late in the list! She must be content to regard the list as proof of the singular fascinations of her champion.' In return, the girls made clothes for their lads. Scuttlers were much more concerned with their appearances than other young men in working-class districts, and the Ancoats scuttler whose tattoos proclaimed his status as a Lothario was also sporting a pair of 'beautiful pictorial socks', lovingly knitted by one of his 'molls'.

There was a clear hierarchy within bands of scuttlers. Just as the gangs aroused fear as well as fascination in the districts in which they congregated, some scuttlers aroused fear even among their own followers. The Ancoats lads described one such character, noted for his

'flashy', rolling walk, his shoulders shrugged somewhat and his head drawn down into them, his hands pulled into his sleeves, one of them often holding the handle of an open knife. It was a wonderfully unpleasant and vivid picture. Sometimes he would ask his 'friends' to stand him a drink, sometimes to lend him twopence, and if they refused the knife was always ready to do its sudden work. He was a 'fair terror'; they were all agreed upon that.

Like Alexander Devine before him, the Wanderer in the Slums was convinced that scuttling flourished only in the absence of healthier forms of leisure. He concluded, 'If every boy had the opportunity of playing football there would soon be less of it than there is now.'

By 1890, the Manchester scuttler and his moll 'had achieved a notoriety as widespread as that of any gangs in modern times'. Yet the city's gang wars stretched back over two full decades before Alexander Devine's account was published in the *Manchester Guardian*. Scuttling first made headline news in the local press during the early 1870s, when reports of an eruption of violence caused alarm and bewilderment among the city authorities and terror among the respectable, law-abiding population. Scuttling was the first modern youth cult. It is no coincidence that it developed in the world's first industrial conurbation.

CHAPTER 2

Shock City

'...THE GREATEST STREAM of human industry flows out to fertilise the whole world. From this filthy sewer pure gold flows. Here humanity attains its most complete development and its most brutish; here civilisation works its miracles, and civilised man is turned back into a savage.' This startling observation of Manchester was made by the French travel writer Alexis de Tocqueville in the 1830s. The hub of England's Industrial Revolution, Manchester more than any other city captured the spirit of the age. Economic vitality, however, came at a price: a widening gulf between rich and poor and ever-more squalid living conditions amid the accumulation of great wealth. If Manchester offered glimpses of the future, this 'shock city' fore-told of danger as much as progress.[4]

Vast fortunes were made by local merchants and manufac-turers and, as Manchester's factory districts grew at a staggering rate, tens of thousands of people poured into the city in search of work. Many of the early migrants were from the surrounding Lancashire countryside. Increasingly, however, they came from further afield: from all corners of England and then, in huge numbers, from Ireland during the Great Famine of the 1840s. The new arrivals, many of them destitute, were crammed into the ring of factory districts around the city centre: Ancoats,

---

4 The phrase 'shock city' was used by the historian Asa Briggs to describe the Manchester of the 1840s. As Briggs pointed out, 'Manchester forced to the surface problems of "class", of the relations between rich and poor.'

Angel Meadow, Red Bank, Chorlton-on-Medlock and Hulme. By the mid-nineteenth century, Manchester was a byword not just for industry and commerce, but for poverty, overcrowding and ill-health.

Manchester was 'the chimney of the world', notes historian Stephen Mosley. By 1870, there were more than 1,600 textile works in the city and neighbouring Salford, and nearly 2,000 chimneys – many more than were to be found in any other conurbation. Most industry was coal-fuelled, with more than three million tons consumed in the city each year. The chimneys belched black, sulphurous smoke, blocking out the sun, destroying vegetation and covering buildings in thick layers of soot. The term 'acid rain' was coined in Manchester in 1872 to describe the environmental damage wreaked by this great concentration of industry and visitors to the city found the acrid clouds of smoke inhibited their breathing and stung their eyes. With so much smoke and soot in the air, fog formed all too readily – and Manchester's fogs were unusually pungent, reeking of sulphur.

At ground level, the city's streets reeked of a 'chaotic combination of pungent odours', domestic and industrial. Noxious vapours from the factory chimneys mingled with the stench of decomposing refuse and animal and human excrement. Ancoats had the worst of it: here the smoke was so dense that no object was visible at a distance of a few hundred yards and 'brilliant' sunshine never penetrated – unlike the foul odour of the 'night soil' depot at nearby Holt Town. Where there was smoke, there was incessant noise. Most adults wore clogs and horse-drawn trams and carts ran on wheels with cast iron rims. The rumble on granite-paved streets was deafening and on busy thoroughfares only shouted conversations were possible.

Long hours of physically draining labour, low wages, poor diets and cramped housing failed to dull the lust for life in the factory districts. If anything, the opposite was the case: the drab monotony of the working week seemed only to heighten the excesses of the weekend. Friedrich Engels, one of the foremost commentators on the new industrial age, saw mass drunkenness as the inevitable result of the degradation of the city's workforce: 'On Saturday evenings', he mused in 1845, 'when the whole working-class pours from its own quarters into the main thoroughfares, intemperance may be seen in all its brutality. I have rarely come out of Manchester on such an evening without meeting numbers of people staggering and seeing others lying in the gutter.' Manchester was a thirsty place, served at the time Engels was writing by more than 1,500 public houses and beershops – one for every 150 inhabitants. Under the terms of the Beershop Act of 1830, any ratepayer could obtain a licence to sell beer on his premises, and in the working-class districts of Manchester, beerhouses were frequently opened in the front rooms of terraced houses.

A Saturday night in the heart of the city was something to behold. Pubs, gin-shops, 'singing-saloons' and music halls all did roaring business. *Morning Chronicle* reporter Angus Reach, touring Manchester in 1849 to investigate the impact of industrialisation on the lives of ordinary men and women, was captivated by the noise and bustle of London Road: 'The gin-shops are in full-feather – their swinging doors never hang a moment still. Itinerant bands blow and bang their loudest; organ boys grind monotonously; ballad singers or flying stationers make roaring proclamations of their wares. The street is one swarming, buzzing mass of people. Boys and girls shout and laugh and disappear into the taverns together.'

Even the carnival atmosphere of London Road did not prepare him for a Sunday night in Ancoats. Reach was horrified when he realised that the Sabbath in Ancoats was celebrated in much the same way as a Saturday:

In returning last Sunday night, by the Oldham-road, from one of my tours, I was somewhat surprised to hear the loud sounds of music and jollity which floated out of the public-house windows. The street was swarming with drunken men and women; and with young mill girls and boys shouting, hallooing and romping with each other. Now, I am not one of those who look upon the slightest degree of social indulgence as a downright evil, but I confess that last Sunday night in the

Oldham-road astonished and grieved me. In no city have I ever witnessed a scene of more open, brutal and general intemperance. The public-houses and gin-shops were roaring full. Rows, and fights, and scuffles were every moment taking place within doors and in the streets. The whole street rung with shouting, screaming, and swearing, mingled with the jarring music of half-a-dozen bands. A tolerably intimate acquaintance with most phases of London life enables me to state that in no part of the metropolis would the police have tolerated such a state of things for a single Sunday.

Manchester was by no means an irreligious city. Reach himself was hugely impressed by the work of the local Sunday schools, but even 'this vast moral and educational engine' had done nothing to dampen the Sunday night Saturnalias in Ancoats.

The failure to observe the Sabbath among Manchester's poor was the source of enduring anxieties for the city's religious leaders and philanthropists. In the spring and early summer of 1854, the Manchester and Salford Temperance Society conducted a survey of 'Sunday Tippling in Manchester'. The society's members counted the comings and goings at around 350 'low' pubs, beerhouses and gin shops. They counted more than 215,000 customers: 120,000 men, nearly 72,000 women, and no fewer than 23,000 children fetching beer or whisky on behalf of their parents. In Ancoats, they observed 'a very great amount of drunkenness' and plenty of fights. On the afternoon of Sunday, June 4, two men came out of the Royal Cricketer's Rest in Mill Street and began to fight. When one of the men ran away, the other followed, brandishing a knife, and a third man ran out of the pub with a poker. A large crowd of boys quickly gathered, but there was not a policeman in sight even though the nearest police station was only two hundred yards away.

In nearby Angel Meadow, the haunt of thieves, beggars and prostitutes as well as poorly paid factory workers, the scenes were more shocking still: 'Angel Street, Dyche Street, Charter Street, Ludgate Hill, and adjoining streets, at two o'clock on Sunday, May 28th, were crowded with men, women, and children, in rags and filth, some drinking in the streets, others gambling; in fact, this district can only be described as a very hell upon earth.' Well-dressed strangers were not welcome in 'the Meadow'. The temperance workers keeping watch on the beerhouses here had to change places every half-hour or so: 'some were driven off by mobs, and others stoned'.

The other slum districts were almost as bad. 'No pen could describe' the fearful state of the hovels of Deansgate, where the Hop Pole Inn on Hardman Street was frequented by 'the very lowest dregs of society'. The temperance volunteers were stationed here in threes following a series of assaults by the irate landlord. Some of the Deansgate pubs boasted singing rooms. As on Oldham Street, these were especially popular with young people of both sexes. The district between Oxford Road and London Road was little better than Deansgate. One man was seen entering the Lass o' Gowrie on Charles Street 'with nothing on but his shirt and shoes'. The observers noted that 'A fearful state of demoralization exists about this house.' Only three of the fifty-seven children counted entering the Earl Grey in nearby Ashton Street were wearing clean clothes: 'One little fellow, covered in rags and filth, came at three o'clock for a pint of whisky, and again at half-past four for a pint of ale; such was his wretched appearance that a gentleman followed to see where he lived. [The boy] went into a filthy cellar, not fit for a pigsty, where several persons were drinking.' There were no reports of intoxicated children, although drunken youths were a common sight.

Between Deansgate and Oxford Road lay the infamous 'Little Ireland'. Many here preferred to drink at home, sending their children to the local beerhouses with jugs. Engels visited the district shortly before the worst of its slums were demolished to make way for Oxford Road railway station:

In a rather deep hole, in a curve of the [River] Medlock and surrounded on all four sides by tall factories and high embankments covered with buildings, stand two groups of about two hundred cottages, built chiefly back to back, in which live about four thousand human beings, most of them Irish. The cottages are old, dirty, and of the smallest sort, the streets uneven, fallen into ruts and in part without drains or pavement; masses of refuse, offal and sickening filth lie among standing pools in all directions; the atmosphere is poisoned by the effluvia from these, and laden and darkened by the smoke of a dozen tall factory chimneys. A horde of ragged women and children swarm about here, as filthy as the swine that thrive upon the garbage heaps and in the puddles.

In later decades, the adjacent district was known as Gaythorn and was one of the hotbeds of so-called 'Criminal Manchester'. The inhabitants were fiercely clannish and notoriously hostile to the police.

In Hulme in the spring of 1854 the workers of the Manchester and Salford Temperance Society found a number of sporting pubs, renowned for the rowdiness of their customers, in the district bounded by Great Jackson Street, Stretford Road and Chester Road. Several fights broke out, they noted, at which no police appeared. One beerhouse was filled with pigeon-flyers, who spent the whole afternoon and evening flying their birds from the front of the house. Another was 'filled with dog-fighters, with their dogs, during the evening. There was one dog fight, and two fights among the men frequenting the house, at none of which any policeman interfered.' The absence of the police during disturbances was an all-too-frequent theme of their reports. On the other hand, no fewer than fifty-four police officers had been spotted entering licensed premises whilst on duty.

The survey of 'Sunday Tippling in Manchester' was presented to local Members of Parliament. The Temperance Society was appalled by the catalogue of debauchery and crime its members had recorded. With 'agencies for evil so potent and subtle' and 'temptations so numerous and widely spread', what hope was there, the Society asked, for 'the triumph of pure religion and virtue among our debased and sensual population?' Twenty years on, the situation was little different. By 1873, there was one licensed premises for every 139 of the city's inhabitants. Arrest rates revealed a still more shocking state of affairs: one in forty of the city's population was apprehended for drunkenness that year. The comparable arrest figures for drunkenness in Birmingham and Leeds were one in 126 and one in 164 respectively. Little wonder Sir John Day, one of the judges on the Northern Circuit, quipped that 'the shortest way out of Manchester' was through the pub doorway.

Few of those who frequented the city's low beerhouses left records of their experiences. But in the spring of 1869, two contributors to the Manchester satirical magazine the *Free Lance* made a surreptitious visit to one of the dens of Deansgate. Dressed as artisans, they ventured into the dark, narrow side streets off the busy thoroughfare. They picked out a house with a rough illuminated canvas hung above the door, lit by the lamps which flared behind it. Half a dozen girls in their teens stood on the pavement outside, their status as prostitutes 'impossible to mistake'. Ignoring their solicitations, the intrepid explorers stepped inside:

> Three narrow deal tables were in the room, and wooden benches were placed on each side of them. There was hardly space for another visitor. The apartment was nearly full of women, half dressed, and men, if men they could be called, who were not yet out of their teens. Upon the end of one of the tables a 'hurdy-gurdy' stood, and behind, a middle-aged woman, the only one in the room decently dressed. When we entered she was singing a filthy song, with a chorus in which the company was expected to join.

Amid much dancing and merriment, drink was being consumed by lads and lasses alike at a rate which appalled the observers. What worried them most, however, was the overt sexuality on display. The clientele was young but far from innocent, as evidenced by the gusto with which they greeted each innuendo-laden chorus.

ANGUS REACH's sketches of the London and Oldham Roads in the middle of the century highlighted one of the most striking features of Manchester's population: its youth. Young workers were cheap and nimble, making them attractive to mill and factory owners, and many of those who moved to Manchester in search of work were single and aged in their teens or early twenties. Those families who settled in the factory districts often depended on their children's wages to lift them out of poverty. Demand for juvenile labour in Manchester during the latter decades of the nineteenth century generally exceeded supply, and it was said that any boy, upon leaving school, could find employment within two hours. Working-class boys and girls alike left school as early as possible, starting full-time work between the ages of eleven and thirteen. Their strong economic position was recognised by their parents. Whilst living at home, they were expected to 'tip up' the bulk of their wages to their mothers, but most received 'spends', or pocket money, in return. This gave them money for magazines, fashionable clothes and visits to music halls, theatres, pubs and gin shops. Their precocious independence alarmed many middle-class commentators, who saw the freedom of the young leading only to moral ruin.

Young people formed the majority of the weekend audiences at Manchester's 'low' music halls. This was tragically illustrated at the Victoria in July 1868. Popularly known as Ben Lang's, the Victoria could house audiences of 2,000, and with admission prices of twopence and threepence it offered one of the cheapest nights out in Manchester. On July 31, nearly 3,000 people crammed inside. The bill featured a sack race, scheduled for ten o'clock. As the twelve competitors lined up on stage, some lads in the 'pit', or stalls, took hold of a gas pipe attached to the lower gallery and attempted to lift themselves up above the heads of the people in front to gain a better view. The pipe cracked under their weight. The escaping fumes caused alarm among those in the pit, which turned to terror when a voice yelled, 'Fire!' The effect was devastating. The audience rushed as one for the doors, and the occupants of the top gallery ran down the stairs into the gallery beneath before jumping on top of the people in the pit. An iron rail on the stairs leading down to the entrance hall gave way, and more than a hundred people fell down into the landing below. Amidst scenes of 'indescribable confusion', twenty-four people were fatally crushed. Dozens more suffered serious injuries. With a handful of exceptions, those who died were aged between twelve and twenty. They were slum-dwellers from the nearby districts of Salford, Ancoats, Angel Meadow and Red Bank.

Manchester's unruly street life, which made such an impression on Angus Reach in 1849, was still flourishing twenty years later. On weekend evenings the young took to the streets in droves, many of them heading into 'town' – Manchester city centre. The great magnet on a Saturday night was Smithfield Market at Shudehill. With no means of storing fresh foodstuffs over the weekend, stallholders sold off meat and fish for next-to-nothing late every Saturday night. And while married women headed to Shudehill in search of bargains, the young flocked there for fun. Myriad gas lamps illuminated enchanting pleasures. Factory lads and lasses could have themselves weighed and measured for a ha'penny, endure mirth-inducing shocks from 'galvanic batteries'; shoot at targets on tiny rifle ranges; listen to lectures on the workings of the human body; and jig to the strains of Scottish fiddlers. Crowds swarmed through Shudehill on Saturday nights in their thousands, pushing, elbowing and swaying to and fro between the stalls.

On Sunday evenings, young people promenaded in single-sex groups along Oldham Street and Market Street, Hyde Road or Stretford Road with the aim of pairing off, or 'clicking', with members of the opposite sex. The scenes on Stretford Road in Hulme on a Sunday night in November 1869 appalled a writer for the *Free Lance*. Young ruffians aged from around ten to sixteen assembled in batches of a dozen or more to assail female passers-by. Lewd comments were accompanied by equally explicit gestures. Not content with this, 'they tear off shawls, hats, bonnets, collars, or any other article of dress that may catch their fancy, and run off at the top of their speed'. This custom – known as 'bonneting' – was widely practised in Manchester's poorer districts. It was intended to discomfort those of superior social standing, or aspirations. Worse still, the *Free Lance* noted, there had been numerous instances of late in which respectable young women were assaulted on Stretford Road in full view of the passing crowds.

The parades on Oldham Street, the principal thoroughfare from the city centre to Ancoats, were the most tumultuous of all. The *Free Lance* complained in 1870: 'Oldham-street on a Sunday night appears to be given up to the carnival revels of Manchester's vagabonds. Here scenes may be witnessed which are unparalleled in any city or town in England.' Shrieks, yells and curses filled the air. The unfettered ribaldry and sexual licence was startling:

> Urchins with bare heads, singing snatches of vile comic songs, assemble in droves, many with pipes in mouth, which are drawn out only to express some disgusting foulness to girls, also *minus* head-gear, and equally wicked, passing by. Shambling along, with similar bad intentions, are lads of decenter appearance, each of course with his bit of clay or penny twisted leaf, blaspheming at almost every step, and rudely jostling girls of a like age, who, seemingly, only too well relish the contamination.

Worse still, in the eyes of the anti-Semitic *Free Lance*, crowds of apparently respectable young women joined the throng, untroubled by the presence of groups of Jewish lads from Red Bank.[5]

Nowhere was Manchester's love of fashion displayed with more zeal than on Oldham Street on a Sunday evening. The *City Lantern* described the scene in August 1875:

> From end to end is a surging mass of human beings overflowing from the broad pavement into the roadway. Every grade of juvenile workers is represented. The shopman, attired in ready-made garments of the most alarming pattern and extravagant cut; the shop-girl and mill-hand, gorgeous in

---

5 Manchester's Jewish community grew significantly from the 1860s following an influx of impoverished migrants from Russia and Poland. Most settled in the dilapidated slums of Red Bank, situated in the heavily polluted valley of the River Irk on the northern fringe of the city centre. They met with a vituperative response from the local press.

cheap jewellery, feathers, and silk; the youthful mechanic, disguised in broadcloth and a clean shirt; the lower order of factory operative, in fustian, and the proverbial shawl and clog; and the bullet-headed, ragged, shoeless street Arab, happy in his dirt.

Keeping up appearances mattered every bit as much to young men as it did to young women.

Echoing the concerns voiced in the *Free Lance* five years earlier, the *City Lantern* noted that if the behaviour of these gaggles of lads and lasses on Oldham Street was frequently coarse, their language was worse:

Ribald jests and lewd observations are the rule, and the conversation one overhears, bandied between young men and young women, leaves no doubt that they are well acquainted with every kind of vice, and rather glory in the knowledge. One amusement is very popular here with both sexes. A gang of young ruffians, linking their arms together, extend themselves across the footway, and, walking or running along the street, jostle as many of their companions as possible into the road. The scuffles and amatory encounters which result from this proceeding, and the opportunities it affords for the use of choice oaths, render it peculiarly enjoyable and exciting.

Publicans benefited handsomely. Their brilliantly illuminated vaults were jammed full and the sounds of pianos, conversation and laughter reverberated across the street. At closing time, drunken revellers spilled back out onto the pavements, already looking forward to the following weekend.

WITHIN THE home, Manchester's young workers were subject to the authority of their parents. Parental discipline was strict and often violent, even towards older sons and daughters about to get married themselves. On the streets, however, young people revelled in their freedom and independence. Their promenades and excursions to city-centre markets, music halls, and beer-houses took them well away from the watchful eyes of their parents. Their presence in large, often boisterous, groups was the source of frequent alarm among the wider population.

In drink, these young 'roughs' were all the more contemptuous of their elders. Jests and taunts all-too-easily ended in violence, and those who chided youths for their impudence risked severe beatings. This was never more apparent than in the autumn of 1866. A gang of two dozen youths spent the afternoon of Wednesday, September 26, in the Beehive beer-house on Jersey Street in Ancoats. By the time they spilled out at half-past five, they were much the worse for wear. A boatman named Edward Jewell was leading his horse along Jersey Street at the time, his wife Ellen walking a few steps behind. Joe Rodgers, aged nineteen, ran up to Mrs Jewell, threw his arms round her neck and then ran away laughing. Furious at his impertinence she followed him into Bengal Street, where she 'upbraided' him fiercely. When Rodgers took off his coat as though preparing to fight, Mrs Jewell prudently doubled back onto Jersey Street to re-join her husband. Rodgers followed, as did the rest of the gang. They surrounded the couple and began to pull the horse about. John Dorning, eighteen, jumped onto the terrified creature's back. When Edward Jewell protested, he was punched.

William Lee, a spinner from Bradford Road in Ancoats, witnessed the altercation. He told the youths to leave the couple alone, but the gang's blood was up and they turned their fury onto him instead. Dorning 'bonneted' him and Joe Rodgers felled him with a punch. Lee got to his feet, only for Henry Holland to knock him down for a second time. The rest of the gang crowded round and kicked out repeatedly with their brass-tipped clogs until Lee was motionless. Lee's companion ran for a policeman. The sight of a single constable was enough to scatter the youths, but the officer's arrival was too late to save William Lee. A group of women from Bengal Street tried to lift him up, but he died in their arms.

Seven local 'roughs' aged between eighteen and twenty-three

were subsequently rounded up by the police. They stood trial for manslaughter at the South Lancashire Assizes on December 7. Five of the prisoners were found guilty. Henry Holland, who inflicted the fatal kick, was sentenced to fifteen years' penal servitude. Joe Rodgers, who sparked the row by molesting Ellen Jewell, got ten years. Two other youths, both of whom kicked William Lee as he lay on the ground, got five. John Dorning was jailed for eighteen months with hard labour. Reports of 'the Jersey Street Outrage' in the national press made Manchester a byword for violence. De Tocqueville, it appeared, had been right: civilised man was indeed reverting to a state of savagery. Within Manchester, Ancoats earned a lasting reputation as 'the Kingdom of the Rough'.

The working lads of Manchester and Salford were fearsome enough on their own. Quick to take offence, they battered and bloodied each other in 'fair fights' with their fists even when they were disposed to settle their differences amicably. When affronted, they reached for weapons without the slightest hesitation. And when they banded together to form gangs, they terrified the entire city. Now the swaggering independence, fierce pride and legendary rowdiness of Manchester's youth were to find a new outlet, in a kind of mob warfare never witnessed before.

CHAPTER 3

The Rochdale Road War

IN 1700, ANGEL MEADOW afforded views of vale and river, hill and woodland. One hundred and fifty years later, this once-heavenly landscape was one of Manchester's worst slums. Bounded by Rochdale Road, Miller Street, Cheetham Hill Road and Gould Street, Angel Meadow covered thirty-three acres on the edge of the city centre. The London-based journalist Angus Reach had been appalled by what he found there in 1849: 'The lowest, most filthy, most unhealthy, and most wicked locality in Manchester is called, singularly enough, "Angel-meadow". It is full of cellars, and inhabited by prostitutes, their bullies, thieves, cadgers, vagrants, tramps, and, in the very worst sties of filth and darkness, by those unhappy wretches the "low Irish".'

In the lodging-houses of Charter Street, Reach encountered 'squalid, hulking fellows' and 'coarse-looking and repulsive' women. The latter, he was in no doubt, were 'the worst class of prostitutes'. The men were their 'bullies', or pimps, and their partners in robberies. Lodging-house keepers charged fourpence per bed, per night. The beds were crammed into 'filthy unscoured chambers, with stained and discoloured walls, scribbled over with names and foul expressions'.

The occupants of the lodging-houses were mostly English-born. The rapidly growing Irish population of Angel Meadow occupied the cellar dwellings. Reach descended into one of these subterranean holes:

38

The place was dark, except for the glare of a small fire. You could not stand without stooping in the room, which might be about twelve feet by eight. There were at least a dozen men, women and children on stools, or squatted on the stone floor, round the fire, and the heat and smells were oppressive … the inmates slept huddled on the stones, or on masses of rags, shavings and straw, which were littered about. There was nothing like a bedstead in the place.

The cellar's occupants told Reach that they came from Westport in County Mayo, on Ireland's west coast. They had fled the Great Famine only to find themselves in the foulest slum of the new, industrial age. The most infamous spot in the Meadow was the former parish burial ground of St Michael's. Forty thousand paupers were buried there between 1788 and 1816, when it was finally closed. The ground lay unpaved for almost forty years until flagstones were finally laid; it was known to local people thereafter as 'the Flags'. A resident of Rochdale Road testified to its condition in the years that followed:

There [was] at some time a boundary wall, of which but very few bricks remain; the others were taken during the hours of darkness to make and repair various pigsties and cottages in the neighbourhood. Upon the Back Style-street side it is raised about 6ft. and this deposit consists of ashes and fæcal matter flung upon its surface by the people of that street. There was at one time a number of gravestones covering the remains of some dear lost ones, but these have been removed, and a few are to be seen in some of the cottages, forming part of their flooring, and others performing the same office to some of the common privies. Very often are the bones of the dead exposed and carried away, and a human skull has been kicked about for a football on the ground. The ground is very often the arena for various gladiatorial exhibitions, such as a fight generally got up in some of the low drinking places of the neighbourhood. I have often seen some hundreds of the poor inhabitants of this district congregated together to witness two of their species stand up to be knocked down, and frequently kicked while in that condition; and this takes place over a spot where 40,000 bodies are said to be buried. Upon the Sabbath Day it is the great centre for a number of gamblers at pitch and toss.

The two populations of Angel Meadow – vagrant English and destitute Irish – maintained an uneasy and often fractious co-existence. During the 1850s they were frequently at war: 'Periodical invasions, amounting to actual riots, were often made at that time on each other's territory, by the Celtic inhabitants of Angel Meadow and the wandering tribes of Charter-street,' recorded local author B. A. Redfern. Tensions increased during the 1860s in the wake of Fenian operations in Britain. Dedicated to the violent overthrow of British rule in Ireland, the Fenians brought the fear of terrorism to all of Britain's major cities, not least to Manchester. In September 1867, two leading Fenian prisoners were freed in a raid on a police van en route to the Manchester City Gaol at Belle Vue. Sergeant Charles Brett of the City of Manchester Police was shot and killed during the raid. The prisoners escaped, but no fewer than twenty-eight men were arrested as police combed the city's Irish quarters. Seven men were sentenced to penal servitude. Three others, the 'Manchester Martyrs', were sentenced to hang. The convictions were based on patchy evidence and the subsequent executions provoked storms of protest both in Manchester and further afield. In Angel Meadow, relations between the English and Irish communities deteriorated sharply.

The police treaded carefully in 'the Meadow', mindful of the perils of interfering in disputes in this quarter. As a Manchester detective noted in 1869, 'When a row breaks out here, it is nasty. They use all sorts of weapons, pitch pots out of the upper windows, use feet, knives, and anything which comes handy.' The *Manchester Weekly Times* agreed. 'Pugilism is common there', the paper noted, 'and women have been seen half stripped, fighting like men. Very recently two women were on the ground, not only fighting, but biting one another, in what they called "true Lancashire fashion".' Yet for all the protestations of the police and the press, Charter Street did adhere to a fighting code which was instantly recognisable in society at large. In mass brawls weapons were used freely enough, but when two grown men fell out they were expected to settle their differences in a fair fight. In Charter Street, as elsewhere across England, fights were usually scheduled for Sunday afternoons. The Flags, the old burial ground, was the preferred spot.

One memorable fight there during the early 1860s was described by Redfern:

> Perhaps the most noted event which has occurred for the last few years was a most vindictive fight between two one-armed beggars, which was witnessed by many hundred people, who were drawn together by the oddness of the conflict. 'Bacup Billy' was a quiet enough fellow till roused, when he came 'dangerous'. Stumpy was a bully, and more 'dangerous' still, besides that he had been a 'navvy' and was 'strong as a horse.' Some bullying of Stumpy's led to a challenge from Billy, which was eagerly accepted. The fight was all in Stumpy's favour, much to the disgust of the spectators, until about the sixth or seventh round of the most close and determined character of fighting, when, Billy having been thrown, Stumpy gave him a crashing kick in the ribs as he lay. Then the spectators threw themselves on Stumpy, and would have torn him limb from limb but for Billy, who screamed out with tears of rage that the fight might be allowed to continue. This at last was permitted, and afterwards Stumpy became cowed, and all went in 'Bacup's' favour. Once the men were rolling on the ground when the bigger villain bit through Billy's hand (completely through), and the consequence was that the crowd smashed him into a crushed, shapeless and bleeding mass, in their indignation at such foul play.

Bacup Billy never recovered from the fight and died from his injuries the following year. Stumpy did recover, but he had no choice but to leave Manchester. Having breached Charter Street's fighting code, he was an outcast among villains.

By the late 1860s, the notoriety of Angel Meadow was secure. The lodging-houses of Charter Street remained a magnet for tramps, scamps, outcasts, thieves, swindlers, hawkers, umbrella menders, knife grinders, ballad singers, sellers of prize-fight broadsheets and tinkers. Dotted among the lodging-houses were beershops, pawnshops, and 'tommy' shops, the latter selling all manner of delicacies from boiled spare ribs of pork to pea soup at a halfpenny a pint. The beerhouses served as the headquarters for the more dangerous denizens of the lodging-houses: 'the elder thieves, the fighting men, those who are both, the swindlers, and the more mutilated mendicants'. The Irish community, who made up roughly half of the population of Angel Meadow, eked out a living as hawkers, labourers and factory hands. It was among the boys – English and Irish – of this densely packed, dangerous, poverty-haunted locality that 'scuttling' was to develop into the first modern youth cult.

ON 19 JULY 1870, France declared war on Prussia following a dispute over the Prussian claim to the vacant throne of Spain. The French forces soon suffered a series of catastrophic defeats, culminating in the surrender of Napoleon III on September 3 and the overthrow of the French monarchy. The new Republic fought on, but Paris fell the following January and the remaining French forces surrendered within a week. A final peace treaty was signed in May 1871.

Given its far-reaching implications for the balance of power in Europe, the Franco-Prussian War received extensive coverage in the British press. In Manchester, some of the war's most avid followers were schoolboys, who began to re-enact the continental battles in the streets of New Cross, the district wedged between the slums of Angel Meadow and Ancoats. New Cross became the battleground in what the Manchester press was soon to label the 'Rochdale Road War'. The 'German' army was initially recruited from Protestant boys attending the Lancasterian School in Marshall Street. Their sworn enemies, the 'Frenchmen', were otherwise known as the scholars of St Joseph's, the Catholic school nearby. Boys flocked in their hundreds to join battle. At half past two on the afternoon of Sunday, 2 October 1870, between 300 and 400 'Frenchmen' gathered in an alleyway off Miller Street in Angel Meadow, armed with sticks, wooden swords and pistols. Led by a single standard-bearer carrying a paper flag on which was painted the word 'French', they marched in a body onto Rochdale Road where an equal number of 'Prussians' were posted. Blank cartridges were fired to signal the commencement of hostilities.

Hand-to-hand fighting had barely begun when four police officers charged onto the battle-field. The two armies scattered. Many of the combatants were mere boys and they were no match for the City of Manchester police. Eight were arrested; their ages ranged from ten to eighteen. They were brought before the magistrates at Manchester City Police Court the following morning, when one of the arresting officers produced the French flag in evidence, along with a pistol and sword. The presiding magistrate fined each boy in turn ten shillings and sixpence, with fourteen days' imprisonment in default of payment.

By November, the Rochdale Road War had intensified. Police in Manchester's 'B' Division were receiving a stream of reports of disturbances in New Cross and Angel Meadow, where the warring parties of Germans and Frenchmen had taken to stoning each other in the streets on a nightly basis. Police inquiries suggested that, whilst the conflicts might be understood in ethnic and sectarian terms – English versus Irish as much as Protestant versus Catholic – they owed just as much to the boys' simple love of fighting. The conflicts rapidly spread, north along Rochdale Road into Collyhurst and east across Oldham Road into Ancoats. Other boys were quick to emulate the scholars of the Lancasterian School and St Joseph's. The *Salford Weekly News* described the disturbances as 'a civil war in Manchester'.

For more than twelve months, battles raged across the slums of Rochdale Road and Oldham Road. Most of the early skirmishes involved volleys of stones. These were weapons of convenience, easily collected, and they could be hurled from a distance by those unwilling to fight at close quarters. As scuttling spread, however, older lads joined the battles in ever greater numbers. And they resorted increasingly to knives, iron swords and firearms. Severe injuries were inflicted. These served only to raise the level of violence further as scuttlers stockpiled weapons for 'self-protection'. Not surprisingly, injuries were by no means restricted to the belligerents. As Superintendent Godby of 'B' Division complained, 'The injury done to people passing along the streets has been fearful, many persons having had their heads broken, and been otherwise seriously injured.'

Considerable damage was also done to property. Publicans and shopkeepers feared for their plate glass windows and mill owners suffered systematic damage as scuttlers turned to vandalism as a diversion from the on-going feuds between rival gangs. More than 150 windows were broken in one mill over a period of five months. The owner of a glassworks in Jersey Street, Ancoats, complained to the Manchester magistrates that thirty-six windows at his works had been broken in one month alone. One pane had been shattered by a bullet fired from a rifle. The landlord of the Mechanic's Arms pub in Henry Street, off Oldham Road in Ancoats, told how the neighbour-hood had been in uproar for three or four months. Henry Street had been plagued by riots and the constant outbreaks of scuttling had cost the publican much of his trade.

The police response was determined, but ineffectual. Superintendent Godby had one of the most difficult jobs in Manchester. Responsible for maintaining order on the streets of Angel Meadow, Rochdale Road and Oldham Road, he told the Manchester magistrates that outbreaks of scuttling had given him a great deal of trouble. This was an understatement. Four or five officers were constantly deployed in Angel Meadow, 'parading the streets so as to prevent fights'. Moreover, it transpired that Godby had been obliged to rouse officers on night duty from their beds in the middle of the day to reinforce detachments sent out to suppress outbreaks of scuttling. Despite such measures, the superintendent was forced to admit that the disturbances 'were no sooner put down in one place than renewed in another'.

Officers from 'B' Division made regular spates of arrests from October 1870 onwards. By the following March more than 150 boys had been arrested for stone throwing. Notices were posted throughout the districts at the lower ends of Rochdale Road and Oldham Road, 'by order of the Chief Constable, cautioning persons against the practice, and informing them that they are liable to a penalty of forty shillings for the offence'. This was a huge sum in a period when many working men earned fewer than fifteen shillings in a week. The *Manchester City News*, noting that the fines would generally have to be paid by the boys' fathers, was hopeful that parents would join forces with the police in suppressing what the paper termed the 'stone throwing nuisance'.

Stone throwing resulted in at least two deaths in Manchester during the spring and summer of 1871. Neither was connected to the scuttling epidemic, but both cases served to highlight the menace posed by the Rochdale Road War. In March 1871, thirteen-year-old James Casey appeared at the South Lancashire Assizes charged with the manslaughter of a boy named Augustine Hopkins. The two lads had been playing together, but they fell out and fought. Casey threw a stone at Hopkins following 'some provocation'. At the Assizes, Casey pleaded guilty to manslaughter. The judge, however, refused to accept a plea of guilty from 'one so young, who could not understand the legal meaning of it'. Having read the various witness statements and medical evidence, the judge was satisfied that Hopkins' death had been caused not by the blow from the stone, but by an infection which had subsequently got into the wound. In the judge's view, Hopkins' death might have been prevented by proper medical care and the case therefore ought not to proceed. The counsel for the prosecution agreed. The jury duly returned a verdict of not guilty and James Casey was discharged.

Two months later, eight-year-old William Hales, from Every Street in Ancoats, was returning from a Sunday afternoon outing to Philips Park with a group of friends when they passed two boys who were quarrelling in the street. One of the boys threw a stone which missed its intended target and struck William on the forehead. He staggered home to Every Street, but his condition deteriorated rapidly the following morning. He lay unconscious for a fortnight before he died. His father searched for the boy who threw the stone, but could not find him, and the police were not told of the incident until after William's death. They too were unable to find the stone-thrower, their inquiries meeting a wall of silence. The jury at the coroner's inquest returned a verdict of death by misadventure and no criminal proceedings followed.

In the autumn of 1871, the Manchester police, in concert with the city magistrates, made a renewed attempt to suppress the 'juvenile terrorism' wreaked by the scuttlers. On the weekend of October 21-22, a special squad of officers from 'B' Division was assembled to deal with the disturbances. The first reported outbreak of fighting was in Whitley Street in Collyhurst. The police rushed to the scene en masse and waded into the two warring factions. They made twenty-one arrests. The prisoners, all lads between the ages of twelve and sixteen, were brought before the presiding magistrate, Charles Rickards, at the Manchester City Police Court on the following Monday morning. Some of the lads were described in court as 'English'. Their adversaries were described as 'Irish', although most had been born in Manchester to parents who had fled Ireland during the Great Famine. Mr Rickards was quickly persuaded of the prisoners' guilt. Rather than pronouncing sentence, however, he ordered that the lads be remanded in custody whilst Superintendent Godby prepared a report on the 'dangerous practice of scuttling'.

When the court sat the following day, Superintendent Godby relayed the story of the origins of scuttling in the feud between the boys of the Lancasterian School and their Catholic counterparts from St Joseph's. He described the lads' formation of armies of Germans and Frenchmen, but cast doubt on the sectarian basis of the disturbances, telling the court that 'he did not think it proceeded from any feelings of religious animosity, but solely from a love of mischief, and what the boys considered fun'. Godby then detailed the spread of scuttling from New Cross into Ancoats and as far as New Islington. He dwelled on the hazards posed to peaceable passers-by, before introducing a procession of civilian witnesses, including a mill owner, to testify to the gangs' record of vandalism as well as violence against the person. Henry Garner, the Chief Inspector attached to the Police Court, told disapprovingly how 'the language of the prisoners when in the cells and the prison van on Monday was the most disgraceful that he ever knew'.

Superintendent Godby calculated that no fewer than 500 lads had been brought before the court for scuttling in the previous twelve months. He read out a list of the fines imposed by the magistrates over that period. Most were of between two and ten shillings, though three unlucky warriors had been required to pay the maximum penalty of forty shillings. In each case, the alternative to payment was imprisonment, usually for seven or fourteen days. Even the common fines of five or ten shillings were severe by Victorian standards. Few families in Manchester's poorer districts could part with such sums lightly. In periods when trade was bad and unemployment soared, many households eked out an existence on less than ten shillings a week. Yet the fines imposed on these warring lads appeared to have been entirely useless as a deterrent.

The magistrates were as keen to get to grips with the scuttling menace as the police, as an exchange between Superintendent Godby and Charles Rickards showed.

Rickards: 'I remember when these cases first came before us they were said to have arisen in connection with the continental war between the French and the Germans, and the fights were represented to be half political and half sectarian.'

Godby: 'That was so. You are aware also no doubt that the chief constable got bills printed and posted throughout the entire district, informing persons what penalty they were liable to for such conduct. That seems to have had no effect, and I must now ask your worship to inflict the full penalty as the only means of putting a stop to it.'

Rickards: 'It was stated here yesterday that in some instances pistols were fired.'

Godby: 'Yes, that is so. There have been both pistols and swords used.'

Rickards: 'Yes, I saw some of the swords, iron ones, which in the hands of a strong, thoughtless lad might be very dangerously used. I also understand that wheelbarrows of stones had been deposited in entries ready for throwing.'

Godby: 'That is true.'

Rickards agreed that exemplary punishments were needed. Before sentencing the twenty-one lads stood before him, he lectured them at some length, knowing that his words would be relayed throughout Manchester by the local press. He told the prisoners that education did not appear to have taught them to obey the laws of their country. He hoped that Manchester Corporation, in its next application for parliamentary powers, would include a clause giving magistrates the power to have such offenders flogged. Rickards added that he was sorry to send boys to prison. He was convinced that if he could order them to be flogged in front of their school-mates, there would be no need to resort to jail sentences.

Rickards fined all twenty-one of the prisoners the maximum sum of forty shillings. In default of payment, they would be locked up for six weeks. A 'great scene' ensued in court. The *City News* noted with some satisfaction that the lads made piteous appeals to their parents to pay the fines. Many of the parents were themselves in tears at the prospect of their sons being locked up for six weeks. According to the *Manchester Courier*, the prisoners' mothers, in particular, were inconsolable.

Charles Rickards expected to be applauded throughout Manchester for the severity of his sentences. Some of the head-lines in the local press bore him out: the *City News* reported his pronouncements at length in an article headed 'JUVENILE TERRORISM IN ROCHDALE ROAD'. However, praise for his stand against the scuttlers was by no means universal. The *Free Lance* mocked him savagely. In a column headed 'THE ROCHDALE ROAD WAR', the *Free Lance* applauded not the avenging magistrate but the 'fighting youths' of Angel Meadow and Ancoats: 'The warriors on each side are armed with wondrous weapons of offence and defence, and they daily meet and fight with all the energy of Britons of the finest possible extraction. Nothing can daunt their courage, or scare them from the field.' With heavy irony, the *Free Lance* professed to being appalled by the magistrate's plea for the power to flog these 'gallant' juveniles. 'This military ardour is a thing to be encouraged. What matter if a few panes of plate glass be demolished, or a confectioner's shop or two be sacked! The blood that Mr. RICKARDS would draw by means of the birch runs in British veins, and boils at the insult!' Apparently forgetting that many of the warriors identified themselves as 'Irish', the *Free Lance* ended with a piece of advice to the magistrate: he should appoint a bodyguard of police officers all to himself, and double it, 'when he perambulates the Rochdale Road – or who can foresee the terrible consequences?'

The police and the magistrates must have hoped that the sentences imposed on the batch of twenty-one scuttlers at the Manchester City Police Court on 24 October 1871 would finally deter the warring juvenile gangs. The annual report on the City Gaol at Belle Vue revealed that 406 juveniles were admitted in 1871, 374 of them boys. Most had been convicted of scuttling. Some local councillors became concerned at the sight of twelve- or thirteen-year-olds languishing in prison because their parents could not afford to pay their fines. The boys themselves saw their plight differently: one signed a letter home, 'The Hero of Belle Vue Gaol.' Any hopes that the spate of jailings would put an end to scuttling were soon dashed. Rather than withdrawing from the fray, the gangs began to extend their operations. New gangs appeared in Red Bank and in the slums of Deansgate, which rivalled Angel Meadow as a hotbed of what journalists termed 'Criminal Manchester'.

MANCHESTER BOASTED the most buoyant provincial press in England during the late nineteenth century. The *Manchester Guardian*, founded in 1821, the *Manchester Courier* (1825) and the *Manchester Examiner* (1846) were the city's heavyweight morning papers. The *Courier* was Conservative in outlook. The *Guardian*, by contrast, was the foremost Liberal newspaper in England, with a wide national readership and a circulation of 48,000 by the 1890s. The *Examiner* was to the left of the *Guardian* in its politics. The readerships of all three were largely middle-class. The *Manchester Evening News*, first published in 1868, was half the price and reached a much wider readership. By 1891, it claimed a circulation of 152,000. Its politics were Liberal. The *Manchester Evening Mail*, first published in 1874, was avowedly pro-Conservative. Manchester was also served eventually by three weekly newspapers: the *Weekly Times* (1857), the *City News* (1864) and the *Weekly Post* (1879). All of the city's newspapers, whether daily or weekly, reported on cases heard by the Manchester magistrates. Columns of 'Police Court News' provided picaresque galleries of brutish husbands, loutish youths and habitual thieves, prostitutes and drunkards.

Weekly satirical journals flourished in Manchester during the 1860s and 1870s, with the *Free Lance*, the *Sphinx*, the *City Jackdaw* and the *City Lantern*. The satirical press declined after 1880, although several new titles including the *Parrot*, the *City Bells* and *Spy* were launched. They were short-lived and *Spy* in particular veered from the scurrilous to the libellous. However, the satirical journals subjected Manchester's leading citizens to intense scrutiny, and alongside biting political sketches they provided outlets for a good deal of social comment. They specialised in explorations of Manchester 'low life'. In a city rigidly divided by social class, they allowed the middle classes to glimpse the seamy side of life in Angel Meadow or Ancoats from the comfort of their own armchairs.

BY THE summer of 1872, Manchester City Council was increasingly alarmed by the reported increase in violent crime. Some feared that the very reputation of the city was once more at stake. According to stipendiary magistrate Charles Rickards, nearly all of the perpetrators of serious, 'aggravated' assaults were Irish, either by birth or by descent. In Rickards' view, Manchester's

Irish population was 'belligerent' and 'undisciplined' and the police had little control over them. He gave five examples he had dealt with in the past few weeks. In the first case, 'a giant of a fellow' brutally assaulted an infant. The other four victims were all women, one of whom had jumped from a first-floor window to escape a beating from her husband, whilst another had been badly assaulted by her own son. Rickards linked these cases of domestic violence to the sectarian 'faction fights' – outbreaks of scuttling – which had flared in Angel Meadow during the Franco-Prussian War. He admitted he 'did not know how these things were to be remedied' and wondered whether scuttlers brought before the magistrates should automatically be sent for trial at the Assizes, where the most serious criminal cases of all were heard, so that 'the judges might be made aware of the condition of things in Manchester'. However, as the clerk to the Manchester justices pointed out, such cases could not be sent to the Assizes unless the lads had been charged with cutting and wounding. Even then, the clerk added, the judges were unlikely to impose stiffer sentences than the magistrates.

Rickards had another idea. He suggested that 'it would be well if the children of all denominations, Protestant and Roman Catholic, were schooled and educated together', believing this would help do away with the prejudices that existed among them. This proposal was immediately opposed by one of Rickards' fellow magistrates and it found little favour in the city as a whole. If the local leaders of the Catholic and Protestant churches agreed on one thing, it was that each church should be responsible for those born into its own faith. Most parents wholeheartedly agreed.

Charles Rickards' instinctive description of scuttling as an Irish problem masked the enthusiasm with which the English-born, Protestant scholars of the Lancasterian School in Marshall Street fought the Rochdale Road War. The magistrate's eagerness to blame Manchester's Irish population for the apparent increase in violence drew upon the enduring English stereotype of the Irish as a lawless people, fond of drink and quick of temper. Tellingly, Mr Rickards described scuttles as faction fights.

During the 1850s and 1860s, English journalists commonly referred to the tradition of faction fighting in rural Ireland. These huge brawls between men from rival villages or counties were generally viewed as a form of community entertainment, and were governed by a number of rituals. According to the historian Carolyn Conley, a formal faction fight, which might involve hundreds of men on each side, usually began with the ritual of 'wheeling', which included chants, stylized gestures and insults. 'The traditional wheel included the names of the person(s) issuing the challenge as well as the intended opponent. For example, "Here is Connors and Delahanty. Is there any Madden will come before us?" The setting was often prearranged and faction fights were routine at fairs, markets and other large gatherings.' Sticks and stones were the customary weapons and fatalities occasionally resulted, but the Irish judicial authorities rarely intervened and, when they did, jurors were reluctant to convict. In the wake of the Great Famine, faction fights between rival groups of Irish migrants on the streets of Manchester were reported regularly in the local press. Hostilities which stretched back for generations were, it appeared, being maintained on the streets of districts like Angel Meadow.

Yet Charles Rickards' readiness to blame the Irish for the growth of scuttling conveniently, and perhaps wilfully, obscured the traditional love of fighting among the English. Continental Europeans had long regarded the English as an alarmingly violent people. In the 1690s, the French travel writer Henri Misson famously remarked, 'Any Thing that looks like Fighting is delicious to an Englishman.' Throughout the eighteenth century and for much of the nineteenth, the prize-fight was one of the best-loved English spectacles. In Manchester and Salford, bare-knuckle bouts were generally organised by publicans and beerhouse keepers, often with bookmakers in attendance. Some erected rings on their premises, but fights were also staged in parks, on canal banks, or at more remote locations on the fringes of the city such as Throstle Nest, near Old Trafford, or remoter still, at Baguley Moor in Wythenshawe.

Gilbert Owen, who was born in Ordsall in 1907, remem-

bered his grandfather – 'a bit of a villain' – as a noted pub
fighter:

> The men in my family, they were rough. A lot of the fun they
> got out of it, if you don't mind me telling, was by fighting. A
> lot of fighting went on. Each pub had its own fighter. And it
> was called a pub fight. And when it got mad, they used to egg
> the men on, they'd give 'em a pint, and then another pint.
> And then they'd say, 'You know so-and-so? He said he'd do
> you,' and all that. And then they used to make their way to
> what they used to call 'the hollow' [a patch of open ground
> near to Throstle Nest]. They used to make their way down
> there, and they used to have to dog out [keep watch] for the
> police. Then they used to fight, these fellers, bare fists. My
> granddad was one. He was one, and so was my uncle, he was
> a mad fighter.

Such men were maintaining a neighbourhood tradition which
stretched back well into the nineteenth century.

Notable local fighters during the 1830s included Bob Heald,
who worked for many years as a blacksmith in New Bailey Street,
Salford. Heald was born in Stockport in 1817, and took up
prize-fighting at the age of eighteen. He fought several bouts on
Baguley Moor before venturing further afield for fights in
Warwickshire and Derbyshire. Heald was known by two aliases:
'the Stockport Vulcan' and 'the Sledge-hammer'. His career as a
pugilist was interrupted for six months when he was jailed after
a police raid on one of his fights. His final 'stake' fight was in
June 1839, when he took on Bill Preston, alias 'Bill Butcher',
from Preston. The fight, or 'dust', was originally scheduled to
take place on Horwich Moor, but the police got wind of it and
the fighters narrowly escaped arrest. They decamped with their
supporters to a field outside Turton, near Blackburn, where they
fought for stakes of £50 a-side. The early rounds went to the
Sledge-hammer, with the odds falling to three-to-one by the end
of the fifth. By the eighteenth, however, the fight was tilting in
favour of Bill Butcher and the odds were reduced to evens. The

fight continued for another thirty-seven rounds. During the last five, the ring was broken and the bout ended in acrimony following complaints from the Sledge-hammer's supporters that Butcher 'had not come to the scratch in time'. After a bitter squabble, Heald was finally declared the victor and carried triumphant from the field. The exhausted fighters had battled it out for an hour and forty-five minutes. Heald had had much the worst of the later rounds and it was just as well he was carried from the ring, as he was in no state to walk.

Heald gave up prize-fighting after the punishing encounter with Butcher. He returned to his forge, but continued to train up-and-coming fighters in Salford for the next four decades. When the *Salford Reporter* interviewed him at the age of seventy-nine, he was still an avid follower of the ring and had attended a clandestine bout in 'the bar parlour of a well-known Salford public house' only two weeks previously.

During the 1860s, magistrates around Manchester expressed alarm at reports that prize-fighting was on the increase. The police forces of both Manchester and Salford were instructed to take action. Salford Borough Police posted two officers at Throstle Nest every Sunday during the autumn of 1863, 'as it was the practice of a number of persons to congregate that day to take part in and to witness prize-fights'. The pugilists and their supporters were quick to take evasive measures. For major bouts, they decamped to still more remote venues such as Barton Moss, ten miles from the centre of Manchester. However, regular bouts were surreptitiously staged behind locked doors in low public houses throughout Manchester and Salford. Jerome Caminada, who joined the City of Manchester police in 1868, identified the slum streets off Deansgate as the principal haunt of the city's pugilists at that time. 'In several of the beerhouse garrets there were regular rings of stakes, ropes, etc, and some of the "spriest" men known have stripped there,' he wrote. 'When these battles were stopped, the fights took place in kitchens, stables, cellars, or in any other place where the police were not likely to put in an appearance.' The same venues were used for illicit dog-fights and badger-baiting, or 'drawing the badger'.

Prize-fights were by no means the only time-honoured manifestation of the English love of fighting. Indeed, Manchester men with longer memories than Charles Rickards acknowledged that scuttling itself was by no means a recent phenomenon. James Bury traced its origins as far back as the 1820s in an essay published by the *Manchester City News* in 1879. Bury's account was perhaps romanticised, for he insisted that in former times scuttling had been an honourable pursuit. Nonetheless, his recollections made it impossible to blame scuttling upon those Irish migrants who had settled in Manchester since the 1840s:

> Scuttling in Manchester is no new pugnacious indulgence, for between fifty and sixty years ago it was very prevalent amongst the rough boys, rising youth, and not thoroughly developed manhood of those times; but neither sticks nor dangerous weapons were used, nor were the public assaulted. It was an expression of pluck and a trial of physical strength, fists, clods of grassy earth, with an occasional shower of pebble stones, being the missiles used in a general mêlée, varied by single pitched battles amongst the lads of neighbouring districts.

Feuds akin to those of the scuttling gangs of the 1870s were fought during the 1820s between the lads of Ancoats and those of 'Bank Top', which subsequently became London Road. Shooter's Brook flowed between the two districts and the crofts on either side became regular battlegrounds. According to Bury, this feud 'outrivaled for bitterness that of the Capulets and Montagues'. The western edge of Shooter's Brook was the battleground in another long-running feud between the boys of a school on Back Mosley Street and the lads of Granby Row National School. Bury recalled 'many a pair of brilliant black eyes' given and taken in these encounters.

Pitched battles were fought between the lads of different factories as well as between those of rival schools. These fights were encouraged, and even set in motion, by older men who appear to have regarded the subsequent mêlées as a form of spectator sport. James Bury recalled that: 'The dyers and calico-printers at the several works on the banks of the river Medlock, between the Downing Street bridge and Clayton bridge, set their boy assistants, technically called blue-dippers and tier-boys, against each other.' Within workplaces, there was a recognised hierarchy in which youths were graded according to their fighting prowess: 'At each works one lad, by force of fist, reigned supreme over his fellows as "cock of the walk", which dignity he had to hold against each new-comer, or be beaten.' Each workplace had its own recognised fighting ground. The lads of Statham's dye-works in Tipping Street, for example, fought in the lanes behind the George and Dragon in Ardwick Green, still a country pub during the 1820s.

The first recorded use of the term 'scuttling' dates back to the 1860s. Its origins are unknown, but as a term to describe a fight between rival gangs of youths it was distinctive to the Manchester conurbation. In 1864, a contributor to the magazine of St Paul's Literary and Educational Society in Manchester compiled a glossary of boyhood slang. The noun 'scuttle' was defined as:

A fight. — When boys of one street take offence at boys of another street, they often fall to fighting in a body. This is called a 'scuttle'. There is an English word 'scuttle' meaning a short run, a quick pace, and as many run away rather quickly from such combats, we are inclined to think that this is a reasonable derivation.

It is not clear from the glossary whether the term was a recent invention or of longer standing. However, the term 'scuttler' was certainly in widespread use in Manchester by the late 1860s. In September 1867, Lieutenant-Colonel Charles Gordon, the future hero of Khartoum, visited Manchester and wrote at length from the city to his sister Augusta. Gordon was shocked by the poverty he witnessed, although he acknowledged that conditions had improved since the Cotton Famine of the early 1860s, when the American Civil War interrupted the supply of raw cotton to Lancashire's mills, resulting in short-time working and mass lay-offs.

'Your heart would bleed to see the poor people here,' he told his sister, 'though they say there is no distress such as there was some time ago; they are indeed like sheep having no shepherd, but, thank God, though they look forlorn, they have a watchful and pitying eye over them. It does so painfully affect me, and I do trust will make me think less of self and more of these poor people. Little idea have the rich of other counties of the scenes in these parts.' Gordon continued: 'The poor scuttlers here, male and female, fill me with sorrow. They wear wooden clogs – a sort of sabot – and make such a noise.' Gordon's brief note on the scuttlers suggests that they already formed a distinct grouping among the young people of the city. Moreover, they were far from a discreet presence. Quite the reverse: they announced themselves by the noise they made, and if their choice of footwear was anything to go by, their distinctive fashions.

Speaking during the summer of 1872, Charles Rickards was already behind the times when he described scuttles as sectarian faction fights. As scuttling spread across the slum districts which ringed Manchester city centre, the conflicts rapidly lost their overtly sectarian edge. Gangs increasingly sought confrontations with any like-minded gatherings of youths, whenever and wherever they encountered them. The hostilities between 'English' and 'Irish' lads within Angel Meadow or Ancoats appear to have subsided, eclipsed by wider territorial animosities. And the level of violence continued to grow. Many of those taking part in scuttling expeditions were now aged in their mid-to-late teens. They were powerfully built youths, often working as outdoor labourers or carters or performing heavy labouring work in factories or iron foundries. This new breed of scuttler still carried pockets full of stones to hurl at the onset of a scuttle but he also fought at close quarters with knives and belts. When in the company of his gang, he was a formidable prospect.

CHAPTER 4

Greengate Roughs

THE BRIDGES OVER the River Irwell joined Salford to Manchester city centre and to the slums of Strangeways, Deansgate and Hulme. Angel Meadow and the borders of Ancoats were also only a short walk away. Indeed to outsiders, Salford was part of Manchester, forming, in effect, the city's West End. Yet Salford was an independent county borough with a population of 125,000 by 1870. Salford had its own Members of Parliament, its own system of local government and its own institutions of law and order. Many of Salford's inhabitants worked in Manchester, many others had once lived there. But the borough was proud of its independence and those young people who grew up in Salford displayed a fierce local pride. They were adamant that they did not come from Manchester.

The slums of Salford were as grim as those of Angel Meadow or Ancoats. Friedrich Engels classified Salford in 1845 as:

one large working men's quarter, penetrated by a single wide avenue … an old and therefore very unwholesome, dirty, and ruinous locality is to be found here, lying opposite the Old Church of Manchester, and in as bad a condition as the Old Town on the other side of the Irwell … All Salford is built in courts or narrow lanes, so narrow, that they remind me of the narrowest I have ever seen, the little lanes of Genoa. The average construction of Salford is in this respect much worse than that of Manchester, and so, too, in respect of cleanliness. If, in Manchester, the police, from time to time, every six or ten years, makes a raid upon the working-people's districts, closes the worst dwellings, and causes the filthiest spots in these Augean stables to be cleansed, in Salford it seems to have done absolutely nothing. The narrow side lanes and courts of Chapel Street, Greengate and Gravel Lane have certainly never been cleansed since they were built ... Exactly the same state of affairs is found in the more distant regions of Salford, in Islington, along Regent Road, and back of the Bolton railway. The working-men's dwellings between Oldfield Road and Cross Lane, where a mass of courts and alleys are to be found in the worst possible state, vie with the districts of the Old Town in filth and overcrowding.

As Salford's factory districts expanded to the south and west over the decades that followed, new residential districts – street upon street of two-up, two-down terraced houses – were built to accommodate the rapidly growing working-class population. The new districts, such as Ordsall, to the south of Regent Road, were much more salubrious than the slums that so horrified Engels. The streets were wider, and the houses were built with back yards and entries, or alleyways, running between them. But Greengate and the other slums of Old Salford were to change little over the course of the century.

Situated just a few minutes' walk from Manchester Cathedral, Greengate was a byword for crime. Attacks on the police were commonplace and officers could expect little help from the local populace. At around six o'clock one evening in August, 1871, constables Cain and Butler of the Salford Borough Police were patrolling the area when they encountered a corner gang on the pavement opposite a well-known public house called the Three Legs of Man. The gathering included a number of local 'Greengate roughs' and some nefarious characters from low districts in Manchester. The roughs resented being told to disperse and instead of moving on they attacked the police officers, both of whom were badly battered. P.C. Cain fared worst: he was struck, his whiskers were pulled, and he was kicked and then knocked down. Other beat bobbies were alerted by the shouting and rushed to help. Between them, they managed to apprehend Henry Hoggard. The prisoner, a twenty-one-year-old, hailed from Hulme, but was living in a lodging-house in Hardman Street, Deansgate. As the police led him away, the crowd renewed their attack in a bid to rescue him. A second arrest was made: John Carroll, of Dean's Court, Greengate.

Hoggard and Carroll were brought before the magistrates at the Salford Police Court the following morning and were both convicted of being drunk and disorderly and assaulting the police. They were sent down for six months with hard labour, the maximum sentence for assaulting the police permitted under English law. Jane Kennedy, from Oldham, another member of the crowd that night, was sentenced to fourteen days for drunkenness and attempting to rescue a prisoner. She was no stranger to fights with the police; the magistrates heard that she had assaulted another officer only the previous evening. Police subsequently issued a warrant for the arrest of two more men, including Andrew Hoggard, brother of Henry. Aged twenty-four, Andrew described himself as a tailor but was known to the police as a prize-fighter. He was arrested three weeks later, charged with assaulting the police, and jailed for a month.

Scuttling spread into Salford during 1871 and the first reports in the local press surfaced in September that year. At around nine o'clock on the night of Friday, September 15, a large number of young men took part in a scuttle between two gangs in the district known as the Adelphi, an impoverished slum downhill from St John's, the Catholic cathedral on Chapel Street. The Adelphi vied with Greengate for the title of Salford's worst slum. The entire district lay permanently shrouded in nitric acid fumes from the local factories. Few local people complained, not least since the worst offender, the vast Broughton Copper Works in Ford Lane, provided regular work for hundreds of local men and youths. Many of the inhabitants of the Adelphi were Catholics, and Irish by birth or descent. They were reputedly ferocious street fighters and the police ventured into Silk Street and Cannon Street only with great caution, even when in pairs. The youths hurled stones at each other and fought with a variety of improvised weapons, including a truncheon and a strip of board into which two-inch nails had been hammered at one end. Amid the chaos and confusion, a passer-by named Henry Clarke was knocked unconscious. Clarke was an engine driver at Lemming's mill, close to the scene. As he tried to walk round the edge of the fray, he was hit by a number of missiles and was then struck on the head by the scuttler armed with the board of nails. A group of Clarke's workmates from Lemming's were watching the fight and, when they saw what happened, they rushed into the brawling mass of scuttlers and grabbed hold of fifteen-year-old Michael Carr.

Carr, who lived nearby in Corporation Square, was handed over to the police. When searched at the police station, he was found to have twenty-four stones of various sizes stashed in his pockets. The stones were produced in evidence when he appeared at the Salford Police Court, along with the board of nails which had been abandoned at the spot where Henry Clarke fell. Sir John Iles Mantell, the stipendiary magistrate for Salford, demanded to know whether Carr had been seen throwing stones. The police, however, were unable to state categorically that that was the case. The stipendiary then interrogated Michael Carr.

Sir John: 'Boy, you must have been very improperly engaged to have such a large number of stones in your pocket.'

Prisoner: 'But, sir, I did not throw any. There was one lot of boys against another.'

Sir John, to the police: 'Is there any damage done to property?'

Police officer: 'Some windows were broken, but no-one could say exactly which of the boys it was that broke them.'

Sir John: 'Then I can do nothing with the case. I cannot find out who hit the man, and I shall discharge the prisoner. (To the prisoner:) You had better take care of yourself in future, or you will be bound over to keep the peace.'

In Manchester, where the magistrates were much more alert to the problem of scuttling, Carr would without doubt have been heavily fined and might well have been locked up in default of payment.

The police officers who attended Salford Police Court to testify to the disturbance in the Adelphi described the incident as 'a dangerous game called scuttling'. The term had evidently been adopted by gangs of lads in Salford, who took to the pastime with every bit as much fervour as their counterparts in Manchester. No mention was made of any sectarian dimension to the Adelphi affray, even though the district was renowned as one of the major areas of Irish settlement in Salford. The *Salford Weekly Chronicle* did not specify whether Michael Carr was English or Irish. Instead, it labelled him 'a young rascal of the Arab race'. The term 'street Arab' was widely used by Victorian social commentators to describe boys from the slums of the major cities, many of whom earned their living on the streets and spent most of their leisure time there too. The term was highly derogatory, but it bore no trace of the sectarian animosity displayed by the self-styled Frenchmen and Germans busily fighting the Rochdale Road War across the River Irwell.

The ready resort to violence in the slums of Manchester had many parallels in Salford. On New Year's Day in 1872, Joe Smith, a velvet finisher from Queen Street, Greengate, went for a celebratory drink with John Pennington at the British Rolla, a public house in nearby Collier Street. When Smith and Pennington left the pub, they met a crowd of young men on the street corner engaged in an animated discussion about fighting. Emboldened by drink, Smith approached them and declared, 'If I were put to it, I dare say I could mill [fight] any of you.' Smith then began to walk away but was followed by John Savage, a twenty-eight-year-old labourer, who was determined to put Smith's boast to the test. The two of them started to fight in the street and Savage quickly knocked Smith down. When Smith got back to his feet, he was attacked for a second time. Twenty-year-old Alf Prophet rushed to join in the assault, followed by his brother, Thomas, a twenty-one-year-old carter. Together with Savage, they beat Smith back to the ground.

It was only when the fight was over that Smith realised that he had been stabbed in the head. He was treated by a surgeon, who found that he was suffering from shock as well as a severe head wound. Doctors at the Salford Dispensary feared for his life for the next ten days. Savage and the two Prophet brothers were all neighbours of Smith's from Queen Street. His challenge to their fighting prowess had evidently been too much for them to stomach in front of a crowd of their friends. Smith's assailants were all charged with assault by stabbing and committed to the Assizes. However, when the case came to trial it quickly collapsed. Smith could not say which of his three assailants had used the knife and there were no witnesses willing to identify the perpetrator in court. Savage and the two Prophet brothers were found not guilty and discharged.

Queen Street – an 'un-Queenly nest of filth and squalor' according to local printer and trade unionist W. H. Wood – lay at the heart of Greengate. This was the oldest part of Salford and by far the most notorious. The cramped courtyards off Queen Street were reputed to be hotbeds of drunkenness, crime and vice. The population of Greengate, it was said, would fight anyone on the slightest provocation. The *Sphinx* reported in June 1869 that:

Greengate and Broughton Road, Salford, are acquiring an unenviable notoriety as the scenes of numerous pugilistic encounters, chiefly among the youthful portion of the community. In this populous district, dedicated to the exhala-tions of the adjoining river, and the aromatic odours of sundry copper, chemical and other works … there are 'mills' to be seen of a nature other than those of Messrs Langworthy Brothers & Co. We do not allude to the establishments of Mr Bill Brown, pugilist, or Mr James Hancock, pedestrian, nor to our old friend the Stalybridge Infant, who is frequently to be seen in this quarter. These are peaceable citizens, who pursue their professional avocations at intervals, in retired spots, in a legal illegal sort of way.

The entertainments to which we allude are given in the open street. Sometimes they take place about the time when the factories are loosed, are sometimes not. The neighbour-hood is pugnacious, and even the dogs which abound in it, and the cocks and hens which pass their days on the street, and their nights in a cellar, are always at it. We have been an unintentional witness at several of these gratuitous exhibitions. A few weeks since, two lads, who looked about fifteen years of age, but were probably older, as human growth is stunted in this quarter, had what sporting papers facetiously term a merry little mill, consisting of several rounds, aided by backers and bottle holders.

It took place on a Sunday evening, as the bells were ringing for church, within fifty yards of a certain well-known church and an independent chapel, which stand against each other, like two competing theatres. Within the last seven days we have been a witness of two other affairs of a similar nature. One of these was also between two lads who showed considerable gameness which might be utilised for better purposes. This performance occurred at half-past one p.m., and was numerously attended.

The third encounter was between two young women.[6] The *Sphinx* drily noted that the police were conspicuously absent on all three occasions.

With its thinly veiled references to dog-fighting and cock-fighting, and its listing of prize-fighters known to frequent the district, the *Sphinx* portrayed Greengate as a place in which violence was both endemic and admired. The hulking Sam Hurst, 'the Stalybridge Infant', was the bareknuckle champion of England during 1860–61. Jem Mace, who took his title, later recalled that Hurst had given him 'the toughest eleven rounds I ever fought'. Hurst, he recalled, 'was a huge fellow, well over six feet in height, and big in proportion. When he came at me his arms were waving in the air like windmills. He had huge hands and arms, and could have felled an ox with one blow.'

WHEN GANGS of scuttlers from Manchester began to cross the River Irwell into Salford they no doubt expected a hostile

---

6 This incident is described in Chapter 16.

response. One of the first documented incursions was in April 1872. A gang from Red Bank crossed the river and made their way to Oldfield Road, where they confronted a number of local youths. The Manchester lads appear to have been more practised in the arts of scuttling. They attacked with their belts, aiming the oversized metal buckles at the heads of their opponents. Two Salford lads suffered serious head injuries when they were struck on the head with the buckle swung by sixteen-year-old James Coulburn. The Red Bank scuttler was arrested close to the scene and he subsequently appeared at the Salford Police Court. The magistrates fined him £5 with the alternative of one month's imprisonment.

Raids by Manchester gangs into Salford continued throughout the summer and autumn of 1872. In October, a band of scuttlers from Angel Meadow ventured across Blackfriars Bridge and roamed the back streets off Chapel Street until they encountered a gang of Salford scuttlers in Worsley Street. The two gangs hurled volleys of stones at each other, but a contingent of beat constables arrived before a full scuttle commenced. One lad from the Meadow, Thomas Quinn, was arrested at the scene and subsequently convicted of riotous and disorderly conduct. The prospect of feuds with youths from Salford must have held great appeal to the scuttlers of Angel Meadow and Ancoats as well as the emerging gangs from Deansgate. The Salford lads proved to be worthy opponents, so they were a good test of the mettle of the more established Manchester gangs. And the scuttlers of Angel Meadow and Ancoats, who were by now easily recognised by the officers of 'B' Division, were not yet known to the Salford constabulary.

Regular skirmishes took place in each of the streets leading onto the bridges across the Irwell. Hampson Street, one of the main thoroughfares leading into Salford from the slums of Deansgate, was a favoured meeting ground. Salford gangs congregated here each night, ready to repel bands of marauding youths from Manchester and sending out raiding parties of their own across the Irwell. In July 1872, a gang from the Adelphi confronted a Manchester gang in a Sunday evening row in Irwell Street. Two months later, a beat constable from Manchester's 'A' Division was stoned by scuttlers when he chanced upon sixty lads fighting in Bridge Street and Gartside Street, on the Manchester side of the river. P.C. Dunncliffe was struck a number of times on the helmet and once on the head.

Salford's magistrates were initially prepared to sanction informal punishments of boys convicted of stone throwing. When Dan Taylor was convicted of riotous and disorderly conduct by throwing stones during a scuttle in Hampson Street in May 1872, he was fined two shillings and sixpence. The fine was waived following discussions between the magistrates and Taylor's mother after she promised to give her son 'a sound thrashing'. She returned to court to report that the deed was done, to the evident satisfaction of both the magistrates and the court reporter for the *Salford Weekly News*. The publicity was probably as painful as the beating for Dan Taylor. By September 1872, stone throwing between rival gangs came to be regarded by Salford's magistrates as 'only a milder form of scuttling'. Accounts of more brutal affrays had been all too common in the Salford press that summer. In July, four young men and one young woman were fined twenty shillings each following a scuttle in Gravel Lane and Queen Street in Greengate. One of their adversaries had been beaten with a belt. Superintendent Williams told the Salford Police Court that, 'These disturbances were getting very frequent and serious in the neighbourhood. They were known locally by the name of "scuttling". It appeared that a band of young men would get together and assault anyone they came across.' Mary Ann McFay, arrested with four of her male companions following the assault was one of the first young women to be convicted of scuttling.

Salford scuttlers began to emulate their Manchester counterparts by adopting belts as their customary weapons. In September 1872, another batch of five scuttlers appeared at the Salford Police Court. According to police evidence, 'The prisoners and a number of other lads had formed themselves into a gang, and assaulted by means of belts with large heavy buckles attached everyone who passed.' The *Salford Weekly News* commented, 'We should state that this nuisance is getting serious in Salford, and we have heard of persons being severely injured. The police will do well to keep a sharp eye on such offenders.' Salford's police, who were doing their best to contain the violence, must have been exasperated to say the least by the newspaper's strictures.

The dangers posed to the police themselves were amply demonstrated on the night of 1 October 1872. At around eight o'clock, three beat constables were dispatched to break up a scuttle in Brown Street, off Chapel Street. Constables Snelson, Brierley and Pritchard were confronted by a crowd of youths fighting with sticks, stones and a range of other missiles. As the officers approached, they were greeted with a shower of stones. Tommy Whitehood, a seventeen-year-old from Posey Street, threw a bottle at P.C. Snelson and then hurled a five foot plank of wood at him. P.C. Snelson managed to dodge the missiles, both of which struck the unfortunate P.C. Brierley instead. P.C. Pritchard came off even worse: he was hit in the eye with a stone. The constables managed to arrest Whitehood and he duly appeared at the Salford Police Court. The magistrates were remarkably lenient with him. Whitehood was bound over to keep the peace for three months, albeit with sureties totalling £20 which he and his relatives would forfeit should he come back before the magistrates.

SCUTTLING SPREAD quickly from Angel Meadow and Ancoats across the vast slum districts which ringed Manchester city centre and into the heart of Salford. In Deansgate, which bordered Salford, police were deluged with complaints of scuttling in the autumn of 1872. Dozens of lads were fighting pitched battles which spilled into city centre thoroughfares such as Bridge Street. Beat constables tried valiantly to disperse the combatants, but were subjected to volleys of stones in return. In Chorlton-on-Medlock, to the south, boys as young as nine reportedly entered into the affrays alongside lads in their teens. The increasing resort to weapons posed a growing threat to gang members and passers-by alike.

By late 1872, scuttling was firmly established as part of the turbulent street life of the low parts of Manchester and Salford.

Gangs of heavily armed youths roamed as far as three or four miles in one night in search of opponents. Encroaching into another gang's territory laid down a clear and deliberate challenge. Scuttlers were obliged to fight to uphold the honour both of the gang itself and of the neighbourhood from which it was drawn. It was now difficult for boys aged in their teens to move freely across any of the districts to which scuttlers laid claim. From Newton Heath in the north of the city to Chorlton-on-Medlock and Hulme in the south, the gang wars raged.

As conflicts continued to grow over the course of the decade, filling the police court news columns of the local newspapers with seemingly endless tales of violence and depravity, even the satirical *Free Lance* became alarmed. Having previously admired the pugnacious spirit of the warriors of Angel Meadow, the *Free Lance* came to regard the practice of gangs of lads fighting with weapons and stoning each other in the streets as no laughing matter. The mounting anxieties in the local press were justified. The civil war in Manchester had three decades to run.

CHAPTER 5

Young Savages

IN 1862, ENGLISH society had been gripped by fear of 'garrotters'. This apparently new breed of criminal typically worked in pairs: one man seized the victim from behind and choked him, while the other rifled his pockets. The gentlemanly highwayman of the past, it appeared, had given way to a plague of brutes loitering in the darkened corners of England's cities. A national outcry was raised that July, when the Liberal Member of Parliament for Blackburn, James Pilkington, was garrotted in Pall Mall while walking back to his London residence at one o'clock in the morning after a late-night sitting of the House of Commons. Outraged by an assault upon one of its own, Parliament was quick to respond. A Security from Violence Act was passed the following year, reinstating the penalty of flogging for the crime of robbery with violence. The punishment had only been abolished two years previously.

The garrotting panic peaked in December 1862 when *The Times* raged against 'the insecurity of life and property' in the Metropolis. By the time the Security from Violence Act came into force in July 1863, the panic had already subsided and the numbers of such crimes reported to the police was falling. However, in later years, the reintroduction of flogging was widely cited as the *reason* for the decline in garrotting. In the minds of most of the newspaper-reading public, the message was clear: flogging worked. Where lengthy terms of imprisonment had conspicuously failed to deter criminals, the 'cat o' nine tails' was the cure.

The lessons of the garrotting panic lived long in English memories. A dozen years later, readers of the *Manchester Evening News* were presented with a first-hand account by a former convict who had himself been 'under the lash'. This one-time garrotter had recently returned from the term of penal servitude which followed the infliction of the cat. He was now living by honest means. Still a relatively young man, he was of slim build and below average height, but his face was 'an intelligent one', displaying none of the brutish features commonly associated with members of the 'criminal class'. He freely admitted to his past exploits, telling an *Evening News* investigator that, before his time in prison, he had been part of a 'beech-buzzing' mob, a gang of itinerant pickpockets working the 'gaffs' or fairgrounds of northern England and Scotland.

He abandoned his life of crime when he got word that his mother had been taken ill. He returned to Manchester immediately, vowing to settle down and get married. However, his past quickly caught up with him. Quite by chance he found himself involved in a fracas in Wood Street, off Deansgate. He was arrested at the scene and promptly charged with garrotting. On this occasion, he swore, he had been innocent: 'It was a put-up job, for I never screwed the man who was robbed.' He fully expected to be freed following his trial at the Manchester Assizes, and was shocked when the jury found him guilty. He knew he was in for 'something hot', having already served a 'drag' (three months), two sentences of six months and one of four years. Nonetheless, he was staggered by the severity of the sentence: a 'seven-stretch' (seven years' penal servitude) and two dozen lashes.

The 'bashing' (flogging) was scheduled to take place in Strangeways a week after the trial. The wait was terrible: 'I kept trying to feel what the strokes of the lash would be like.' On the appointed day:

> I was led from my cell into the yard and stripped to my trousers. It was cold as could be, for it was December, and I shivered and felt just as bad as ever I did in my life. I was taken to a wall and saw two rings in the bricks about as high as my

shoulders and two posts of wood, standing a bit apart and away from the rings, with a cross piece that seemed as if it could slide up and down. At the bottom of the posts was a kind of box with two round holes in the top. They opened this like you might pull a drawer out of a cupboard, and I was made to stand in it. My feet were fitted into the corners, and then they closed it and screwed it up. My legs were just fixed in the holes now up to over the knee, and I was as fast as in a vice. My hands were put into the rings and the cross-piece of wood fitted across my chest by the doctor. I was as tight as a drum, and my back was a little bent and forced out and my arms stretched full length. I couldn't bend my knee or shift about in any way, for everything was fixed up so as to keep me in that same state till I'd got my dose. One of the screws [warders] had got the cat in his hand, and he was a big fellow, but not half a bad 'un. He said to me he hoped I shouldn't think any worse of him for it, but if he didn't do it some'un else would. The doctor stood by with his chronometer in his hand and then I got my bashing.

The first stroke went right across my shoulders, and it was something awful. I'd never felt anything like it before, and I howled out sharp, and roared loud as I could. Just where the lash went it seemed to burn right up into me, and the skin felt as if it had swelled up and was going to burst. It went through me, and if a hot iron had scorched me it wouldn't have been half as sharp. I'd been told by the old 'uns in the gaol that it was best to shout, as the doctor might think it was hurting me bad, and I might get off with half the dose, and I kept on all the time it lasted. It was only a bit of kidment to scheme the doctor, but it didn't work. It was slow time, for I counted thirty before I got number two, and that came as sharp as the first. The doctor stood close by, and pointed where every stroke was to drop, and the screw put it down just where he shewed. He was a bad 'un, that doctor, for every cut was as bad as the others, and the pain was just like dying over and over again. The doctor would point, and I waited till I heard the whip coming, and then I cried out louder every time. Sometimes it would drop on one of the cuts that had gone before and it was – bad then. I could have sworn my back was as big again as it should be, for after the cat was pulled sharp back the flesh went after it, and rose up till I knew I was bleeding, and that the skin had burst. The blood ran down into my trousers thick, no cheese [mistake] about it. Every now and then the cat lapped round my chest, and that was the worst of all. It knocked me out of wind, my breath went as if I'd jumped into cold water, choking like, and my mouth as dry as could be. I'd nothing to chew, so I hung onto the rings with my hands as hard as I could, and this only pulled my chest across the wood and made my back tighter. I bled a good deal, but I got the two dozen, and I felt every odd 'un [each one]. The last was as bad as the first.

He was held in the Manchester City Gaol at Belle Vue for thirteen weeks before he was sent to 'the Bank' for ten months. Millbank was a tough London prison, previously used to hold prisoners prior to transportation. He ended up in Dartmoor, the bleakest of England's Convict Prisons, where hard labour consisted of cutting pieces of turf on the Devon moors under armed guard – a much more punishing task than 'grinding air', or working the treadwheel, at Belle Vue.

Within Manchester, this 'garrotter's confession' helped to cement the belief that flogging offered a solution to the problem of crime. In fact, more sober analyses of the impact of the cat suggested no such thing. The first judge to utilise his new powers under the Security from Violence Act in the summer of 1863 had been Mr Justice Lush, sitting at the Leeds Assizes. He ordered floggings in each case of robbery with violence brought before him. Mr Justice Lush eagerly awaited the next sitting of the Assizes at Leeds to gauge the results of his salutary sentences. He was dismayed to learn from Mr Justice Keating that the floggings appeared to have had no deterrent effect whatsoever. Quite the reverse: the number of cases of robbery with violence had considerably increased – so much so, that Judge Keating had felt obliged to impose very severe sentences of imprisonment. Opinion among Her Majesty's judges as to the value of flogging as a deterrent was keenly divided. It was less so among the nation's newspaper editors and their readers, for whom the myth of the powers of the cat held enduring appeal.

As fears of street robbery receded during the 1870s, English society was gripped by new anxieties. A reported proliferation of violence for its own sake led to growing fears of brutalisation among the urban poor. In August 1874, a twenty-six-year-old porter, Richard Morgan, died after he was repeatedly kicked during a drunken row in Tithebarn Street, one of the central thoroughfares of Liverpool. Morgan was walking home with his wife and brother following a day by the sea at New Ferry when he was accosted by a gang of roughs demanding money for beer. His refusal prompted a frenzied assault. Equally shocking was the behaviour of the crowd at the scene. Dozens of people stood and watched as Morgan was kicked from one side of the street to the other. No-one intervened apart from the victim's brother, who was himself assaulted by members of the crowd. Two youths were later hanged for Richard Morgan's murder.

In March 1875, a police constable was fatally stabbed during a riot in Navigation Street, reputedly the roughest place in Birmingham. Twenty-year-old Jeremiah Corkery was convicted of murder and hanged; four of his associates were sentenced to penal servitude for life. 'Liverpool and Birmingham do not stand alone,' commented *The Times*. 'They may be worse than their neighbours, but their neighbours are bad enough, and in every large town there is a population of ruffians who live in habitual defiance and violation of the law.' According to *The Times*, these criminals were at war with society.

Nowhere was this more apparent than on the streets of Manchester. In September 1874, the *Manchester City News* observed:

Brutality is still in the ascendant. Day after day the shameful and sickening catalogue runs on. No morning comes now without its black calendar of disgusting crime. Neither the sentences of justice, such as they are, nor the protests of the press, seem to be of the slightest avail. The ruffians are too much for us; and we are only expressing the feeling which is shared by all decent persons, whether rich or poor, when we say that this is a condition of things altogether unendurable by a civilised people.

The following month, the Conservative government led by Benjamin Disraeli established an enquiry into the state of the laws relating to assault. Disraeli's government had already embarked upon a wider programme of social reform, addressing factory working hours, slum clearance and public health. Violence was added to a growing list of pressing social problems. At the behest of the Home Secretary, Richard Cross, a circular was sent to the Assize circuit judges, the recorders presiding over courts of Quarter Sessions and the stipendiary magistrates throughout England and Wales. Recipients were asked whether the existing punishments for brutal assaults were sufficiently stringent. They were also asked whether flogging had been effective in putting down offences of robbery with violence.

The circular was sent to the three most important jurists in Manchester: the city's stipendiary magistrate, the Recorder of Manchester and the chairman of the Salford Hundred Quarter Sessions. The stipendiary, Francis Headlam, was convinced that the reintroduction of flogging had led to a steep fall in garrotting in Manchester. Nonetheless, he advocated longer prison sentences rather than flogging for common assaults and assaults on the police. Recorder Henry West conferred with the grand jury at the Manchester Quarter Sessions in January 1875. The jurors were strongly of the view that assaults should be punished more severely, whether at the police courts or at the Quarter Sessions. W. H. Higgin replied in his capacity as chairman of the Salford Hundred Quarter Sessions. He argued that whipping should be added to the range of punishments permitted for unlawful wounding and inflicting grievous or actual bodily harm.

Amongst the judicial authorities in and around Manchester, there was clear support for the introduction of heavier punishments for crimes of violence. This was echoed across England and Wales, with recorders and stipendiary magistrates alike pointing to an upsurge in violence which they blamed on rising wages and a corresponding increase in drunkenness. Many were adamant that the epidemic could be halted if flogging were sanctioned for severe cases of assault as well as robbery with violence. In the event, the only significant change in the law during the 1870s was the Matrimonial Causes Act of 1878. This gave magistrates the power to grant separation and maintenance orders to women who were assaulted by their husbands. Out of step with much of public opinion, Parliament was not ready to sanction the wider use of the cat. In Manchester and Salford, the courts were therefore left to rely on their traditional powers in their increasingly desperate attempts to stem the rise of scuttling.

Against this backdrop, commentaries on scuttling in the local press became increasingly harsh in tone. The satirical *Free Lance* had mocked Charles Rickards for over-reacting to the Rochdale Road War of 1870-71. Yet over the course of the decade, the magazine's own columnists were to become increasingly shrill in their condemnation of the bands of disorderly youths infesting the city's streets. As the magistrates began to impose mandatory prison sentences in the wake of the more serious outbreaks of scuttling, they found themselves applauded rather than derided. 'Every one who has had occasion to pass along any of our more rough neighbourhoods, such as Ancoats, Salford or Red Bank,' the *Free Lance* insisted, 'must have noticed, if he has not actually been annoyed by, these premature miscreants, and it is very satisfactory to find that magisterial severity is being exercised with the view of repressing street outrages such as would disgrace the lowest purlieus of the least-civilised city in Europe.' Such judicial severity was prompted by a steady stream of woundings and assaults carried out by 'mere lads'.

EVEN AS scuttling spread out across the Manchester conurbation, Ancoats remained a hotbed of gang fighting. One of the most active gangs emerged from the cluster of streets off Prussia Street, a densely packed slum quarter crammed between Oldham Road and the Rochdale Canal. According to officers of 'C'

Division, the Prussia Street scuttlers were a terror to the neighbourhood. They savagely assaulted any local adult foolhardy enough to complain about the gang's activities or cause offence to one of its members. Any unfamiliar youth who attempted to pass through Prussia Street was stopped and interrogated for the faintest sign of association with a rival gang.

In the winter of 1875, the Prussia Street lads overstepped the mark. On the evening of Saturday, November 27, they were patrolling Prussia Street when they spotted a boy they did not recognise. They stopped him and demanded to know if he was a scuttler, adding that if he was, they would 'stick a knife into him'. The boy managed to persuade them that he was not a gang member, and they let him go.

The Prussia Street scuttlers walked on only a few yards when they encountered an old man by the name of Charles Finn. Without warning, they seized hold of him and began to push him about. When Finn tried to get away, Tommy Rigby tripped him up and Matthew Melia stabbed him in the back with a large table knife, inflicting a wound one inch deep. Jimmy Gerrard kicked the old man, and then threw a half-brick at him. The brick missed, but the gang had not finished. Another of the Prussia Street lads named James Burns struck Finn on the back with an iron-headed hammer. A crowd gathered to watch the assault, but no-one dared to intervene on the old man's behalf. The gang's reputation was enough to deter all but the bravest of bystanders, but Burns took no chances. Waving his hammer in the air, he shouted to the on-lookers that if anyone stepped in, he would 'do for them'. The scuttlers left their elderly victim bleeding on the ground. What, if anything, Finn had said or done to cause them offence is not known. Immediately after the attack on the old man, the Prussia Street lads encountered a youth by the name of England. They seized hold of him in turn and Matthew Melia struck him with a belt before stabbing him in the side of the head with his table knife.

Knowing that the assaults were likely to be reported to the police even if no names were given, the Prussia Street lads made themselves scarce for a couple of hours. On this occasion, their notoriety was their undoing. Sergeant Chambers from 'C' Division was dispatched to Prussia Street with two constables and they apprehended five of the local scuttlers later that night. Matthew Melia, Thomas Rigby, James Gerrard, William Ackers and James Burns were charged with two counts of assault by stabbing. They appeared together at the Manchester City Police Court the following Monday morning, when the magistrates heard how the gang had 'run amok' on the Saturday night. Melia was known to the police as the ringleader of the Prussia Street scuttlers. He was sent down for four months. The other four got two months each. The *Manchester Weekly Times* labelled them 'YOUNG SAVAGES'. The *Manchester Guardian* reported that the gang had been 'temporarily broken up' following the police action.

Despite this concerted action by the police and the magistrates, scuttling continued to flourish in Ancoats. By the late 1870s the most infamous gang in the district hailed from Pollard Street, a squalid slum wedged between the Ashton Canal and the River Medlock. They waged long-running vendettas against gangs from Miles Platting and Newton Heath, to the north, and Bradford, to the east. On Saturday, 22 September 1877, the Pollard Street lads took advantage of the half-day's holiday to gather their forces and head into Bradford for a major showdown. At the appointed time of five o'clock, they marched to a brickfield, where no fewer than 500 lads assembled in two vast mobs armed with knives, belts, sticks, pokers, bricks and stones. The scene was set for one of the biggest scuttles since the days of the Rochdale Road War.

The two sides faced each other in a tense stand-off. Ned Lynch, a twenty-one-year-old iron foundry labourer, was at the front of the Pollard Street mob. The Bradford scuttlers were headed by George Worthington, aged eighteen. Egged on by the baying mobs behind them, the two 'captains' stepped forward. Lynch challenged Worthington to fight one-on-one. Worthington accepted, and the two gangs edged closer together, weapons drawn, forming a ring around them. Lynch and Worthington stripped to their waists. They eyed each other warily, knowing that no quarter would be given even in a 'fair' fight.

Before the two captains could come to blows, however, a squad of police officers rushed into the crowd. The police had been tipped-off that a scuttle was to take place that afternoon and Sergeant John Smith from the Bradford Police Office had assembled a force of constables to break it up. Smith was a brave officer, but on this occasion he was foolhardy. In the face of such numbers, his officers had little chance of making arrests and they might have been better off seeking merely to disperse the two mobs. As the police charged into the crowd, the rival gangs joined forces to 'stone the bobbies'. Two of the constables were floored by missiles hurled from all directions, and beaten with sticks and belts as they lay on the ground. Sergeant Smith was hit on the head by a stone and knocked unconscious. He was carried home, where doctors maintained constant watch over him for three days.

Five scuttlers were arrested over the course of the following week. They were committed for trial at the Salford Quarter Sessions, where they appeared on October 22. They were identified in court as Thomas Porter, aged eighteen, a moulder; James Moran, nineteen, moulder; Henry Heathcote, sixteen, brickmaker; Thomas Dalton, twenty-four, seaman; and Edward 'Ned' Lynch, twenty-one, labourer. The jury found the five guilty of unlawful wounding and riot. They were all jailed, with Lynch receiving the longest sentence of twelve months. Porter, one of Lynch's henchmen in the Pollard Street gang, had served a three-month sentence for theft the previous year. He also had two previous convictions for assault. However, his record paled beside that of his captain. Ned Lynch was widely acknowledged as one of the terrors of Ancoats. By the age of twenty-one he had amassed twelve convictions for assault and drunkenness. Although he worked alongside his father in an iron foundry, he also moved on the fringes of the local underworld and in August 1874 he had been jailed for twelve months at Manchester Quarter Sessions for uttering base coin, or forging money.

Lynch's release from Strangeways in October 1878 coincided with a renewal of hostilities between Ancoats and Bradford. On the night of October 26 – a Saturday, the favoured day for many scuttles – the Pollard Street gang intercepted a Bradford youth named Thomas Dwyer, who was walking through Ancoats on his way home and demanded to know where he was going. When the terrified Dwyer refused to answer, he was set upon and stabbed, once on the shoulder and twice in the back. He was treated by a surgeon at the Ancoats Dispensary, who deemed the wounds to be extremely serious both on account of their position and the resultant loss of blood.

Two sixteen-year-olds were arrested the following morning and appeared at the Manchester City Police Court on the Monday, when police officers informed the magistrates that Ancoats was suffering yet another resurgence of gang fighting. The surgeon told the court that no fewer than five cases of stabbing had been treated at the Ancoats Dispensary following affrays between rival scuttlers that month. The magistrates warned that they had debated whether to commit the pair for trial at the Quarter Sessions since they meant to make an example of everyone brought before them for scuttling. In the event, both lads were sentenced to two months' imprisonment.

Six months later, Ned Lynch was himself back before the magistrates. Police from 'C' Division arrested four scuttlers, Lynch included, following a fierce clash in Pollard Street in which a number of youths were stabbed. Lynch was convicted on two separate counts of assault and sentenced to four months with hard labour. He was living with his parents in Burke Street, off Pollard Street, at the time. His face heavily scarred and his hands covered in tattoos, he cut a fearsome figure even on the streets of Ancoats. He had by now served fourteen terms of imprisonment, including two separate stretches of twelve months in Strangeways. Modelled on London's Pentonville, Strangeways Prison was opened in 1868. It housed up to 1,000 prisoners on six wings radiating outwards from a 234-foot tower. From the outside, Strangeways was grand and imposing. The cells, by contrast, were dingy and sparse, measuring just thirteen feet by seven.

The autumn of 1879 saw a lively feud develop between Pollard Street and a newly formed gang from Newton Heath to the north. The population of 'the Heath' had grown rapidly during the 1860s and 1870s and new factories and workshops now nestled between the Oldham Road, the Rochdale Canal and the Lancashire and Yorkshire railway. The opening of the 'loco sheds', a vast locomotive repair works, in 1877 brought an influx of railway workers, adding to the hive of industry. The streets here were more uniform and better paved than in the central slum districts, and the neat two-up, two-down cottages were little palaces compared to the back-to-back hovels of Ancoats. However, the Newton Heath lads had to pass through Ancoats to reach the city centre and whichever route they took, they were unwelcome. Opting for safety in numbers, they formed a gang of their own and, to prove their mettle, they took on the Pollard Street mob.

According to the police, the 'nightly custom' of the two gangs was to 'meet, under the leadership of self appointed captains, and wage war on each other in the streets, stones being thrown on each side, and even knives being resorted to'. On the night of Saturday, November 8, the Newton Heath lads launched a raid on Ancoats, swarming through the streets between Pollard Street and Every Street. In Price Street, they spotted sixteen-year-old Thomas Tetlow, who they took to be a member of the Pollard Street gang. Tetlow was knocked down and kicked 'until he was insensible'. When he regained consciousness, he got to his feet and started to walk away. The Newton Heath lads had other ideas. Matthew Stringer, aged seventeen, had set out that night with a pistol. He fired one shot at Tetlow, hitting him on the arm.

Eight lads were subsequently arrested. Their ages ranged from fifteen to seventeen. They initially appeared at the Manchester City Police Court where they were charged with unlawful assembly and disturbing the peace by scuttling. Charles Rickards committed them to the Manchester Quarter Sessions, declaring that scuttling on this scale was too serious a matter for the magistrates to deal with. The whole batch of scuttlers appeared at the Quarter Sessions on December 12. They were now charged with unlawful wounding, but the case was more complex than it at first appeared. It transpired that the eight prisoners included members of both gangs, yet only the Newton Heath lads had any motive for the assault on Thomas Tetlow. Six of the eight prisoners were discharged on the grounds that the evidence against them was insufficient to sustain the indictment. Before discharging them, the recorder warned that, had they been found guilty, they would have been 'deprived of their liberty for a very long time'.

The two remaining prisoners were then dealt with in turn. The charge against Charlie Chatburn, from Pollard Street, was reduced to common assault. The jury found him guilty, and the Recorder sent him down for twelve months. This was an exemplary sentence. Matthew Stringer, who had shot Thomas Tetlow in the arm, was found guilty of unlawful wounding. The Recorder sent him down for fifteen months, noting that he had been convicted at the Quarter Sessions before, whilst his testimony in the present case had shown him to be a liar as well as a lout.

It is possible to profile this group of eight scuttlers in some depth as they appear in one of the few surviving nineteenth-century registers of Strangeways Prison. Seventeen-year-old Matthew Stringer was just under five feet tall. He had a 'fresh' complexion, brown hair and brown eyes. His arms were heavily tattooed. On the right arm was an anchor, a star and the initials 'MS' and 'W'; on the left arm, 'MS', an anchor and 'other blue marks'. Some of these tattoos had more than likely been acquired during his previous spell in prison; the Strangeways register shows that he had served one sentence of fifteen months whilst in his mid-teens. Stringer had grown up in Newton Heath, yet at the time of his arrest he was living with his parents in Boundary Street, Greenheys, several miles to the south. He gave his occupation as glass-blower and his religion as Church of England. He was illiterate.

Stringer's adversary, Charlie Chatburn, was also aged seventeen. He lived on Pollard Street with his mother and step-father and worked as a labourer. The Strangeways register does not record Chatburn as having any tattoos, but does note that he was scarred between the eyebrows. He had also already served one lengthy prison sentence: twelve months in Strangeways. It appears that Stringer and Chatburn were picked out from the batch of eight scuttlers at the Quarter Sessions on account of their criminal records; they were the only two to have previously served prison sentences. Stringer received the longer sentence on this occasion on account of his use of a pistol and the seriousness of the injuries sustained by the unfortunate Thomas Tetlow.

The Strangeways register also provides some interesting clues to the basis of the feud between the two gangs. It does not appear to have been sectarian. Six of the prisoners were Protestants, including both Stringer and Chatburn. Pat Connell, one of the Newton Heath lads, was a Catholic – as was the leader of the Pollard Street mob, Ned Lynch. Several of the Newton Heath lads were employed as glass-blowers and it is likely that they were workmates. The gangs thus appear to have drawn on a combination of occupational groupings and territorial loyalties. The latter were loosely defined, not least since many working-class families moved house at frequent intervals during the late Victorian period. As Matthew Stringer's case showed, scuttlers might stay loyal to gangs in the districts where they had grown up, even if their families moved two or three miles away. The Strangeways register suggests that all eight scuttlers were habitual street fighters. Six of them bore facial scars, mostly on their cheeks and foreheads, testifying to the frequency with which gangs fought with knives. Scars elsewhere on the body were rarer and this points to a shared fighting code in which scuttlers generally sought to inflict highly visible, but not life-threatening, wounds upon their rivals.

Ned Lynch, the captain of the Pollard Street scuttlers, maintained a lifelong, one-man feud with the constables of 'C' Division of the City of Manchester Police. At the age of thirty, Lynch was arrested during a Saturday night fracas in Ancoats by P.C. Samuel Gilbert, who needed help from three fellow officers to drag Lynch to the police station in Fairfield Street. By the time they reached the station, both the arresting officer and his prisoner were so badly injured that they had to be carried on stretchers to Manchester Royal Infirmary. It took ten days for Lynch to recover sufficiently to appear before the Manchester magistrates. He was promptly sent down for six months. By this time, Lynch had no fewer than twenty-eight previous convictions, almost all of them for assaulting the police. .

WHILST THE gangs of Ancoats were more feared than any others in Manchester, the spread of scuttling beyond the city's eastern boundaries was the cause of growing concern. In the 1870s, Bradford, Gorton and Openshaw were still independent townships in their own right, prior to their incorporation by Manchester over the following two decades.[7] Gorton and Openshaw were renowned as manufacturing districts. The Beyer-Peacock locomotive works at Gorton alone employed more than 1,000 men by 1875. Employment opportunities were on the whole much better in these districts than in the slums of Ancoats, where many lads and men depended on unskilled and irregular labouring work. The Bradford district lay to the east of Ancoats, a short walk from Pollard Street. Bradford was famous for its coal pit, sunk beside Forge Lane opposite the Bradford Ironworks. A giant gasometer, opened in 1869, loomed over both. Criminal cases from Bradford, Gorton and Openshaw were tried at the County Police Court, which sat at Strangeways Prison. Cases deemed too serious to be dealt with by the magistrates were committed to the Salford Hundred Quarter Sessions.

Sam Kirkham, who was born in Gorton in 1860, recalled that incursions by gangs from surrounding districts were a regular sight during the 1870s:

A gang would cross over Donkey's Common from Miles Platting or Bradford way to meet an Openshaw or Gorton gang. They would be drawn up not in echelon but in mass format. They would approach nearer and nearer. Then the leader would shout their battle cries. The weapons were belts, slings, sticks and

---

7 Bradford was incorporated in 1885; Openshaw and West Gorton followed suit in 1890.

stones. Both sides would give a yell as the police came on the scene, then the two armies would scatter in all directions to meet some other day. Could anyone wonder at such happenings in the past? The combatants hailed from the badly-lighted slum districts of those days. There was nothing for the lads but the streets. No picture houses, no billiard halls. What could anyone expect?

Kirkham claimed that many scuttlers subsequently joined the army, adding that: 'almost without exception they made the best of soldiers'.

The character of Bradford changed dramatically during the 1870s following a rapid influx of families from the slums of central Manchester. They came in search of work at the pit and adjacent manufacturing works. However, their arrival caused dismay among established residents, who feared that the newcomers were generally of the 'lowest classes'. By 1879, the population of Bradford was estimated at 15,500. Yet the township was served by a police force comprising just one sergeant and three constables. Under these circumstances, the tide of gang warfare was impossible to hold back.

The escalation of scuttling in Bradford was first highlighted during the summer of 1877, when the youths of the district found themselves assailed from all sides. Repeated incursions from the west by the Pollard Street lads were interspersed with raids by scuttlers from Openshaw to the east and Gorton to the south. The Bradford youths were forced to seek assistance from lads from the neighbouring district of Beswick. The combined forces of Bradford and Beswick fought a lengthy series of pitched battles with the Openshaw scuttlers on a croft in Gresham Street. During August 1877, the two sides clashed four times on successive weekends, culminating in a huge mêlée involving between 200 and 300 young people of both sexes on the night of Monday, August 20.

The gangs exchanged volleys of bricks and stones before fighting hand-to-hand with sticks and other improvised weapons. The scuttles clearly followed a ritualised pattern.

'They met and commenced skirmishing,' an angry resident wrote to the *Gorton Reporter*. 'Gradually they got worked nearer together, then the melee commenced.' Adult passers-by were injured by the showers of bricks and stones, and no quarter was given when the two gangs came to blows. On one occasion, a youth was 'kicked almost to death', added the letter-writer, who claimed to be a Bradford resident of long standing. The peace of this 'hitherto tolerably quiet neighbourhood' had been shattered by the sudden outbreak of scuttling: 'When I state that neither life nor property is safe where such disgraceful conduct goes on, I am much too mild. Where the police go I cannot imagine.' He further told how he and a friend had called at the Bradford police station on the night of the latest disturbance only to be told that the police were unable to intervene. An approach to a local councillor was equally fruitless: 'He consoles me with the assurance that such things are a matter of course – will be, will happen, cannot well be remedied.' As the letter-writer wryly noted, 'Our local authorities are somewhat short of doing their duty.'

The *Reporter* published the letter under the startling headline 'BULGARIAN ATROCITIES OUTDONE IN OPENSHAW AND BRADFORD', a reference to reports reaching the British press of massacres of Christians by Turkish troops in Bulgaria, then part of the Ottoman Empire. Russia offered support to the Bulgarian Christians, as did nonconformists in Britain, while Prime Minister Disraeli attempted to downplay the massacres and sought a negotiated settlement to the conflict. His efforts failed and by the spring of 1877 the Russians and the Turks were at war. Britain managed to stay out of the conflict, but with great difficulty.

Stung by the adverse, if extravagant, publicity, the Bradford police made valiant efforts to suppress the local scuttling gangs over the course of the following month. At three o'clock on Sunday, September 9, the rival mobs gathered in Gresham Street and began to shower each other with hails of bricks and stones. Two hundred lads took part in the scuttle, surging back and forth across a croft with 'one party beating back their opponents and then being compelled to retreat themselves'. The entire neighbourhood was in 'a state of tumult'. Eventually a troop of police led by Inspector Burke rushed between the two gangs. They took five lads into custody. Their haul included George Worthington, by now well-known to the police as the captain of the Bradford scuttlers. Worthington was convicted of stone-throwing and fined twenty shillings at the Manchester County Police Court, with the option of fourteen days' imprisonment. The four lads arrested alongside him were fined ten shillings each.

Perhaps inspired by the coverage of their activities in the *Gorton Reporter*, the Openshaw scuttlers had taken to calling themselves 'the Russians'. The lads of Bradford and Beswick were quick to respond, christening themselves 'Turks'. The Russo-Turkish War, it appeared, was to rage across the eastern townships, just as the Franco-Prussian War had been re-enacted on the streets of Angel Meadow and Ancoats seven years earlier. George Worthington, who had been at the head of the 'Turkish' forces in September 1877, was at the forefront of another incident involving the Bradford scuttlers the following February. A around four o'clock on a Saturday afternoon, Worthington was at the head of a twenty-strong gang of Turks in Coalpit Lane, close to the Bradford–Openshaw border, when he spotted a raiding party of Russians. The two gangs exchanged volleys of stones before rushing headlong into battle. The Russians were quickly overwhelmed. They turned and ran, but two of their number were caught as they tried to flee. George Worthington struck Thomas Connolly on the head with a stick, felling him. A second Russian, John Forrest, was struck on the head with a half-brick and knocked to the ground. Worthington stood over the two prostrate figures, brandishing his knife. He demanded, 'Part with your – money or I'll run it through you.' The Turks were merciless. They robbed Connolly of his cap and two knives. Forrest was stripped of his elaborately decorated belt – a scuttler's most prized possession – as well as his cap, plus one shilling and a penny in money. Before departing the scene, Worthington threw a stone at Connolly, splitting his head open.

George Worthington and four of his fellow Bradford Turks were apprehended by the police later that evening. At the

Bradford police office, Worthington denied wielding a knife, but did confess that he had chased John Forrest. According to the police, Worthington also admitted that he knew who had taken Forrest's money but 'would not tell'. The five scuttlers subsequently appeared at the Manchester County Police Court, where a surgeon testified to the severity of the head wounds suffered by Connolly and Forrest. Sir John Iles Mantell committed all five prisoners to the Quarter Sessions.

They were tried before W. H. Higgin at the Salford Hundred Sessions, where their ages and occupations were read out: George Worthington, aged eighteen, stoker; William Sharp, seventeen, carter; George Taylor, seventeen, collier; George Bryan, sixteen, collier; John Gleaves, aged eighteen, engineer's apprentice. All five were charged with wounding and robbery but the jury found them guilty of wounding only. In a highly unusual step, Mr Higgin sentenced the lads to just three days in prison. He no doubt viewed both sets of scuttlers as inveterate disturbers of the peace. However, whilst the jurors were unconvinced by the allegations of robbery, Higgin was still troubled. He ordered Worthington, Sharp, and Bryan to each pay ten shillings to both Connolly and Forrest to compensate them 'for their trouble and loss of time'. Failure to make the payments would be punished by three months in Strangeways. The monies were duly paid.

Any hope that the financial penalties incurred by George Worthington and his associates might help to quell the spate of disturbances in the eastern townships was shattered the following month when reports emerged of scuttling affrays spreading into Higher Openshaw. Rival bands of scuttlers from the adjacent townships had temporarily shifted their activities to a new site. This served to confuse the police, who were still concentrating their patrols on Bradford. Moreover, as the *Gorton Reporter* acknowledged, it appeared as though the scuttlers aimed to 'give the police as much trouble in taking them to the police office in Bradford as possible'.

The tendency for Manchester scuttlers to assemble in Bradford and the surrounding districts continued for the rest of the decade. On Saturday, 7 September 1878, rival gangs engaged in fierce bouts of stone throwing in the streets of the township. One resident who dared to remonstrate with a gang of youths for breaking his windows was badly beaten. The following day, 300 lads rampaged through the streets of Bradford throwing stones. Not surprisingly, a number of passers-by suffered head injuries and many more irate householders had their windows broken. The police managed to arrest three boys. When the lads appeared at the County Police Court, Inspector Burke said the authorities had been compelled to keep officers in plain clothes on duty in the neighbourhood at weekends to maintain order, but still they had not been able to put down the disturbances. According to Inspector Burke, 'The majority of the offenders came from the lowest parts of Manchester, and when any one of them was caught they clubbed up amongst themselves to pay the fine, and then boasted of it.' On this occasion, the magistrates imposed very heavy fines, one of forty shillings.

In a lengthy commentary on the case, the *Free Lance* noted that scuttlers were usually 'mere lads' driven to lawlessness 'more through a spirit of idle mischief than with any very pronounced criminal intent'. Nevertheless, the journal added, scuttlers ought to be punished by mandatory prison sentences. Echoing Inspector Burke's complaint at the County Police Court, the *Free Lance* pointed out that some of the gangs were so large that even a hefty fine, once shared, amounted to only a 'very trifling outlay' for each individual member.

The disturbances in the eastern townships continued. In March 1879, P.C. Simpson was patrolling the streets of Newton Heath when, turning into Iron Street, he stumbled into a fight between a gang of local scuttlers and a raiding party from Bradford. Around sixty youths were running to and fro. P.C. Simpson managed to hold one of them, only to find that the two gangs immediately joined forces to 'stone the bobby'. Simpson let his prisoner go but only after he had been struck on the head by a stone thrown by a veteran scuttler named Tommy Rigby, originally from Ancoats. Simpson suffered a severe cut on the head which left him unfit for duty for a week. He was able to identify Rigby and another youth, from Bradford, as his principal assailants. Warrants were issued against both lads and they later appeared before Sir John Iles Mantell at the County Police Court, where they were sentenced to the maximum punishment for assaulting the police: six months' imprisonment.

The Easter weekend of 1879 appears to have seen a temporary cessation of hostilities between the scuttlers of Bradford and Openshaw. Extraordinarily, youths from the two townships combined with others from neighbouring districts in Manchester for a 100-strong expedition into the leafy villages of Cheshire. Their chosen destination for Good Friday was Northenden, seven miles south of Manchester city centre and a popular weekend resort for the inhabitants of wealthy suburbs such as Didsbury. The frock parades of Northenden were genteel affairs in comparison with the boisterous horse-play of the proletarian promenades along Oldham Street or Hyde Road.

The motley band of scuttlers left a trail of devastation. Spotted by a police constable in Burnage Lane, they were waving sticks and hurling insults and volleys of stones at everyone they met. Having cleared the street, they began stoning the doors of each building they passed. Stopping off at a shop, one youth entered the premises whilst others stood on the pavement outside banging on the windows. They were approached by a lone beat constable, on whom they promptly turned their fury. The entire mob began to stone him, filling the air with shouts of 'Let's warm the —'. The officer escaped and ran for reinforcements, and seven arrests were made before the mob reached Didsbury. The prisoners were fined £2 each by Sir John Iles Mantell, with the option of fourteen days in Strangeways.

Hostilities between the rival bands of scuttlers were quickly resumed. The afternoon of Sunday, May 11 saw another set-piece confrontation between Bradford and Openshaw. The two mobs, each numbering over 200, gathered in what had become their regular battleground: the neighbourhood of Mill Street and Coalpit Lane. They were armed with sticks, stones and belts. The fighting lasted for around three-quarters of an hour. When the mobs finally dispersed, the streets were littered with stones. A police sergeant and two constables watched the proceedings from the sidelines and only one youth was arrested while the riot was taking place. The police had decided under the circumstances to try to identify as many of those taking part as possible and obtain warrants for their arrest afterwards.

Ten scuttlers appeared at the County Police Court at Strangeways on the following Friday. They were charged with scuttling, which was defined in court as 'a sort of faction fight' between two townships. The prisoners were all working lads, aged between sixteen and twenty-one. Three worked as colliers, two as foundrymen. The rest gave their occupations as dyer, tailor, labourer, hawker and cotton factory operative respectively. Mr H. T. Crofton, leading the prosecution, claimed that scuttling had escalated in Bradford to such an extent that 'neither life nor property was safe. Street lamps and windows of houses were repeatedly broken, and those who remonstrated with the offenders were usually ill-treated, so that a reign of terror almost existed.' He argued that the fines inflicted on scuttlers in the past had been entirely ineffectual, since 'the comrades of those convicted subscribed to pay them, so that no punishment was suffered by the offenders. In case they could not raise sufficient money amongst themselves they went round to the shopkeepers and obtained subscriptions from them by intimidation.' Mr Crofton urged the magistrates to commit the prisoners for trial at the Quarter Sessions, so that they could be severely punished. He knew the Court was loath to jail young men, particularly if they were in work, but the prisoners' conduct could no longer be tolerated. A superintendent confirmed that the police had received a stream of complaints about scuttling, both from residents of Bradford and from members of the local council.

Two civilian witnesses were then called to give corroborative evidence. Councillor Frederick Chappell confirmed that there had been constant damage to street lamps in the district following bouts of stone-throwing by scuttlers. There had not been a council meeting in the previous six months without some complaint of damage being received from property owners, he said. A man from Longsight testified that he owned property in Bradford and visited the township every day. In his experience, damage to property was a constant occurrence. Only a month previously he had put new windows in some houses from top to bottom, only to find them all broken a few days later. He had a difficulty in finding tenants for the same reason, and said another speculator had told him that he was delaying building houses in Bradford until 'this ruffianism' was put down. The magistrates committed all of the prisoners to the Quarter Sessions.

The next sitting of the Salford Hundred Quarter Sessions took place on May 27. W. H. Higgin, Q.C., presided. The ten scuttlers were charged with having, at Bradford, 'together with divers other evil-disposed persons to the number of 500 and more unlawfully and riotously assembled to disturb the public peace, and then made a great riot and disturbance, to the terror and alarm of her Majesty's subjects there being'. Witnesses for the defence, including a number of women, provided character references for several of the prisoners. The jury, however, was swayed by the police testimony and had little hesitation in finding all of the prisoners guilty.

If Henry West, the Recorder of Manchester, was an aristo-cratic Liberal known for his old-world courtesy, William Housman Higgin was the opposite. A 'stern, unbending Tory' and down-to-earth Lancastrian, Higgin was nearly sixty. Educated at Lancaster Grammar School, he had been called to the Bar in 1848 and 'took silk', joining the elite ranks of Queen's counsels, in 1868. The following year, he was appointed chairman of the Salford Hundred Quarter Sessions, to preside over cases referred from the Salford Police Court and the County Police Court at Strangeways. Higgin was a grave, imposing and, within the courtroom at least, entirely humourless figure. According to a fellow judge, he seemed to embody the phrase 'the majesty of the law'. Higgin was a firm believer in long terms of penal servitude for habitual offenders. As he saw it, the offender who was constantly in and out of prison was both 'a source of anxiety and wretchedness for his family and a dangerous nuisance to the public'. The habitual thief belonged in one place only: the gaol. And in Higgin's view, the scuttler belonged beside him.

Before passing sentence, Higgin addressed the court at some length. The prisoners, he proclaimed, 'were guilty of a most disgraceful riot'. Indeed, he exclaimed, 'The whole case was most disgraceful, from one end of it to the other.' The conduct of the witnesses for the defence was nearly as bad as that of the scuttlers themselves. Higgin pointed to several of the female witnesses, reminding the court that they had stated on oath that the prisoners were 'orderly and respectable', only to confess later that they had known all along that the prisoners had been convicted of similar offences in the past. 'Those women,' said Higgin, 'seemed to think nothing of deliberately and calmly telling lies upon oath, and if they found themselves indicted for perjury it would be their own fault.' He was clearly exasperated by what he viewed as a general conspiracy against the law. Finally, he warned that if the exemplary sentences he was about to pass did not put scuttling down, he would authorise the police superintendent present to ask the magistrates to send each and every scuttler for trial at the sessions in future. Then he sentenced George Bryan, John Curley, John Hill and Benjamin Winterbottom, all of whom had previous convictions for scuttling, to nine months' imprisonment. The remaining six prisoners were each given four months.

Nor was the police operation against the two gangs yet over. Four months after the trial, another Bradford scuttler was brought before the magistrates. John McGregor 'had been out of the way up to this time'. He too was convicted of riot and sent to Strangeways.

EVEN WHEN Manchester's young roughs were not embarking on scuttling expeditions, their habit of carrying knives meant that the most trifling arguments could rapidly escalate into life-threatening violence. On the afternoon of Saturday, 18 November 1876, John Calligan, a sixteen-year-old dyer, took part in a card game in Hadfield's public house in Lower Cambridge Street on the southern edge of Manchester city centre. A dispute broke out among the gamblers and Calligan was turned out of the pub along with four of his friends. The youths were all the worse for drink and carried on the argument in the street, quickly coming to blows.

When a middle-aged labourer named John Bailey tried to break up the fight, the youths turned on him instead. Bailey was powerfully built but found himself fending off not just John Calligan but Thomas Ryan, a fifteen-year-old porter, and another youth named Garrity. Calligan stabbed Bailey on the arm. A married woman tried to intervene but she too was stabbed by one of the youths. The disturbance was heard by the occupants of the nearby houses, one of whom, a twenty-six-year-old tin-plate worker named John Pennington, came to his front door to see what was going on. Pennington happened to be the son-in-law of the beleaguered John Bailey. He immediately ran across the street to help to fight off the three youths. Pennington traded punches with Thomas Ryan, only for Calligan to come across and 'dig' him in the ribs with a knife. John Pennington died from his injuries in Manchester Royal Infirmary two weeks later, but not before identifying the knife-man.

Calligan was tried for wilful murder at Liverpool Assizes. Opening the prosecution, Henry West, Q.C., the Recorder of Manchester, said that 'the crime arose out of one of those violent street disturbances for which Manchester has gained an unenviable notoriety'. Despite the defence claim that it was Garrity who had inflicted the fatal wound, the jury took only fifteen minutes to find Calligan guilty of murder. However, they recommended mercy on account of the prisoner's youth. Calligan was then asked, 'Have you anything to say why sentence of death should not be passed upon you, according to law?' He promptly burst into tears, crying out, 'Oh, Lord Jesus in heaven, I am innocent. Have mercy on me!' His mother was in the public gallery and shouted out repeatedly, if incongruously, 'Judge, have mercy on my orphan,' until two police officers bundled her out of court. The judge donned the black cap before passing sentence. While giving an assurance that he would pass on the jury's recommendation to mercy to the 'proper quarter', he warned Calligan not to anticipate a reprieve even on account of his youth. He then pronounced the sentence of death. Calligan, not surprisingly, was 'much agitated' during the judge's remarks, shouting, 'God in heaven knows I am innocent,' as the sentence was passed and continuing to protest his innocence as he was dragged down from the dock.

John Calligan was reprieved early in 1877. He was moved to H.M. Convict Prison, Portsmouth, to begin a life sentence. His trial attracted a good deal of coverage in the local press, but even the initial publicity surrounding the sentence of death appeared to have little deterrent effect among the more warlike elements of the rising generation in Manchester. The city's law-abiding inhabitants felt increasingly threatened by the packs of armed boys and youths roaming the streets. In September that year, a resident of Longsight wrote an anguished letter to the *Manchester Evening News*:

> Sir, – Will you please to insert this letter in your paper?
>
> On Saturday nights it is quite dangerous for any person to come up or down New Bank Street, Longsight, on account of the rough lads who infest Gray Street and Red Bank Street tearing down the palings for weapons, and using belts with buckles on them. Last Saturday night they paraded up and down the street for above two hours, and, whenever they [caught] a glimpse of a policeman, they were off. What it requires is a plain clothes' man to watch them and take them in the act. I am sure that all respectable people will agree with me that strenuous efforts ought to be made in order to put down scuttling, which is now becoming a perfect pest in more places than ever.
>
> A RATEPAYER.

The *Free Lance* heartily agreed, asserting that the real menace of scuttling lay not so much in the fights between rival bands as in random assaults on unsuspecting and inoffensive passers-by. The *Free Lance* conjured a nightmarish vision of gangs of scuttlers lying in wait for their victims in dark corners, armed with anything from 'a railway sleeper to a handful of Cayenne pepper'.

The cumulative effect of the feuds of the 1870s was to establish scuttling as one of the principal threats to law and order across the entire Manchester conurbation. Gang conflicts extended from the north of the city to the south and ranged across the townships to the east of the city boundaries. Scuttlers were sent in increasing numbers for trial at the courts of Quarter Sessions so that they might be made to feel the full force of the law. Yet heavier prison sentences appeared to have little effect. On the other side of the River Irwell in Salford, matters were no better. Some local commentators feared that, if anything, they were worse.

CHAPTER 6

Rowdy Salford

IN AUGUST 1876, the Manchester satirical magazine the *City Jackdaw* published a startling indictment of the level of violence on the streets of Salford. In a lengthy front-page article headed simply 'ROWDY SALFORD!' the anonymous author, himself a resident of one of Salford's leafier suburbs, catalogued a series of cases heard in a single week at the borough's police court and the Salford Hundred Quarter Sessions. The court proceedings had been reported throughout the local press and the assorted headlines made disturbing reading. According to the chairman of the Quarter Sessions, W. H. Higgin, the recent spate of violence in Salford was 'disgraceful'. The stipendiary magistrate, Sir John Iles Mantell, was no less appalled – but he was not shocked either. As he drily noted, 'I am not taken by surprise at anything that occurs in Salford.'

The *City Jackdaw* listed the following cases heard by Sir John at a single sitting of the Salford Police Court on Monday, 21 August 1876: Joseph McKie, violent assault upon a youth in the Adelphi, committed to the Quarter Sessions; William Jordan, violent assault in Whit Lane, committed to the Quarter Sessions, bail refused; John Whittle, kicking in the abdomen without provocation, two months' imprisonment; William West, assault upon a woman with a bayonet scabbard, to find sureties for good behaviour; William Lacy, stabbing a boy, committed to Quarter Sessions. As the *Jackdaw* noted, this was 'a pretty good day's work for Sir John Iles Mantell'. He faced further cases of assault in the days that followed.

W. H. Higgin, presiding at the Quarter Sessions, had had an even grimmer week. On the second day of the sessions, he dished out sentences for a number of attacks all committed in Salford: Henry McKay, wounding Sarah Ogden, two years' imprisonment; John Purcell, unlawfully wounding George Bottomley, fifteen months; Catherine Flynn, unlawfully wounding Mary Agnew, fifteen months; Eliza Pears, unlawfully wounding Jane Taylor, nine months; Ann Kearns, for striking Mary Maguire with a clog, nine months; Betty Carpenter, unlawfully wounding Sarah Brown, six months. In Salford, it appeared, the women were almost as violent as the men.

The cases tried on the third and final day of the sessions made even more alarming reading for the citizens of the metropolis. The *Jackdaw* listed headlines from reports on the various cases in one of Manchester's daily newspapers:

BRUTAL ASSAULT IN SALFORD: MALICIOUSLY
WOUNDING WITH A KNIFE

A KICKING CASE IN LOWER BROUGHTON

SERIOUS CASE OF STABBING IN PENDLETON

KNOCKING A MAN'S EYE OUT IN SALFORD

ASSAULT WITH A POKER IN SALFORD

BREAKING A WOMAN'S JAW IN PENDLETON

ASSAULT UPON SALFORD POLICE CONSTABLES

ANOTHER ASSAULT ON THE POLICE IN SALFORD

The cases ranged over the entire borough, from the slums of Greengate to the more respectable districts of Pendleton to the west and Broughton to the north. As the *Jackdaw* pointed out, 'Here is a table of crime which rakes together and carefully distils the essence of all the most horrible crimes committed week by week in the United Kingdom.' Drink, the magazine noted, was 'the primary or aggravating cause of the mischief' in almost every case. The *Jackdaw* concluded that the Salford magistrates needed to look carefully at the borough's licensing arrangements, for if drunkenness could be curbed then violence would surely diminish in its wake.

The stipendiary magistrate for Salford, Sir John Iles Mantell, had himself frequently been the object of the *Jackdaw*'s ire. The stipendiary was a controversial figure, to say the least. The eldest son of a doctor from Farringdon in Berkshire, he was born in 1813. The first twenty-five years of his legal career were spent in The Gambia, as a Queen's Advocate and then as Chief Justice. He was knighted for his services in West Africa. In 1869, he was appointed as stipendiary magistrate for the borough of Salford and the Manchester division of the County Police Court at Strangeways, covering the independent townships such as Bradford and Gorton on the outskirts of Manchester. As the *Manchester City News* later recalled, his manner in court was decidedly brusque and 'did not conduce to the comfort of witnesses, nor ease the way of the accused. His idea was to dispose of the cases as quickly as possible, and in the process he was apt to be stern and appear to lack sympathy.' His mocking of the impoverished and often uneducated people brought before him was unsparing, and the justice he so abruptly dispensed often appeared harsh.

In December 1875, Sir John jailed a working man named Henry Bennett for three months under the terms of the Vagrancy Acts. Bennett was destitute and homeless. His crime had been to sleep rough beside a night watchman's fire. A beat constable found him and took him into custody. When Bennett was brought before the Salford Police Court, Sir John treated him as a rogue and vagabond. The sentence unleashed a storm of protest, which rapidly worked its way into the columns of the national press. The sentence was partially remitted by order of the Home Secretary, and Salford Borough Council promptly began to discuss the procedure for appointing a separate stipendiary magistrate to serve Salford alone. The *City Jackdaw* was unsparing in its condemnation of Sir John. 'His reign,' it opined, 'has been marked by a want of that discretion and good temper which should distinguish all who hold the scales of justice, and his erratic mode of dealing with cases has time after time caused discontent in the minds of those who have listened to his decisions … His whims are too numerous to be detailed, and his occasional bursts of spleen are so unrestrained, that every one, prisoner, witness, and solicitor, is alternately bullied and threatened.' One London newspaper recommended that the Home Secretary send Sir John back to The Gambia to 'sleep out' there and 'see how he likes it'.[8]

YOUTHS HELD no monopoly on violence in Salford. Pub brawls between older men were just as prevalent, whilst rows between neighbours could escalate into free-for-alls involving dozens of adults of both sexes. Behind closed doors, wife-beating was so commonplace that only exceptional cases, involving the threat of murder or permanent injury, were likely to be reported to the police. Much of this violence was drink-fuelled. Men who endured long hours of heavy toil in Salford's factories, workshops and pits felt that they had earned the right to enjoy themselves in the evenings and especially at weekends. Their cramped dwellings offered few opportunities for relaxation and, in any case, it was easier to forget their troubles in the beery camaraderie of one of the borough's 600-plus pubs and beerhouses. Salford's drinking dens were warm and convivial but were not for the faint-hearted. The most trifling argument, or the mere suspicion of an insult, could provoke a fight at any moment. Men who spent heavily on beer inevitably left their wives short of money for housekeeping. Most of the violent disputes between husbands and wives were triggered by arguments over money; husbands resented their wives' nagging, whilst women were understandably furious at their husbands' irresponsibility and reckless neglect. It was little wonder, many local journalists noted, that so many of the women in the slums of Salford frequently turned to drink themselves.

The young people of Salford, following the example of their

8 Sir John Iles Mantell was relieved of his duties in Salford two years later, when Joseph Makinson was appointed to the newly created post of Stipendiary Magistrate for Salford, leaving Sir John to preside over the County Police Court.

parents' generation, did much to cement the borough's notoriety during the 1860s and 1870s. Salford had its own equivalents to the parades on Oldham Street in Manchester: the Crescent, Regent Road and Eccles Old Road would all fill with hundreds of lads and lasses on Saturday and Sunday nights. Allegations of ruffianism and depravity abounded. In October 1869, a 'lover of decency' wrote to the *Manchester Courier* to complain about the promenades on the Crescent:

> In wending my way homewards on Sunday evening last along Cross Lane, I happened to overhear the following conversation between a party of young lads: 'Cressing it tonight, Tom?' Tom replied, 'Proper here, nowt to stop.' Naturally enough I wondered what they meant by 'cressing it'; and as I was going the same way as they were I thought I would watch them. Getting on the Crescent they commenced insulting young girls, and because I interfered they commenced to use the most abusive language I ever heard. I think it is high time such things were stopped, as they are a disgrace to Salford, and our authorities have been reminded enough lately.

The anguished lover of decency perhaps failed to realise that Salford lasses generally gave as good as they got in these exchanges of banter and innuendo. Not content with eyeing up potential sexual conquests, young people of both sexes jostled adult passers-by, pushing them off the pavements and subjecting them to crude taunts. Those respectable young women who sought to stay aloof from the proceedings were 'bonneted', their hats knocked off and trodden into the ground to whoops of approval from the watching crowds.

In these tumultuous streets, scuttling flourished. Gangs formed throughout the borough's poverty-stricken, 'low' working-class districts. The most feared congregated in the slums of Greengate, most notably in Queen Street. The courts and alleys here contained some of the most wretched hovels to be found in Salford. The natural enemies of the Greengate scuttlers were the gangs of the neighbouring district known as the Adelphi.

Divided by Blackfriars Road, Greengate and the Adelphi were both renowned as districts of heavy Irish Catholic settlement. However, proximity bred only resentment among the youths of the two districts. Bands of scuttlers from Manchester also made sporadic raids into Greengate throughout the 1870s, seeking to prove their mettle in confrontations with the worst gangs in Salford.

Scuttling spread deeper into Salford over the course of the decade. Gangs were found in the maze of streets off Hope Street and Oldfield Road in the heart of the borough and in the newly built terraced streets off Ordsall Lane to the South. In Pendleton, scuttlers emerged in Ellor Street and Chaney Street, Hanky Park, and in the mining district of Whit Lane. Salford's scuttlers cultivated their notoriety. As their fame, or infamy, spread, some of the more prominent figures within the gangs acquired reputations spanning the breadth of the borough and beyond.

THOMAS INGLIS was one of the most avowedly respectable youths in Greengate. He was a devout Christian and a regular at Sunday school. Employed as an iron glazer, he was a hard worker and a dutiful son, 'tipping up' his entire wage packet to his parents. Despite repeated requests, Inglis refused to join the local band of scuttlers, the King Street lads. They were determined to teach him a lesson of their own.

At around eight o'clock on the evening of Sunday, 19 January 1873, Inglis, aged eighteen, escorted thirteen-year-old Thomasina Nabb home from Sunday school. As they passed along King Street, they stopped to talk to one of Thomasina's friends, only to see a twenty-strong gang of scuttlers turn into the street. When the King Street lads spotted Inglis, they began to shout, 'That's him, we want him!' One of the scuttlers ran up to Inglis and struck him with the buckle end of a belt. Inglis and Nabb fled, running across Blackfriars Road towards their homes in Picton Street. The scuttlers ran after them. Inglis was caught and punched by one of the chasing pack. Some of the scuttlers were carrying straps with stones fastened to the ends; others had stones tied in knots in the corners of handkerchiefs. 'Hold on,' pleaded Inglis, but to no avail: he was surrounded and beaten with sticks, stones and belts. When the blows ceased, Inglis picked himself up and ran to the door of his parents' house.

The scuttlers followed, their ranks swelled by a crowd of local urchins. They stood en masse on the opposite side of the street, yelling curses and threats. Inglis's brother handed him a fire-rake with an iron handle so that he might defend himself. Inglis hurled the rake at the crowd of scuttlers. It landed on the flags, or paving stones, in front of them, bounced up and lodged in the skull of ten-year-old John O'Toole. Alice Rhodes, aged fourteen, watched the proceedings from the doorway of her home in Picton Street. When she saw O'Toole fall to the ground, she ran across and tried to pull the piece of iron out of his head. She tugged with all her might, but was unable to dislodge it. A boy went to help her and between the two of them they managed to pull it out.

John O'Toole was taken to Salford Royal Hospital. The house surgeon found a wound two inches behind his left ear and noted that O'Toole had been rendered 'partially insensible'. He died at around eleven o'clock that night. Inquiries by the police quickly led them to Thomas Inglis, who was arrested at his parents' house. Inglis was held overnight in a cell at the Salford Town Hall. The following morning, he was charged with the wilful murder of John O'Toole. Inglis made no reply. A post-mortem examination carried out later that day revealed a hole in John O'Toole's skull three inches deep and extending to the brain.

Inglis stood trial for murder at the South Lancashire Assizes. The counsel for the defence, William Charley, Conservative MP for Salford, explained to the court that Inglis himself had initially been the victim of repeated assaults by scuttlers. Charley presented Inglis as an industrious worker, a model son and a committed Christian. He was, said Charley, a 'good boy', who had positively declined to join the band of scuttlers. He was an honest lad, and earned a weekly wage, being 'the main prop of indigent parents and a younger brother'. Charley then relayed the story of the scuttlers' unprovoked attack on the night of 19

January: 'The prisoner was knocked down and severely beaten. Escaping from his assailants, he ran to his father's door, where the piece of iron was thrust into his hand by his brother, and, yielding to an irresistible impulse, he threw it, not among, but towards the crowd of boys, who had rushed up to the door and then rushed back again. The iron fell upon the pavement in front of the crowd, and then rebounded and struck O'Toole.' The direction of the wound was crucial to Inglis's defence. Medical evidence showed that the rake handle had lodged horizontally in O'Toole's skull, indicating that it had indeed bounced up off the pavement.

In the light of the medical testimony, the judge, Baron Pollock, ruled that the case was one of manslaughter rather than wilful murder. The jury found Inglis guilty of the reduced charge, but urged the judge to show mercy. Baron Pollock deferred sentence for one day. When the court resumed, he declared that, in the eyes of the law, Inglis was guilty of manslaughter. However, the prisoner had been 'very much excited by the ill-treatment he had undoubtedly received'. Moreover, Baron Pollock was swayed by the character witnesses, who had spoken so persuasively of Inglis's previous good conduct and his prospects of 'a life of industry and honesty'. Baron Pollock sentenced Thomas Inglis to two weeks' imprisonment.

GREENGATE WAS the epicentre of scuttling in Salford. Here, as in Manchester and the surrounding townships, gang fights could involve huge numbers. In January 1875, Detective Inspector Hargreaves of the Salford Borough Police claimed that scuttles were breaking out on a nightly basis in the area around Queen Street, with as many as 200 boys and youths fighting with sticks, stones and belts. Similar fights were almost as frequent, and just as fierce, in other thoroughfares nearby, most notably in New Blackfriars Street and in Broughton Road. Pedestrians were frequent casualties during bouts of stone throwing. Residents of those streets worst affected were forced to stay indoors whenever fighting broke out, while shopkeepers were obliged to shut their premises. Large-scale affrays broke out in all of the districts to which scuttlers laid claim. In February 1875, a Sunday night battle involving 300 lads was reported in the Islington district, which lay between Chapel Street and Ordsall. The local scuttlers had paraded the streets all day in anticipation of the fight.

In Cross Lane, a fight between scuttlers from Ordsall and Pendleton involved between 200 and 250 boys and young men. Stones flew 'furious and fast' across the street as the battle raged for forty minutes without a police officer in sight. A resident wrote to the *Manchester Courier* telling how one shopkeeper appealed to the scuttlers to 'go further away and to mind his windows', but he 'might as well have spoken to the stones'. Salford's scuttlers armed themselves with a fearsome array of weapons. In addition to the belts and knives favoured by their counterparts in Manchester, many carried 'slings', or catapults, which they used to fling stones at their enemies, while members of one Greengate gang even made swords out of pieces of old iron.

In September 1876, a series of scuttles in Salford led to a deluge of complaints to the police. On Saturday, 30 September, the Chief Constable, Captain Torrens, took the unusual step of attending the borough police court in person. Four scuttlers were due to appear before the Salford magistrates that morning in connection with three separate affrays and Captain Torrens was determined to add his weight to the testimony against them. He listed their arsenal – belts, bludgeons, stone slings, and 'other dangerous weapons' – and declared that their nuisance was now so great that constables had been placed on special duty in plain clothes to check the disturbances. 'Shopkeepers have been compelled to put up their shutters and close their premises,' he told the magistrates, 'and a feeling of terror exists in the different neighbourhoods where the battles take place.'

A youth from Nuttall's Court, Queen Street, was brought before the court charged with scuttling in Blackfriars Street the previous evening. A stone fastened to a string had been found in his pocket. A constable explained how 'this was swung round the head, and when it had attained sufficient force it was loosed, regardless of any injury or damage it might do'. The scuttler was sent down for fourteen days. Two others were brought into the dock, charged with taking part in a scuttle between gangs from Greengate and Pendleton on the same night. They were apprehended by two constables, one of whom was hit on the shoulder by a stone as he struggled to restrain his prisoner. Again, the scuttlers received fourteen days. Finally a lad named John Castleton was charged with scuttling in Collier Street, Greengate. A police constable told how Castleton had a stone in his hand when he was apprehended. He too got fourteen days.

Playing to the gallery of assembled court reporters, stipendiary Sir John Iles Mantell was in fine form. 'These cases are frightful,' he said, 'and can scarcely find a parallel in the most lawless and uncivilised part of the world. The next boy that is brought before me for this offence I will send to a reformatory for five years, because it is a practice that must be checked with a strong hand in order to prevent murder. I say it advisedly, and after deep consideration of the matter.' The stipendiary and the Chief Constable were evidently in agreement about the gravity of the problem and the need for stiff sentences.

THE REFORMATORY School (Youthful Offenders) Act of 1854 had given magistrates the power to send any offender aged below sixteen to a reformatory. The minimum sentence was to be two years, the maximum five. In all cases, offenders were to serve at least fourteen days in prison first. The aim was to save children from the corrupting influence of hardened offenders in adult prisons, but also to remove them from the degrading home environments which reformers believed bred the criminal child.

The Manchester and Salford Reformatory for Juvenile Criminals was opened at Blackley in North Manchester in 1857. The Manchester reformatory was certified to hold ninety boys and although the majority of inmates during subsequent decades were from Manchester and the surrounding areas, others were admitted from as far away as London. Likewise some of the juvenile offenders brought before the magistrates in Manchester and Salford were sent to reformatories elsewhere, notably to the two reformatory ships moored on the River Mersey at Birkenhead: the *Akbar* for Protestant boys and the *Clarence* for Catholics. Separate institutions were established for children between the ages of seven and fourteen who were found to be vagrant and destitute – in other words, homeless – under the terms of the Industrial Schools Act of 1857. A further Act of 1861 established four categories of children to be sent to industrial schools: those apparently under the age of fourteen who were found begging; those under fourteen found wandering without any home or visible means of support or in the company of thieves; those under fourteen whose parents declared them to be beyond their control; and those aged below twelve who had committed an offence punishable by imprisonment.

The daily schedules of reformatories and industrial schools were very similar. Heavy emphasis was placed upon industrial training. In effect, the youthful inmates endured long days of forced labour in addition to conventional schooling and religious instruction. Lengthy sentences were intended to ensure that by the time of their release, inmates would be prepared for lives of honest toil. Yet sentences of up to five years appeared extraordinarily harsh for offences such as petty theft. And however philanthropic the reformers' motives, there is no doubt that, from the perspective of the youthful inmates, reformatories and industrial schools alike were highly oppressive institutions.

FIGHTS BETWEEN neighbourhood gangs generally took place at weekends, often on Saturday nights. During the mid-1870s, however, scuttles were also frequently fought between gangs of boys from different workplaces.[9] In October 1874, Matthew Bailey, general manager of the Manchester and Liverpool Screw Bolt Works in Oldfield Road, sought the assistance of the police to suppress outbreaks of scuttling between his employees, or 'hands', and those of Worrall's dye-works in nearby Ordsall Lane.

---

9 This was a tradition that stretched back to the 1820s, at least (see Chapter 3).

He alleged that, over a considerable period, the boys from Worrall's had done their utmost to frighten his lads from entering their place of work. In mid-October, Mr Bailey was tipped off that an attack was to be made by the Worrall's lads during their dinner break. Three Salford detectives and a uniformed sergeant took up positions in the screw bolt works, so that they could see what took place. At two o'clock, a number of lads returning from their dinner break were set upon by youths from Worrall's, who pelted them with stones. Missiles crashed through the windows of the works. The detectives rushed out into the street and arrested three of the hands from Worrall's: James Oates, aged sixteen, Jim Richardson, aged eighteen, and thirteen-year-old Michael Igo. All three were charged with stone-throwing and disorderly conduct. When they appeared at the Salford Police Court, Mr Bailey testified that knives, sticks, belts and a poker had been used in the attack. A detective told the court that 'this kind of attack was termed "scuttling", and not long since a lad was fatally injured in a similar attack'.[10] The three lads were bound over to keep the peace for three months.

The following year saw a feud between the hands of Kendal and Gent's machine works in Springfield Lane, Greengate, and those of the nearby Langworthy's mill. Certain factions among the two sets of employees were in the habit of fighting during their meal breaks. Complaints to the police became so numerous that plain-clothes officers were instructed to stem the violence. So when the police received a tip-off that a scuttle was planned for the morning of Saturday, 18 September, six officers arrived in Springfield Lane shortly before the nine o'clock meal break and hid themselves in twos at each end of the street and in the middle. They watched four boys pass down the length of the street: it later transpired that this was a group of 'pickets' sent out to see if any police were in the neighbourhood. The pickets gave the all-clear and returned, followed by a group of fifty armed with sticks, stones and other weapons. The police rushed out of

---

10 This appears to be a reference to the death of ten-year-old John O'Toole in January 1873.

the houses and with some difficulty managed to arrest four youths aged between fourteen and seventeen. The prisoners included the captains of the respective gangs: Billy Tyrell and Jimmy Handley. All four were given fourteen days. The magistrates told them, 'There must be an end to this practice, and though we are sorry to send to gaol lads so young, under the circumstances we cannot do otherwise.'

Affronted by the growing notoriety of the Salford mobs, gangs from Manchester made repeated incursions into the neighbouring borough throughout the 1870s. At around half past ten on the night of Saturday, 16 February 1878, a gang of around forty scuttlers from Ancoats launched a raid into Greengate. They took up a position under a dimly lit railway arch with the aim of ambushing any of the local scuttlers who passed by. At around a quarter to eleven, they spotted their prey. Five local youths left the Bridge Inn and walked along Greengate towards the arches. As the Greengate lads approached, the Ancoats scuttlers stepped out of the shadows. At the head of the Ancoats gang was their captain, Peter Murphy, a seventeen-year-old iron turner who lived off Oldham Road. Murphy waved his knife in the face of Jimmy Chappell, a chimney sweep from nearby Broughton Lane. Chappell told Murphy to go away, but Murphy continued to brandish the knife. Finding themselves outnumbered and surrounded, the Greengate lads decided that attack was the only possible means of defence. Chappell punched Murphy in the mouth. In response, one of the other Ancoats lads struck Chappell's companion, John Kelly. Chaos erupted and in the commotion, Chappell and Kelly managed to break through the Ancoats ranks. The Greengate lads ran for all they were worth. Peter Murphy ran after them. He managed to catch Kelly and he plunged his knife into the Salford youth's back, raking the blade from his shoulder to his spine.

Kelly, a factory labourer from Birtles Square in Greengate, was taken to Salford Royal Hospital. Doctors found the wound in his back to be two and a half inches deep and not surprisingly he had lost a great deal of blood. Peter Murphy was apprehended and appeared at Salford Police Court six days after the attack. The court heard that Murphy had been released on licence from a

SALFORD

reformatory for juvenile offenders. He had previously been convicted of assaulting the police and was widely acknowledged as a gang leader. He was committed to the Salford Hundred Quarter Sessions on a charge of unlawful wounding and just three days later was tried before W. H. Higgin. The jury convicted Murphy and Higgin sentenced him to a year's imprisonment.

Gangs of scuttlers would walk as far as three or four miles to seek out members of rival bands. On Saturday, 6 September 1879, a gang of Openshaw scuttlers ventured as far as Oldfield Road in Salford, where their captain – Thomas Wetherby – had a stand-up fight with a local youth named James Moss. Beat constables found the two fighting in the middle of a crowd of fifty youths on a patch of vacant land in Factory Lane. Moss, a gold beater, was a scuttler of some local renown. His reputation counted against him on this occasion. The Salford magistrates fined him seven shillings and sixpence. Wetherby was discharged.

There were signs of the emergence of a distinctive gang culture in Salford during the 1870s. Scuttlers' belts – often their most prized possessions, as well as their favourite weapons – were increasingly viewed as trophies to be captured during fights. To rob a belt from a rival scuttler was to score a symbolic victory and gang members needed to be cautious if they walked out alone with their belts on display. In October 1872, Joe Jones from Heap's Court in Salford's Hope Street district, was accosted by half a dozen rival scuttlers in Oldfield Road. According to Jones's account, they tried to take his belt and when he refused, they beat him severely. One of his attackers was subsequently jailed for assault.

For those youths growing up in neighbourhoods colonised by scuttlers, gang membership was increasingly viewed as the norm. Many joined gangs in self-defence, since only by entering the ranks of the local scuttlers could they protect themselves from marauding bands from other districts. Those who refused to take part in scuttles faced retribution. In March 1879, thirteen-year-old Horatio Barlow, from Nangreave Street near Oldfield Road, was beaten by the local band of scuttlers. He had repeatedly refused to join them in their scuttling expeditions. Punishment was meted out one night as Barlow made his way home from Worrall's dye-works. He was waylaid by John McNally, who knocked Barlow down in the street and kicked him as he lay on the ground. Barlow's parents lodged a complaint and McNally, who was well-known to the police as a scuttler, was caught while sleeping rough in a brickyard the following night. He was sentenced to two months' hard labour.

Salford's scuttlers, like those of Manchester, did not threaten only rival gang members. Unfamiliar pedestrians were always at risk of insults, or worse, if they passed a corner where a gang of scuttlers congregated. Even those local adults were who known to the gangs might be targeted if they complained about the gang's activities or testified against the gang's members in court. One June evening in 1874, a joiner named James Gibson took a stroll with his wife in Salford's Peel Park. As they returned home they spotted 150 scuttlers gathered by the park gates. The Gibsons kept on walking, making sure that they did nothing to attract the mob's attention as they passed. Their discretion was not enough to keep them safe. Without provocation or warning, John Whipday rushed out of the crowd and struck James Gibson two fierce blows on the head. Whipday, a carter from Ordsall, was known to the police and he was subsequently sentenced to two months for assault.

In December 1876, three scuttlers were apprehended following an incident in Greengate. On this occasion, the trouble began when John Castleton threw a dead cat in the face of a mechanic named George Morris. Castleton, who had been jailed for scuttling two months previously, was one of the noted local 'terrors'. He appears to have assumed that Morris would not dare to retaliate. He was wrong. Morris was a resident of Birtles Square, one of the toughest places in Greengate. W. H. Wood described Birtles Square as a 'den of sin and infamy' whose inhabitants appeared to live beyond the reach of the forces of law and order. As Wood put it, the Square was 'a perfect Alsatia'.[11]

---

11 In seventeenth-century London, the 'Alsatia' district of Whitefriars, situated between the Thames and Fleet Street, had afforded sanctuary to

Morris was no shrinking violet. He clouted the impudent youth and thought no more of it. However, at six o'clock the following evening, Castleton appeared in Birtles Square at the head of a formidable body of scuttlers and stood outside Morris's house.

'Let that man come out now and we'll kill him,' shouted Castleton. 'I'm not by myself now.'

Morris wisely stayed indoors. After three and a half hours he ventured out, only to find that the scuttlers were still waiting at the bottom of the street. The youths launched a furious assault, lashing out at Morris with their belts and knocking him to the ground. As Morris struggled to his feet, John Castleton struck him on the forehead with a knife. Morris ran back into his house, where he remained until one of his neighbours was able to get a message to the police. He eventually sought treatment at the dispensary at Salford Royal Hospital. Doctors dressed his head wound, which was an inch and a half long and had penetrated to the bone.

Castleton was arrested later that night and appeared the following morning at the Salford Police Court, where he gave his age as sixteen and his occupation as factory labourer. Two others were arrested later that week. John Rafferty, aged fifteen, from King Street in Greengate, had been in court twice before: once for gambling in the street and once for stealing a pair of boots. James Leighton, aged fourteen, had been convicted of scuttling in September 1875 when only thirteen. Castleton was committed to the Salford Hundred Quarter Sessions on a charge of unlawful wounding, while Rafferty and Leighton were dealt with by magistrate W. W. Goulden, who heard from a police witness that 'The boys assembled in a gang of perhaps a hundred, and shopkeepers had to put up their shutters to protect their windows.' Goulden declared that 'steps must be taken to stop this abominable practice' and sentenced Rafferty to fourteen days' imprisonment, to be followed by five years in a reformatory school. Leighton was bound over to keep the peace for three months.

John Castleton was tried before W. H. Higgin early in the

---

criminals and debtors alike.

New Year. A police witness stated that Castleton was aged fifteen, rather than sixteen as the prisoner had claimed at the Salford Police Court. Castleton was convicted of unlawfully wounding George Morris with a belt. Mr Higgin sentenced him to twelve days' imprisonment followed by five years' incarceration in a reformatry. To Castleton, this was a disaster. Like many fourteen- and fifteen-year-olds, he had given his age as sixteen precisely to ensure that he would be dealt with as an adult offender. On this occasion the ruse had failed, leaving Castleton to a much lengthier period of confinement as a juvenile in need of 'character training'.

Alf Richardson of the Queen Street scuttlers was brought before the Salford magistrates on a number of occasions during 1877. In January, Richardson, aged seventeen, took part in a fight between Queen Street and the Bury Street scuttlers. Richardson chased an opponent into an alleyway where he clubbed him over the head with the buckle end of his belt. In court, Richardson admitted that he and his friends had been fighting but protested nonetheless that they 'were not scuttling'. The magistrates were not convinced; they sent Alf Richardson down for two months.

Immediately after the sentence had been passed, Richardson's married sister, Mary Wood, was brought before the magistrates. She was accused of threatening one of the witnesses in the case. Esther Edwards had agreed to testify against Alf Richardson only for Mary Wood to threaten that 'she would kill her if she came downstairs after the case'. Mary Wood admitted making the threat, but claimed in her defence that Edwards had given false testimony against her brother. She was bound over to keep the peace for six months.

The Richardsons were a notorious family, even by the standards of Greengate. The head of the household, Edwin Richardson, was an iron turner. He ought to have been able to provide comfortably for his wife and five children, but his addiction to drink was his ruin – and theirs. His frequent bouts of idleness forced his wife Mary to take a job as a silk winder in a nearby mill, but she did not earn enough to keep the family on her own.

During the early 1870s, the Richardsons lived in a cramped, courtyard dwelling off Gravel Lane. They fell on harder times by the middle of the decade. Edwin Richardson lost his job, and the family flitted from house to house before settling in a cellar in Bombay Street. Edwin Richardson eventually found new employment as a warehouse porter, but by now the family's reputation was sealed. Both of his sons were well-known to the Salford police. William worked as a spindle-maker, but he was widely recognised as one of the Queen Street scuttlers. Alf, the younger of the two, had been sent to a reformatory school as a child, only to join the Queen Street gang within days of his release.

Alf Richardson was back before the Salford magistrates by the end of May 1877. He was charged on two counts of assault following an outbreak of anti-Semitic violence in Greengate. The victims were Isaac Rosenthal, a Polish-born slipper maker, and his son, Wolf. One night the Rosenthals passed through Greengate on their way home to Moreton Street in Strangeways. In New Bridge Street, six-year-old Wolf, who had been lagging behind his father, suddenly cried out for help. Isaac Rosenthal turned round to see a gang of youths striking his son and calling him 'a —— Jew'. When Rosenthal went to his son's aid, he was manhandled and pulled by his hair before Alf Richardson punched him to the ground, knocking out one of his teeth. Rosenthal grabbed hold of Richardson and managed to restrain him until a beat constable arrived.

Detective Inspector Hargreaves told the magistrates that the entire neighbourhood of Queen Street was dangerous for pedestrians on account of the gangs of youths who insulted passers-by. He added that, 'If the persons aggrieved ventured to remonstrate they were instantly attacked by the gang, who would use stones or any weapon within reach, and resort to kicking also.' The police were frequently forced to post extra officers there. As for Alf Richardson, the inspector reported that since his release from a juvenile reformatory he had been convicted of several minor offences in addition to the assault on a Bury Street scuttler four months previously. Richardson was convicted of assaulting both Isaac and Wolf Rosenthal and received the maximum penalty for common assault – two months' imprisonment with hard labour – on each count.

Richardson's growing reputation as one of the terrors of Greengate was cemented during the early 1880s, when he became one of the henchmen of the much-feared Sam McElroy. In the meantime, the antics of the Queen Street scuttlers suggested to many observers that the youth of Salford's poorer districts were running wild. There is surprisingly little evidence of attempts by the older generation to curtail their activities. Parental authority was usually strict enough within the home. But tackling bands of young people, many of them armed, on the streets was a different matter. Even the police were wary of gangs.

As scuttling intensified on the streets of Salford during the 1870s, a number of high-profile scuttlers emerged from the ranks of the gangs. Among the most prominent were the Bellis brothers. They exercised something akin to a reign of terror in Greengate, subjecting any well-heeled stranger foolish enough to enter the district on foot to taunts, intimidation or worse, and showing flagrant disregard for the police.

CHAPTER 7

A Professor of Riot and Disorder

THE BELLIS BROTHERS first hit the headlines in September 1872 following a scuttle between around one hundred youths from rival workplaces in Greengate. The police had been tipped off in advance and a detachment of officers from the Salford force was dispatched to the scene. They managed to arrest just one of the combatants and even then found themselves besieged by the prisoner's friends. A Manchester detective went to help his Salford colleagues, but he in turn was assaulted. Prominent among his assailants was Joe Bellis, a seventeen-year-old apprentice dyer. He had a wooden leg, which he allegedly used to knock the detective down during the fracas. He was eventually restrained and arrested along with his brother Bill, a twenty-one-year-old porter. Joe got fourteen days in Strangeways while Bill was fined. Bill was back before the Salford magistrates the following February, when he was fined five shillings for assaulting Edwin Johnstone. The unfortunate Johnstone had tried to interfere when he spotted the brothers and their fellow scuttlers destroying a cart. He grabbed hold of Joe Bellis and was immediately set upon by Bill, who punched him in the mouth.

By the mid-1870s, Bill Bellis was one of the most-feared scuttlers in Salford. The police had identified him as the leader of the much-feared Broughton Road gang and they were determined to see him behind bars. In July 1875, they saw their chance. A youth named Charles Kay complained to the police that he had been assaulted by Bill Bellis while walking down Springfield Lane, Greengate, in broad daylight. Kay, who was not a scuttler, told the police that Bellis had accosted him in the street before punching him twice without provocation. The police immediately issued a summons against Bellis and when he came before the magistrates, Detective Inspector Hargreaves testified to his notoriety: according to the police, he was the leader of a gang who infested the entire neighbourhood of Broughton Road. The magistrate decreed that Bellis pay £40 in sureties to keep the peace for six months or spend six months in gaol. This was an extraordinary sum, as the magistrate knew perfectly well, representing more than a year's wages for Bellis. To emphasise the point, the magistrate told him, 'I hope you will have to serve out the time in gaol.'

The following year, it was Joe Bellis's turn to appear before the bench following another scuttle in Greengate. On this occasion, one of the brothers had been worsted. Joe told the court how he had been knocked down and dragged along Broughton Road before being assaulted by four members of an opposing gang, and named his assailants in court. They in turn alleged that Bellis had been at the head of his own gang at the time and had himself 'seriously ill-used' one of their friends. The stipendiary, Sir John Iles Mantell, was probably correct when he told the five youths that they were all as bad as each other. He discharged two of Bellis's alleged attackers but required the other two to provide sureties for their future peaceful conduct.

Joe Bellis's 'career' as a Broughton Road scuttler was curtailed at least temporarily three months later. At around 11.30 p.m. on Saturday, 3 February 1877, he was stood on the corner of Broughton Road and Greenbank with his gang when Charles Heaton, a smartly attired commercial traveller from nearby Cheetham, passed by. Angered by Heaton's apparent air of superiority, the scuttlers barged him as he passed and pushed off his glasses. When Heaton protested, Joe Bellis punched him in the mouth and twice in the ribs. Heaton crashed to the pavement, dislocating his shoulder as he fell. Salford police did not need long to identify the perpetrator. Arresting Joe Bellis was a different matter. Police called for him at his home in Greenbank the following morning. Bellis reacted furiously, biting the finger of one constable in the ensuing struggle. A local shopkeeper subsequently testified that he saw Bellis knock Heaton down. Bellis was committed for trial at the Quarter Sessions, where he was sentenced to twelve months' imprisonment.

WALTER ARMSTRONG first came to the attention of the Salford police during the winter of 1874-5. He was the leader of an up-and-coming band of scuttlers from the Adelphi and his reputation spread rapidly in the wake of a series of showdowns with rival gangs from both Salford and further afield in Manchester. Then aged sixteen, Armstrong was living with his parents in Kirkley Street. He was one of nine children to George Armstrong, a carter, and his wife Maria. The family of eleven lived in a two-up, two-down terraced house. They somehow found room for two of George's nieces as lodgers. Walter Armstrong was working as an errand boy at the age of eleven. By fourteen, he was working full-time in a factory. He was known throughout Salford by his street name 'Doll' on account of his taste for fashionable clothes.

On the evening of Sunday, 28 February 1875, the Salford Borough Police learned that a scuttle had broken out in Factory Lane, off Oldfield Road. Superintendent Hall set off to quell the disturbance with a party of six constables. They arrived to find a seething mass of sixty lads fighting with sticks, stones and belts. The officers managed to arrest seven of the combatants: five from Salford and two from Manchester. All seven were convicted of riotous and disorderly conduct at the Salford Police Court the following morning and were either fined or bound over to keep the peace, although Richard Jones, a sixteen-year-old steam-hammer driver from Deal Street in Salford, was jailed for three months as he was unable to find two sureties of £5. The Salford lads included both Doll Armstrong and his fourteen-year-old brother Robert.

The convictions did nothing to deter the Armstrongs. On a Friday evening at the height of the summer of 1876, John

Conway, a nineteen-year-old forgeman from Rockley Street in Pendleton, was walking home following a visit to a beerhouse with Tom Morton, his friend and workmate. The pair were well-known scuttlers and they felt safe enough in their own territory after a quiet night out. As they made their way along Broad Street, Pendleton, they spotted a rival gang in their path. Prominent in this group was Doll Armstrong. Conway recognised him straight away; the two had clashed during a scuttle in Cross Lane, Salford, twelve months earlier. Emboldened by drink, Conway walked up to Armstrong and accosted him.

'Doll, what did you pull the knife out to me for that time when the scuttle was on?'

'I'll pull another one out,' warned Armstrong.

Conway responded in kind: 'I'll kick your – head off.'

Conway and Morton began to walk away. The challenge to Armstrong had been clear enough and all of those present assumed that another scuttle between the two gangs would follow soon enough.

Doll Armstrong, however, was unwilling to suffer so public an insult. He charged after Conway and Morton, running twenty yards along Broad Street to confront them. As Conway turned to face him, Armstrong yelled, 'You big-headed sod, what do you mean?' One of Armstrong's associates tried to pull him back, but he wriggled free, pulled a knife from his pocket and plunged it into Conway's chest. Conway staggered, shouting to Tom Morton, 'I'm stabbed.' Armstrong walked away, his honour satisfied.

Morton took Conway to Pendleton Dispensary only to find that the doctor was not in. They called at the surgery of another local doctor, but he was not in either. As Conway drifted in and out of consciousness, Morton enlisted a passer-by to help carry his friend to another surgery. This time the doctor was in. Examining Conway, he found a puncture wound on the left breast, between the fourth and fifth ribs, roughly one and a half inches deep, which appeared to have been inflicted with a double-edged weapon. There was a lot of internal bleeding and the doctor feared Conway would die before the night was out.

He sent a message to the Pendleton police office, saying that a murder inquiry would more than likely soon be underway. A police inspector immediately arranged for a deposition, or sworn witness statement, to be taken from Conway by one of the Salford magistrates. Conway knew that these words might be his last. He swore that he had been sober when he left the beer-house, having drunk only one glass of beer. He identified Walter Armstrong as the youth who had stabbed him and ascribed his motive to their heated exchange in Broad Street. He admitted there was bad blood between them, telling the magistrate how Armstrong had lunged at him with a knife during the scuttle the previous summer. On that occasion, said Conway, 'I think he only meant to get my cap.'

The Salford Borough Police searched in vain for Doll Armstrong on the Saturday. At around six o'clock on the Sunday morning, he was spotted by P.C. Goodman in East Market Street. He appeared to be heading towards his home in Kirkley Street. P.C. Goodman gathered one of his fellow constables and the two set off for Kirkley Street, where one took up a position at the front of the house and the other went round to the back. Moments later Armstrong appeared in the back yard, whereupon the waiting officer kicked the yard door down. Armstrong promptly climbed up a water spout onto the roof of the house. The constables sent for reinforcements and the house was surrounded by a group of eighteen policemen. Several officers climbed up onto the roof of a house at the end of the terrace and started to edge their way across the slates, only to find that Armstrong had vanished. The police searched Kirkley Street for two hours. In the middle of the search, an officer named Cassidy fell through the roof of one of the houses, landing in a bedroom in which an entire family was asleep, apparently oblivious to the drama unfolding above their heads. Armstrong was eventually captured in the garret of one of the houses adjoining his own, having slipped in through a skylight. By the time the police dragged him out into the street, the entire neighbourhood was in uproar.

Armstrong was brought before Salford Police Court on the Monday morning. He was charged with attempted murder and remanded in custody for one week pending Conway's recovery and further inquiries by the police. Armstrong had been working as a hawker, and reporters noted that he was a 'rough-looking youth'. By the time of his second court appearance, a week later, Conway's condition was beginning to improve. Armstrong was remanded for a further week by which time, it was hoped, the victim would be well enough to testify. Armstrong was brought before the magistrates for the third and final time on Monday, August 14. Conway was able to attend, although he was too weak to stand and had to be provided with a special seat from which to give evidence.

P.C. Cooper of the Salford Borough Police told the court that he had arrested Armstrong on the morning of July 30 and had charged him with attempting to murder John Conway. 'I did not attempt to murder him,' replied Armstrong, adding: 'He told me he would kick my – head off, and then I went into him.' When P.C. Cooper asked, 'What with?' Armstrong replied, 'With a knife.' Stipendiary Sir John Iles Mantell then turned to the assembled police witnesses.

Sir John: 'What is known of the prisoner?'

Detective Inspector Hargreaves: 'He is a notorious character. He has been frequently brought before the court on various charges. He has only just completed a term of six months' imprisonment for robbery with violence in Manchester.'

Sir John: 'Is he one of these scuttlers?'

D.I. Hargreaves: 'He belongs to a very bad family, and he is ready for anything, either scuttling or thieving.'

Sir John committed Armstrong for trial at the Quarter Sessions on a reduced charge of unlawful wounding. After being cautioned, the defendant told the court, 'I did not do it wilfully; we were wrestling at the time, and I dropped onto him.'

Armstrong appeared at the Quarter Sessions before W. H. Higgin, Q.C., on August 25. Mr Higgin was appalled when the evidence presented to the magistrates was relayed once more. He declared that all of those concerned in the case 'ought to have been in bed at their fathers' homes' at that time of night, rather than being out on the streets or in beerhouses. In Higgin's view, it was a pity that 'these young fellows had not had a stick taken to their backs and been sent to bed'. He further lamented the wages offered to boys upon leaving school, claiming that rising wage levels were fostering a potentially deadly lack of discipline among the young:

> It was a fact that nowadays wages were so high that a child just out of the cradle could earn money, and they became independent, left home, and assumed the rights, and acted as men; and it was this which was eating its way into the best part of the social system. A degree of lawlessness was abroad nowadays, especially among the young, which was very difficult to contemplate, because it was most difficult to say where it would end. There was a degree of independence which if legitimately exercised was a very noble spirit to display, but there was a kind here which was fast degenerating into absolute lawlessness. It was quite time something were done to put a stop to this kind of conduct, and to bring these young people back to a sense of decency.

Mr Higgin was ready to make a start. He sentenced Doll Armstrong to the maximum term for unlawful wounding: five years' penal servitude. He said that the knife had been deliberately thrust at Conway's heart and concluded that Armstrong would certainly have forfeited his own life had Conway died. Higgin furthered warned, 'If the prisoner and the class of boys which he represented would assume the character of men, and would commit crimes that were usually committed by men, it was not astonishing, nor must they complain, if they were punished as men.' Armstrong showed no emotion as the sentence was pronounced and appeared utterly unmoved by the proceedings. When he left prison it was for the army, one of the few legitimate routes out of Salford for the youth of the Adelphi.

AT HALF past four in the morning on Monday, 5 July 1875, Mrs Jane Hopkins, of Mobberley's Court, Queen Street, was woken by a disturbance outside her bedroom window. She looked out to see a youth named John Appleby swinging a cat around by its tail and striking its head against the wall of her house, egged on by a gang of lads. Mrs Hopkins woke her husband, James, and the two of them rushed downstairs and ran out into the street to chase the youths away. Mrs Hopkins went to fetch a policeman, but by the time she returned with a beat constable the youths were nowhere to be seen. At around seven o'clock that evening, however, Mrs Hopkins spotted Appleby again. She asked him what he had done with the cat. Appleby responded with a stream of abuse and then punched her in the face. He was quickly joined by around twenty other lads, a number of whom took off their belts and began to hit her. James Hopkins ran to his wife's defence but was in turn struck with belts and kicked in the head. The gang then ran off, leaving the couple dazed and covered in blood.

Three youths who lived nearby were subsequently arrested. Tommy Hyman was a painter, as was Dick Cawley, while John Appleby worked as a labourer. They were charged with violently assaulting Jane Hopkins. Mrs Hopkins had brought the charges herself and she and her husband hired a lawyer named Bennet to lead the prosecution. Mr Bennet told the court that the prisoners formed 'part of a gang of the worst lads in the Borough, commonly known as scuttlers. They swarmed the streets with belts in their hands, and if any person approached them they were certain to be assaulted.' He said his client was struck in the face by the prisoners, and her husband received a kick in the eye, and he hoped any punishment would not only deter them in future, but would also be an example to their companions.

James Hopkins told the court that the youths had surrounded his wife 'like a swarm of bees'. Mrs Hopkins herself described the assault in graphic detail, adding that she had since been victimised and Cawley's mother had threatened 'to be the death of her' if she prosecuted her son. Other neighbours, however, sickened by the attack, were unusually willing to step forward and testify in court. A local married woman, Elizabeth Smith, told how she had witnessed Appleby strike Jane in the face. Another neighbour stated that he 'saw the blood pouring from Mrs Hopkins like a stream of water'. Police witnesses identified the three youths as members of the much-feared Queen Street scuttlers. Detective Sergeant Kirk confirmed that Queen Street was their headquarters, saying at times it was almost impossible to pass the street because of them. The magistrates were as appalled as the Hopkinses' neighbours had been. The three youths were each ordered to find £20 in sureties to keep the peace for six months with the alternative of six months in prison. No-one in court was surprised when the prisoners were jailed.

John Appleby's sureties were subsequently paid and he was released part of the way into his sentence. By October 1875, however, he had been brought back before the magistrates. Late on a Saturday night, Superintendent Hall of the Salford Borough Police heard a woman crying 'Police!' in Duke Street. He ran to the scene, where he was stoned by Appleby and another Queen Street scuttler, Thomas Mosley. The distressed woman told Superintendent Hall that they had assaulted her. Both Appleby and Mosley were well known to the police and were quickly arrested. They were brought before Sir John Iles Mantell and charged with riotous and disorderly conduct, common assault, and assaulting the police.

Superintendent Hall was the principal trial witness. He stated that the victim of the original assault had come to the police station the day before the court hearing to state that she had been struck by the two boys 'by accident'. Hall then told the magistrates how he had been bombarded with stones. Thomas Mosley's mother was next to address the court. She claimed that the boys had been messing around and had only been throwing stones at each other. Sir John was not impressed. His anger was palpable when he was told that both defendants had previous convictions for scuttling. 'I will ensure the prisoners are not in court again in a hurry,' he thundered. 'This scuttling is a most unlawful proceeding. I mean to make an example of these prisoners.' He sentenced them both to twenty-one days in Strangeways, followed by five years in a reformatory school.

Mrs Mosley was aghast. When the sentence was announced she protested so vehemently that she was invited to re-enter the witness box.

'I don't want my boy to be sent to a reformatory,' she wailed. 'He can read and I don't want him to be sent there.'

'But they have been mischievous,' replied Sir John.

'I know you are a gentleman, Sir John,' she pleaded. 'Don't send them there.'

Detective Inspector Hargreaves then chipped in. 'I may say, Sir John, that this woman was brought before the court a short time ago by Detective Sergeant Kirk for keeping a brothel.'

Sir John: 'I shall most decidedly send the prisoners to a reformatory.'

TOMMY HYMAN, one of the trio who beat up Jane Hopkins, rejoined the Queen Street scuttlers on his release from Strangeways early in 1876. Over the next fifteen months, he was in and out of court on charges of drunkenness, theft and assault. In March 1876, he was convicted of assaulting a woman walking through an alleyway with a baby in her arms. Hyman confronted her with a stream of 'abusive language' and knocked the child out of her arms. He was fined ten shillings with the option of two weeks in prison.

In the spring of 1877, Hyman embarked on a spree of thuggery that brought him before the magistrates yet again. One Friday night, a fitter named William Litherland was walking down Greengate towards his home in nearby Springfield Lane. Hyman, who was loitering in the street with four other youths, suddenly ran at Litherland and struck him on the side of the head. Litherland, who had offered no provocation, suffered a severe injury to his ear. When a passing female mill worker remonstrated with Hyman, he punched her in the mouth. A crowd quickly gathered at the scene. P.C. Minogue of the Salford Borough Police was the first officer to arrive. He managed to take hold of Hyman, but struggled to drag him to the police station. Hyman kicked out and issued a string of threats, telling P.C. Minogue that if he had a knife he would 'run it through his gizzard' and if he got twelve months, he would 'run a knife into his heart when he came out'.

Hyman appeared in court the next morning, when Detective Inspector Hargreaves said that Hyman had been using the alias 'George Graham' in an attempt to trick the police into ignoring his previous convictions. Now aged nineteen, Hyman was still working as a painter. He lived at 2 Queen Street, one of the most notorious addresses in Salford. Inspector Hargreaves told the court that he was obliged to station as many as six plain-clothes constables at a time in Queen Street, such was the danger of assaults on passers-by. Hyman was a prominent member of 'a group of roughs, who assembled there, and indulged in what was known as bonneting – striking persons' hats. When parties so ill-used remonstrated with these roughs, they would grossly insult them.'

Hyman was sent down for three months. In a sardonic commentary on the case, the *Free Lance* labelled him a 'professor of riot and disorder':

Salford continues to assert itself as a centre of brutality and violence almost without a rival throughout England. The pleasant and exhilarating practice of scuttling – lying in wait for unoffending pedestrians at street corners with the view of savagely kicking and otherwise maltreating the unwary – has bated not one jot of its popularity as a healthy and spirit-stirring exercise. A 'notorious' young miscreant of several aliases, whose exploits in the character of a drunkard, thief, professor of riot and disorder, etc, have upon many previous occasions occupied the attention of the authorities, was upon the evening of Friday last the hero of an exciting adventure in Greengate. Surrounded by a posse of his myrmidons this precocious ruffian committed a violent personal assault upon an individual named Litherland, brought his fist into unpleasantly close contact with a young girl who ventured to interfere, and capped the exploits of the evening by inflicting serious bodily injury upon an officer of the law, whose life he proclaimed his intention of taking on the earliest fitting opportunity.

Under the circumstances, the *Free Lance* suggested, Hyman might justifiably have been locked up for a year. The magazine advised P.C. Minogue to 'make his will, purchase a coffin, and arrange for his decent interment upon the expiration of the current quarter'.

CHAPTER 8

The Police and the Gangs

IN 1871, THE Manchester City Police numbered 691 men. They served a population of just over 351,000, a ratio of one officer per 508 people. They were organised into five divisions, each headed by its own superintendent answerable to the Chief Constable, Captain William Henry Palin, and his deputy. By 1901, the force's strength had increased to 993, although the city boundaries had extended too and the population had reached 540,000. Divisions 'A' to 'D' were territorial and divided into beats, each of which was patrolled by constables – either singly or in pairs – on a strict timetable. 'E' division was the detective department. The Salford Borough Police was a wholly independent force with its own Chief Constable. In 1891, when the population stood at almost 200,000, the Salford force was only 300-strong. The ratio of one officer per 667 people was considerably higher than in Manchester. Given Salford's reputation it is no surprise that the borough's beat constables, in particular, faced a hard time on the streets.

Senior officers in both forces were generally recruited from military backgrounds. Constables were often former industrial workers or agricultural labourers. Relatively few were local men, and superintendents were careful to ensure that Manchester-born officers did not patrol the districts where they had grown up. Familiarity with the local people would all too easily compromise them in the execution of their duties. Constables were generally young men recruited on the basis of height – and brawn. There were few written examinations for aspiring officers before 1900. The average length of service in 1870 was seven years and those who left the force were given character testimonials to help them find jobs in local industries.

The best-known police officer in Victorian Manchester was Jerome Caminada. Born in the city in 1844, Caminada spent five years in the Royal Lancashire militia. By the time he applied to join the police, at the age of twenty-four, he was working as an iron dresser at the Salford ironworks of Mather & Platt. Caminada initially served as a constable in 'A' division, where his beat included the slums of Deansgate and Angel Meadow. He recalled the Deansgate quarter in 1870 as 'the rendezvous of thieves and a very hot-bed of social iniquity and vice. The women of the locality were of the most degraded class, and their chief victims were drunken men, collier lads, and country "flats" [simpletons], whom they picked up and rifled with impunity.' Beerhouses such as the Dog and Rat, the Old Ship and the Green Man attracted raucous crowds, many of them youths. Prostitutes lived in the upstairs rooms, with the beerhouse-keepers acting as their bullies, or pimps. Many of the beerhouses were in fact shebeens, and Caminada assisted in closing many of them down as the civic authorities strove to cleanse Deansgate of its unsavoury reputation.

Caminada transferred from 'A' division to the detective department, 'E' division, where he rose quickly to the rank of inspector. He was soon recognised as the outstanding detective on the Manchester force. His dealings with thieves, burglars, swindlers and counterfeiters led to a series of high-profile trials and press coverage made him a household name in Manchester. He retired as Chief Detective Inspector in 1899.

In 1885, the *Manchester City News* described a Saturday night in the fortress-like Goulden Street police station. Lying between Oldham Road and Rochdale Road in the maze of slums streets that separated Angel Meadow from Ancoats, Goulden Street was one of the toughest beats in the city, but its officers were well versed in dealing with the local population. Most of those taken into custody as the pubs closed were drunk; many were maudlin rather than cantankerous once they were locked up:

The busiest hours are from eleven p.m. till about two on Sunday morning. Most of the cases are of the ordinary drunk-and-rowdy class, sometimes aided by women and sometimes not. We can only describe one here and there. This case just now to the fore is rather more serious than the majority; but the man charged comes up smiling and seems to make very light of it. He has been arguing too excitedly with his mother-in-law, not a very unusual occurrence; but he has supplemented his arguments with a poker and the woman has had to be taken to the Infirmary in a seriously-injured condition. 'I think,' says our inspector suavely, 'you have been here on some other occasion.' 'Yes.' 'Wasn't there something about a poker that time?' 'Oh, yes. But that was the other man, you know.' This prisoner is jaunty enough; but nothing is more striking in the demeanour of the majority than their craven heartedness. There is little of the defiant gloriousness of the prisoners depicted in the 'Penny Dreadful', and they are for the most part a weeping, miserable lot of fellows. They have been splendid enough all the evening, drinking, fighting, scuttling, insulting respectable females and what not; but when brought to book they become lach-rymose, penitent and broken down. One thinks of his poor father, a second of his situation [job], and a third of his wife and children waiting for him at home.

'Ordinary' drunks were difficult to take into custody. They frequently resisted arrest and, as often as not, their friends tried to rescue them from the clutches of the police. The scuttler was an even more difficult proposition. He was invariably armed and all too often willing to use his weapons to evade arrest.

Resentment of the police was particularly fierce in the slum districts of Victorian Manchester. Arrests for minor public order infringements often led to mass assaults on the arresting officers. On one infamous occasion during the 1840s, a storm of protest had followed the arrest of two off-duty soldiers after a row in a beerhouse in Bengal Street, Ancoats. An angry crowd broke into a nearby police station and severely beat a number of constables.

Order was only restored when a detachment of troops arrived. By the 1870s, relations between the police and the inhabitants of the city's poorer districts had thawed – but only to an extent. Ordered to keep the streets clear of 'disorderly persons', beat constables were placed in the unenviable position of having to move on drunks, break up knots of gamblers and disperse street corner gatherings of youths who, in many cases, had nowhere else to spend their evenings or weekends. For those brought up in cramped homes, the streets formed a vast, outdoor play-ground. However, the presence of gangs of roughs lurking on street corners worried more 'respectable' passers-by. Night after night, beat constables harassed the corner gangs, ordering knots of surly youths to move or face arrest for obstructing the highway. Assaults on the police were commonplace; at pub closing time in districts such as Angel Meadow or Ancoats, they were routine. And when scuttlers were involved, they were often made with an array of potentially lethal weapons.

Scuttling gangs were extraordinarily difficult to police. Their operations spread over a vast area and the local police forces found it impossible to pinpoint precisely when or where scuttles would break out. When rival gangs clashed, their numbers were such that beat constables frequently left them to it. How could one or two officers armed only with truncheons disperse a crowd of scores or even hundreds of youths fighting with belts and knives? Yet the police could not ignore scuttling, for each outbreak brought fresh demands from outraged citizens for the restoration of order and the break-up of the gangs.

The police adopted a series of measures to contain, if not eradicate, the violence. They flooded noted trouble spots such as Greengate in Salford with additional officers, mounting nightly patrols and hidden surveillance operations in their effort to drive the most dangerous gangs from the streets. They frequently waited for scuttles to subside before pouncing and arresting the wounded, though sometimes the police did wade in between warring factions. Like gang members, police officers cultivated reputations for toughness and for refusing to dodge confronta-tion. Scuttlers were generally wary of the bobbies, not least since police operations against particular gangs could last for months on end. Nonetheless, scuttlers frequently retaliated, launching mob attacks upon isolated policemen, some of whom were beaten almost to death.

Jerome Caminada reflected on the menace posed by gangs of scuttlers in a volume of memoirs published after his retirement:

> From time to time the people of Manchester are startled by some scuttling outrage, and the cry is raised 'Where are the police?' These are about the worst cases with which the police have to deal. Very little credit is given by the public to the man who interferes in such an affray, yet he is frequently injured in so doing, and is sometimes in peril of his life; for the ruffians who mix up in these battles will stand at nothing when their blood is up. Even in quarrels amongst themselves the knife is drawn on the smallest provocation. Many a good tussle have I had with other classes of criminals, but I would rather face the worst of these than a scuttler; for though the former will use their hands and feet freely enough, the knife is seldom thought of.

Caminada was insistent that a scuttler would use his knife on his own associates or even his 'sweetheart', never mind the police.

As a raw constable, Caminada learned the folly of interfering single-handed in scuttles when he wandered into a frenzied skirmish between gangs from Clock Alley in Manchester and Greengate in Salford.[12] The Greengate mob had repelled a raid by the Clock Alley lads and chased the intruders out of Salford over Victoria Bridge. The Manchester scuttlers gathered reinforcements before making another stand. Caminada intervened.

> I happened to be passing at the time, and having, perhaps, too exalted an opinion of the powers of a police officer and the

---

12 Clock Alley lay between Withy Grove and Balloon Street, a few minutes' walk from Victoria Station. Once occupied by fustian cutters and smallware weavers, it was named after the 'clock lace' produced for use in the collars and cuffs of military uniforms. The street was demolished in 1891 to make way for an extension to the wholesale department of the Co-operative Society.

majesty of the law, I went in between them. If I had expected them to dissolve at the sight of my uniform I was soon disillusioned. The streets at that time were not kept so free from stones and missiles as they are now; in fact, it was nothing new at that time for scuttlers to pull up the boulder stones which formed the pavement. After a succession of minor bruises, I was at length hit on the spine with a large stone weighing some pounds. Well built and strong as I was, I went to the earth, where I lay prostrate. The two factions, resenting my interference with their little amusement, had combined in making the 'bobby' the target for their shots … This proved an object lesson to me upon the folly and uselessness of interfering single-handed between gangs of scuttlers for the purpose of keeping the Queen's peace.

Many of Caminada's fellow officers were to learn the same painful lesson for themselves.

DURING THE 1870s, the Salford police received innumerable complaints regarding the conduct of crowds of unruly youths who gathered on corners across the poorer districts of the borough to play 'pitch and toss' on Saturday and Sunday afternoons. Pitch and toss is a simple form of gambling in which three coins are spun into the air and bets are made on the proportion of heads to tails as they fall. These 'schools' of gamblers included many scuttlers and their mere presence on the streets intimidated passers-by. Local councillors and religious leaders wondered whether the youths' money might not be better spent on more respectable pursuits and from time to time, as pressure to clamp down on street gambling mounted, the police organised raids on the pitch and toss schools, bringing batches of lads (and some older men too) before the magistrates, who duly issued fines accompanied by stern moral lectures.

One such clampdown was launched in Salford during the summer of 1873. Constables were dispatched in pairs, wearing plain clothes, with instructions to sweep the gambling schools off the streets. On the afternoon of Saturday, August 30, constables Baker and Minogue were sent out to comb the streets between Chapel Street and the River Irwell. The officers, neither of whom was in uniform, swooped on a gang playing pitch and toss in Yorkshire Street. P.C. Baker grabbed a boy named William Doyle but found it difficult to keep hold of him. Doyle proved 'very obstinate' and P.C. Minogue was forced to go to Baker's assistance, leaving the other youthful gamblers to escape. The two officers began to drag Doyle towards the police office at Salford Town Hall. The boy struggled for all he was worth, loudly proclaiming his innocence.

William Doyle's cries of protest quickly drew a large crowd. Few of those present were minded to assist the police. In the eyes of the crowd, the police were the villains of the piece, picking on a mere boy whose harmless Saturday afternoon pastime hardly constituted a crime. Becoming angrier by the minute, the crowd began to hoot and shout at the constables. In Wilkinson Street, thirty-eight-year-old James Farrer stepped forward, telling the officers, 'Let the lad away; he has done nothing.' The constables warned Farrer that if he did not move back he would face arrest himself. As Farrer retreated into the crowd, stones were flung at the police. The first passed over the constables' heads. The second flew in between them. The third stone struck P.C. Baker on the side of the head, near the left temple. He fell forward onto the pavement, his helmet rolling down the street, blood oozing down his cheek. P.C. Minogue shouted to the crowd that Farrer had thrown the stone. Farrer was well known to the Salford police: he had two previous convictions, one as a 'rogue and vagabond', the other for assaulting a constable.

The only person who went to the aid of the police was a passer-by named Henry Stanley. A 'gentleman' of independent means, Mr Stanley resided at Fox Hill, near Barton Moss, eight miles outside Salford. He helped P.C. Minogue to take P.C. Baker to a nearby chemist's shop, where the head injury was dressed. Mr Stanley then accompanied the constables to the Town Hall, where William Doyle was charged with playing pitch and toss in the street. Another officer, P.C. Drysdale, went out in search of James Farrer. By five o'clock, Farrer too was in custody at the Town Hall. Constables Baker and Minogue both identified him as the man who had thrown the third stone.

P.C. Baker went back out on duty. He patrolled the streets of Salford for three hours before complaining that he felt too ill to finish his beat. By the time he was taken to a doctor's surgery, P.C. Baker was in a state of 'giddiness and stupor' and unable to walk properly. The doctor ordered him straight to bed. The constable returned to his lodgings at the Regent Road police station in Ordsall, where he was put to bed at nine o'clock. George Baker never awoke. He died at around three o'clock in the morning. The doctor subsequently stated that, 'No human skill could have prevented death once the injury had been sustained.' A native of Gosport in Hampshire who had joined the Salford Borough Police only the previous year, Baker was aged just twenty-one.

James Farrer was charged with wilful murder at six o'clock that evening. 'I am innocent,' he protested. 'I never threw the stone.' The following morning, he was brought before the magistrates at the Salford Police Court. He was described as a married man, living in Johnson Street. His occupation was given as carter. P.C. Minogue told the court that he had seen Farrer 'in the act of throwing a stone at Baker. The stone struck Baker on the left side of the head, and he fell forward on his hands and face.' Asked whether he was certain that it was Farrer who threw the fatal stone, Minogue replied that he was. In Minogue's account, Farrer was stood no more that twelve yards from the officers and there was no doubt he was the stone-thrower.

Two civilian witnesses were called: a clogger, whose premises were nearby, and a young girl. Both told the court that they saw P.C. Baker being hit by the stone but did not see who threw it. At the suggestion of the Chief Constable, Farrer was remanded in custody for five days. Meanwhile, the inquest was held. The key witness was again P.C. Minogue. The clogger who had testified before the magistrates now told the coroner's jury that he 'heard a great deal of hooting and shouting in the street ... and saw a piece of flag thrown which hit one of the policemen on the head.' The flag, or paving stone, was ten inches long, five inches wide, and one and a half inches thick. The coroner declared that it was quite clear that P.C. Baker had died from this wound; if the jury were convinced that Farrer had thrown the piece of stone, they had no choice but to convict him. The jurors were uneasy. A number of them regarded the police testimony with some scepticism. Moreover, they pointed out, no evidence had been presented in Farrer's defence. The coroner urged them to find Farrer guilty of murder; but the jurors would not be swayed. They refused to return a verdict on account of the paucity of the evidence presented to them.

Farrer made his second appearance before the Salford magistrates on September 6. He once more vigorously denied the charge and, as the *Salford Weekly News* pointed out, the only evidence against him was the testimony of the deceased officer's colleague, P.C. Minogue. Yet if Farrer did not throw the stone, then who did? As the *Weekly News* noted, 'It is impossible for Farrer, or anyone else in the crowd, to have lifted and to have thrown so large a stone without being observed by several of those who were around, and consequently there must be people in Salford, in addition to the constable, who saw Farrer, or some other person, throw the stone.' The paper regretted that 'the authorities have been unable to produce additional witnesses in regard to this vital point of the case'. In effect, the *Weekly News* was issuing a challenge not just to the police but to the people of Salford. For if Farrer was not guilty of Baker's murder, then there were dozens of people, at least, who were shielding the real killer. Farrer's counsel told the magistrates that 'he was prepared to prove by seven witnesses that the prisoner was not the man who threw the stone which hit the deceased; the stone was thrown ten yards from where the prisoner was standing', but stipendiary magistrate Sir John Iles Mantell was prepared to trust the testimony of a police officer. He committed Farrer for trial at the Assizes on the charge of wilful murder.

James Farrer stood trial before Baron Pollock at the Manchester Assizes in December 1873. A surgeon told the court that death had been caused by a blow from a stone which had severed an artery within the skull. The principal witness for the prosecution, yet again, was P.C. Minogue. The officer gave what was by now his standard account of the incident in which he firmly identified Farrer as the man who threw the stone that hit P.C. Baker on the head. When P.C. Minogue mentioned that neither officer was in uniform on the afternoon in question, the judge interjected.

Baron Pollock: 'Why not?'

P.C. Minogue: 'We were detailed for special duty in plain clothes.'

Baron Pollock: 'Do you call picking up a boy for playing pitch and toss in the street special duty?'

P.C. Minogue: 'Yes, that was what we were detailed for, to look after lads gambling.'

Baron Pollock: 'Is it common to send out constables on service of that kind?'

P.C. Minogue: 'Yes.'

Baron Pollock was evidently unimpressed. If anything, he appeared to share the concern of many in the crowd that witnessed the arrest of William Doyle: did the police not have better things to do?

Henry Stanley, the 'gentleman' who had helped the police, now appeared as a witness. He told the court how he had heard Farrer shout, 'Let the boy go.' He was adamant, however, that Farrer had not thrown the third and fatal stone. In fact, he asserted, when the stone was thrown Farrer himself turned to the crowd and shouted, 'Who the hell threw that?' Several additional witnesses were called, all of whom swore that the fatal stone was thrown by another, unidentified, man outside the main body of the crowd. The jury found Farrer not guilty and he was discharged. No-one else was ever charged with the murder.

The Salford Watch Committee resolved to pay a gratuity of £10 to P.C. Baker's mother. This was scant compensation for the loss of a son.

ASSAULTS ON the police in Salford were common throughout the 1870s, to the consternation of the stipendiary magistrates,

Sir John Iles Mantell and his successor from 1878, Joseph Makinson. Both raged against the savage mistreatment of the police by 'Salford roughs'. Officers were most vulnerable on Saturday nights, when drink-fuelled arguments spilled onto busy thoroughfares such as Chapel Street and Cross Lane. Late one Saturday night in June 1874, two constables patrolling Chapel Street encountered a crowd of between 200 and 300 people gathered in the busy road. In the middle of the crowd were two men, stripped to the waist, engaged in a stand-up fight. The constables ran into the crowd and managed to apprehend one of the pugilists. Their interference sparked huge resentment among the onlookers, one of whom, a well-known bruiser from the Adelphi, made a determined effort to rescue the prisoner, punching both constables in the process. The would-be rescuer was arrested and dragged to the police office at the nearby Town Hall. He was later jailed for a month.

Beat constables patrolled Salford's rougher quarters in pairs, but this was rarely enough to ensure their safety. Constables Tatton and Lane were on plain clothes duty in Greengate late one Saturday night in July 1876 when they witnessed a fight breaking out among a group of twenty lads and girls in Norton Street. When the officers intervened, P.C. Lane was thrown to the ground by Robert Tarpey, a nineteen-year-old labourer. Lane was surrounded and kicked repeatedly before his colleague eventually managed to chase off the youths. Lane was left bleeding profusely and unable to walk. Four of the youths were later rounded up and brought before the magistrates. Captain Torrens, the Chief Constable, appeared as a witness and told the court that the Watch Committee had awarded P.C. Lane six weeks' paid leave, plus a gratuity of £2, to compensate him for his injuries. P.C. Tatton, whose acts of bravery had been commended on more than one occasion, had been awarded a merit badge for his efforts in saving his fellow officer. The Chief Constable added that no fewer than 208 people had been brought before the Salford magistrates for assaulting the police during the previous twelve months. Sir John Iles Mantell remarked that he had jailed many of the offenders, to no effect. He concluded, somewhat forlornly, 'I don't think you can find this borough equalled by any in the kingdom for cases of brutal assault.'

A surgeon from the Salford Dispensary told the court that P.C. Lane was brought in at half past eleven on Saturday night. He found the constable to be 'suffering from a compound fracture of the right nasal bone, and a cut on the forehead about an inch long. His right eye was very much congested, and the soft parts of his nose were completely cut through. The sides of his body had also been injured. It was very likely that his nose would be permanently disfigured.' Remarking that the prisoners were 'evidently a rough, lawless set of fellows', Sir John committed them for trial at the Salford Hundred Quarter Sessions, where they were convicted of assaulting P.C. William Lane and sentenced to terms ranging from six to twelve months. The heaviest sentence was meted out to John Cassels, whose criminal record included convictions for theft and possession of stolen goods.

Two weeks after the frenzied assault on P.C Lane, on another rowdy Saturday night, P.C. Joseph Gilmore was called to the public baths in Greengate. The baths superintendent had taken a boy into custody and requested that the police should arrest him. P.C. Gilmore made the arrest and set off back to Miller Street police station with the prisoner and the superintendent in tow. They had not ventured far when they were stopped in the street by a 'rough-looking young fellow' called John Pennington, who stood directly in front of the constable and told him that he should not take the lad into custody. The officer warned Pennington that he would be arrested too, to which Pennington replied, 'I'll be damned if I'll let you take him.' The constable handed his prisoner over to the baths superintendent and seized hold of Pennington before setting off again for the police station. When they reached Queen Street, however, they were quickly engulfed by a hostile crowd of scuttlers. P.C. Gilmore was thrown to the ground and kicked all over his body as he struggled to get back to his feet. One man held him down, shouting, 'Let's kill the –'. P.C. Gilmore eventually struggled to his feet, somehow still holding Pennington, and dragged him down the street for another 100 yards before he was knocked down again.

At this point, the brave constable was also struck on the shoulder with a bottle and on the hands with a stick; according to a witness, he was 'knocked about like clothes in a washing tub'. P.C. Gilmore was finally forced to relinquish Pennington and staggered to the Royal Dispensary for treatment.

John Pennington and four other young men were arrested by detectives over the course of the following week and tried at the Quarter Sessions before William Higgin. Having jailed four other Greengate youths for the assault on P.C Lane just three days before, Higgin was in no mood for leniency. The five 'roughs' charged with the assault on P.C. Gilmore were all identified in court as painters, their ages ranging from seventeen to twenty-four. They were all convicted of unlawfully wounding the constable and jailed. Pennington, who got the longest sentence of fifteen months, had nine previous convictions for drunkenness and assault.

GREENGATE WAS by no means the only part of Salford where the police faced constant harassment. The neighbouring district of the Adelphi, renowned as an 'Irish' quarter, likewise saw frequent assaults on beat constables when they attempted to make arrests for fighting, drunkenness or minor breaches of the peace. Two constables were patrolling the Adelphi at around midnight on Saturday, 25 March 1876, when they apprehended a man in Arlington Street for wounding his wife. On the way to the police station, the man began to resist and in the struggle one constable's helmet was knocked off. The prisoner grabbed the helmet and threw it among a nearby crowd of fifteen to twenty roughs. Seizing the opportunity to taunt the constables, the roughs promptly embarked on an impromptu game of tossing the policeman's helmet. One officer rushed at the crowd and managed to apprehend a dyer from Cannon Street, who was later convicted of drunken and disorderly conduct. The helmet was never recovered; in all likelihood, it adorned an Adelphi mantelpiece for some time afterwards.

Anti-police sentiment persisted in the Adelphi for many years. In November 1880, two plain-clothes constables spotted a shoemaker named Thomas Kenny embroiled in a fierce argument outside a pub in Pine Street. When the constables took him into custody, Kenny lashed out with punches and kicks. The officers managed to drag Kenny towards the police station, but a crowd tracked them, throwing bricks and stones and hitting them with sticks. One was struck on the eye by a brick and severely wounded. Eighteen-year-old Michael Burns, alleged by the police to have been the ringleader of the crowd, was later imprisoned for one month for beating one of the officers with a stick. Thomas Kenny was by no means chastened by this incident. In September 1884, he was arrested on another charge of being drunk and disorderly and assaulting two police constables. Superintendent Donohue informed the Salford Police Court that Kenny had by now amassed nine convictions, adding that: 'He was an Adelphi rough, and a worthless, lazy fellow.'

In the summer of 1882, Superintendent Donohue had complained bitterly that 'the district was a very low one, and it was very difficult to get the people to assist the police'. Indeed, local people were more inclined to thwart the police than to help them make an arrest. One Saturday night that May, P.C. Radford of the Salford Borough Police was called to a pub in the Adelphi where a man named Kelly was drunk and causing a nuisance to other customers. P.C. Radford asked Kelly to go home, but Kelly refused and knocked the constable down. Undaunted, P.C. Radford took Kelly out of the public house and marched him in the direction of the Silk Street police station. Moments later, they were set upon by a gang led by John Kelly, the prisoner's son. A second constable rushed to the aid of the beleaguered Radford. The two officers were repeatedly assaulted and Radford was thrown down in the street and kicked all over his body, but still the constables managed to take the Kellys to the police station. Both were subsequently sent to Strangeways.

BEAT CONSTABLES and detectives alike were frequently tempted to get their retaliation in first. They were steadfastly supported by the magistrates, who saw the use of violence as an inescapable part of maintaining public order. Joseph Makinson, Salford's stipendiary from 1878 to 1911, tended to dismiss allegations of police brutality, telling prisoners that they ought to have complained to the desk sergeant at the time of their arrest if they had been assaulted by officious or over-zealous policemen. Some prisoners were given severe beatings behind closed doors. There were no civilian witnesses within the confines of a police station and officers who had themselves been subjected to violence on the streets were not shy of seeking revenge in the cells. When a Salford labourer called Blackie appeared at the police court in April 1874, charged with being drunk and disorderly and assaulting three constables, the officers told the court that the prisoner had attacked them and damaged their uniforms. Blackie made a counter-allegation against a constable named Jones in court.

'Didn't you strike me and give me a pair of black eyes, and also cut my head?' he asked the constable.

'No,' said P.C. Jones.

'I should have been murdered if it had not been for Detective Kirk, who was in the police office at the time,' retorted Blackie.

Detective Sergeant Kirk told a different story. He said Blackie had been very disorderly at the station and attacked the officers in the charge room several times. Another detective told the court that the prisoner had previously been convicted of assaulting the police. Blackie was fined twenty shillings, plus nineteen shillings to cover the damage to police uniforms. Unable to raise the money to pay the fine, he was sent down for one month. He left the dock threatening to take out a summons against the constables for assault.

CHAPTER 9

The Bengal Tigers

DURING THE MID-1880s, the formidable confidence of the Victorians was shattered by economic depression and wide-spread unemployment. British agriculture was hit by the growth of American wheat production and by innovations in refrigeration that allowed the import of meat from Australia and New Zealand. The prospects for British industry were equally gloomy: export markets were being lost in the face of increasing competition from Germany as well as the United States. As the Royal Commission on the Depression in Trade and Industry concluded grimly in 1886, 'We are beginning to feel the effect of foreign competition in quarters where our trade formerly enjoyed a practical monopoly.' In London, a demonstration by 20,000 unemployed dockers and building workers in February 1886 turned to looting in Piccadilly; for two hours, *The Times* complained bitterly, the West End 'was in the hands of the mob'. The decade also saw growing recognition of the problems of the slums in England's great cities. Although average wages were rising, so was the gulf between those who were comfortably off and the poor. Churchmen and social investigators highlighted the chronic poverty and overcrowding in London's East End, exposing a shocked nation to the sheer depth of misery, crime, destitution, filth, and prostitution in 'Outcast London'. Parallel investigations revealed similar conditions in 'Outcast Manchester', 'Blackest Birmingham', and 'Squalid Liverpool'.

In Manchester, new charities were launched to augment the meagre provision of the city's Poor Law guardians. Notable among the charitable works was the Wood Street Mission in Deansgate, founded in 1869. The mission's original aim was to give help to the 'street arabs, neglected children, outcasts and the poor people of our slums'. By the 1880s, its provision of free meals for women and children was extended to include men without work; 3,200 meals were provided specifically for the unemployed during the winter of 1884–5. Temporary shelter was given to those who suddenly found themselves homeless. However, despite heroic efforts on the part of the mission's workers and those of their colleagues at the Manchester and Salford Methodist Mission, founded in 1886, such philanthropic ventures did little to improve living conditions.

Fred Scott, the secretary of the Manchester and Salford Sanitary Association, investigated a sample district in Ancoats in 1889. In a paper published by the Manchester Statistical Society, he revealed that fifty per cent of households could be classified as 'very poor'. By this he meant 'those who are always face to face with want', living on incomes of less than four shillings per adult per week. A further twenty-three per cent were 'poor', living a 'hand-to-mouth existence' on incomes of less than six shillings and threepence per adult per week. Only twenty-seven per cent of the households in his sample had incomes which provided for luxuries, over and above the bare necessities of life. Scott insisted that his survey had been undertaken during a period of 'exceptionally full employment. How aggravated [conditions] must be when trade is bad and employment scarce!'

Violence, like poverty and disease, was most densely concentrated in the central slum districts: in Angel Meadow and Deansgate, still the haunts of 'Criminal Manchester', and in the slums of Ancoats, where rival gangs patrolled each of the principal thoroughfares. The ferocity of the Ancoats gangs was legendary. Prussia Street, Bengal Street, Alum Street and Pollard Street were constantly at war, if not with each other then with the infamous Meadow Lads or the denizens of Lime Street or Holland Street in Miles Platting. In the eastern townships, gangs from Bradford, Gorton and Openshaw continued to vie for territorial supremacy, their bitter local conflicts periodically interspersed with clashes with mobs from further afield: from Ancoats, or from Chorlton-on-Medlock and Hulme to the south. And all of the gangs of Manchester had one thing in common: a fierce loathing of Salford.

This welter of scuttling was arousing increasing concern among the judicial authorities. The magistrates, apparently powerless to stem the repeated outbreaks of youthful gang fighting, began to commit increasing numbers of scuttlers for trial at the higher courts. Where the magistrates had failed, perhaps the recorders at the Quarter Sessions and the judges sitting at the Assize Courts might succeed? The judges of the Northern Circuit were accustomed to violence in all of its forms. However, even they were shocked by the sheer lust for mayhem among Manchester's scuttlers.

BY THE mid-1880s the most powerful gangs in Ancoats were the Bengal Tigers and the Prussia Street lads. The Tigers took their name from Bengal Street, and drew their members from the mesh of narrow streets and slum courts bounded by Great Ancoats Street, Oldham Road, German Street and Union Street, the latter running alongside the Rochdale Canal. The area had acquired an 'evil' reputation following the Jersey Street Outrage of 1866. Five years later, the *Manchester City News* pointed out that Bengal Street itself, with the huge Murray's Mill complex at one end, was 'tolerably respectable'. The same could not be said, however, for the side streets off it such as Primrose Street – 'full of evil cellars and populations to match' – or 'the even more wretched courts which opened off these streets, and the dirty and overcrowded warrens, such as McKay's buildings, which existed in close proximity'. These dilapidated courtyards, often named after the jerry-builders who had erected them five or more decades earlier, stood in perpetual darkness. Some were reached by passages eight yards long and only thirty inches wide, which few outsiders dared enter.

By the following decade Bengal Street had lost any glimmer of respectability. With a population of around 5,600 crammed into a grid of just thirty-six acres, the district was a 'phthisis nest' – a

A young man displays some of the street fashions of the 1890s, including pointed clogs, a white muffler, and cap worn on the back of the head to display the fringe.

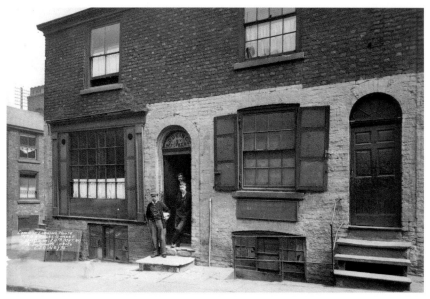

Angel Street in Angel Meadow, the heart of 'Criminal Manchester' and haunt of the feared Meadow Lads. Many scuttlers lived in the district's squalid and overcrowded lodging houses.

Lodging house interior, 1890s.

The chimney of the world: the industrial district of Ancoats in the 1890s.

Pollard Street, one of the principal Ancoats thoroughfares, seen here from the back. The Pollard Street scuttlers fought fierce battles with gangs from surrounding areas.

Goulden Street police station in New Cross was a veritable fortress, built to withstand sieges and entered through a heavy, metal-studded gate.

Manchester police officers pose for a divisional portrait during the 1880s.

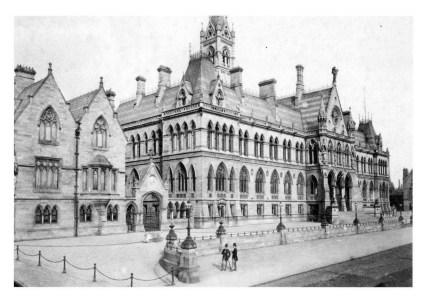

The neo-Gothic splendour of Manchester Assize Courts, the grandest building many scuttlers would ever set foot in.

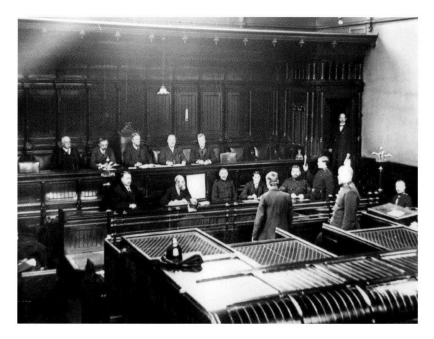

Inside the City Police Court at Minshull Street, Manchester, where hundreds of scuttlers appeared before the magistrates.

A cell block at the Manchester City Gaol at Belle Vue. Local councillors grew concerned at the number of twelve- and thirteen-year-old boys held in the prison during the 'Rochdale Road War' of 1870-71.

An example of the meagre fare in Strangeways Prison. Victorian prisoners complained often of hunger and many suffered rapid weight loss in the early stages of confinement.

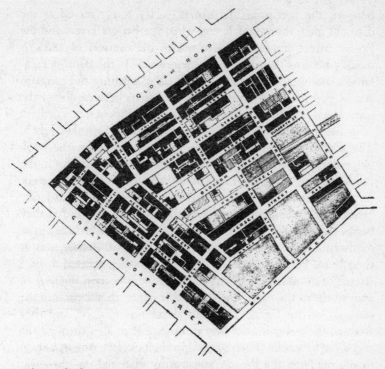

*The grid of streets around Bengal Street, in the heart of the factory
district of Ancoats, home of the Bengal Tigers.*

hotbed of tuberculosis, with deaths from the disease running at
more than double the national average. The Medical Officer of
Health for Manchester noted that many of the houses were back-
to-back and, with no effective ventilation, were constantly damp,
their timbers rotting and fusty. In winter, the smoke from thousands of domestic hearths, and from the huge factory chimneys
that stood above the maze of streets like megaliths, cast a choking
pall over the entire district. The very air seemed to threaten life
rather than feed it.

Prussia Street, which was almost as squalid, lay less than five
minutes' walk to the north. Canal wharves, stretching from
Portugal Street to Jersey Street, formed a natural dividing line

between the two gangs' territories. Jersey Street served as the district's main thoroughfare and when the Bengal Tigers and the Prussia Street scuttlers went to war in the summer of 1884, it quickly became their regular battleground. As the conflict escalated many were wounded on both sides, pushing the gangs to acts of ever greater reciprocal ferocity. Theirs became one of the great feuds in the turbulent history of the Manchester scuttlers.

It began with a set-piece battle, arranged for Saturday, July 5. The scuttle was the talk of the neighbourhood for the week beforehand; in workshops and mills, on street corners and in the public-houses, there was mention of little else. At half-past eight on the appointed evening, the rival armies marched into Jersey Street. The Prussia Street gang numbered over 150 and as they began to walk south towards Bengal Street, they filled the entire roadway. Dennis Tracey, a sixteen-year-old iron dresser, was at their head. Passing the Jersey Street Mills, they entered a short stretch of no man's land: a flint glass works stood on the left, an iron works to the right. Once past this point, they were into the territory of the Tigers. The road ahead was straight, and they strained their eyes for the first glimpse of their foes through the ever-present smoke. Their brass-tipped clogs clattering in unison in the roadway, the Prussia Street army marched on, their war cries echoing off the soot-stained factory walls.

The Bengal Tigers filed out onto Jersey Street in even greater numbers. Every likely-looking lad in the neighbourhood had been pressed into service, swelling their ranks to close to 200. Tommy Neild, a seventeen-year-old labourer, led them forward. The two mobs filled the street, their curses and threats reaching a crescendo as they squared up. The younger Prussia Street lads hurled a barrage of sticks and stones high into the air, which rained down onto the Tigers, who instantly retaliated in kind. Seconds later, the two mobs charged headlong into combat.

The Prussia Street lads were quickly routed – the Tigers were too many, and too fierce. Tommy Neild, already a veteran street fighter despite his youth, lunged at his enemies with a knife in one hand and a belt in the other. He stabbed John McCormick, a private in the 6th Lancashire Militia, in the chest before lunging at Dick Hughes. He plunged the knife into Hughes's shoulder and as Hughes fell, he turned to face Billy Jackson. At twenty-four Jackson had long given up scuttling, but he had re-joined the Prussia Street mob to boost their front line for the night.

Neild was not cowed by Jackson's superior strength. He raised his knife over his head before plunging it into Jackson's chest. Neild turned to see four of his fellow Tigers, Jimmy Johnson, Bobby Fisher, Tommy Dixon and Pat Connor, closing in on the captain of the Prussia Street gang, Dennis Tracey. The Bengal Street boys showed no mercy. Johnson and Fisher stabbed Tracey in turn before all four Tigers beat him to the ground with the buckle ends of their belts. Seeing their leader fall, the Prussia Street lads fled. Tommy Neild walked across, reached down over the stricken figure of his rival, and plunged his knife into Tracey's back.

The battle had been brief but brutal. By quarter to nine, three of the Prussia Street scuttlers lay in the Ancoats Dispensary. The resident surgeon, Dr Robertson, was used to treating stab wounds inflicted by scuttlers, but even he was shocked by the state of the three lads before him. All three were 'more or less exhausted' from loss of blood. The doctor treated Jackson's chest wound before tending to Hughes's shoulder. Tracey's condition caused most immediate concern: he had been stabbed in the face, but much more serious was the wound in his back. Dr Robertson was fearful that the knife had punctured a lung. He sent a message to Kirby Street police station and Sergeant Wild promptly went to the Dispensary to investigate. He obtained the names of four of the Tigers, including Thomas Neild, and arrested all four later that night. One had a knife and a scuttler's leather belt in his possession when he was arrested; the knife was stained with blood. Another also had a belt in his possession. All four lads were held in the cells at Kirby Street over the weekend.

The following evening, warrants were used to round up other prominent Tigers, and six young men and two young women were taken into custody. These eight were charged not in relation to any specific incident but with 'scuttling' in Ancoats for 'some time past'. One of them, Joe Brady, aged just fifteen, was already making a name for himself as one of the most fearsome up-and-coming scuttlers in Ancoats, while Joe Armstrong and Alf Finch had previously been inmates at Barnes Industrial School in Stockport. Finch had only been released a few months earlier.

Two batches of Bengal Tigers were brought before the Manchester magistrates on Monday, July 7. The eight prisoners arrested the previous day were placed in the dock first. 'The prisoners, with a number of others, have been going about the neighbourhood of Oldham Road for some time past breaking windows, assaulting people in the streets, and creating disturbances,' said Sergeant Flowers, the senior arresting officer. 'The police have held warrants for a number of the young scoundrels for several days past, and about a dozen of them were caught on Saturday and Sunday evenings.' The prisoners were dealt with immediately: each was fined twenty-one shillings with the option of one month's imprisonment.

Tommy Neild, Jimmy Johnson, Tommy Dixon and Pat Connor were then brought into the dock. All four were charged with scuttling in Jersey Street and stabbing Dennis Tracey, Billy Jackson and Dick Hughes. Jackson testified that he had been 'walking quietly along Jersey Street' on Saturday night when Neild suddenly came running towards him and stabbed him in the chest 'without the slightest provocation'. Jackson was adamant that he had no previous quarrel with Neild and did not know any of the other prisoners. Dr Robertson described the injuries suffered by the three Prussia Street lads. He then addressed the bench with some exasperation: 'This sort of thing was becoming an intolerable nuisance in the neighbourhood, scarcely a week going by without such cases being brought to the hospital.' The prisoners were remanded in custody for four days.

At their next court hearing the magistrates again pressed Billy Jackson, demanding to know whether he, too, was a scuttler, before proceeding with the case against the four Bengal Street lads. Jackson insisted that: 'He had never belonged to either of the two gangs of scuttlers who fought in that neighbourhood, nor had he ever taken part in the street fights.' There was little more that the magistrates could do. They committed the four prisoners for trial at the forthcoming Assizes.

As they languished in prison, skirmishes continued to rage between the gangs of Ancoats. One clash between junior members of the Bengal Tigers and an invading army from Alum Street, on the other side of the Rochdale Canal, was witnessed by a reader of the *Manchester Guardian*. The Alum Street mob tried to cross the canal bridge at Henry Street, but were met by a handful of Tigers who stood fast under a hail of rocks and quarter bricks. 'When I got to the bridge I saw three heroes keeping it, and defiantly facing the crowd, beyond which we could only hear and not see,' wrote the eyewitness. 'These three lads on the bridge were in a shower of stones and brick-bats and were running a great risk. I must say it was very inspiriting, and something low in my nature prompted me to have a go at it.' He resisted the urge, but was sufficiently moved to write a rare defence of scuttling as the outcome of 'the want of natural outlets for the superfluous vigour of healthy lads'.

The four Bengal Tigers arrested in the wake of the Jersey Street battle – Neild, Johnson, Dixon and Connor – appeared at the Manchester Assizes on July 17 before the formidable Mr Justice Day. The spectacular Assize Courts had been designed by the celebrated Liverpool-born architect Alfred Waterhouse in his favoured Gothic style and completed in 1864. Waterhouse went on to design Strangeways Prison, Manchester Town Hall and the Natural History Museum in London, among many other public buildings. The court was by far the most imposing edifice the four Tigers had ever set foot in. Their ages ranged from fifteen to nineteen and they all worked as labourers. They were charged together with unlawfully wounding Dennis Tracey, whilst Neild was indicted on a second count of unlawfully wounding Dick Hughes and Billy Jackson. Knowing that the evidence against him was damning, Neild pleaded guilty on both counts. The three other lads pleaded not guilty.

Witness accounts of the fight between the two gangs prompted Justice Day to remark that there appeared to be 'great fault in the administration of the police' in Manchester. Sergeant

Flowers of the City of Manchester Police replied that the police were faced by overwhelming numbers, adding that he 'did his best to put a stop to it'. Justice Day responded that he did not wish to blame particular officers: 'He had no doubt individual constables did their duty to the best of their ability, and indeed he had on numerous occasions highly commended them; but the existence of this scuttling led him to blame those who were responsible for the public peace.'

The jury found Johnson, Dixon and Connor guilty of unlawful wounding. Before passing sentence, Justice Day addressed the court at some length on the menace of scuttling. The prisoners, he said, had been convicted upon the very clearest evidence of 'an atrocious outrage'. He could hardly believe it possible, until he heard it proved in a court of justice, that ruffians armed with knives and belts could launch such attacks night after night. Responding to the character references presented on behalf of the prisoners, the judge commented that they might well bear 'good characters as to their working capacity; but it was absolutely necessary for the preservation of the peace of the city that an example should be made of them'. Justice Day was in no doubt that the prisoners were aware of the wickedness of their actions. He could not, he said, entertain pity for men who, in a gang of four, could 'rush upon a helpless fellow-creature with knives in their hands and stab him in the brutal, infamous way the prisoners stabbed Tracey'. He added that, were he permitted to do so in law, he would 'have the prisoners thoroughly well flogged, more than once, and would then send them back to their work'. A few doses of the cat would ensure that 'they would take no more part in riots and outrages'. Under English law, however, flogging was still only permitted in cases of robbery with violence. Woundings inflicted without robbery were punishable only by jail. With great reluctance, Justice Day pronounced sentences of imprisonment with hard labour: Neild, eighteen months; Johnson, eighteen months; Dixon, six months; Connor, three months.

Dennis Tracey recovered from his multiple stab wounds. His companion Billy Jackson did not fare so well. Throughout the trial proceedings, Jackson was receiving treatment as an out-patient at the Ancoats Dispensary for the knife wound to his chest. Towards the end of July, his condition worsened and he was admitted to Manchester Royal Infirmary. His doctors suspected that a tumour had formed in the vicinity of the wound. Jackson remained in hospital for three months. By the end of October, his doctors decided that surgery was necessary. The operation was not a success. Severe bleeding set in, and Jackson died on November 4. A post-mortem examination revealed a series of blood clots around the wound and a tumour 'about the size of a hen's egg, in which the nerves and other vessels were involved'. At the coroner's inquest, the jury returned a verdict of manslaughter against Thomas Neild. The Deputy Coroner declared that an example ought to be made of Neild to put a stop to the practice of scuttling, adding, 'If Jackson had died at once, in all probability Neild would have been hanged.'

Neild appeared back before Mr Justice Day at Liverpool Assizes on November 20. The judge decreed that although the legal aspect of the case was altered by Jackson's death, the prisoner's 'moral guilt' remained the same. The judge saw no grounds to amend Neild's sentence: the term of eighteen months would stand.

SUCH LENIENCY was out of character. John Charles Frederic Sigismund Day was born in 1826. The son of an army officer, he was educated at London University, called to the Bar in 1849, appointed a judge in June 1882, at the age of fifty-six, and knighted later that month. He was a staunch Catholic and a determined upholder of tradition. Deploring the advent of the railway age, he once cantered between Assize Courts on horse-back. He was said to have 'no deep interest in the law', but he had strong views on criminals. As one of his sons later observed, 'Mr Justice Day decided that he would do most good by devoting his main energies to enforcing the moral law, and to deterring criminals from further offences against God and society by means of severe sentences including, when possible, the use of the lash.' As a judge, he had no use for 'theories of penology' or the 'pseudo-scientific sentimentalism which would excuse all sin on the score of insanity'. As his son recalled, 'His pity went to the victim, and only increased his indignation against the ruffian who had inflicted the wrong.'

With his long, bewhiskered face, close-set eyes peering from the twin circles of his metal-framed glasses, and his prim, tight mouth, Day cut a lugubrious figure to those miscreants unfortunate enough to face him from the dock. His willingness to order floggings earned him a fearsome reputation and the nickname 'Judgement' Day. He was said to have sentenced more than one hundred criminals to be flogged, imposing nearly 4,000 lashes in total. His severity shocked many lawyers, however, and at times outraged public feeling too. On one occasion, he sentenced a seventeen-year-old to penal servitude for life. Day was also an enthusiastic yachtsman, spending his holidays sailing and walking with a fellow judge, and was an avid art collector. His collection of paintings, valued at more than £100,000, included works by Jean Baptiste Camille Corot and Jean-Francois Millet, although these were not to the taste of his first wife, the banker's daughter Henrietta Brown, and it was rumoured that he had to smuggle his purchases into the house.

THE BENGAL Tigers were undaunted by the capture of their captain. In such charged times, they did not restrict their violence to members of opposing gangs but routinely assaulted anyone who offended them, often on the slightest of pretexts. On Saturday 11 October 1884, one of the gang's leading figures – an eighteen-year-old labourer called Stephen McLoughlin – had a furious argument with his moll in George Leigh Street. McLoughlin's cap fell off during the quarrel and was picked up by Christopher Collins, aged nineteen, from nearby Primrose Street. Collins trailed McLoughlin to his house, knocked on the door and returned the cap. McLoughlin asked Collins if he wanted to fight. Thinking this was a joke, Collins said, 'Yes.' He was immediately set upon – not just by McLoughlin, but also by John Connor, another Bengal Tiger who was present. The unfortunate Collins was hit on the forehead with the buckle of a belt and stabbed in the shoulder and on the back of the head.

Collins bravely reported the assault to the police. The following afternoon, he went to Bengal Street, accompanied by two constables, to point out his assailants. The search was not difficult. As the constables walked some distance behind, Collins was promptly set upon by McLoughlin and Connor again. McLoughlin was arrested at the scene; Connor subsequently surrendered at Kirby Street police station. The two Bengal Tigers appeared at Manchester Assizes, where they called two witnesses, both of whom swore that Collins himself started the fight by striking the prisoners with a belt.

The jury agreed that Collins's wounds had been caused by a knife, but they could not agree which of the prisoners had used it. They found McLoughlin guilty of assault only, while Connor was acquitted. Justice Smith jailed Stephen McLoughlin for six weeks, warning him that if it had been proved that the prisoner had used a knife, he would have passed upon him 'such a sentence as he would not have forgotten for some time'. Evidence presented at the trial revealed a desperate state of affairs in Ancoats. The prosecuting counsel read a statement from Dr Robertson, the surgeon who had treated the wounded after the great battle in Jersey Street that summer, who wanted it to be known that he had dealt with no fewer than twenty-five stabbings arising from scuttling cases in Ancoats in the past few weeks alone. The war between Bengal Street and Prussia Street was the bane of his working life.

ON SATURDAY, 6 December 1884, two Bengal Tigers were keeping watch outside the Cross Keys public house in Jersey Street at closing time when they spotted thirty or forty Prussia Street scuttlers heading towards them. As soon as the lads at the door raised the alarm, other Tigers gathered in the pub downed their drinks and ran out into the street. The ensuing exchange of insults and threats was more venomous than ever: the Prussia Street scuttlers wanted revenge for the death of Billy Jackson, while the Tigers were aggrieved that several of their number were serving time in Strangeways. Bricks flung at the Bengal Tigers crashed through the windows of the Cross Keys, but this was only the prelude to a mass brawl in which belts and knives were used on both sides. One Bengal Tiger was knifed in the shoulder, but his wounds paled compared to those suffered by one of the Prussia Street lads.

Edgar Crossland, aged fifteen, was tripped by William Wilson at the start of the fight. As the scuttle raged around him, Crossland lay on the ground, trying to shield himself from the Tigers' clogs. Bobby Fisher drew a clasp knife and plunged it between Crossland's ribs, pushing the six-inch blade in to the hilt. Annie Flanagan – one of the Tigresses – kicked the stricken youth with her clogs as he lay on the ground. The fight was over in seconds. The Prussia Street mob had wrecked one of the Bengal Street lads' drinking dens – but at great cost.

Wilson, Fisher and Flanagan were all arrested over the following week. Meanwhile Crossland lay in hospital, his life in the balance. By the time the prisoners were brought before the magistrates on December 15, Crossland had started to recover. A police witness referred the court to the case of Billy Jackson: 'Both the witnesses for the prosecution and the male prisoners belong to different gangs of scuttlers, and many of them were concerned in the affray in July last in which a young man named Jackson received a wound which ultimately caused his death.' Bobby Fisher, for example, was 'wanted' at the time, but, 'He had left the town, and only returned a few weeks ago.' The defendants were committed for trial on a charge of inflicting grievous bodily harm.

They appeared before Mr Justice Wills at the Manchester Assizes on 24 January 1885. Edgar Crossland had now recovered sufficiently to give evidence. According to his testimony in court, he was walking home with a group of friends when they passed the Cross Keys. His friends were laughing and joking among themselves, but a gang of youths outside the pub mistakenly took offence, believing they were laughing at them. According to Crossland, he was then savaged without provocation.

As the evidence unfurled, however, Crossland's self-depiction as an innocent victim unravelled. Crossland's own companions, summoned as witnesses for the prosecution, admitted that there was a general scuttle with bricks and belts between the two gangs that night. They were further obliged to admit to a wide range of previous convictions. Crossland's associates began to look less and less like a group of inoffensive pedestrians and more like a raiding party of scuttlers. The hard-pressed Dr Robertson of Ancoats Dispensary told the jury that he had dressed Crossland's wound, which was 'between the ninth and tenth ribs, on the left side of the back of the chest. It extended inwards and upwards, and was about six inches long, and penetrated the lung. The wound was of a very dangerous character, and although the most critical period had passed, still the most serious consequences might arise.' Dr Robertson noted that 'with a slight change of direction' the wound would have proved fatal. He added that he recognised two of the prosecution witnesses only too well: he had treated their injuries following previous scuttles.

Summing up the evidence, Justice Wills declared:

One lived and learned with regard to the forms under which crime showed itself. He had sat for four years as Recorder of Sheffield, and thought he knew violence under its various aspects, but anything more shocking than the system which prevailed here, and which must have prevailed for some time to a very alarming extent, one could not conceive. Troops of young scoundrels went about ready to pick a quarrel with any peaceable passer-by and then resorted to deadly weapons to settle these uncalled-for and gratuitous quarrels.[13]

The jury found Bobby Fisher guilty of unlawfully wounding Crossland. William Wilson was found not guilty of wounding but

---

13 The son of a Birmingham solicitor, Mr Justice Wills had served as Recorder of Sheffield from 1881 until his appointment as a judge in 1884. An accomplished mountaineer with an interest in alpine botany and glaciology, he would earn lasting notoriety when he jailed Oscar Wilde for 'gross indecency' in 1895.

guilty of common assault. Annie Flanagan was found not guilty. Justice Wills commended the jury and, addressing Fisher, said that 'it was no merit of the prisoner's that he was not subjected to a trial for murder'. His sentence was five years' penal servitude. Wilson was sent down for two months, as the judge was not convinced he had used a knife. Wilson got off very lightly indeed. As one of the assembled court reporters noted, 'The prisoner, who evidently anticipated a much heavier punishment, shrugged his shoulders and left the dock in a very cheery manner.'

SCUTTLERS' ENDLESS pursuit of honour and status frequently extended to vicious fights over their girlfriends, or 'sweethearts'. At half past nine on the night of Wednesday, 11 February 1885, two Bengal Tigers took a stroll from Ancoats towards Manchester city centre. Michael Noon and Joe Cooper were both aged eighteen. Noon was employed as a dyer; Cooper as a spring-maker. They were headed for the drinking dens and singing saloons of Oldham Street. At the corner of Oldham Road and Goulden Street, they met two of their gang's female members and stopped to talk.

The conversation was interrupted by the sudden appearance of Tommy Ward, a twenty-three-year-old mill worker from Collyhurst. Ward walked to within two yards of Noon and Cooper and began to unfasten his belt. Noon, who was scared of Ward, started to back away. Ward mocked him, pointing out, 'You've got Joe with you.' Noon replied, 'What is it to you whether I am with him or not?' With anger and embarrassment rising, Noon and Cooper pulled off their own belts and lashed out. They brought the buckles crashing onto Ward's head no fewer than five times. Ward collapsed. His two attackers then walked back up Oldham Road towards Ancoats. When their female companions asked what 'the bother' was about, Noon said that Ward had assaulted him three weeks earlier.

A passer-by found Ward bleeding from his head wounds and told him to go to a doctor. Still stunned, Ward at first made no reply, but after a few minutes he got to his feet and walked away.

He collapsed again three quarters of an hour later and was taken to Manchester Royal Infirmary, where the house surgeon quickly discovered that his skull had been fractured. Ward was by now paralysed and could not speak. Further examination revealed five scalp wounds, each of which appeared to have been caused by a separate blow. Noon and Cooper were arrested a few days later and were remanded in custody pending Ward's recovery. Ward regained his powers of speech after three weeks. He appeared to make good progress for several days, before suffering a relapse. Fearing that pieces of Ward's skull had been forced onto his brain, doctors decided to operate. Tommy Ward never regained consciousness. He died on March 17.

The origin of the quarrel between the two youths and the deceased was finally revealed at the coroner's inquest the next day. Eliza Hannon, a tennis net-maker, told the coroner that both Noon and Ward had 'kept company' with her, and Ward was following her about the streets on the night of February 11. Ward, it appeared, had lost her affections to his youthful rival. The two Bengal Tigers were charged with the manslaughter and committed to the Manchester Assizes.

At their trial, before Justice Wills on April 23, counsel for the defence argued that there was no proof of design on the part of the two prisoners to harm Ward. Moreover, since the prosecution could not prove which of the prisoners had inflicted the fatal blow, they ought both to be acquitted. The jury was unconvinced. They found both Noon and Cooper guilty of manslaughter, but coupled their verdict with a strong recommendation to mercy on account of the provocation the youths had endured. Justice Wills clearly listened to their appeal and sentenced both Michael Noon and Joe Cooper to six months' imprisonment. The two lads were fortunate to say the least that they were not identified as scuttlers during the trial. The Manchester Assize calendar at that time included two Angel Meadow scuttlers charged with murder following a street fight in Salford and two of the Lime Street Boys from Miles Platting. Had the judge and jurors learned that Noon and Cooper were scuttlers too, there would have been little prospect of leniency.

The two Lime Street Boys, Alf Elliott and William Jackson, appeared the following week, charged with inflicting grievous bodily harm upon a Bradford scuttler named Jimmy Grimshaw during a scuttle in Miles Platting on the night of Wednesday, April 8.[14] The scuttle began with a cry of one word: 'BOTHER!' The Bradford lads were quickly worsted in the fray and Grimshaw took to his heels. A Lime Street group gave chase and rained blows upon him with their belts. In desperation, Grimshaw took refuge in a shop. The shopkeeper kept the terrified youth inside his premises for an hour and a half, but when Grimshaw finally emerged, he was dismayed to find that the Lime Street lads were still hunting for him. He was quickly spotted and the chase resumed. This time Grimshaw ran to the doorway of a house, where he was struck on the head with a brick. The startled occupants opened the front door, whereupon Grimshaw staggered inside before collapsing unconscious on their sofa. Grimshaw was taken to the Royal Infirmary, where he was found to have a compound fracture of the skull.

Alf Elliott and William Jackson were arrested and eventually appeared at the Assizes, where the shopkeeper who had shielded Grimshaw was called as a witness. The shopkeeper told how Alf Elliott had burst into the shop while Grimshaw was inside, demanding that the lad should be given up, stating that 'they would kill him'. The court was not told what, if anything, Grimshaw had done to cause such offence. The jury found both prisoners guilty. Before passing sentence, Justice Smith told Elliott and Jackson that, had Grimshaw died from his injuries, there was no reason why they should not be hanged. The judge then told the court that while he had great sympathy for impoverished wretches forced to commit petty larcenies, and for former convicts who struggled to find honest employment, he had no sympathy for the prisoners: 'In obedience to the most lawless, unbridled passion … they hunted each other about and

---

14 Jackson lived in Trickett's Buildings, Walker Street, Miles Platting. He was no relation to the Prussia Street scuttler, Billy Jackson, fatally wounded by the Bengal Tigers in July 1884.

threw brickbats at their opponents, who, for anything they knew or cared, might be stunned, killed, or incapacitated for life.' Justice Smith accepted that the prisoners had no previous felonies to their names, and believed every word of the character testimonials submitted on their behalf. Nonetheless, he felt bound to make an example of them. He sent both lads down for eighteen months.

BY THE spring of 1885, the Bengal Tigers reigned supreme among the scuttlers of Ancoats. Yet they had no shortage of enemies. Their notoriety captured the attention of gangs across Manchester, and in Angel Meadow, in particular, resentment towards the Tigers was growing. The Meadow Lads formed a fearsome mob, their ranks constantly replenished by new arrivals at the lodging-houses of Charter Street. Cut off from their families and shorn of any glimmer of respectability, they had nothing to lose and feared no-one. For a brief period in the mid-1880s, this band of itinerant labourers, hawkers, bullies and thieves forged an uneasy alliance with their counterparts from Greengate, Salford, but old feuds could not easily be set aside.

CHAPTER 10

Outcast Salford

BY EARLY 1889, moves were afoot to confront the problems of what the *County Telephone* termed 'Outcast Salford'. A Working Men's Sanitary Association was formed following a public meeting that May in Greengate, attended by both the Catholic Bishop of Salford and the Dean of Manchester. A local man told the meeting, 'The house in which I live is ten feet, six inches in length; eleven feet, six inches in width; and the height from the floor to the ceiling is eight feet. There are two rooms in the house – one up and one down – and for this I pay three shillings and sixpence per week.' To cries of 'Shame!' he added, 'The great cause of the poverty and misery that exist in Salford is the unequal distribution of wealth.' A series of speakers further testified to the appalling condition of much of the housing in Greengate and the adjacent district between Chapel Street and the River Irwell. The courtyards off Queen Street were singled out as 'decidedly unfit for human habitation'.

H. B. Harrison, a Liberal councillor and temperance advocate, then spoke of cases he had seen:

In no. 1, eleven of a family lived in a house of two rooms, with two beds in it. (Shame!) Case no. 2 was a 'one up and one down' house. There were ten of a family and two beds. He called that overcrowding. (Hear, hear.) No. 3 was a cellar with two families of five persons in it. He had thought cellar dwellings had to be shut up. No. 4 was a 'one up and one down' house with two families, or thirteen persons, and two beds. (Shame!) No. 5 was a case of seven persons sleeping in one room, and no. 6 was a case of eleven in a small house. In no. 7 there were 15 persons in one house, with two bedrooms. There were two parents and four children, and they had room to take in lodgers. (Laughter.) In another case there was one sleeping room with two beds – one occupied by the father and mother and the other by five children, the eldest a youth of 19, and the second a girl of 17. Could they have decency under such conditions? (No!) Could they have morality? (No!) He said it was a state of things most destructive to both.

The evangelical fervour of the meeting was dampened by the Dean of Manchester, who asked the speakers to remember that 'there were Christian ladies present'.

Salford Borough Council appointed a committee to report on the dwellings of the poor in June 1889. Five months later, the committee, chaired by the stipendiary magistrate Joseph Makinson, produced a list of streets and courts requiring 'early attention'. The list included large swathes of Greengate and parts of the Adelphi. However, the committee urged caution on the grounds of cost and noted that structural alterations, which landlords could be required to undertake, offered a prudent alternative to wholesale demolition and rebuilding. As a first step the committee proposed the demolition of several rows of dilapidated cottages in Greengate. Three hundred homes would be pulled down and replaced by new 'artisans' dwellings'.

Slum clearance was to be a painfully slow process in Salford and meanwhile the health of the borough continued to suffer. In 1871, Salford was ranked the third unhealthiest town in the country after Newcastle-upon-Tyne and Sunderland. Salford's relative position had not improved by 1900, and by the turn of the century only Preston and Blackburn had higher rates of infant mortality. A Salford child born in 1900 had only a one-in-five chance of surviving until its first birthday. Within Salford itself, there were huge inequalities: the population density in Greengate in 1886 was 119 people per acre. In Ordsall, the figure was seventy per acre; in Broughton and Pendleton, the respective figures were twenty-five and twenty.

THE MOST prominent Salford gang of the early 1880s was the McElroy mob from Greengate. Their leader, Sam McElroy, was born in the slums of Ancoats in 1860. His father, a coal miner, moved the family to Greengate during the mid-1860s. Sam McElroy worked as a market porter. Streetwise and charismatic, he gathered together some of the most battle-hardened scuttlers in Greengate, including the likes of Alf Richardson, with criminal records stretching back to their childhoods. They viewed the police and the courts with equal disdain. The core of the gang was drawn from Queen Street, long notorious as the heartland of what the press called the 'Greengate Roughs', but McElroy's reputation was such that recruits from as far away as Oldfield Road flocked to join him. The McElroy mob ruled the streets of Salford with merciless displays of violence toward any up-and-coming, younger gang who dared to challenge them.

McElroy's closest associate was Amos Briggs. With a string of convictions for assault to his name by the late 1870s, Briggs was well-known as one of the terrors of Greengate. In October 1879, he took part in a vicious assault on Charles Allen, a shopkeeper with premises in Bridgewater Street. Allen heard somebody knocking at the shutters to his premises at quarter past eleven one night. He went outside to investigate and found seven or eight figures gathered on the pavement. One of them – Briggs – struck him a blow and the others followed suit. Allen fell to the ground, where he was kicked and left unconscious. The following day, Sam McElroy's henchman Alf Richardson called at Allen's premises to 'try to make it up'. The shopkeeper refused and instead complained to the police.

The onslaught had been witnessed by the shopkeeper's young son, who subsequently identified Amos Briggs as one of the perpetrators. Richardson and Briggs were both convicted of assault. Richardson, who had only just completed a six month sentence for theft, was sent back to Strangeways for two months.

Briggs was further charged with assaulting an Ancoats scuttler named Bartholomew Trucket, who had been struck several times on the back of the head with a belt during a fight in St Simon Street in Greengate. Trucket had been knocked out and a surgeon from Salford Royal Hospital testified to the severity of his wounds. Briggs was convicted on two counts of assault. He was jailed for two months for his part in the assault on Charles Allen and a further two months for the assault on Trucket.

Such convictions were rare. The McElroy mob inspired such fear in Salford that few of their escapades were reported to the police. Most of their victims suffered in silence, convinced that the law was no protection against McElroy's wrath. In the summer of 1880, however, the gang fell foul of the police following a battle at the fairground beside Salford's Flat Iron market. Their opponents on this occasion were the Cross Street scuttlers, a newly formed gang of younger lads from Greengate. Spotting the Cross Street boys among the fairground crowds, McElroy and his followers pulled off their belts and charged straight at them. The Cross Street scuttlers fled, but one of their number, Joe Jeffers, slipped and fell. The pack was upon him in an instant. George Cookson struck Jeffers on the head with his belt buckle and then held him down while the rest of the gang kicked him with their brass-tipped clogs. Jeffers suffered a depressed wound to his skull and lost one of his fingers in a vain attempt to shield himself from the kicks. His wounds were so severe that he was unable to attend court for a fortnight after the assault. When he eventually appeared before the Salford magistrates, Jeffers told how Cookson led the charge on the night in question, shouting, 'Let's kill the —.'

George Cookson and George Evans were both sent down for two months. Jeffers identified Amos Briggs as another of his assailants, and Briggs too was jailed. A fourth member of the McElroy mob, Bob Knowles, was apprehended in August and he too was sent down. Knowles, like Briggs, had a string of convictions for disorderly conduct, scuttling and assault, prompting magistrate Joseph Makinson to declare, 'The sooner such characters as Knowles are shut up [in prison] the better.'

The McElroy mob rallied round to assist their comrades upon their release from Strangeways. When Amos Briggs was due to be liberated they organised a collection on his behalf, approaching other youths throughout Greengate for contributions. Sam McElroy and his followers stood at the gates of local factories and workshops at mid-day on the Saturday prior to Briggs's scheduled release. Saturday was pay day, so this was the ripe moment for a collection. However, some of those approached were unimpressed. John Castleton, a well-known former scuttler, was accosted by McElroy and asked if he 'was going to give anything to the collection for Amos Briggs'. Castleton said no, he would give nothing as he 'knew nothing about the matter'. McElroy replied that Castleton 'wanted a good kicking'.

When Castleton went to the fairground at the Flat Iron market that night, he was spotted by McElroy. Gathering three of his followers, McElroy led a sudden attack. Castleton was punched, kicked and struck with belts. McElroy and one of his cronies were later apprehended and charged with assault. McElroy had a host of previous convictions, two of them for scuttling. He was now sentenced to what was becoming the standard gaol term for a scuttler convicted at the Salford Police Court: two months' hard labour.

Sam McElroy was back in front of the Salford magistrates the following year, following another clash at the Salford fairground, which he clearly regarded as his fiefdom. Another up-and-coming mob had emerged in Greengate – the Fleet Street lads – and their arrival at the fairground en masse at twenty to eleven on a Saturday night was a direct challenge to McElroy's status as the terror of Greengate. In the affray that followed, McElroy knocked John Mann to the ground. Mann was surrounded and kicked until he was unconscious. He lost most of his teeth. McElroy, George Cookson and John Livesey were all jailed for two months. They were described in court as 'very bad characters'. Two younger lads from McElroy's mob were convicted alongside them.

Within two months of their release from Strangeways, McElroy, Cookson and Livesey were all arrested by detectives once more.

On this occasion, Amos Briggs and Bob Richardson were picked up, too. The five scuttlers had assaulted Joseph Boscow, a thirty-six-year-old wire-maker, who had been enjoying a quiet tea when he heard a disturbance outside his front door. He went out into the street to see what was going on, and found the prisoners beating a young man. Boscow picked the battered youth up off the ground, only for the prisoners to knock him back down again. When Boscow asked them to stop, they knocked him down too and kicked him. The Salford magistrates sentenced McElroy to yet another two months in Strangeways; his four henchmen were to join him there.

SAM McELROY seemed invincible, but his reign as the leader of the Greengate mob came to an abrupt end in the spring of 1885. At ten to eleven on the night of Saturday, March 14, one of his followers, a nineteen-year-old blacksmith's striker from Queen Street named John Holgate, was outside the Eagle Inn in Greengate talking to a girl called Jenny Robinson. Their conversation was interrupted by the arrival of two lads from Angel Meadow. Holgate immediately recognised one of the lads as his workmate, William Murphy. They exchanged greetings, and the three lads filed into the beerhouse together. The Eagle Inn, better known locally as the 'Lamp Oil' on account of the paraffin shop next door, was one of the recognised haunts of the Greengate scuttlers, and Sam McElroy arrived a few minutes later with three of his followers. Two more noted local tearaways, Dick Williams and John Callaghan, joined the party shortly afterwards. John Holgate vouched for the two Meadow Lads and they were accepted into the company of McElroy and the Salford mob.

When the pub closed at eleven o'clock, the scuttlers spilled out into Collier Street. However, their raucous bonhomie was suddenly interrupted by a quarrel between the ever-volatile McElroy and John Holgate. McElroy accused Holgate of hitting a young woman who lived nearby. When Holgate did not reply, McElroy punched him repeatedly. Eventually Patrick

Grant – one of the two Meadow Lads – told McElroy that Holgate had had enough. McElroy's henchmen were enraged at this interference by an outsider and one of them threw Grant to the ground.

This was a situation McElroy's mob had been in many times before: their blood up and their opponents outnumbered. Usually their rivals would crumble and run, or curl up on the floor as the kicks and stomps thudded home. But the Meadow Lads were scuttlers from one of the roughest patches of Manchester, and they were cowed by no-one. As Grant got back to his feet, he turned to his friend William Murphy and asked, 'Shall we start at them?' Murphy pulled out a large clasp-knife with a five-inch blade; Grant whipped off his belt. After a momentary stand-off, the Meadow duo lashed out. Murphy stabbed Alf Hopkins and Sam McElroy in quick succession. Grant then brought the buckle end of his belt crashing down onto McElroy's head. Stunned by the sudden and ferocious onslaught, McElroy beat a humiliating retreat, leading his followers away down Collier Street and into Gravel Lane.

Here McElroy met two more members of his mob: Christopher Sheffield, better known by his street name of 'Midge', and Ned Rafferty. The two younger lads had grown up together in Queen Street and they had been scuttlers since their early teens. They had spent the evening in Manchester city centre, where they attended the Queen's Theatre. They left the theatre at around quarter past ten, and went to Shipton's, one of the Salford lads' favoured city-centre drinking dens, where they quickly downed three glasses of whiskey each before setting off back to Salford. In New Bailey Street, they met a young mill worker named Theresa Glass and the three of them headed to the Salford fairground, stopping for a glass of porter on the way. After a brief walk around the fairground, they headed towards home and, in Gravel Lane, met McElroy. He showed them his hand, which was covered in blood, and they noticed that his head was also bleeding. Rafferty and Sheffield were 'fighting drunk' and were ready to seek retribution there and then, but McElroy told them to bide their time; the Greengate mob would have other opportunities to deal with the Meadow Lads soon enough.

Rafferty and Sheffield continued on their way back towards Queen Street. At the corner with Collier Street, the two parted: Sheffield stayed at the corner to talk to Theresa Glass, while Rafferty headed towards the Lamp Oil. Emboldened by beer and whiskey, he had decided to seek out the two Meadow Lads on his own. He caught up with them at the bottom of Collier Street, where Murphy was showing Grant and Holgate a cut on his hand. Rafferty confronted Murphy.

'You wouldn't have cut your hand if you hadn't used the knife,' he told him.

Murphy waved his knife in the air and shouted, 'I have chivved one and I will chiv another before I go home.'

Grant turned to Rafferty and asked pointedly, 'Is it anything to do with you?' Rafferty clearly felt it was. He challenged Grant to fight one-on-one, telling him, 'If you can do anything, pull off your coat.' Grant immediately obliged. He and Rafferty sparred for a few moments, before Grant smashed his fist into Rafferty's face. Rafferty was too drunk to be any match for his opponent and Holgate grabbed hold of him, telling him, 'Get out of the road.' Rafferty walked away but told Holgate to 'wait there a bit'. He then headed back to the corner of Queen Street, where he had left his mate Midge Sheffield.

John Holgate now told the two Meadow Lads that they had better get out of Salford. 'Don't go down Greengate,' he warned, 'there will be a mob waiting for you.' Holgate took them instead into Springfield Lane, which led to a bridge across the River Irwell into the Strangeways district, a roundabout route back to Angel Meadow but the safest way home for Murphy and Grant that night. Holgate led the Meadow Lads along Springfield Lane; Dick Williams and John Callaghan of the McElroy mob were just a short distance behind. As they passed Langworthy's dye-works, two little lads came running down the street, shouting that 'Midge' and 'Ned' were coming after them with knives.

The Meadow Lads were eager to continue the fight, but this put John Holgate in an impossible position: Murphy was his friend and workmate, but Ned Rafferty and Midge Sheffield were his neighbours, and he had fought alongside them in the Greengate mob for years. Holgate turned back to intercept Rafferty and Sheffield. As they turned the corner into Springfield Lane, Rafferty, who was waving a knife in the air, shouted, 'Come on,' at the Meadow duo. Holgate grabbed Sheffield round the waist, telling him, 'Don't go down there, you will get mollycrushed.' But Sheffield wriggled free, pushed Holgate to one side, and charged at Murphy. As the two came to blows, Murphy grabbed Sheffield in a head-lock and stabbed him repeatedly, digging his knife into Sheffield's neck and shoulder. Sheffield dropped to the ground, where he lay on his side with his hands under his head. Murphy reached down and stabbed him again, before walking away. Patrick Grant calmly walked across to Sheffield, belt in hand, and aimed a blow at the fallen youth's head. He hit the prostrate figure so hard that the brass buckle split in two. Holgate stood in front of Grant and pushed him back. 'Let me have another clout at the bloody sod,' demanded Grant. He delivered one more blow before walking up Springfield Lane to rejoin Murphy.

As the two Meadow Lads finally made their way across the bridge back into Manchester, Holgate went to fetch Midge Sheffield's mother. At the same time, Dick Williams grabbed hold of Rafferty, who was still brandishing a knife, and quietly ushered him away from the scene. A local ironworker had witnessed the fight between Murphy and Sheffield as he was walking home and he ran to find a police constable. He returned with P.C. Tom Patterson, who found Sheffield lying unconscious in a pool of blood in the street. The two men carried the injured youth directly to Salford Royal Hospital.

Sheffield's condition was so serious that the police arranged for him to give a deposition before one of the Salford magistrates on the Sunday morning. Sheffield identified himself as a shoe-maker, of Queen Street, Salford. He told how he had been to the Queen's Theatre with Ned Rafferty and had stopped for whiskey and porter on the way home, but swore that he could remember nothing after he and Rafferty left Shipton's in the city centre; he was too drunk. When asked who had stabbed him in Springfield Lane, Sheffield replied, 'I couldn't tell who did it. I remember nothing. There was a lot there, but I could not recognise them. I believe I'm going to die. It's God's will, and I can't help it.' If Midge Sheffield did know his assailants, he was certainly not going to tell the police or magistrates.

Murphy and Grant were much less discreet. They spent the Sunday afternoon in Angel Meadow, boasting of their exploits the previous night. They spoke first with one of their fellow residents at Holder's Lodging-house in Charter Street. When they went up to the man's room, Murphy was whistling as though he didn't have a care in the world. He proudly announced that he and Grant 'had had a bit of bother last night', adding that 'he had very nearly killed a fellow'. Murphy then took out his clasp knife, saying that he had scoured all the blood off it. When asked who had been stabbed, Murphy replied, 'Midge Sheffield.' He said he had stabbed the Salford lad three or four times, including once in the neck. Grant then pulled his belt off and said, 'Look what I've done.' Half of the buckle was missing. The three then had 'a drink or two' together before Murphy and Grant left.

Their bragging did not stop there. Murphy and Grant left the lodging-house and wandered out to the corner of Simpson Street, where they found another of their drinking partners, Tommy McEverley, a twenty-year-old labourer. McEverley had himself been drinking in the Lamp Oil the previous night, but had left the beerhouse prior to the initial row between Sam McElroy and Holgate. Grant told McEverley that he had struck Ned Rafferty on the nose and that Rafferty had run away. When Rafferty returned with Sheffield, 'Someone copped the knife.' Murphy then showed his knife to McEverley, who noted that Murphy himself had a cut on the head and a torn coat.

Police inquiries focused initially on the McElroy mob. Holgate and Dick Williams were taken into custody after witnesses placed them both at the fracas outside the Lamp Oil and at the scene of the fight in Springfield Lane. Detectives obtained the names of Murphy, Grant and McEverley as the three Meadow Lads who had been seen in Greengate that night. McEverley was apprehended at his lodgings. Murphy and Grant, however, were nowhere to be found. A 'wanted' notice was circulated throughout England and Wales via the *Police Gazette* on Friday, March 20:

> Salford (Borough). For attempted murder – PATRICK or PARKEY GRANT, age about 20, height 5 ft. 1 in., complexion fresh, hair light, moustache slight; dress, black ribbed cloth coat and vest, black cord trousers, white muffler, billycock hat. – WILLIAM MURPHY, age 20, height 5 ft. 4 or 5 in., complexion dark, tender eyes, squints, full round face, turned up nose; dress, dark cutaway coat and vest, light cord trousers, hard billycock or slogger cap.

Even for scuttlers, the two Meadow Lads were extravagantly dressed. Grant, in particular, cut a swell figure, dressed from head to toe in black save for his muffler. The 'billycock' was a bowler-style hat made of felt with a rakish, curved rim two-and-a-half inches wide. It was worn low on the crown of the head. The 'slogger' was Birmingham's equivalent of the scuttler. Grant and Murphy needed to jettison their fashionable headgear fast if they were to evade the police search.

The two lads were eventually arrested in Blackburn, thirty miles from Manchester, on March 25, eleven days after the fight in Greengate. Sergeant Richard Howard was dispatched from Salford to collect them. Sergeant Howard charged the two lads with attempting to murder Christopher Sheffield. Murphy replied, 'I had no knife. I don't remember tackling him. I had had some drink at the time. I got knocked down and was kicked myself.' Grant insisted, 'I had no knife.' He then confessed, 'I used my belt in the row.' Sergeant Howard showed the two lads a portion of a brass buckle, telling them, 'This has been found close to where the row took place.' Grant admitted, 'That is from the buckle of my belt that got broke in the row.'

Williams, Holgate, McEverley, Murphy and Grant were charged with attempted murder at the Salford Police Court.

They were further charged with unlawfully wounding Rafferty, Hopkins and McElroy. All five were remanded for one week, with the police confident they could prove that Murphy had inflicted the most serious wounds. The court heard that there were fears for Sheffield's life. The Mayor of Salford, sitting alongside the stipendiary magistrate, asked Superintendent Donohue: 'It may be a case of murder then?'

Donohue replied, 'I think it will.'

The prisoners were remanded for a further week on April 2. Six days later, Christopher Sheffield died at the Salford Royal Hospital. A post-mortem examination revealed numerous marks of violence on his body:

Excised wound on the left side of the top of the scalp, one inch long and down to the bone. Excised wound behind the left ear, about half an inch long. Punctured wound two and a half inches below the ear and two inches from the spine. Punctured wound three-quarters of an inch above the middle of the collar bone, an inch long; this wound passed downwards, inwards and backwards to the spine, passing between the great vessels of the neck; blood clots extended upwards into the neck and downwards into the chest – this was the most serious wound.

The house surgeon found ten wounds in total; seven of them caused by a knife, the other three consistent with wounds caused by the buckle end of a belt. Death was caused by 'exhaustion' due to the loss of blood from the wound in the neck and damage to the lungs.

Police inquiries were by now focused on Murphy and Grant. The two lads were charged with wilful murder and committed for trial at the Manchester Assizes. The charges of unlawful wounding against Williams, Holgate and McEverley were dismissed following consultations between Detective Superintendent Donohue and the Chief Constable of Salford; the police feared that proceedings against the three for unlawful wounding might prejudice the case against Murphy and Grant. Williams, Holgate and McEverley were warned as to their future conduct and then discharged. All three would testify at the forthcoming murder trial.

When Mr Justice Wills addressed the jury at the opening of the Assizes on April 17, he noted that there were no fewer than six cases to be heard in which human life had been taken. In addition, there were a number of cases of robbery with violence, and some savage assaults on women. Judge Wills singled out the case of Murphy and Grant, remarking that scuttling threatened the safety of every inhabitant of Manchester. 'It was a new thing in his experience,' he told the jurors, 'even in very large towns, and it needed to be put down with a strong hand'. Fifty-eight other prisoners were dealt with before Murphy and Grant were called into the dock the following week, but there was no doubt which of all the trials attracted the most interest.

The case against the Meadow Lads commenced on April 23. Murphy, aged nineteen, was identified as a blacksmith's striker, and Grant, aged twenty, as a labourer. They were charged with the wilful murder of Christopher Sheffield, shoemaker, of Queen Street. Ned Rafferty and John Holgate gave detailed accounts of the events that night, both swearing that Murphy and Grant had inflicted the injuries upon Sheffield: Murphy with his knife, Grant with his belt. Theresa Glass, the mill worker who accompanied Sheffield and Rafferty to the Salford fairground, raised the only laugh during the grim proceedings when she was asked whether the two lads were drunk on the night in question. She replied, 'I could see they had had a good sup.' All the same, she insisted, 'They could walk and talk all right.' James Barden, the Springfield Lane ironworker who witnessed the assault on Christopher Sheffield, told the court that the perpetrators crept away from the scene with 'their faces to the wall' to prevent passers-by getting a look at them.

Frederick Hyde Folkes from Salford Royal Hospital provided the medical evidence. He confirmed that a police constable brought Sheffield to the hospital between midnight and one o'clock in the morning in a state of collapse due to loss of blood. The injured youth appeared to rally in the days that followed, although he remained in a critical condition, but suffered a relapse due to a haemorrhage from the neck wound. He suffered another haemorrhage two days later and 'gradually sank' until he died.

The jury found both Murphy and Grant guilty, not of the capital crime of murder, but of manslaughter. Justice Wills seemed surprised they had escaped the gallows. 'You belong to one of those gangs of ruffians by whom the streets of Manchester have been now for some time disgraced,' he told them. 'You are young both of you, but young as you are, even a long life could scarcely have brought you into a state of mind more merciless or inhuman. It is difficult to realise or understand the pitiless and vindictive passion with which no less than seven cruel stabs were inflicted one by one with no faltering hand upon the unfortunate man who is dead.' For that, they would suffer the consequences 'for many a long year'. Judge Wills sentenced Murphy to twenty years' penal servitude and Grant to fifteen years', by far the most severe sentences imposed on scuttlers since the onset of the Rochdale Road War fifteen years earlier. Casting a glance at the court reporters, Mr Justice Wills declared that he hoped that these sentences might act as a warning to the 'idle and disorderly' of the city: they all ran the risk of the gallows, for 'the hand of justice would be too strong for them in the end'.

AMOS BRIGGS, Sam McElroy's right-hand man during the early 1880s, was playing little part in the Greengate mob's scuttling affrays by 1885. After repeated spells in Strangeways, Briggs moved out of his family home in Salford. He took lodgings in Angel Meadow, the heart of 'Criminal Manchester' and the first resort of many hardened lags upon their release from prison. In the lodging-houses of Angel Street and Charter Street he befriended some of Manchester's most nefarious villains. Finding it increasingly difficult to secure legitimate employment, he turned instead to crime.

In January 1885, Briggs appeared at the Salford Police Court alongside a fellow denizen of the Charter Street lodging-houses. The pair had attacked two men returning home from a dinner at a pub in Chapel Street and had stolen their hats, punching one of the men in the process. The hats were worth no more than five shillings for the pair, a paltry sum in relation to the fines imposed by the magistrates. Briggs and his accomplice were fined twenty shillings each, with the alternative of fourteen days' imprisonment. Briggs might have been a much-feared scuttler in his youth, but he was an inept robber and an even worse burglar: he kept getting caught. He would go on to be punished for a string of trivial thefts, running up a long criminal record:

Manchester Quarter Sessions, 14 December 1885: convicted of stealing twenty pinafores, nine months' imprisonment with hard labour.

Manchester Quarter Sessions, 8 December 1887: convicted of housebreaking, twelve months' imprisonment with hard labour and three years' police supervision.

Salford Quarter Sessions, 4 November 1889: convicted of stealing thirty-six pairs of boots from the shop of Sarah Ann Walker, twelve months' imprisonment with hard labour.

Salford Quarter Sessions, 6 February 1891: convicted of breaking and entering the dwelling house of Charlotte Sophia Rowley, 187, Great Cheetham Street with attempt to commit a felony, eighteen months' imprisonment with hard labour.

On the last occasion, Briggs was discovered by a beat constable at 1 a.m. during a routine patrol. The bobby noticed that the door to the yard of the house had been unlocked. When he went to investigate, he saw Briggs drop down into the coal-hole. He hauled Briggs out, and asked what he was doing there, to which Briggs replied smartly, 'I wanted a night's lodgings.' He had a jemmy and a knife in his possession.

At the time of his appearance at the Salford Quarter Sessions in November 1889, Briggs was living with his common-law wife, Kate Calligan, back in Queen Street, Greengate. They shared their lodgings with another thief named Henry Hall, who, like Briggs, was under police supervision as a habitual criminal. On the night of September 17, their drinking spree included a visit to the Dyer's Arms in Chapel Street. Next door was a shop, and when the owner opened up the next morning, she found that a number of slates had been removed from the roof and three dozen pairs of boots were missing. Briggs and Kate Calligan were apprehended after Calligan took several pairs to a Greengate pawnbroker. The pawnbroker's assistant was immediately suspicious and followed Calligan back to Robinson's Buildings in Queen Street. He informed the police, who found Briggs wearing one of the stolen pairs of boots. Briggs immediately confessed to the burglary, although he swore blind that Calligan knew nothing about it. They were both aged twenty-seven. She gave her occupation as 'rag sorter' but her criminal record was as sorry as his: at the age of sixteen, she had been jailed for stealing a handkerchief. At eighteen, she was jailed for two months for stealing two shillings, plus an additional four months for assaulting the police constable who made the arrest. By the age of twenty-seven, she had amassed twenty-three convictions, many of them for prostitution and brothel-keeping.

Amos Briggs was rarely out of prison for any extended period of time over the next fifteen years. By 1899, he had amassed a long string of convictions for theft in addition to seventeen minor offences, mainly vagrancy, drunkenness and assault. But his last conviction for scuttling had been way back in 1882, at the age of twenty – the normal 'retirement' age for a scuttler.

KATE CALLIGAN was the kind of loose-living girl that many a scuttler hooked up with. Prostitution was rife in the poorer districts of both Manchester and Salford. The police generally preferred to ignore it, although prostitutes and, more rarely, brothel-keepers, were periodically rounded up and brought before the magistrates to demonstrate police 'efficiency'. Deansgate and Greengate had both long been known for their brothels and street walkers, but the centre of Manchester's trade in vice was Angel Meadow. John Mercer, Reverend of St Michael's in Angel Meadow, claimed during the 1890s that the women of his parish were more degraded than the men:

> The class of fallen girls and women is very large and aggressive. Of the 42 streets of the parish, only 18 can be said to be free from this class, and many of these 18 even are doubtful. The following figures will give some idea of the state of the two principal streets:
> *Angel Street*, with 54 houses, has only 8 quite free.
> *Charter Street*, with 79 houses, has only 21 quite free.
> Further, there are 15 lodging houses which are practically quite given up to this class of women, and a large number lodge in the mixed lodging houses with the men who live on their earnings.

Mercer reported that a group of 'rescue workers' from London who worked for a time in Angel Meadow found 'a more vicious state of affairs than prevailed in even the worst parts of Whitechapel'. In East London, they pointed out, most brothels were kept by women. In Angel Meadow, 'it is frequently young men who hold girls in their power, and who pass idle, dissolute lives on the earnings of their poor slaves'. Reverend Mercer's solution to this state of affairs was a radical transformation of society. 'We must see,' he asserted, 'that there is no underpaid female labour, that women's economic interests are protected as well as men's; that there shall be more enlightened social sympathy shown to those girls whose temptations are often so great, and a more serious fostering of social purity and chivalrous spirit among men.'

Such enlightened times were a long way distant.

THE DEMISE of Sam McElroy created a power vacuum in Greengate during the mid-1880s. A new generation from Queen Street, led by Stephen Callaghan and Joe Sullivan, set about claiming McElroy's mantle. In the autumn of 1886, Callaghan led the Queen Street lads in a series of raids on the Adelphi on successive Sunday afternoons. So on November 14, the Adelphi scuttlers set a trap for him. Unbeknown to the two mobs, so did the police. Callaghan took his followers into Cannon Street, in the heart of the Adelphi. Armed with knives and belts, they were confident of chasing off any of the local scuttlers who dared to oppose them. On this occasion, however, the Adelphi lads had gathered reinforcements and their sheer weight of numbers forced Callaghan's mob to back off. The Queen Street crew were swept into the clutches of a posse of police officers, who cut off their retreat in Ford Lane. The constables grabbed Callaghan and a labourer called Tom Hughes.

The two lads appeared at the Salford Police Court the following morning. The Chief Constable of Salford attended the court himself to emphasize the seriousness of the problems posed by the resurgence of the gangs. He told the magistrates that 'great complaints' had been made to the police, and special detachments of officers had to be assembled to deal with the scuttlers. Callaghan and Hughes were both aged seventeen. Callaghan worked in a Greengate mill as a doffer. This was poorly paid, repetitive work, taking full bobbins of cotton off the throstles, or spinning machines, and replacing them with empty ones. It was traditionally allocated to boys and girls aged between twelve and fifteen. Hughes gave his occupation as labourer. Joseph Makinson sent down Callaghan for fourteen days and fined Hughes ten shillings.

On Guy Fawkes Night the following year, a gang of scuttlers from Ancoats ventured into Greengate to test the mettle of Callaghan's mob. The Ancoats lads went from pub to pub along Greengate, determined to flush out the local scuttlers. They met no opposition in the Hat and Feathers, so they proceeded to the White Hart. As soon as they crossed the threshold, the Ancoats lads realised their mistake: Callaghan's entire mob was crammed inside. The Ancoats lads turned and ran; in an instant, the beer-house emptied after them. The interlopers ran into Queen Street, where one of them was caught and mercilessly beaten. The rest carried on, turning into Ashton Street, where one of the

Ancoats mob was caught. Joe Sullivan set about him with his belt. The bloodied and battered youth was left to stagger back towards Manchester and was picked up by two beat constables in Blackfriars Street. When he told them what had happened, the constables sent for reinforcements: there was no way that they were going to enter Queen Street on their own. Sergeant Drysdale led a squad of officers into Greengate. They apprehended Joe Fitzpatrick, a well-known member of Callaghan's mob, whose belt was heavily bloodstained. P.C. Prendergast and P.C. Wells were ordered to take Fitzpatrick to the station, whilst Sergeant Drysdale led the rest of his men to the White Hart. When the police reached the beerhouse, the scuttlers were nowhere to be seen.

The Greengate lads had already set off to rescue Joe Fitzpatrick. Joe Sullivan led the charge, hurling bricks at the two constables dragging Fitzpatrick along the street. Fitzpatrick immediately began kicking out for all he was worth. P.C. Wells left his colleague to deal with Fitzpatrick and ran among the crowd of scuttlers towards Sullivan. This was a near-fatal mistake. Sullivan lunged at P.C. Wells and hit him with a brick. The rest of the mob then surrounded P.C. Prendergast and began flailing him with their belts. Prendergast was only saved by a passing carter, who pulled the beleaguered officer onto his cart and took him to Salford Royal Hospital. The house surgeon found six cuts on Prendergast's head; one of his ears had almost been severed.

Joe Sullivan, Joe Fitzpatrick and Stephen Callaghan were all subsequently arrested. When they appeared at the Salford Police Court, they were charged with assaulting the Ancoats scuttler as well as assaulting the police. Detective Superintendent Donohue told the court that he had been instructed by the Chief Constable to call attention to the condition of Queen Street:

It was in a very bad state, and lately he had been obliged to increase the number of officers on duty in that neighbourhood on Saturday nights. On the 29th of October, a determined attack was made on the police and two persons were convicted. On Saturday night the Chief Constable sent a sergeant and a number of men down there, but they got disorganised, and were only able to apprehend the three prisoners. The Chief Constable appealed to the bench for a substantial penalty to stop these serious assaults. The roughs were becoming entirely masters of the situation down there.

Stipendiary Makinson assured the superintendent that the magistrates were determined to prevent this scuttling. If need be, they would send the offenders to the Quarter Sessions to 'get them out of the way for five years'. Sullivan and Callaghan were both imprisoned for six months. Joe Fitzpatrick got three months.

JOSEPH MAKINSON was a native of Salford. Born the son of a solicitor in the wealthy suburb of Higher Broughton, he was educated at Cambridge University and was called to the Bar in 1869, practising as a barrister on the Northern Circuit until he replaced Sir John Iles Mantell as stipendiary magistrate for Salford in 1878. He would hold the post for thirty-three years. Like Sir John, he was a man of strong views and was not afraid to air them in court. His pronouncements frequently blended legal judgements with moral ones, delivered with sweeping rhetorical flourishes – and an eye to the assembled reporters. A ready wit, he poked fun at prisoners and witnesses alike. His rapport with some of the borough's habitual offenders, most notably Susan Wilson, became the stuff of local legend.

Makinson's real passion was not the law, but cricket. He captained the university team at Cambridge, made numerous appearances for the All-England eleven and was a leading member of Broughton Cricket Club, where he gained a reputation as a bowler in the round-arm style and an accomplished batsman. He played for Lancashire County Cricket Club in its inaugural first-class match in 1865, and in later years, as a member of the club's committee, Makinson's presence at matches at Old Trafford was de rigueur. It was often noted that on match-day mornings his police court cases were dispatched with remarkable speed. During the winter months, with no cricket to occupy his mind, he paid regular night-time visits to Wood Street Mission in Deansgate, where he wandered among the tramps, determined to study 'the raw material of the criminal'. The tramps' responses to his nocturnal vigils were not recorded.

CHAPTER 11

The Killing of Joe Brady

PATRICK AND MARGARET Brady raised four sons in Blossom Street, off Bengal Street, during the 1860s. Patrick was a wood-turner; Margaret worked in one of the nearby mills. By the middle of the following decade their two oldest sons had also found employment as mill-hands. With four wage-earners, the family was relatively prosperous, at least by the standards of Ancoats. Their third son, John, was born in 1868. He found work as a dyer and, like his brothers, was a steady worker. Margaret Brady came to depend heavily on her sons' earnings after her husband died suddenly in the early 1880s. To save money, she moved the family to Caldwell's Buildings, a slum court off Garrick Street, five minutes' walk east of Bengal Street.

John Brady was better known on the streets of Ancoats as 'Joe'. At the age of thirteen, he was one of a group of lads from Blossom Street recruited by the Bengal Tigers. At fifteen, he was sufficiently well-known to be rounded up in the police operation against the gang following the great Jersey Street battle of July 1884. By eighteen, his name was known throughout the slums of north and east Manchester. 'Joe' Brady was one of the gang's most ferocious street fighters.

By the mid-1880s, the Bengal Tigers' fiercest enemies were the scuttlers of Angel Meadow. Their former great rivals, Prussia Street, were no longer a force to be feared, but the Meadow Lads were a different proposition altogether. Many, though by no means all, of the Ancoats scuttlers held regular jobs in factories or workshops. Some of the Meadow Lads laboured in local industries, but they were more likely than their counterparts in Ancoats to find work as market traders or hawkers, and some of them lived by their wits, enduring persistent harassment from the police and repeated prison stretches.

The two gangs fought regular battles on the streets of New Cross. Two decades earlier, this slum quarter wedged between Rochdale Road and Oldham Road had been the epicentre of what became known as the Rochdale Road War. Throughout the 1880s gangs from Angel Meadow, to the west, and Ancoats to the east were equally determined to claim the streets of New Cross as extensions of their own territory. Incursions by one gang were viewed as provocation by members of the other. If Ancoats lads paraded New Cross lasses as their sweethearts, the Meadow Lads became incensed and vice versa. A series of encounters during the summer and autumn of 1886 saw members of both gangs stabbed and bludgeoned with belts and pokers. Many of the combatants were hospitalised but few were jailed, as most of the clashes took place without police interference.

On the afternoon of Sunday, 23 January 1887, a 'fair fight' was arranged between Joe Brady of the Bengal Tigers and nine-teen-year-old Owen 'Oney' Callaghan from Angel Meadow for a purse of twenty shillings. The location was kept secret from all but long-standing members of the two gangs. The police knew nothing of it, nor did the local press. The outcome of the fight is unknown but Brady might well have beaten the slightly built Callaghan, since the Angel Meadow scuttler was left nursing a bitter grievance. The Bengal Tigers had acquired a fresh grudge of their own against the Meadow Lads since the turn of the year. Two sixteen-year-old girls from Primrose Street, off Bengal Street, had begun 'walking out' with lads from New Cross who had aligned themselves with Callaghan's mob from the Meadow. Kate McTighe, a mill-hand, and Martha Gray, a rag-sorter, must have known how their actions would be interpreted – but if anyone in Bengal Street chastised them, they could fetch the Meadow Lads at any time.

The two gangs fought repeated skirmishes in the weeks that followed the Brady-Callaghan bout. The night of Saturday,

February 5, saw running battles in the streets of New Cross for two hours. During one skirmish, Jim Carroll, one of Joe Brady's closest associates, was chased to a house in Back Holgate Street, where he took shelter at around half-past nine. When the fighting finally subsided, Brady and a handful of his followers stationed themselves in a public house, the Land o' Burns, on Lees Street. They were joined by Brady's moll, Mary Jane Judge, and her friend Mary Ann Collins. The two young women lodged in the house where James Carroll had taken shelter: 23 Back Holgate Street.

At around quarter to eleven, Brady set off on the short walk to Back Holgate Street, where he planned to carry on drinking. As he turned into the street, accompanied by Judge and Collins, he was accosted by one of Owen Callaghan's gang, nineteen-year-old Charlie Burns. A private in the 63rd (Manchester) Regiment, Burns was in full military uniform, although he was on furlough from the barracks at Ashton-under-Lyne. Burns and Brady traded insults, then punches. Both were 'fighting drunk' but Judge and Collins dragged Brady down the street and up the short flight of steps to number 23. Once inside, they bolted the front door. Brady, Carroll, Mary Jane Judge and Mary Ann Collins began to swap stories of the night's scuttling and carousing.

Fifteen minutes later, they heard shouting in the street outside. Soldier Burns had returned with Callaghan and more than twenty of the Meadow Lads. Burns was waving a knife in the air.

'Come out, Joe Brady, and face this,' he shouted.

Heavy kicks drummed on the door to the house. It flew open to reveal five of the Meadow Lads stood around the steps. The knife-wielding Burns was at the front with his older brother 'Sonny' on one side and Callaghan at the other. Joe Brady went to the doorway to face them; Jim Carroll stood behind him.

'Draw your knives!' Callaghan ordered the rest of the Meadow Lads.

One of them lunged at Brady, who immediately cried out, 'I'm stabbed!' Callaghan warned Jim Carroll to keep back or 'he would do the same for him'.

'You'll have to suffer for this,' said Carroll.

'I'll suffer for you if I get you outside,' snarled Callaghan.

Brady tumbled down the steps into the street, where he was surrounded, kicked, and struck with pokers and knives. He begged for mercy, pleading, 'Oh, don't kill me!' But Callaghan gave the order: 'Let's finish him.' Callaghan and his followers were urged on by Kate McTighe and Martha Gray, both of whom were shouting, 'Go on!' Most of the lads standing over Joe Brady held knives and one of them now stabbed him in the heart. He died almost instantly. The shout rang out, 'Murder!' and the Meadow Lads turned and ran.

Leaving Carroll in the house for his own safety, Mary Jane Judge and Mary Ann Collins headed out to report the killing to the police. Judge carried a knife that Charlie Burns had dropped in the doorway. They were confronted in the street by Sonny Burns, Owen Callaghan, Martha Gray and Kate McTighe, who demanded the return of the knife. When Judge refused to hand it over, her jacket was torn from her and she was kicked and knocked down. She held on to the knife. Her screams were so fierce that Callaghan and Burns ran off, fearful of attracting the attention of any passing beat constables. Judge and Collins took the knife to Goulden Street police station and two constables were dispatched to Back Holgate Street, where they found the body of Joe Brady. The first arrest was made that night. Constables from 'B' Division found Charlie Burns drunk in Back Holgate Street at around 11.30 p.m. He was taken to Goulden Street where, at quarter past one the following after-noon, he was charged with the wilful murder of Joe Brady. Martha Gray and Kate McTighe were apprehended with him.

At the inquest, on February 9, Jim Carroll told the jury that Owen Callaghan had stabbed Brady with a clasp-knife. A labourer named Tommy Dixon told how he had seen the Meadow Lads chase Carroll to Back Holgate Street. Dixon claimed that he had also witnessed the killing of Joe Brady:

[Charlie] Burns called out to Brady 'Brady come and face this' and held up a knife. Brady then went to the door and Burns hit him and I then heard Brady say 'Oh, I'm stabbed.' He fell and they all got round and kicked him and Ryan hit him with a poker. Brady said, 'Oh, don't kill me.' 'Oney' Callaghan said 'Let's finish him at once.' He had an open pen knife in his hand and he made a hit at Brady with it. He also kicked him. They all then ran away.

The jury returned a verdict of murder against Charles Burns, Martha Gray and Kate McTighe, plus four Meadow Lads – all of whom were wanted by the police: Owen Callaghan, John Brennan, Joseph Ryan and Sonny Burns.

Ryan, a twenty-one-year-old umbrella maker, was arrested later that day. Along with Burns, Gray and McTighe, he was charged with murder and remanded in custody whilst the police continued their inquiries. John Brennan, a twenty-two-year-old labourer, was the next to be arrested when police found him in Angel Meadow on the afternoon of February 24. Owen Callaghan, aged nineteen, was out of work – 'except jobbing about'. He dodged the police on the night of the killing. The following morning, he walked to Oldham. From there he tramped to Halifax, and then on to Leeds, where he worked for a fortnight as an outdoor labourer.

A 'wanted' notice posted on the front page of the *Police Gazette* described Sonny Burns, a brushmaker, as aged about twenty-three, stout, with fair hair and a slight squint in his left eye; Callaghan, a moulder, was of medium height with a 'fresh' complexion; while Brennan was tall for a lad of the time at about 5ft 8in, with dark brown hair and a moustache. With their distinctive uniforms of black clothes, mufflers, bell bottoms and billycock hats, the three Meadow Lads were hardly inconspicuous. Now officers from every force in England and Wales were on the look-out for them.

On Friday, February 25, police in Bradford, Yorkshire, were informed that a young man matching Callaghan's description had set off for Bradford that day. P.C. Edwin Lee was dispatched to find him. Lee, who was wearing plain clothes, spotted the youth walking along Manchester Road, Bradford, at four o'clock that afternoon. The constable stopped him and asked where he came from. 'Leeds,' replied the youth. He gave his name as 'John Davies' and his occupation as moulder, adding that he had been working in an iron foundry. P.C. Lee told the youth that he would have to accompany him to the police office at Bradford Town Hall, and warned him 'to be very careful what he said'.

When they arrived at the Town Hall, P.C. Lee sent for the Chief Constable. He then told the youth that he had been brought in 'on suspicion of being Owen Callaghan of Manchester, wanted for murder'. The youth replied, 'You are mistaken, my name is Joseph Davies,' and insisted that he 'belonged to Leeds'. P.C. Lee referred him to the *Police Gazette*, and the Chief Constable then asked him to state his name once more. He now replied, 'Tom Davies.' When P.C. Lee said that he was about to telegraph the Leeds police, the youth crumbled.

'I will not give you any further trouble,' he told the officers. 'My name is Callaghan.'

P.C. Lee told him that he would be charged with the wilful murder of Joe Brady.

'It is no use me saying what I did do or what I didn't do,' replied Callaghan. 'I was there and as bad as the rest. It has been a scuttling do. Me and Brady fought for ten shillings a side a fortnight before. I was coming up the street that night. Brady was on the opposite side and called out my name. The row then commenced. I am very glad you caught me. I wished you had copped me a fortnight before as I have been nearly starved to death.'

Callaghan was willing to admit to his personal feud with Joe Brady – but the charge of scuttling paled beside that of murder. A Manchester police sergeant was dispatched to Bradford to collect Callaghan and the two of them returned to Victoria Station later that night. A large crowd was waiting. News of Callaghan's arrest had leaked out and the Bengal Tigers had gathered, intent on administering justice of their own. 'The greatest excitement prevailed,' noted a reporter at the station, 'and it was with difficulty that the police kept the mob off the prisoner. They were followed by a large crowd to the Town Hall.' Owen Callaghan was safe, for now.

Callaghan and Brennan appeared before magistrate Francis Headlam on March 3. A fresh witness was now called for the prosecution. Joe Cooper told the court:

> On the night in question about 12 o'clock I was at the top of Ludgate Street, Rochdale Road, on my way home from Salford. I met Callaghan coming down Rochdale Road. I knew him before. He came up to me and said, 'Halloa, one of your lads has just been dosed.' I said, 'Who is it?' And he said, 'Brady. I am one of them.' With that he walked on. I went home. I knew Brady very well. I used to 'pal' with him & others. Callaghan used to 'pal' with another lot. Charles Burns is one of them.

Callaghan was silent in court, but Brennan vigorously denied any involvement in the fatal affray. When arrested, he had told the desk sergeant at Goulden Street, 'I don't know anything about it. I was never there, if I was to drop dead.' Mr Headlam was unmoved. He committed both of the prisoners for trial at the Assizes on the charge of wilful murder. That left only Sonny Burns, aged twenty, at large.

Burns was eventually traced to a house in Brown Street, Salford. Officers raided the house before dawn. Burns was woken with a start, but still had the presence of mind to give his name as 'Michael Smith'. By the time he reached Goulden Street police station, he was calling himself 'Farrell'. Nevertheless, he was charged with the wilful murder of Brady. In reply, Burns claimed that he had been in his lodgings in Charter Street until 8.30 on the night in question. He had then gone to his sister's house and remained there until 11.45, when he returned to his lodgings. At around midnight, he said, 'Kitty' McTighe and Martha Gray came in. 'They told me about the row there had been in Back Holgate Street. They stayed there all night. I took no notice of what they said till about ten o'clock [the next morning] when I left, as I did not like the idea of being locked up.' Burns's relationship with McTighe and Gray is unclear. He had a common-law wife, living in Angel Street, who confirmed his alibi, as did his sister. Yet he claimed that the two sixteen-year-olds spent the night at his lodgings. Perhaps Burns was exploiting his status as a scuttler to further his sexual conquests. Or was he McTighe and Gray's bully? Either way, the Burns brothers were closely entwined with the two girls, to the fury of the Bengal Tigers.

Of the five male scuttlers arrested for the killing of Joe Brady, only John Brennan had no criminal record. Sonny Burns gave his occupation as brush-maker when he was arrested. However, he was better known to the Manchester police as a petty thief. Detectives and beat constables alike knew him by his alias: 'John Farrell'. His first appearance at the Manchester City Police Court had been in July 1885 when he got three months for stealing 120 rabbit skins. Later that year, 'John Farrell' was brought before the Manchester Quarter Sessions on a charge of housebreaking. On this occasion, he was acquitted. His other conviction was for assaulting a police officer. Joseph Ryan had one previous conviction. He too was better known to Manchester police by an alias: 'John Daley'. He had been jailed for stealing a pair of curtains in 1886. Charlie Burns had two previous convictions: one for assaulting the police, the other for drunkenness. Owen Callaghan, despite his status as a champion scuttler, had just one, also for drunkenness.

Joseph Ryan, John Brennan, Owen Callaghan and the Burns brothers stood trial for murder at the Manchester Assizes on May 5. The hearing, before Mr Justice Wills, lasted for two days. Their two female companions, Martha Gray and Kate McTighe, were charged with being accessories to murder after the fact. The prosecution was led by Henry West, Q.C., who had taken up the post of Recorder of Manchester in 1865 and had tried dozens of scuttlers at the city's Quarter Sessions. For all that, he was a man out of place; according to one of his fellow judges, Edward Abbott Parry, 'Manchester and West had little in common.' Henry West was an aristocratic liberal, born and bred in London. According to Parry, he was 'impartial, honest, and fearless in his administration of the law', but at the same time 'apparently lacking in knowledge of the working class of the North of

England'. As Recorder, West was usually willing to show clemency towards youths and first-time offenders but he had no sympathy whatsoever for scuttlers.

West outlined the 'facts' of the case and identified three of the prisoners as having wielded knives: Callaghan and the Burns brothers. According to West, the most important task facing the jury was to discern which of these three had struck the fatal blow. However, this was likely to be far from straightforward, as Mr West himself admitted: 'Unfortunately some of the witnesses for the prosecution were not entirely sober [at the time of the killing], and those who would be called to say what took place were ignorant persons, and some of them, he feared, had tainted characters.' West knew that the prosecution witnesses were likely to face severe cross-examination. Three of the key witnesses were well-known Bengal Tigers. Two had previously been tried at the Manchester Assizes themselves: for manslaughter and unlawful wounding. West's frank admission cannot have inspired much confidence among the jury.

The testimony of Jim Carroll, who stood immediately behind Brady at the time of the fatal wounding, was a strange blend of certainty and doubt. He said he could not identify any of the prisoners as part of the gang that pursued him into Back Holgate Street earlier that evening, nor did he know why anyone might want to chase him through the streets. He 'could not say' whether Charlie Burns was at the scene when Brady was killed. However, he could recall only too clearly hearing Callaghan's instruction: 'Draw your knives.' And he was quite sure that he saw Callaghan stab Brady. Tommy Dixon gave a similar account of the fracas on the steps of 23 Back Holgate Street, telling of Charlie Burns's challenge to Brady: 'Come on, Brady, face this,' and Callaghan's curt instruction to 'Draw knives.' And Joe Cooper told the court of Callaghan's chilling boast: 'We have just dosed one of your lads.'

As Henry West feared, one of the biggest obstacles facing the prosecution was the character of the witnesses. Dixon, it transpired, had only been released from Strangeways four days before the fatal stabbing, having served a month for 'being drunk and fighting'. He had been in prison 'about six' times. Worst of all, he had been charged with stabbing a youth who had subsequently died of his wounds. Dixon protested vehemently that he 'had only used his fist' on that occasion – the battle of Jersey Street in July 1884, in which Billy Jackson was fatally wounded.[15] For his part, Joe Cooper admitted under cross-examination that he had been imprisoned once for manslaughter and 'five or six' times for drunkenness. His conviction for killing Tommy Ward two years earlier arose, he insisted, not out of scuttling but from 'jealousy'.[16]

Counsel for the defence was equally quick to seize on the contradictory evidence against the defendants and called a series of witnesses to provide alibis. They were no more convincing than those for the prosecution. Samuel Parry, a boy who appeared on behalf of Charles Burns, swore on the first day of the trial that Owen Callaghan was alone when he stabbed Brady. The boy was recalled the following day after it was pointed out to the judge, Mr Justice Wills, that he had previously sworn that Callaghan had another man at his side when the fatal blow was struck. The sister of Charlie and Sonny Burns vouched for Sonny's claim that he had been at her house for most of the evening in question, but under cross-examination by Mr West was forced to admit that she had herself been in prison since the killing, having been convicted of assaulting Brady's companions Mary Jane Judge and Mary Ann Collins. Nonetheless, she protested, she was as 'innocent as the child unborn'. Mary Greaves, who had been living 'over the brush' with Sonny Burns, was also called to confirm his alibi. She too, it transpired, had served a string of prison sentences.

Summing up the prosecution case, Henry West claimed that there was a general agreement among the witnesses for the crown that Owen Callaghan had struck the fatal blow. The case against the Burns brothers, he contended, was if anything strengthened by the evidence of witnesses for the defence. On the question of motive, West remarked, there seemed to be none. These scuttlers

---

15 On that occasion he had been identified as 'John' Dixon.
16 See Chapter 9.

simply behaved 'like different tribes of wild Indians rather than as people inhabiting a Christian country, with apparently no other motive than a ferocious love of fighting'. Mr Justice Wills took two hours to give his summary of the evidence. He urged the jury not to 'shrink from doing their duty, painful though it might be'. To Owen Callaghan and the two Burns brothers, the judge's words held a chilling implication.

The jury did not begin their deliberations until half past five in the afternoon. They were locked in debate for two and a half hours. Three times they stopped to ask the judge for further guidance. Each time, the packed courtroom drew its breath, waiting for the one word that would send one or more of the scuttlers in the dock to the gallows. Finally, at eight o'clock, the jurors returned their verdict. They found Ryan, Brennan and the Burns brothers not guilty of murder. They found Callaghan guilty of manslaughter. Mr Justice Wills was not impressed. Before passing sentence, he described the jury's verdict as 'very merciful'. In his view, 'It was about as bad a case of manslaughter as could be imagined.' He sentenced Callaghan to penal servitude for twenty years. The judge's pronouncement was met with an anguished shriek from a young woman in the gallery. According to the *Manchester Guardian*, it also 'appeared to create a marked impression on a large number of young men who were present in court'.

The following day, Sonny Burns was brought back to the dock to face the charge of being accessory to murder after the fact. Martha Gray and Kate McTighe stood beside him in the dock. Counsel for the prosecution said that, in view of the previous day's result, the crown did not propose to proceed with the charge. Mr Justice Wills, who had heard more than enough of scuttlers and their tangled courtroom tales for one sitting of the Assizes, expressed his approval. As Wills remarked, the trial had shown 'how impossible it was to get an accurate account of what really took place' in scuttles. Addressing the prisoners, the judge said that he understood that Sonny Burns had boasted that, whatever the outcome of the trial, 'he would get three months'. Justice Wills continued:

They must not flatter themselves that they could lead disorderly lives and escape the consequences by light sentences. Scuttling was now pretty well known to all the judges, and they were convinced, as he was, that those who took part in it must, when convicted, be punished with the utmost rigour. Life in parts of Manchester was as unsafe and as uncertain as amongst a race of savages. Manchester and two other towns he could name enjoyed an unenviable reputation for crime of this kind, and elsewhere he had met with nothing like it.

One of the other towns was Salford; the other was Liverpool.

The repercussions from the murder of Joe Brady did not end with the strongly worded warning from Justice Wills. The feud between the Bengal Tigers and the Meadow Lads continued in a spate of tit-for-tat assaults on those who had given evidence at the trial. Joe Cooper, the convicted killer who testified on behalf of the prosecution, was assaulted within hours of Wills's tirade at the Assizes. Walking along Birchall Street with his moll late that night, he was stopped by two Meadow Lads who punched him to the ground. Alf Hey was subsequently arrested and jailed for the assault. As the *Manchester Courier* noted grimly, 'Since the night on which the alleged murder took place several conflicts have taken place between the companions of the respective parties, and the magistrates have had numerous cases of assault before them.'

To Henry West, Q.C., the on-going violence was 'motiveless'. To the participants, of course, it was anything but. Scuttlers' reputations for prowess were hard-won, widely acknowledged and jealously guarded. Their claims to territory – and to the 'ownership' of local young women – were matters of life and death. The Bengal Tigers were honour-bound to avenge the killing of Joe Brady. To the followers of Owen Callaghan, the sentence of twenty years was not so much a deterrent as an incitement to vengeance against all those who had testified against him.

MR JUSTICE Wills's declaration that 'Life in parts of Manchester was as unsafe and as uncertain as amongst a race of savages' divided opinion among the readers of the *Manchester Guardian*. One derided the judge's comment as 'unreal and illogical, and therefore unjustifiable'. Others suggested that Justice Wills had barely hinted at the depth of depravity to be encountered in the streets off the Rochdale and Oldham Roads. A self-proclaimed 'Retired Ancoats Rough' supplied a startling account of street fights that had recently taken place in the district, gleaned – he claimed – from one of the 'decent' female residents. 'It is quite common,' he wrote, 'for ragged, half-naked people to commence fighting, and in a few moments to be on the floor struggling, stark naked, like demons, surrounded by scores of young people of both sexes, each taking his or her own "side," and often joining in the fray.' The former 'rough' claimed that he was 'quite used to this sort of amusement thirty years ago', but was bewildered by the failure of philanthropy to improve the condition of the district over the intervening period.

If the letters page of the *Guardian* was any guide, the public was split between hawks, demanding longer sentences and liberal application of the cat o' nine tails, and social reformers, who blamed the appalling living conditions of the working class. 'If the bloodthirsty ruffians who perpetrate these outrages were to be shot down like mad-dogs when caught red-handed, the law would be only doing a swift duty to all whose lives are [worth more] than those of cats and dogs,' suggested one of the more rabid correspondents. Another, writing under the nom de plume 'The Unlucky One', had been subjected to volleys of abuse when venturing into the side streets of Ancoats and New Cross on business, prompting the comment: 'If the roughs would only take it out of each other in [a] fair fight it would not be a bad plan to let them fight, like the Kilkenny cats, till they had quietened things a little.'

Another reader applauded Justice Wills for speaking out so boldly:

These bloody and desperate contests have been going on for years; they have been gradually increasing in ferocity. Now I ask, in the name of common sense, in the name of public morality and of public order, was it not high time that someone in authority should call public attention to such a shocking and outrageous state of things? As neither the magistrates nor the City Council have attempted to deal with a great scandal, we may be thankful that one of these gentlemen coming occasionally down from London ... has had the good sense to call attention to the matter.

Other *Guardian* readers saw things differently. In keeping with growing concern with the entrenched problems of 'Outcast Manchester', they viewed scuttling as the product of wider social forces. Joseph Billam, a master shoemaker from Ancoats, identified youthful drunkenness as the principal cause and demanded prompt action from the licensing authorities. 'It is always at the week-end, when the passions of our youth are inflamed by drink, that these disgraceful acts are perpetrated,' he wrote. 'It is wrong to assume that these cowardly acts are the work of loafers and corner-boys; they are frequently the work of youths who, apart from drink, live fairly exemplary lives.' According to Billam, unscrupulous beerhouse-keepers plied young people of both sexes with drink 'until they are whipped into a state of savagery fit for the commission of any dastardly act'.

Yet another reader blamed the dullness and monotony of modern industrial life, and the lack of organised leisure activities, contending that Manchester's wealthier citizens had abandoned the city's poor. The toiling 'masses' were herded together in destitution and squalor, only to be noticed by their social superiors when they came under the moral scrutiny of the various religious and philanthropic agencies. Joseph Waddington, of Ancoats, offered the most systematic remedy to these problems. 'Many of the dwellings in Ancoats are unfit for human beings to live in,' he wrote. 'A remedy is needed. Give us cheerful homes; give us useful work, and not useless toil; give us leisure to think and to realise life in all its brightest aspects; give us that precious right that the producers of wealth shall enjoy their full share of the wealth that they produce; give us art, that we may take pleasure with our toil; give us the hand of fellowship, that we may co-operate to make work useful to us all.' Waddington's prescription – socialism – was anathema to the bulk of the *Guardian*'s readership, but his eloquent concern for the plight of the urban poor echoed a growing body of public opinion.

MR JUSTICE Wills's coded reference to Salford and Liverpool at the trial of Owen Callaghan was understandable. The 'High Rip' gangs of Liverpool were making their own headlines at the time of the death of Joe Brady in Manchester in February 1887, and some newspaper columnists bracketed scuttlers and High Rippers together. The *Manchester Courier*, always more hawkish than the *Guardian*, condemned them equally as part of the 'residuum' – that wretched portion of society living, as the *Courier* saw it, in a state of almost hopeless poverty and dependence. The *Courier* recommended flogging as the cure in both cities. Yet the Liverpool gangs were very different in character from the scuttlers of Manchester and Salford. Scuttling gangs were fighting gangs, their feuds driven by the pursuit of status, reprisal and sheer excitement. The High Rippers, by contrast, generally used violence and intimidation in pursuit of profit. They were much more prone to carry out street robberies and it was even alleged that they levied systematic blackmail on the dock labourers of Liverpool's North End.

The High Rippers had first come to the attention of the judges in 1884 following the fatal stabbing of a Spanish seaman. Five youths were charged with murder and they stood trial at the Liverpool Assizes. In his address to the jury, the judge identified seventeen-year-old Michael McLean as 'the leader of the High Rip gang'. McLean and Patrick Duggan, aged eighteen, were both convicted of murder and were sentenced to death. Duggan was subsequently reprieved, but McLean went to the gallows.

Two years later, a startling intervention by Mr Justice Day brought the High Rippers back into the headlines of the national press. The Head Constable of Liverpool, Captain William Nott-Bower, had alleged that the High Rip existed only in 'the imagination of newspaper correspondents'. His comments sparked a furious debate which was still raging in the Liverpool newspapers when Mr Justice Day arrived in the city for the November Assizes. 'High Rippers' were mentioned in two of the cases of wounding brought before him. One arose out of a dispute between members of two rival gangs; in the second, a man was accused of shooting a youth in the foot when he fired a revolver to disperse a 'crowd of High Rippers' outside his house. The *Liverpool Echo* viewed the proceedings as a shocking indictment, not just of the gangs, but of the Head Constable who had sought to deny their existence.

Justice Day weighed into the controversy by announcing that he 'would tour the city and see for himself the situation as regards the High Rip'. He made a midnight circuit of the Scotland Road district, escorted by the Head Constable, two detectives and one of his fellow judges. They saw no sign of the High Rippers – although any lurking predators would have been wise to stay out of the sight of the judge and his unlikely entourage. The following morning, however, Justice Day tried a number of cases of robbery with violence. He imposed sentences of imprisonment to which he added floggings: twenty or thirty lashes, to be administered in two instalments, the second prior to release. The sentences caused a sensation in Liverpool, where the redoubtable judge was promptly christened 'Judgement Day'.

If floggings were the solution, then the streets of Liverpool's North End should have been quietened at a stroke. Six months later, however, Mr Justice Day was faced by four High Rippers brought before him on charges of malicious wounding and robbery with violence. On the day before Joe Brady was killed in Manchester, the four lads were stood on the corner of Westmoreland Street when a man named James Marsden walked by with one of his friends. One of them jabbed at Marsden with a knife, cutting clean through his hat and inflicting a serious head wound. The four youths then embarked on an orgy of violence and plunder. They steamed into a pawnshop, grabbing armfuls of coats and bedding and striking at the owner with their knives as he tried to fend them off with a wooden pole. Next they cut down some articles on display in another pawnbroker's window before charging into a confectioner's shop. A woman came to the doorway with an infant in her arms. One of the youths struck at her with his fist, catching the child in the face. When the woman shouted that the child was 'killed', one of the others kicked her. Two of the woman's brothers came to her rescue; one of them was cut severely on the head, the other was knocked to the ground and stabbed in the back. The High Rippers continued on the rampage, attacking a butcher and two more pawnbrokers, knocking down two women as they charged through one of the side streets off Scotland Road, and striking a small child who got in their way. By the time they were caught by the police, their knives were covered in blood.

The jury found all four prisoners guilty. Mr Justice Day, hardened as he was to the gangs of Manchester, had in all his experience 'never heard such outrageous conduct narrated'. He had hardly considered such things possible in any civilised city in England, or indeed the world. He sentenced them to penal servitude for terms of between fifteen and twenty-one months, remarking that these comparatively short terms would be 'less burdensome to society'. During their sentences, the prisoners were all to be flogged three times: twenty lashes with the cat on each occasion.

If the cat was as sure a remedy for crime as Mr Justice Day supposed, the prisoners would not have been stood before him in the first place. The sentences of flogging he handed out amidst so much controversy in Liverpool six months previously ought to have put a stop to the activities of the High Rippers. In fact, Sir John was handing out similar sentences at the Liverpool Assizes well into the following decade. His reputation as a flogging judge was secure, but so was Liverpool's reputation as a hotbed of robbery with violence.

In Manchester, the feud between the Bengal Tigers and the Meadow Lads had not yet run its course. Clashes between them resulted in a series of court cases during 1888 and 1889. In March 1888, a group of Bengal Tigers spotted some of the Meadow Lads in Smithfield Market. Both sets were dressed to the nines, the Tigers sporting black jackets, white cord bell-bottomed trousers and bowler hats. In the mêlée that followed,

Tommy Hughes from Ancoats was stabbed in the back and 'Duffey' Toole from the Meadow suffered a fractured skull; depositions were taken from Toole in Manchester Royal Infirmary in case he died. Hughes was subsequently charged with unlawful wounding along with a Meadow Lad named Tommy Cunningham. Aged seventeen and eighteen respectively, they both worked as labourers. Since the Manchester Assizes had just sat, the two lads were sent for trial at Liverpool where they appeared before Justice Day, who explained to the jury that scuttling was 'the public recreation of the rising generation of Manchester'. Day sentenced Hughes to twelve months' hard labour. Cunningham went down for one month, having admitted to stabbing Hughes 'in self-defence'.

The Tigers were also not averse to adding their weight to wider communal hostility towards the police. One raucous Saturday night in September, 1888, P.C. Arthur Elvidge arrested twenty-four-year-old Maggie Flanagan outside the Royal Oak Inn on Jersey Street for being drunk and disorderly. In her younger days, Flanagan had been one of the most prominent female members of the Bengal Tigers and she was well-known even to the gang's newer recruits. As P.C. Elvidge began to escort Flanagan to the police station, he was confronted by a group of men and youths who rushed out of the pub. The youths took off their belts and swung a succession of blows at the officer's head and chest. P.C. Elvidge let his prisoner go and attempted to take one of the lads into custody instead. This prompted a renewed, and still more frenzied, assault. James Quinn, an eighteen-year-old labourer, smashed the heavy buckle of his belt into the constable's face. The blow cut the officer's right eye clean out of the socket. He also suffered a broken jaw.

James Quinn was subsequently arrested along with two other eighteen-year-olds: Mick Robinson and John Burke. The three all had previous convictions, though Robinson and Burke's were only for drunkenness. Quinn's record told a very different story. In December 1882, at the age of twelve, he had been convicted of stealing lead and sentenced to one month's imprisonment to be followed by five years on the *Clarence*, the reformatory ship for Catholic boys moored on the River Mersey at Birkenhead. Since his release, he had quickly amassed a further ten convictions, mainly for drunkenness and assault. Quinn, Robinson and Burke were initially charged with assaulting a police officer, but the charge was upgraded to one of unlawful wounding and they were committed for trial at the Manchester Quarter Sessions. 'Not only did the constable lose the right eye,' the jury heard, 'but the sight of the left one was affected, and he was altogether incapacitated for duty as a policeman.' Belt buckles were said to be 'the favourite weapon amongst the Ancoats roughs'. The Recorder of Manchester, Henry West, Q.C., sentenced Quinn to fifteen months' imprisonment and Robinson and Burke to nine months each.

Far from quelling the operations of the two gangs, the killing of Joe Brady had only served to deepen the enmity between them – and towards the police. The Meadow Lads were to figure prominently in the escalation of scuttling in the years that followed.

CHAPTER 12

The Wars of the Townships

WHILE BATTLES RAGED between the scuttlers of Angel Meadow, Ancoats, and Salford, the townships on the eastern fringes of Manchester were barely less troubled. Every youth entering Bradford, Gorton or Openshaw was viewed with suspicion; every unrecognised face deemed a threat. On Saturday, 4 October 1884, Edwin Walker was walking through Gorton when he was stopped by a gang who demanded, 'Are you a scuttler?' Walker replied that he was not. His interrogators were not satisfied. Tommy Seal, a seventeen-year-old labourer, punched Walker in the eye. Walker tried to run but was caught and stabbed in the head. Seal was later arrested along with two other Gorton youths: John Flattely, aged sixteen, and fourteen-year-old John Elliott. All three were convicted of unlawful wounding. Flattely and Seal were both jailed for nine months by W. H. Higgin at the Salford Hundred Quarter Sessions. Elliott's youth counted against him: at the age of fourteen, he was liable to a longer term in an institution for juvenile offenders. He was jailed for twenty-one days. He was then to be sent to a reformatory for five years.

Mr Higgin dealt with two further cases of scuttling at the same meeting of the Quarter Sessions. James Kelly, another fourteen-year-old, was convicted of unlawfully wounding Ben Wood at the Miles Platting wakes on August 23. The unfortunate Wood dropped a penny in front of a nut stall. Kelly picked it up, whereupon Wood immediately seized it from him. Kelly gave a shrill whistle, which beckoned the other members of his gang to the scene. Once Wood was surrounded, Kelly took out a knife and stabbed him on the shoulder. Mr Higgin declared that an example must be made of Kelly 'as a check to the terrorism which at present existed'. Kelly was treated as an adult prisoner would be: he was jailed for twelve months.

The following day, Mr Higgin was faced with a batch of eight lads from Hulme and Ardwick. They were part of a much larger gang that had taken to spending Sundays afternoons terrorising the respectable south Manchester suburb of Rusholme. On Sunday, October 12, fifty young roughs, armed with iron rods, sticks, bludgeons, stones, brickbats, and broken bottles, marched 'like an army' through the streets to the cricket ground at Platt Fields, where they spotted a number of local youths. They shouted challenges to the Rusholme lads but a squad of police officers, alerted by concerned passers-by, inter-vened before any fighting took place. Those arrested were all labourers aged between fifteen and seventeen. They were already hardened scuttlers.

Witnesses at the Quarter Sessions told how, on successive recent Sunday afternoons, Rusholme had been 'overrun by gangs of roughs, who have not only done damage to property, but have attacked and beaten unoffending persons'. Windows had been broken, and one boy had been seriously hurt. The jury found all eight guilty of riot. Mr Higgin was appalled by the evidence of the lads' conduct. He referred the court to the plight of Jimmy Knowles, a nineteen-year-old from Gorton, 'at present hovering between life and death' after a knifing by the Openshaw scut-tlers. It was not to be tolerated, thundered Higgin, 'that on a Sunday a suburb of a great city like Manchester should be invaded by an army of roughs who were to disturb decent and respectable people and make a scandalous and riotous distur-bance in the streets.' Before passing sentence, Higgin stated boldly that 'the court intended to see whether it was stronger than the scuttlers'. He sent six of the prisoners to Strangeways for twelve months. The remaining two, neither of whom had previously been convicted, got nine months. A number of women in the public gallery screamed and one cried out, 'My innocent child!' The gallery was cleared by police.

The assailants of Jimmy Knowles, the Gorton youth referred to by Mr Higgin, were brought before the Quarter Sessions on December 2. The court heard how, on the evening of August 20, Knowles was walking through Pottery Lane in Openshaw when he was accosted by a gang forty-strong. They demanded to know where he lived. Knowles's reply – Gorton – prompted a horrific assault. Joe Siderfin, an eighteen-year-old labourer, began the onslaught, hurling a bottle which hit Knowles on the forehead. Philip McDermott took off his belt and struck Knowles a fierce blow on the back of the head. Other members of the gang bombarded Knowles with stones, before lashing out with their belts as he lay on the ground. John Gibbons plunged a knife into Knowles's ribs. The Openshaw lads walked away, leaving Knowles writhing on the ground. 'Let's go back and finish him,' shouted one of the Openshaw lads, but his companions had no appetite for murder.

The jury found six of the defendants guilty: two of unlawful wounding and four of inflicting grievous bodily harm. The oldest was nineteen and the youngest fifteen. Mr Higgin now opted to use the strongest measures at his disposal. Siderfin and Gibbons, both of whom were aged eighteen and worked as labourers, were sentenced to five years' penal servitude, the maximum permitted under English law, while three of those convicted for grievous bodily harm were sent down for fifteen months: again, the maximum sentence. Court reporters noted that the pronouncement was met with anguish by a large number of young men – 'friends of the prisoners' – who had gathered at the back of the public gallery.

W. H. Higgin no doubt expected sentences of five years to have a salutary effect. The police posted bills throughout the eastern townships, warning people against scuttling and giving details of the sentences passed on the Openshaw six. Any hopes that the sentences would prove a deterrent were shattered just five days later, however, by a renewal of hostilities in Gorton. At five o'clock on the afternoon of December 7, the Openshaw scuttlers arrived in Gorton en masse: they were looking for the Gorton scuttlers who had given evidence against their friends at the Quarter Sessions.

The Gorton lads routed the intruders. Michael Slater, a sixteen-year-old labourer from Gorton, chased an Openshaw lad named James King into a shop in Gorton Lane. Slater threw a bottle at King, who picked up a chair to defend himself. When the female shopkeeper emerged from the store room, Slater ran back out into the street. The shopkeeper went to the front door to find between forty and fifty scuttlers outside. They demanded that she turn King out of her shop. She refused, and instead went to fetch a constable who escorted the Openshaw lad to the police station. At the station were three other Openshaw scuttlers, all of whom had taken refuge in houses in Gorton Lane and nearby Garden Street. The four lads told the police that they had been on their way to chapel when they were set upon by scuttlers armed with belts and sticks.

The Openshaw scuttlers were detained at the police station for three hours. At eight o'clock, they were allowed to go. Two plain-clothes police officers followed them in an attempt to prevent them being further molested. The officers' efforts were in vain: the lads were immediately set upon once more. Five of their assailants were eventually apprehended. They were charged with riot and committed for trial at the Quarter Sessions.

Two of the defendants pleaded guilty and the jury took little time in convicting the others. Two of them had only been released from Strangeways on November 28 after serving two weeks for assault. Mr Higgin sentenced all five of the prisoners to twelve months in Strangeways. He appeared to accept the tale of an unprovoked assault on four respectable young men making their way to chapel, but most of those present in court knew differently. Perhaps Higgin did, too, but his principal concern was to persuade the jurors to convict the five Gorton lads in the dock.

AT AROUND nine o'clock on the night of Wednesday 1 July, 1885, 150 youths took part in a scuttle in Wardle Street, Newton Heath. This was a territorial skirmish: the warring factions identified themselves simply as 'Newton' and 'Beswick'. The rival mobs hurled barrages of missiles at each other until a contingent of police officers intervened. George Waterhouse, the leader of the Newton Heath scuttlers, was arrested along with his brother Joe and four other youths. The six lads were aged between seventeen and nineteen, and they were all employed as labourers. Two had previously been convicted of stone-throwing, while the Waterhouse brothers had also been before the magistrates: Joe for obstructing the footpath and George for vagrancy. Tired of the gangs' unceasing violence, the magistrates committed all six for trial at the Manchester Assizes on the charge of riot.

They appeared before Mr Justice Lopes on July 24, when all bar one of the prisoners pleaded not guilty. The Waterhouse brothers and co-defendant Billy Walker were adamant that they had taken no part in the disturbance, insisting that they had been at a music hall at the time. Walker's mother testified on her son's behalf. She swore that she had collected him from the door of the 'show' at five to nine, five minutes before the riot broke out, and taken him straight home. This was an unlikely story, given the much treasured independence enjoyed by working lads aged in their teens, but Mrs Walker's account was confirmed by another woman who told the jury that she had seen William with his mother at the time of the riot. Mrs Walker's dogged defence of her son was to be rewarded, even though other witnesses identified him among the ranks of the rioters. The jury found William Walker not guilty, and he walked free from the court. The mother of Ellis Cuff, another defendant, swore that her son was at home from half past seven until half past nine on the night in question, during which time he was 'never out of her sight'. In Cuff's case, the jury was more readily persuaded by eye-witness accounts of his participation in the disturbance. The remaining four prisoners were found guilty of riot. Along with Samuel Murphy, who had pleaded guilty, they got four months.

THE OPENSHAW scuttlers spent the afternoon of Saturday, 24 September, 1887, playing football on a local croft. Their game was interrupted by the unexpected appearance of the Grey Mare Boys, a fearless band of colliers from Bradford. The mutual hatred between the two gangs was long-standing. Cries of 'Here's Openshaw!' from the Bradford lads were followed by a volley of stones, one of which felled James King, a prominent member of the Openshaw mob. His was a notable scalp. When he got to his feet, King found John Queenan standing in front of him holding a pistol. Queenan turned to the rest of the Grey Mare Boys.

'Shall I fire?' he asked them.

'Yes,' someone replied.

Others suggested King ought to be spared, but Queenan pulled the trigger. The pistol had been loaded with a mixture of powder and stones, and the force of the shot knocked King back to the ground. Queenan, a fifteen-year-old labourer, was arrested and brought before the Manchester magistrates. He vehemently denied having been present at the croft, but was nevertheless committed for trial at the Manchester Assizes on a charge of unlawful wounding.

He was tried before Mr Justice Day on October 29. The jury heard that the fight was part of a long-running feud between Openshaw and Bradford. Summing up the case, 'Judgement' Day declared that the one punishment that would do the most good judges were not allowed to inflict, and that was to give such 'good-for-nothings' – when they were found with knives or pistols upon them – one or two 'good whippings', and send them out to earn their own living. The jury found Queenan guilty and, before passing sentence, Mr Justice Day returned to his earlier theme. If he could have his own way, he said, he would not 'contaminate' the prisoner by sending him to associate with criminals, to his almost certain ruin, but would 'adopt the reasonable and rational course of having him so whipped that he would shudder at the very thought of a pistol, and certainly never commit such an offence again'. He sentenced Queenan to three years in a reformatory.

James King and his companions drank in the Alma Inn on Ashton Old Road. The concert room of the Alma was frequented chiefly, if not entirely, by the Openshaw scuttlers, both male and female, many of whom stayed on the premises into the early hours of the morning. Police patrols targeted the premises on a nightly basis after a constable was badly beaten by two of its habitués. So notorious was the Alma that it became known locally as 'the Dogs' Home' and 'the Scuttlers' Den'.

THE GREY Mare Boys had few allies but many enemies. They launched seemingly endless raids into both Openshaw and Gorton. In October 1889, their feud with the Gorton scuttlers escalated following an affray in which a Grey Mare Boy named John Gilbert was knifed. He lay in Manchester Royal Infirmary for ten days, his life hanging in the balance, before he showed signs of recovery. The Bradford mob made repeated raids on Gorton to seek revenge, arriving in force at a croft in School Street, close to Gorton Monastery, where the Gorton scuttlers habitually gathered.

A week after Gilbert was stabbed, a Gorton scuttler named Lyons suffered serious facial injuries when he was hit with a brick. With John Gilbert still in mortal danger, the Grey Mare Boys' lust for revenge was far from satisfied. At five o'clock the following afternoon, a Sunday, they assembled at a Gorton beer-house before swarming into School Street, taking over the croft and issuing the boldest of challenges: 'Come on, Gorton, we'll show you what the Bradford boys can do! We'll teach you what scuttling is.' The Gorton scuttlers pulled themselves together and rushed at the Grey Mare Boys, who in turn hurled a volley of bricks and stones before moving forward, belts and stones in hand, for the fray.

The ensuing carnage lasted for fully half an hour. Dozens of windows in nearby houses were smashed. Arriving beat constables saw a crowd of between 200 and 300 'lads and lasses' fighting hand to hand and were forced to seek reinforcements, running back to the Gorton police office, where the sergeant hastily assembled a squad of half a dozen constables. The sergeant led them to the scene of the scuttle and the officers burst among the ranks of the Grey Mare Boys, catching no fewer than eleven of them.

The dishevelled prisoners appeared the following morning

before J. H. P. Leresche, the stipendiary magistrate at the County Police Court at Strangeways. Police officers gave graphic accounts of the riot on the croft and an inspector said that he had spoken to a number of anxious local residents the previous evening, several of whom had declared their willingness to attend court and give evidence. However, 'something had interfered, and they had not arrived'. Mr Leresche replied that the court was determined to ensure that witnesses could come forward without fear of reprisal. He committed all eleven prisoners for trial at the Salford Hundred Quarter Sessions on charges of riot.

The Grey Mare Boys appeared at the sessions before Mr W. H. Higgin on October 22. When their names and addresses were read out in court, it became apparent that the gang drew its core members from the Bradford Colliery: ten of the prisoners worked together at the pit. Eight of them lived in the immediate vicinity while the remaining three were from the neighbouring districts of Beswick and Clayton. Their ages ranged from sixteen to nineteen and five of them had previous convictions for scutling. Having been caught at the scene, seven of the accused pleaded guilty as charged. The other four denied the charge of riot. Two police constables described the mêlée and pointed out that the prisoners were 'only a few' of those involved. One resident came forward to describe the effects upon the neighbourhood: 'When it came dark at night the inhabitants for some time past had been afraid to leave their houses, as bricks were flying about in all directions.'

Three of the accused presented alibis. The mother of one – a 'stout grey-haired woman' – caused considerable mirth in court. She declared firmly that her son, Charlie Gregory, 'was not in this affray', before adding that one of her other sons 'was out on Sunday night and got locked up for standing at the street corner. He had just been at a christening.' The prosecuting counsel, Mr Watson, demanded to know how Mrs Gregory was able to state with such certainty the times that her son had been at home on the Sunday afternoon.

'He was in the house from half past two until the church bells began to ring, so he could not have been one of the scuttlers,' she said.

'How do you know that it was half past two?' asked Mr Watson.

'I can always tell that by the beerhouses shutting up.'

'A very good clock to go by!' interjected Mr Higgin.

Little respect was shown to the defence witnesses. In his address to the jury, W. H. Higgin dwelled instead on the need for severe punishment to serve as a warning to scuttlers. The jury duly found the remaining four prisoners guilty.

Before passing sentence, Mr Higgin asked Superintendent James Bent to step into the witness box. Superintendent Bent told the court that scuttling fights were a serious nuisance and had forced Gorton police to increase their strength by eight men. It was, he said, 'a case of township against township'. The lads who took part were absolutely lawless, and no one could feel safe when darkness set in. The fights broke out so suddenly that even the increased police force struggled to suppress them. Prompted from the bench, the superintendent reminded the court of the plight of John Gilbert, stating that 'at the present moment a youth is lying at the infirmary in a serious condition through being attacked by scuttlers'.

Before sentences were pronounced, two of the Grey Mare Boys asked for permission to address the bench. Jim Lockridge asked Mr Higgin whether, instead of jailing the prisoners, he would be 'kind enough to lash them, so that they might not lose their work'. Tommy Costello suggested that they should be bound over to keep the peace for twelve months. Their comments prompted laughter and smirks from their companions in the dock, and the prisoners' general air of flippancy was noted by the assembled court reporters. Mr Higgin did not share the joke. He had no legal authority to order the lads to be flogged in any case. Instead, he sentenced all eleven to nine months, adding that the punishment for any scuttlers brought before him in future would be doubled. The Grey Mare Boys put on a show of defiance, banging their clogs on the walls of the courtroom as they were taken down to the cells.

The *Manchester Weekly Times* devoted an editorial to the case, describing Gorton as 'that rather unpleasant Manchester suburb'. As the *Weekly Times* saw it:

Two gangs of youths had a pitched battle on some vacant land. If these young roughs confined their violence to their own ranks – if they simply belaboured each other – there would be less reason to complain. But this they will not or cannot do, and peaceable citizens suffer severely from this rowdyism. It was stated at the trial that people are afraid to go out at night because of the lawlessness which exists. This, be it observed, was said of a district not in Ireland but within a few yards of the Manchester Town Hall. Such a state of things cannot be allowed to continue, and the magistrates both in the city and the county are determined that it shall cease.

Superintendent Bent prolonged the police operation against the Grey Mare Boys after the trial. A twelfth member of the gang was arrested the following week and by the time of his trial he was joined by another. The two lads were charged with scuttling. One was acquitted but the other got nine months.

After a lengthy stay in Manchester Royal Infirmary, John Gilbert recovered from the injuries he sustained at the hands of the Gorton scuttlers. Three of his assailants were eventually brought to trial, where two were convicted of unlawful wounding. Both went down for nine months with the customary hard labour thrown in. One of them, Charlie Stansfield, alias Lee, had already served three separate terms of two months in Strangeways: two for theft and one for assaulting the police.

The Gorton scuttlers continued to pose problems for Superintendent Bent of the County Police during 1890. On the evening of Saturday, February 8, they clashed with a raiding party from Openshaw in Gorton Lane. John Fulton from Openshaw was stabbed repeatedly during the affray. Doctors found one wound to be near-fatal, a blade having narrowly missed his right lung. Three members of the Gorton gang were arrested and subsequently found guilty of unlawful wounding.

When the foreman juror announced the verdict, he added that, 'They thought a sound wholesome flogging would do good in cases such as these.' Mr Higgin, presiding, told the jury that he agreed entirely. In his view, 'The uncivilised condition of these lads was most alarming.' Higgin told the court that he was determined to use his powers to 'civilise these Gorton lads', despite allegations in some sections of the local press that long prison sentences were making such youths 'hard-hearted and rendering them altogether unfit for amelioration'.

There was no sign of any civilising influence a month later when the Gorton scuttlers ran amok on the night of the St Patrick's Day celebrations. A crowd of 300 youths paraded around the streets, taunting shopkeepers and shouldering passers-by off the footpaths. Two beat constables watched the vast mob turn into Gorton Lane. When some of the youths began to hurl stones at the windows of the houses, the officers ran towards them. Robert Carnegie, the leader of the Gorton scuttlers, stepped forward. His lieutenant, Alex Smith, was at his side. As the constables approached, Carnegie shouted, 'Now, lads, don't let's be taken. If they touch us, belts off!' The officers turned and ran back towards the Gorton police station to summon assistance. The mob gave chase, bombarding the constables with stones.

Carnegie, an eighteen-year-old driller, and Smith, a nineteen-year-old labourer, were arrested later that night, while two of their followers were caught the next day. The four were committed for trial at the Salford Hundred Quarter Sessions, and when they appeared before W. H. Higgin they were indicted for riot. The jury found Carnegie and Smith guilty after police witnesses firmly identified them as the ringleaders of the disturbance. The evidence against the other two lads was much less compelling and they were both acquitted. Before passing sentence, Higgin railed against the scuttlers of Gorton yet again, declaring that, 'Gorton in these days was nothing but a pandemonium. Decent and respectable persons could not leave their houses or carry on their lawful business with any degree of safety whilst this class of youths paraded the streets.' Once more, Higgin threatened to impose harsher and harsher sentences until scuttling finally ceased. His sentences, however, did not match his rhetoric. Carnegie was jailed for just six months. Smith received the now-customary sentence for scuttlers of nine months, but only after a previous conviction for larceny was taken into account.

If Gorton was a pandemonium, it was no worse than any of the other factory districts which ringed Manchester city centre. It was now twenty years since the 1870 Education Act established a system of universal state schooling, yet somehow the rising generation appeared more unruly than ever.

CHAPTER 13

Scuttlers and the Lash

The Scuttler Boy to the war has gone,
On his fiendish pranks you'll find him;
A big-buckled belt he has girded on,
And a poker hid behind him.
And all aglow with 'that stern joy
Which warriors feel' is the Scuttler Boy!

The Scuttler Boy, with a wild, weird cry,
Works well at the task assigned him;
And the passer-by must mind his eye,
Or the Scuttler Boy will blind him.
For to ruin and wreck, despoil, destroy,
Is the noble aim of the Scuttler Boy!

The Scuttler Boy skips to and fro
With the Scuttler Girl behind him;
Huge stones at the foe it is his to throw,
It is hers those stones to find him.
And the Scuttler Girl with gruesome joy
Sees the gruesome work of the Scuttler Boy!

The Scuttler Boy is a plague, a pest,
Let the law in its fetters bind him;
And we trust, Father Antic, you'll do your best
A taste of the lash to find him.
For the pains of the brute will alone destroy
The admixture of brute in the Scuttler Boy![17]

---

17 First published in the *Globe* on 16 December 1890, this poem, *The Scuttler Boy*, was reproduced in local newspapers such as the Salford *County*

THE SCUTTLERS' REIGN of terror came to a head in the years 1889 to 1890. In Salford, a cluster of high-profile trials in February 1890 sparked a panic which rumbled across the borough for the remainder of the year. In Manchester, the trial of a band of Harpurhey scuttlers in August 1890 (see Chapter 1) led to calls for a deputation from Manchester to the Home Secretary in London. The object was nothing less than a change in the laws of England. By the autumn of 1890, it was claimed that there were more youths being held in Strangeways for scuttling than for any other offence. According to the civic authorities of Manchester and Salford, this scuttling epidemic would only be curbed by the introduction of the lash – the dreaded cat o' nine tails.

For a period of eighteen months from June 1889, Salford's scuttlers were seldom out of the local headlines. The streets of the borough appeared to be almost engulfed by warring young roughs. Reports of outbreaks of gang fighting stretched from the slums of Greengate and the Adelphi to the supposedly more respectable districts of Pendleton to the west and Ordsall to the south. In Greengate, where the ranks of the Queen Street scuttlers had been replenished, a new generation of tearaways was intent on claiming that mantle that had once belonged to the feared Sam McElroy. William Gaffney, a labourer, got into an argument with members of the gang at pub closing time on Christmas night in 1888. The scuttlers – including the fearsome Billy Watts, who boasted convictions for assault, unlawful wounding and attacking the police – surrounded Gaffney and subjected him to a savage beating with their belts. Dazed, cut and bruised, Gaffney was carried to Salford Royal Hospital, where the house surgeon found several cuts on his head had gone clean to the bone. Watts was sent down for two months. Two other Queen Street lads joined him in Strangeways the following week.

Three months later, the Queen Street scuttlers turned their ire on Jimmy Horrocks from Ryland Street in Greengate. On this occasion, their motive was clear: Horrocks had prosecuted

---

Telephone. 'Father Antic' refers to 'old father antic the law' in Shakespeare's *Henry IV.*

Jimmy Gallagher, one of the gang's members, for assault the previous September. Gallagher had served fourteen days in Strangeways as a result. Horrocks was walking home through Gravel Lane at half past eleven on a Saturday night when the scuttlers spotted him. Around thirty of them were spread out across the street. Bert Childs shouted, 'Here's Jimmy Horrocks, who did Gallagher.' Childs struck Horrocks and knocked him down, screaming, 'We will kill you!' The scuttlers crowded round to administer their customary beating with buckles, lashing him unconscious. Childs walked away with Horrocks's hat while one of the other lads stole his muffler.

P.C. Patterson of the Salford Borough Police found Horrocks lying insensible in Gravel Lane and hailed a horse-drawn cab to take him to Salford Royal Hospital. The intrepid P.C. Patterson then rounded up four of the Queen Street scuttlers that night, including Bert Childs, who had led the attack. Childs's sister attended the subsequent court hearing where she claimed that her brother had not worn his scuttler's belt since Mr Makinson cautioned him on a previous occasion. The stipendiary was not convinced. He jailed Childs and one of the other lads, and fined the other two.

The Queen Street scuttlers found their arch enemies in an up-and-coming gang from the Adelphi, thus continuing a tradition of hostility between the two neighbourhoods which stretched back into the 1870s. When Queen Street raided the Adelphi at pub-closing time on Saturday, 19 January 1889, 300 lads took part in a battle royal in Cook Street. Two beat constables bravely tried to disperse them but managed only a single arrest, an Adelphi lad named John Cooper, who kicked one of the officers severely before they restrained him. He was later convicted of 'scuttling with belts and knives', throwing stones and assaulting the police and got two months.

The leader of the new generation of scuttlers in the Adelphi was Joe Slavin. The Salford Borough Police kept a watchful eye on Slavin, repeatedly taking him into custody for minor breaches of the peace. On the afternoon of Sunday, 9 March 1890, P.C. Mather spotted Slavin and his followers in Mount Street in the

Adelphi. The constable approached the crowd and accused them of being drunk and disorderly. They responded with a torrent of abuse before turning to walk away. P.C. Mather grabbed one of the stragglers, fifteen-year-old Robert Cox, and took him to the police station at Salford Town Hall. Shortly afterwards, P.C. Mather spotted the gang in Bury Street. He rushed towards them, and the lads ran into Chapel Street. The determined constable kept up the chase and managed to take hold of Joe Slavin. Conveying Slavin to the police station was no easy task. He kicked the constable repeatedly, and even renewed the assault once he was inside the police station.

Slavin and Cox appeared together before stipendiary Joseph Makinson the following morning. Slavin was aged nineteen and worked as a silk stitcher. His mother, Annie Slavin, a forty-seven-year-old widow, appeared as a character witness. Mothers typically appeared on behalf of their sons in court – fathers were generally conspicuous by their absence. In part, this was because fathers were more likely to be in work, but also mothers could appeal to the chivalry of the magistrates, and they frequently pleaded that only their son's wages enabled them to make ends meet. Mrs Slavin swore that her son was 'a good, quiet lad', but even in the dock his 'impudence' gravely offended Mr Makinson, who sentenced him to one month's hard labour. Cox got fourteen days.

Slavin was back at liberty for only six weeks before his next brush with P.C. Mather. On May 17, the constable spotted Slavin 'obstructing the footpath' in Rosamond Street. Slavin swore at the officer, adding, 'That was the – sod who gave me one month.' The unbending Mather arrested Slavin once again. When the case came before Salford Police Court, the constable told how he had witnessed the prisoner 'pushing young girls off the footpath'. Mather was adamant that, 'Slavin was as big a scuttler as was to be found in the Adelphi.' The magistrates took a sanguine view; they fined Joe Slavin five shillings for obstructing the footpath and 'using profane and abusive language'.

The notoriety of the Adelphi scuttlers was enhanced by the conduct of the gang's female members. One of Joe Slavin's neighbours, seventeen-year-old Lizzie Gordon, appeared at the Salford Police Court in February 1890 when she accused John Green of assaulting her. According to Gordon's version of events, she had been playing with a group of other girls in Gun Street in the Adelphi on a Monday night when Green hit her repeatedly in the face and kicked her. Green had a very different tale to tell. He claimed that Gordon had been abusing his wife; he went out into the street to chastise her, and 'hit her lightly on the face'. Gordon and two of her companions took off their clogs and tried to strike him with them. She threatened to 'get a – poker to him' and banged at the door of a nearby house, demanding a poker from the startled occupant, a Mrs Greaves. When Mrs Greaves refused her request, Gordon confronted Green at his own front door, warning him, 'I will get a – knife and stick it through you the same as I have done Paddy Melling.' Several of John Green's neighbours appeared in court on his behalf. They confirmed that Gordon was one of a gang of girls who assembled in Gun Street every night, to the perpetual annoyance of the neighbours. Joseph Makinson threw out the charge of assault against John Green, commenting that the girls were evidently 'a bad lot'. The stipendiary's fears were confirmed when another batch of 'scuttleresses' came before him later that year. Lizzie Gordon's younger sister, Sarah Ann, had been assaulted after their mother refused to allow the two girls to associate with the local scuttlers any longer.

The reputation of the Adelphi scuttlers was such that they were repeatedly targeted by gangs from Manchester. At around three o'clock on the afternoon of Sunday, 17 March 1889, the Bungall Boys from Fairfield Street ventured into Salford to fight a pitched battle with the Adelphi scuttlers in Chapel Street.[18] The two gangs fought with stones and belts, but quickly dispersed upon the arrival of officers from the police station at nearby Salford Town Hall. Three of the Adelphi lads ran into a

---

18 By the mid-1890s the Bungall Boys were one of the most-feared gangs in Manchester. The exploits of their then-leader, Tommy Callaghan, are described in Chapter 18.

side street, where a woman offered them sanctuary. Her husband told them to hide upstairs before the police arrived, but Sergeant Tom Quick of the Salford Borough Police found them under the couple's bed. When the three were brought before the magistrates, Superintendent Donohue told the court that the shopkeepers of Chapel Street were plagued by gangs of scuttlers. Six extra officers had been detailed to patrol Chapel Street, yet scuttling remained a nightly occurrence. The three lads were convicted of riotous and disorderly conduct, and fined.

The machinations of the Adelphi scuttleresses aroused heated local debate following a raid by a gang from Angel Meadow in December 1889. The Meadow Lads turned up at around half-past eleven on a Saturday night, as the pubs were chucking out. As they marched into the heart of the Adelphi, their chant echoed off the walls of the factory buildings: 'We are the merry boys from the Meadow! We fear no man, woman or child!' When they found the local scuttlers in Blackburn Street, an almighty row ensued. Stones flew back and forth across the street as dozens of young men and boys waded into combat with pokers, knives and belts. A passing beat constable tried to order them to disperse but a group of Meadow Lads broke away from the fray and attacked him. The officer warded off a fierce blow from a poker before retreating to Salford Town Hall for reinforcements.

The Adelphi scuttlers were routed on their own turf. Their retreat was far from orderly; they split up and ran in all directions, desperate to flee the whirling belts of the Meadow Lads. Jim Preston, a sixteen-year-old labourer, ran into nearby Flax Street and made straight for the house of a fellow Adelphi lad, Ned Barry. The door was open and Preston flew inside, slamming the door shut behind him. Seconds later, a shower of bricks and stones hit the door, followed by blows from pokers. Edward Barry senior, a forty-four-year-old bricklayer's labourer, realised instantly what was afoot. He put his shoulder to the door to prevent it from being kicked open and did not move for twenty minutes. When Mr Barry finally ventured out into the street, he was accompanied by his oldest son, Patrick, a twenty-one-year-old labourer, as well as a nervous Jim Preston. The Meadow Lads were still waiting. One of them struck a fierce blow at Preston with a poker. Another lunged at Patrick Barry. Edward Barry senior waded into them, kicking out at the crowd of youths. Four or five of them closed on him, lashing out with their pokers and the buckle ends of their belts.

Four Meadow Lads were subsequently rounded up following a prolonged operation by Salford detectives. When they appeared at the Salford Police Court, Mr Barry senior told the court that 'some girls, who were the instigation of it all, should be in the dock'. The prisoners were tried at the Quarter Sessions for riot and unlawfully wounding Edward Barry. Mr Barry told the court how Jim Preston had come running into his house shouting 'the Meadow!' When he finally ventured out into the street, Mr Barry continued, he 'got a clout with a belt and another big clout with a poker'. The Meadow Lads' only defence was that Preston had assaulted one of them two or three days before the row. The jury found all four prisoners guilty and recorder Joseph Maghull Yates sent them all to Strangeways: Jimmy Martin and Ted White for seven months, the other two for four. Martin was not surprised at the severity of the sentence. At the age of eighteen, he had already served two terms of imprisonment for theft and he had three further previous convictions for assault.

Two more Meadow Lads were apprehended in the days following the trial at the Quarter Sessions. Eighteen-year-old Paddy Callaghan had left Manchester as police inquiries gathered momentum. He found employment in Liverpool, and stayed there until the trial was over. He then returned to Manchester, assuming that the police would now let the matter drop, only to be arrested a few days later. He was brought before the magistrates and charged with disorderly conduct and assaulting P.C. Moore, the officer attacked during the battle. Callaghan was sentenced to two months' hard labour. Thomas Kelly, also aged eighteen, was brought before the magistrates the following week. Like Callaghan, he had vanished in the wake of the affray. Kelly claimed that there was nothing suspicious about his apparent disappearance: he had lost his employment and 'went to sea'. The magistrates were more impressed by the testimony of P.C Moore, who described how Kelly had wielded a belt during the scuttle in Blackburn Street. Kelly was jailed for one month. Jimmy Worsley, who gave evidence on Kelly's behalf, was himself charged with threatening a witness in the case, a girl, after she told the magistrates that Worsley had threatened to 'put her in a hole in the ground'. Stipendiary Makinson promised to punish severely anyone who molested witnesses, only to undermine his own bombast by allowing Worsley to go free.

WHILE GREENGATE and the Adelphi had been recognised as hotbeds of scuttling since the 1870s, Pendleton, on the western fringes of Salford, had generally been regarded as a more respectable, law-abiding district. Pendleton, admittedly, had its own legendary 'hard' men, not least among the rugged colliers of Whit Lane, but in general the area was regarded as being a cut above the slums of the Adelphi.

Perceptions of Pendleton began to shift in the late 1880s, following the emergence of two formidable gangs of scuttlers. The Chaney Street gang hailed from 'Hanky Park', a small slum in the heart of Pendleton. Their adopted pub, the Red Lion, at the corner of Chaney Street and Pimlot Street, was known in later years as 'the Mad House'. According to local lore, the nickname stemmed from the strength of the beverages supplied by Chesters brewery in Ardwick: Chesters 'fighting mild' was the stuff of local legend. Like the Adelphi scuttlers, the Chaney Street gang owed much of its notoriety to its female members.[19] In November 1889, Chaney Street was raided by the Queen Street scuttlers. Running battles saw the Hanky Park lads chased into Hankinson Street, where two of them were stabbed. Alf Blakely and John Donohue were attacked after the scuttle between the two gangs appeared to have subsided. They were stood at the corner of Hankinson Street and Franchise Street, discussing the fight that had just taken place, when three of the Queen Street lads sprang at them from a nearby alleyway. George Mottershead, a nineteen-

19 See Chapter 16.

year-old cooper from Greengate, stabbed Donohue on the arm and William Sewell, a seventeen-year-old moulder, followed up with a blow from a piece of iron.

Mottershead and Sewell stood trial for unlawful wounding at the Manchester Assizes, along with Frank Lord, a seventeen-year-old labourer from Chaney Street. A number of Hanky Park residents came forward as witnesses. Clara Downey from Chaney Street told the court she had overheard a conversation between the Queen Street lads in which Mottershead said to one of his companions, 'I'll run at him [Donohue] if you drop him.' She then claimed to have seen the Queen Street scuttlers again after the attack; at this point, Mottershead took a knife out of his pocket and stated, 'There is no blood on it; I don't think it has hurt him.' Eddie Taylor, one of Donohue's neighbours, told the court that Mottershead brandished a knife at him, threatening to 'run it into my bleeding heart'. However, Downey and Taylor were far from neutral witnesses. As residents of Hanky Park, it was to be expected that their testimonies would cast the Queen Street lads in a bad light. Nonetheless, the jury was convinced. They found all three prisoners guilty and they were sent down for six months.

The Whit Lane scuttlers drew inspiration from the five-month visit to Salford of 'Buffalo Bill's Wild West' show in 1887-8. Led by 'Buffalo' Bill Cody, the legendary U.S. army scout, the performance featured ninety-seven Lakota Indians, part of the Sioux nation, as well as 180 broncos and eighteen buffalo. The Wild West show had been the centrepiece of the American Exhibition at Earl's Court, London, staged as part of the Golden Jubilee celebrations for Queen Victoria in May 1887. In December, Cody and the Lakota set up camp on the Manchester Racecourse in Ordsall, where ten thousand people gathered for the inaugural performance. Daring scenes of gun-slinging and horsemanship delighted the crowd. The *Manchester Weekly Times* commented that Cody 'looks as great a hero in person as he does in his pictures'. The Whit Lane scuttlers were mightily impressed, and quickly renamed themselves 'Buffalo Bill's gang'. They could hardly have been less like the wild horsemen of the plains. The core of the gang was a group of colliers in their late teens who worked together at the Pendleton pit, reputedly the hottest in Britain and the most difficult for extracting coal.

In October 1889, Buffalo Bill's gang raided Hanky Park in search of the Chaney Street scuttlers. The Whit Lane lads spread out across Hankinson Street with knives and belts in their hands, threatening any youths who passed and assaulting those who dared to answer back. One refused to kowtow to the intruders and was badly beaten by Joe Allen, an eighteen-year-old collier, with a belt.

When Allen subsequently appeared at the Salford Police Court, he was followed into the dock by a second member of Buffalo Bill's gang. Seventeen-year-old Jimmy Foley was accused of assaulting Edward Thomas, a resident of Gill Street in the gang's own neighbourhood of Whit Lane. Mr Thomas had tired of the youths' antics. When he finally confronted the scuttlers, asking them to move away from his front door, he was subjected to a string of curses and threats. Mr Thomas was furious. He walked up to Jimmy Foley and pushed him in the chest, only for Foley to unleash two blows to his head with the buckle end of his belt. Foley and Allen were both jailed. The same pair were arrested again on the night of Saturday, 18 January 1890, following an attack upon John Cunliffe, another Whit Lane collier. On this occasion, they were charged with unlawful wounding. Two female members of Buffalo Bill's gang, Amelia Higginbottom and Agnes Garforth, stood trial alongside them (see Chapter 16).

The arrest of four of their members did nothing to dampen the spirits of Buffalo Bill's gang. In a determined show of strength, they made another raid on Chaney Street the following Saturday night. The local scuttlers were initially nowhere to be seen, so the Whit Lane mob began to comb the streets of Hanky Park. They eventually spotted one of the prominent Chaney Street lads, Tommy Gledstone, in Peel Street. Gledstone was out walking with his sweetheart, Maggie Cavanagh. The Whit Lane lads did not concern themselves with the etiquette of the fair fight. They charged at the startled couple and swung at Gledstone with their belts. He managed to run into a shop and, having vaulted over the counter, fled through the back door. Maggie Cavanagh ran into Chaney Street, but the Whit Lane lads soon caught up with her. Dick Wilcock called out, 'Off with your – belts,' and struck the first blow to Cavanagh's shoulder. To his amazement, she grabbed the end of the belt and refused to let go. An unseemly tug-of-war was interrupted by the unexpected arrival of two beat constables, who managed to arrest Wilcock. He was jailed for a month.

November 1889 saw the inauguration of a new court of Quarter Sessions for the Borough of Salford. Joseph Maghull Yates, Q.C., was appointed to preside over the court as the first Recorder of Salford. The first sitting was held on Monday, November 4.[20] The second prisoner brought before Mr Yates was the twenty-seven-year-old former scuttler Amos Briggs, charged with the theft of thirty pairs of boots from a shop in Chapel Street. After sentencing Briggs to four months' imprisonment and seeing him removed to another stint in Strangeways, the recorder adjourned to a grand lunch with assembled civic dignitaries at the Salford Town Hall.

The first active scuttlers to appear at the Salford Borough Quarter Sessions were brought before Joseph Maghull Yates at the second sitting of the court on Tuesday, 4 February 1890. Mr Yates was confronted by three separate batches of scuttlers, accounting for no fewer than fourteen of the thirty-five prisoners brought before him. They included well-known members of gangs from Manchester as well as Salford: the four Meadow Lads charged with riot and unlawfully wounding Edward Barry in the Adelphi on December 7; four members of Buffalo Bill's gang charged with assaulting John Cunliffe on January 18; and six members of another Salford gang – Hope Street – charged with unlawful wounding following a clash with their avowed enemies from Ordsall Lane.

---

20 Cases from Salford had previously been committed to the county quarter sessions – the Salford Hundred Quarter Sessions – along with cases from the townships to the east of Manchester such as Bradford, Gorton and Openshaw.

In his opening address to the grand jury, Mr Yates drew attention to the cluster of scuttling cases, pointing out that when gangs of young men and women combined to inflict injuries, all of those taking part were equally guilty irrespective of who struck the blows. It was, declared Yates, a serious thing for law-abiding citizens that gangs of scuttlers were resorting to 'that most un-English weapon', the knife. The jury heeded Yates's advice. They found thirteen of the fourteen scuttlers guilty as charged. Yates sentenced all fourteen to hard labour; half of them for terms of five months, or longer. The recorder was applauded for his severity in the local press; at last, here was a judge prepared to come down with the full force of the law.

However, these exemplary sentences did not have the deterrent effect that Yates envisaged. Salford witnessed renewed outbreaks of scuttling during February and March 1890. And on April 7, a Bank Holiday Monday, a renewal of hostilities between Hope Street and Ordsall Lane led to an intensive police operation in which seventeen people were arrested. Their trial in June prompted apocalyptic newspaper headlines. By the summer of 1890, the anxieties surrounding scuttling in Salford were at boiling-point. At the same time, alarm was rapidly mounting in Manchester, where it reached a crescendo in August.

THE APPEARANCE of five Harpurhey scuttlers at the Manchester Quarter Sessions on August 12 brought the debate on how to deal with the menace of scuttling to a head. The Recorder of Manchester, Henry West, sentenced two of the prisoners to terms of five years' penal servitude. However, the jury called upon the Recorder to have the scuttlers flogged. West could only declare that he possessed no such powers under English law, before calling for a public debate on the punishment of scuttlers. Two days later, Charles Lister told a meeting of his fellow Manchester magistrates that he intended to move a resolution at their next meeting, calling upon the Home Secretary to introduce a bill to authorise corporal punishment for those convicted of assaults with knives and other dangerous weapons. As Lister saw it, recourse to the Home Secretary was the only option left in the wake of the recent spate of affrays and the repeated pleas by local juries for the introduction of the cat. Many people in Manchester harked back to the 'garrotting' episode of the 1860s. It was still widely reported in the press that the lash of the cat o' nine tails had rendered the streets safe on that occasion. Many jurors fervently believed it could so again.

Charles Lister had qualified as a solicitor in 1864. He was a devout Anglican and a staunch Conservative. After joining the ranks of the Manchester magistrates, he developed a keen interest in prison reform and especially in the plight of first-time offenders. He was convinced that greater clemency – a friendly warning from the bench, followed by acquittal rather than imprisonment – was the most likely means of assisting their 'moral recovery'. As Lister saw it, many of the younger first offenders found themselves before the magistrates through thoughtlessness rather than premeditation. He frequently expressed these views not just to his fellow magistrates but to the wider Manchester public through letters to the newspapers. He urged that these relatively harmless offenders should be spared both the stigma of imprisonment and the risk of 'contamination' by older prisoners. However, Lister's concern for the well-being of the youthful miscreant did not extend to scuttlers.

The next meeting of the Manchester magistrates was held on August 28 at the City Police Court in Minshull Street. Scuttlers had appeared here in droves over the course of the previous two decades; now the magistrates gathered as a body to ponder how the city might finally rid itself of them. Lister's resolution demanded that 'the attention of the Home Secretary be called to the most dangerous practice of scuttling as at present practiced in this and other large towns, and that he be asked to introduce a measure as early as possible enabling magistrates and courts of Quarter Sessions to inflict corporal punishment upon persons convicted of violent assaults, and especially assaults with knives and other dangerous weapons'.

As Lister remarked, the problem was only too familiar to all of those present. Scuttling had reached an intolerable level; it was clear that the existing penalties were inadequate and that imprisonment was no remedy. Confirming that he had been moved to bring the resolution following the appearance of the five Harpurhey scuttlers at the Quarter Sessions, Lister read a lengthy extract from the *Manchester Guardian*'s report of the trial. The magistrates listened in grim silence to the tale of scuttlers marching, like an army, into a desperate combat with knives and belts in which terrible wounds were inflicted. Lister reminded his fellow magistrates that the Recorder of Manchester had called for introduction of corporal punishment at the end of the trial; the chairman of the Salford Hundred Quarter Sessions, W. H. Higgin, was well known to be in agreement.

Lister concluded that there was only one cure for scuttling: the offenders 'should have a taste of corporal punishment'. Nothing was to be gained by sending rough lads to prison only to see them emerge as hardened criminals, or 'gaol-birds'. In some of the cases tried by Higgin at the Quarter Sessions, scuttlers had been jailed for nine months for a first offence, then eighteen months for the second. In several instances, 'Directly they came out of gaol, they had simply gone straight away and started the thing again.' Referring to the sentences of five years imposed upon John Dumphy and Jimmy Barlow from Harpurhey, Mr Lister asked, 'Would it not have been better to have given those youths a good sound flogging rather than to have sent them into penal servitude for five years? If youths chose to use knives upon other people it was only right that they should have a taste of pain themselves.' At present, Lister added, there were more youths in Strangeways for scuttling than for practically any other offence. Flogging might put a stop to scuttling; in any case, it was better than filling the prison with lads.

Francis Headlam, Manchester's stipendiary magistrate, spoke strongly in support of the motion. 'It is quite evident that the present system does not deter people,' he said. 'There is no doubt that these young scoundrels are great cowards and bullies, and corporal punishment is therefore more likely to deter them than imprisonment, for bullies dislike pain more than anything else. That was clearly shown in the garrotting cases. When flogging was allowed, garrotting ceased.'

Thomas Horsfall, pioneer of the Manchester Art Museum in Ancoats Hall, one of the city's boldest experiments in social reform, told his fellow magistrates that Ancoats was terrorised by these lads and many people went in fear of their lives.[21] However, he suggested that many of the youths involved were themselves the victims of terror: 'They joined an organisation which contained only a few pronounced ruffians, and when a row began they dare not desert their comrades, because they knew that they themselves would either be knocked down or cut ... The fact that these lads went on with these disgraceful rows was not a proof of pluck but rather a proof of cowardice.' Horsfall claimed that the origins of the problem lay in Manchester's schools. Few boys learned games in school; those that did had nowhere to play apart from the streets, which only served to bring them into conflict with the police. The result was that by the time they began full-time work, at the age of twelve or thirteen, lads in districts such as Ancoats had already grown to regard the law as their enemy.

Charles Lister's resolution was passed. The magistrates appointed the Mayor of Manchester along with Lister and Headlam to form a deputation to confer with no less a person than the Home Secretary. Support for Lister's resolution was also forthcoming from the county magistrates. At a meeting on September 8, they in turn resolved to appoint a deputation to meet with the Home Secretary to press for powers to inflict corporal punishment upon those convicted of 'the violent and brutal practices known as scuttling'. Support also came from Salford. The Mayor of Salford had already written to the borough's three Members of Parliament seven months earlier, requesting that they should lobby for the introduction of a bill to authorise the flogging of scuttlers convicted at the Quarter Sessions. The new recorder, Joseph Maghull Yates, was not an advocate of flogging but the Salford magistrates showed no such

---

21 Horsfall saw art as a means of ameliorating 'the dullness and miserableness of the life of our towns' and thus combating the spread of vice, crime and pauperism. His Art Museum, which opened in 1886, contained oil and water colour paintings, engravings, etchings, photographs and pieces of sculpture.

qualms. They unanimously endorsed Lister's resolution at a special meeting convened by the Mayor on October 17.

WHILE JUDICIAL authorities across the conurbation debated the problem of scuttling throughout the autumn of 1890, on the streets of Manchester, Salford, and the eastern townships the gang wars raged unabated. On August 5, with the exploits of the Harpurhey scuttlers already gathering headlines following their desperate affray with the Bengal Tigers in Lees Street, three more scuttling cases were tried at the Manchester City Police Court. Four lads were jailed for one month each following an affray in Butler Street in Ancoats. It was reported that one of the youths wore his army uniform during the fight. A Beswick scuttler was sent down for four months following a gang fight in Chancery Lane; the gangs stopped fighting and joined forces when a police constable tried to break it up. Two brothers from the Deansgate district were arrested after they ambushed a Salford youth outside the Dragon public house on Bridge Street. One of the Deansgate lads had previously been locked up for an assault on a member of a touring Midget Minstrel troupe.

On the following Sunday afternoon – just two days before the Harpurhey scuttlers appeared at the Manchester Quarter Sessions – the Whit Lane scuttlers were on the prowl once more in Pendleton. On this occasion, the target of Buffalo Bill's gang was a youth named Francis McCoy. Dick Wilcock ran up to McCoy in Shuttleworth Street, shouting, 'I will cut your bleeding heart out!' McCoy fled, taking refuge in the house of a man named George Acton. When Mr Acton went out into the street with a poker to chase the scuttlers off, they attacked him with their belts. Mr Acton put his hands up to shield his head. The force of one blow shattered one of his fingers. Four of the scuttlers were later arrested and were remanded in custody for a week after the Salford magistrates heard that their victim's finger might have to be amputated. Three of the Whit Lane lads were eventually convicted of scuttling and unlawful wounding and were jailed. One had only just completed a six-month sentence imposed in February, while another had served one month following a conviction for scuttling in January. Reports on the case in the local press appeared to provide ample support for Henry West's call for the introduction of flogging for scuttlers.

The following month saw a spate of scuttling in the Manchester district of Hulme. The Bungall Boys from Fairfield Street raided Vine Street in Hulme on the night of Saturday, September 6. The customary belts and knives were freely used in the row. One of the combatants even grabbed a hammer belonging to a local woman to use in the fray. When she demanded it back, one of the scuttlers threatened to 'rip her up'. Arthur Hilton of the Bungall Boys was identified by the police as the ringleader of the disturbance. He had two previous convictions for scuttling and the magistrates now gave him six months.

At around midnight on Saturday, November 1, police were called to Holland Street in Miles Platting following cries of 'Murder!' The first two constables to arrive were stunned to find no fewer than 500 lads fighting with knives and belts. Reinforcements were summoned from 'B' Division of the Manchester police before any attempt was made to disperse one of the biggest mass scuttles ever witnessed. When the police finally went in, they went in hard. Charging with truncheons drawn, they managed to clear the street, taking three lads into custody. Thomas Cannon, one of the Holland Street scuttlers, later appeared in court alongside two of his opponents, John McClelland and Charlie Mulholland of the Meadow Lads, who had been among a mob that had marched through the heart of Ancoats into Miles Platting. The prisoners, described by court reporters as 'rough-looking young fellows', were each sent down for one month.

HULME LAY to the south-west of Manchester city centre. For much of the Victorian era, it had been regarded as a more respectable district than Angel Meadow or Ancoats. Nonetheless, life in Hulme, as elsewhere in the ring of factory districts that surrounded the city centre, was characterised by overcrowding, ill-health and grinding poverty. Most of the housing stock had been jerry-built during the 1830s and 1840s. By the closing decades of the century, Hulme was widely regarded as a slum. Sir Thomas Thornhill Shann, Lord Mayor of Manchester from 1903 to 1905, spoke of 'drink-cursed, God-forsaken Hulme', and Charles Russell observed that the district's vast population was almost entirely working-class: 'Among the 80,000 inhabitants ... is to be found only a tiny minority of persons of much education or refinement, these being with rare exceptions doctors, or ministers of the various religious denominations, and their wives.' Local families tended to be headed by semi-skilled or unskilled manual workers, who found employment in the factories and mills within Hulme itself or in the neighbouring districts of Chorlton-on-Medlock and Salford.

During the autumn of 1888, Hulme was terrorised by a young man pretending to be Jack the Ripper. Stephen Rourke, who lived in nearby Ardwick, reportedly took to prowling the streets of neighbouring districts at night, searching for women out alone. Around midnight on October 9 – just nine days after a gruesome double killing by the 'Ripper' in Whitechapel in London's East End – Rourke headed into Hulme. He spotted a woman and followed her to her home in Clopton Street, pestering her all the way, hissing threats and telling her he was 'Jack'. Rourke was arrested and brought before the magistrates. The woman, however, failed to appear to testify. Subsequent police inquiries revealed that she was 'a woman of dissipated habits' whose husband refused to live with her. Rourke's employers, on the other hand, gave him an 'excellent character', stating that he had been in their service for eight years. The case was dismissed, leading the *Manchester Guardian* to describe the allegations as 'trumped up'. We will never know what Rourke did, or did not, get up to, but press reports of 'WOMEN TERRORISED IN HULME' told their own story. The Whitechapel terror had gripped Manchester, however fleetingly.

Clopton Street, in the heart of Hulme, was plagued by scuttlers during the early 1890s. In March 1893, twenty of the street's residents petitioned the Watch Committee of Manchester

City Council to protest at 'the gangs of youths of both sexes who have molested us in various ways'. The gangs had taken to stoning adults who complained about their activities; one of the signatories to the petition had lost an eye as a result. Disorderly young women supplied the missiles 'from their aprons', while lads and lasses alike had bonneted the terrified residents. Bonneting – knocking someone's hat off in the street – was a traditional means of humiliating those with 'airs and graces' and it is likely that Clopton Street was the site of mutual loathing between local young roughs and the district's more genteel inhabitants. The scuttlers even stripped advertising posters from nearby hoardings, rolling them up to use instead of belts to torment their accusers.

William Luby was born in a street off Clarendon Street, a stone's throw from Clopton Street, in 1883. His grandfather had fled Kilkenny in County Waterford during the Great Famine of the 1840s and settled in Hulme, where he raised seven children. According to William, when he was interviewed at the age of eighty, the extended family was close-knit and clannish. The men were prodigious drinkers and, as a child, William's job was to replenish the beer bucket which stood on the family's dinner table. Fighting was a way of life. 'It was very common,' recalled Luby. 'The workshops, the public houses at the time of Sullivan or Corbett, the men were always fighting. In fact, behind my grandfather's house there was a canal and a croft. Any quarrels which my grandfather and any of his sons had with anybody would be settled by one son on the Sunday morning on this croft. Because one son was kept for that purpose, fighting. He was a fighter for the family. Bare fists ... And very often his opponent was knocked out. They'd throw him in the canal and then bring him out when he'd recovered. 'Course, often enough a ducking would be enough [to bring him round].'

John L. Sullivan and 'Gentleman Jim' Corbett were fighters of international repute when Queensberry Rules finally came to govern heavyweight championship prize fights during the early 1890s. Sullivan had fought the last bare-knuckle heavyweight title fight against Jake Kilrain in 1889. Corbett then defeated

Sullivan with padded gloves in New Orleans on 7 September 1892 to become the first professional champion under Queensberry Rules. William Luby, who heard all about the fight from his father and uncles in Hulme, was nine years old at the time.

THE JOINT civic deputation from Manchester and Salford met with Henry Matthews, Home Secretary in the Conservative government of Lord Salisbury, at the House of Commons at one o'clock on Friday, December 12. The deputation was introduced by Lees Knowles, the Conservative M.P. for West Salford. Its members included the Mayor of Manchester, Alderman John Mark, and the stipendiary magistrates for Manchester, Salford, and the eastern townships: Francis Headlam, Joseph Makinson and J. H. P. Leresche. Charles Lister joined them in his capacity as a prison visitor at Strangeways Prison.

For the benefit of the Home Secretary, the Mayor defined scuttling as 'faction fights' in which gangs of young men and women fought regular territorial battles against rivals 'armed with such weapons as leather belts with heavy brass buckles attached, loaded sticks, sticks studded with spikes or nails, knives, pieces of iron, short pokers, stones, and clogs'. Specimens of such weapons retrieved by the police after scuttles were then shown to Henry Matthews. As the Mayor pointed out, such weapons were often used to wound policemen as well as rival scuttlers; in some cases, officers had been so badly beaten as to render them unfit for further duties. Much damage was done to property during gang brawls and peaceful passers-by were often assaulted. The Mayor then pleaded on behalf of the city for the introduction of corporal punishment, echoing Charles Lister's view that young men were better dealt with by whipping than by imprisonment. Fines were quite useless, the Mayor added, since scuttlers banded together to raise the money to pay them and levied any outstanding sums by blackmailing shopkeepers. When scuttlers emerged from prison, they were treated as heroes and elevated to the status of 'captain'.

Francis Headlam proposed that the severity of corporal

punishment should be determined by the prisoner's age: the birch rod should be used on younger scuttlers, whereas the older ones ought to be flogged with the cat. Headlam was convinced that the cat would put a stop to scuttling, just as it had reputedly put a stop to garrotting and robbery with violence. Joseph Makinson told the Home Secretary that the power to impose corporal punishment should be given to the magistrates, so that offenders could be promptly dealt upon conviction at the police courts, before the feelings stirred by these outrages 'cooled down'. Makinson raised the case of Peter Moffatt, the leader of the Ordsall Lane gang from Salford, who had served a nine-month prison sentence for scuttling only to renew hostilities on the very day that he was released (see Chapter 14). As Moffatt's behaviour showed, imprisonment seemed to be futile as a deterrent.

Henry Matthews, a distinguished lawyer prior to his appointment as Home Secretary in 1886, listened intently to the deputation's case. His response, however, was lukewarm. He pointed out that it would be difficult to frame a legal definition of scuttling which would distinguish it from other cases of assault, unlawful wounding or inflicting grievous bodily harm. Moreover, 'It would be a startling proposition to say that all such cases are to be punished by flogging.' In any case, the Home Secretary continued, 'It would be hopeless to propose that to the House of Commons in its present mood, as they were very averse to punishment by flogging, especially in the case of big boys and men.' The Home Secretary invited the members of the deputation to devise a legal definition of scuttling themselves, assuring them that he would be extremely glad to see it. Yet his response held out little hope that the Conservative Government would come to Manchester's aid in dealing with the gangs. Lees Knowles was left to thank the Home Secretary for his courtesy in receiving the deputation, adding meekly that 'they had partly attained their object by directing public attention to the question'.

Henry Matthews was a good judge of the mood of Parliament. Moreover, even within Manchester, the local press was by no means united behind the demand for the whip for scuttlers. The avowedly Conservative *Salford Chronicle* was hawkish and railed against the apparent indifference of the Home Secretary. Yet the liberal *Manchester Guardian*, the only local newspaper to command national influence, remained unconvinced of the utility of flogging as a deterrent and feared that its introduction would degrade prison staff. In pointing out that 'the punishment has been altogether abandoned in every civilised country except our own', the *Guardian* was much closer to parliamentary opinion than the city's magistrates.

Francis Headlam, Manchester's stipendiary, attempted to devise a legal clause to be applied in scuttling cases. Headlam came from a very different social universe from the lads who were posing so much trouble on the teeming streets of industrial Ancoats and Salford. Born in 1829, his father was Rector of Wycliffe and Archdeacon of Richmond, Yorkshire. Francis was educated at Eton College and Oxford, where he became a fellow, and then bursar, of University College. He left to become a barrister in 1858 and practised on the Northern legal circuit, mainly at the Quarter Sessions at Berwick, Durham and Northumberland. Headlam was appointed as stipendiary magistrate for the city of Manchester in 1869 and was to hold the office for more than thirty years. He acquired a reputation for being firm, yet merciful. He rarely courted publicity, in stark contrast to his counterparts in Salford, and his adjudications were frequently terse. Many offenders were sent down with a curtly muttered, 'Fourteen days' hard labour,' or, 'Three months.' The satirical *Free Lance* observed in 1876, 'His decisions are, as a rule, mumbled forth in tones almost inaudible, and he seldom ventures to give a reason.' Nonetheless, the *Free Lance* praised Headlam's abilities: 'If the stipendiary is not a brilliant luminary, he is at least painstaking and leans, generally, to the side of mercy.'

In January 1891, still hopeful of an Act of Parliament to address Manchester's tribes of warring youths, Headlam proposed that scuttlers might be defined as: 'Any person or persons armed with dangerous weapons, intending to cause a riot or commit a breach of the peace and commit an assault with any such weapon.' However, Manchester's plea for legislation fell on deaf ears; no Act was forthcoming. If gangs of scuttlers were to be driven from the streets, then means other than the lash would have to be found.

CHAPTER 14

Vendetta

THE HOPE STREET district of Salford has been described as 'the classic slum'. In many ways, as local author Robert Roberts pointed out, the district functioned like an urban village: an almost self-contained community of around thirty streets and courts, bounded by railway lines to the north and south, Oldfield Road to the east, and Cross Lane to the west. Most of the houses dated from the first half of the nineteenth century. According to Friedrich Engels, writing in the 1840s, the district vied with the Old Town of Manchester in filth and overcrowding. During the 1880s and 1890s, the population of the district was still overwhelmingly working-class. Skilled artisans, shopkeepers and publicans formed a local elite. The bulk of the population, however, were semi-skilled and unskilled manual workers and their families, eking out a living on low and often precarious wages.

The standard of housing varied greatly. Most families aspired to a four-roomed terraced house. With two rooms downstairs, two bedrooms upstairs and a backyard, such properties were cramped enough for those with large families, but they were spacious indeed when compared to the older courtyard properties that had appalled Engels. Derbyshire Court, off Hope Street, comprised four houses, each of which contained only two rooms: one up, one down. There was one communal tap in the courtyard, and two outdoor lavatories between the four houses. Some of the houses were home to as many as nine or ten people.

Ordsall lay south of Hope Street. It consisted for the most part of more uniform streets of terraced houses built during the

1860s and 1870s to accommodate the workforces of Haworth's mills and Worrall's dye-works in Ordsall Lane. Like Hope Street, Ordsall was predominantly working-class. Many families were headed by factory workers, but outdoor labourers, many of Irish descent, arrived in large numbers during the construction of the Manchester Ship Canal prior to the opening of the Salford docks in 1894. The excavation of the docks was a vast enterprise: it took thousands of men and boys to move the required 44 million cubic yards of earth. Ordsall acquired a reputation as an 'Irish' district, even though the majority of residents were in fact English-born Protestants.

An infantry barracks occupied a nine-acre site on Regent Road on the northern fringe of Ordsall. As the pioneering trade unionist W. H. Wood noted in 1890, the barracks were a good source of business for local shopkeepers and publicans. Wood was too delicate to say so, but they also lured large numbers of prostitutes to the pubs and beerhouses on Regent Road. A number of brothels opened in nearby Providence Street, which was quickly named 'the She Battery' by a local wag. Providence Street was legendary for the frequency and ferocity of its drunken street brawls. The residents of the She Battery fought among themselves as often as they waylaid unsuspecting outsiders, but the entire neighbourhood would join together to take on the police.

One scene from the 1880s typified the difficulties the police faced. Two detectives and a beat constable from the Salford Borough Police went to Providence Street with a warrant for a woman's arrest. They apprehended their prisoner, but as they attempted to escort her to the Regent Road police station, John Wood ran out of a neighbouring house and felled one of the detectives with a single blow to the side of the head. Wood promptly ran off, leaving the detective lying dazed in the street. When the detectives returned to Providence Street later that afternoon to look for John Wood, all hell broke loose. They chased Wood into one of the houses, only for a group of women to rush inside and surround the fugitive. One of the women set about the detectives with a porcelain dog. The officers eventually managed to drag Wood outside, only to find themselves surrounded once more. A large crowd of men and women gathered and began to pelt the police with bricks and stones, many of them supplied by Elizabeth Ann McGarry, who brought out an apron-full of missiles. The detectives retreated, before returning with reinforcements and a further ten warrants. Five men and five women were eventually convicted of assaulting the police. Nine of them were jailed, their sentences ranging from fourteen days to two months.

Austin Oates, the secretary of the Salford Catholic Protection and Rescue Society, discovered that during the 1880s most of the houses in the She Battery were sub-let: 'A person, man or woman, rents a house with five or seven rooms, pays the landlord, say, a weekly sum of six shillings or seven shillings. The tenant sub-lets the rooms he does not occupy to casual lodgers for two shillings and sixpence, two shillings, or one and six, according to size.' The overcrowding which resulted was terrible to behold:

> We enter another house. The adult lodgers are crowding the front parlour. Not an honest-looking face among them. Our business tonight is more upstairs than down. In the room over the parlour we find on the floor, in one bed, a woman of some thirty years – a girl of two years and a baby of eight months lie on either side of her. Bedclothes – the rags which cover them during the day. At the foot, stretching across the floor towards the window, lies the husband, with a youth of sixteen, and one of eleven years. The back room contains four inmates – a mother, her sister, and two children; the sister, a girl of seventeen, a new recruit to the She Battery. The attic discloses a man and two children, aged respectively eleven and nine years. 'Where is the mother?' 'Doing six months.'

The mother's cell in Strangeways provided much more spacious accommodation.

Despite the reputation of the She Battery, Ordsall was by no means the worst district in late Victorian Salford. Greengate and the Adelphi, to the north-east of Hope Street, were generally regarded as both poorer and considerably rougher by police and journalists alike. Scuttling gangs formed in the Adelphi, or Queen Street in Greengate, enjoyed fearsome reputations simply on account of the districts from which they were drawn. Gangs from Hope Street or Ordsall had to earn reputations the hard way: in the streets.

IN HIS sharply observed account of growing up in the Hope Street district, Robert Roberts described the local scuttling gang as a 'fraternity of some thirty to forty teenagers'. With a handful of exceptions, they all lived within the tightly bounded Hope Street 'village'. Most lived with their parents, who appear to have viewed scuttling with a degree of tolerance in accordance with the traditions of Salford's working-class neighbourhoods. The lads were mainly Protestants, in keeping with the wider population of the village. The Hope Street scuttlers congregated at the junction of Hope Street and Oldfield Road and, at weekends, in the nearby Prince of Wales beerhouse. Alexander Devine met some of the Hope Street scuttlers in his capacity as police court missionary at Strangeways, and noted that the lads displayed Prince of Wales' feathers as insignia on their belts.

At the height of its notoriety, from 1889 to 1890, the gang's leaders were John Allmark and Jimmy Heaton. The Allmarks were a powerful local family, three generations of whom lived in Hope Street and the surrounding streets. They were coal merchants, and employed many of the lads who joined the ranks of the Hope Street scuttlers. Jimmy Heaton was the son of a local stonemason, but he did not follow his father's trade. He worked instead as a carter for the Allmarks. Most of the Hope Street scuttlers came from large families, often with five or more children, living in four- or even two-roomed terraced houses. For example, John Dunn lived with his widowed mother, six sisters and a seventeen-year-old male lodger in a two-roomed house in Clegg's Court, near Hope Street. Dunn also worked for the Allmarks as a carter. Not surprisingly, he spent most of his free time as well as his working life on the streets of Salford.

The Allmarks' notoriety was not due solely to their lads' exploits as scuttlers. In January 1890, Fred Allmark – 'son of a well-known coal dealer', noted the *Salford Reporter* – married Mary Fletcher. The marriage met with some disapproval within the neighbourhood and a crowd of women and children assembled to wait for the bride and groom's return for the wedding party. The celebration was to be hosted by the groom's aunt and uncle at their house at 61 Hope Street. When the newly-wed couple arrived, they were showered not with rice, the customary greeting, but with rattlejacks and ashes, spoiling their wedding clothes. This was clearly the crowd's intention: rattlejacks were pieces of coke bought by the bagful from the gas works in Albion Street by those who could not afford coal. Not content with ruining Mary's dress, the protestors threw stones and old boots through the windows of the house, breaking five panes of glass in the parlour window and three in the bedroom for good measure. An elderly woman named Ellen Johnson was said to be the ringleader in the disturbance and witnesses described her as 'so excited with drink that she frothed at the mouth'.

Hannah Allmark, the groom's aunt, issued summonses against six women, including Ellen Johnson. The defendants appeared before Joseph Makinson at Salford Police Court, charged with malicious damage and using obscene language. One had tipped a bag of ashes over the bridegroom. Another 'danced about derisively' in the doorway, mocking the newly-weds as they were about to cross the threshold. Worse still, some of the protestors had grabbed bricks stashed outside a neighbouring house and begun to hurl those about the street. One of the defendants protested her innocence, claiming that 'she did not know how to fight'. Hannah Allmark replied that 'only the other day [the defendant] struck her own husband with a gallon can'. Ellen Johnson claimed that Mrs Allmark had thrown a bucket of water over her from an upstairs window during the row. Joseph Makinson remarked drily that the whole affair was 'not a creditable one' and fined all of the defendants.

A clue to the cause of the crowd's disapproval was provided by one female champion of the bridegroom. She had told the protesting women to leave him alone as 'he could not marry them all'. Fred Allmark, it appears, had been careless with his affections before choosing one woman with whom to settle down. It is perhaps significant that the protestors at the wedding party were all either women or children. Any local men or youths protesting at the behaviour of the Allmarks in this way would most likely have been severely dealt with, without resort to the courts.

The Hope Street scuttlers faced dozens of criminal charges during 1889 and 1890, whilst the gang's notoriety was at its height. Beat constables from the Salford Borough Police repeatedly broke up their street corner gatherings, making arrests for obstruction, abusive language and disorderly conduct. The police also targeted the Hope Street crew during periodic clampdowns on petty offences such as gambling at pitch and toss and bathing in the canals. The scuttlers retaliated with regular assaults upon the police.

Jimmy Heaton, who led the gang alongside John Allmark, was born in 1872 and lived with his parents and four younger brothers in Waterloo Street. Heaton was seldom out of the clutches of the police for long. He was arrested repeatedly between 1890 and 1892, facing charges of riot, unlawful wounding, assaulting the police (twice), attempting to rescue a prisoner from custody, and being drunk and disorderly. He was sentenced to six months' imprisonment in June 1890 and a further month in October 1891. His last conviction for scuttling was in 1892. Like Joe Slavin, his counterpart in the Adelphi, Heaton found that individual beat constables made a point of singling him out for attention.

Even junior members of the Hope Street gang were subjected to intense police surveillance. They too were brought before the magistrates with great frequency to face a curious mix of trivial and more serious charges, as the case of Sam Thornhill illustrated. During June 1889, at the age of fourteen, Thornhill made four appearances at the Salford Police Court in twelve days. On June 6, he was fined five shillings for bathing in the Bury and Bolton canal the previous afternoon. Three others, including another well-known Hope Street scuttler, were convicted alongside him.

Then, on the night of Saturday, June 8, the Hope Street gang ventured mob-handed into Greengate. Prowling the streets at midnight, they accosted a local youth by the name of Andrew Hind and asked him for 'a chew of tobacco'. When Hind refused, they set about him. Hind was punched, kicked and stabbed in the back. A patrolling beat constable ran to the aid of the stricken youth, only to be set upon in turn. The constable heard one of the Hope Street scuttlers shout at Hind, 'Such as you ought to be killed.' Two lads were arrested at the scene, but the rest of the gang – including Thornhill – escaped. Thornhill was taken into custody at 7.45 a.m. the next day, but his arrest had nothing to do with the stabbing of Andrew Hind. He was arrested during a police raid on an early morning gambling school, along with a fellow Hope Street scuttler. Thornhill and his mate were both fined five shillings at Salford Police Court the next morning.

Two days later, Thornhill was re-arrested; this time in connection with the stabbing of Andrew Hind. He was remanded in custody until June 17 when, along with three other scuttlers, he was found guilty of unlawful wounding. He got fourteen days. 'The borough should be cleared of these scoundrels,' declared Joseph Makinson. The stipendiary's strictures had little effect on Thornhill, who returned to the ranks of the Hope Street gang as soon as he was released from Strangeways. Thornhill's scuttling 'career' saw him endure repeated bouts of imprisonment. In October 1890, he got nine months for wounding an opponent during a scuttle in Manchester. Sam Thornhill was still aged just fifteen.

THE MEMBERSHIP of the Ordsall Lane gang was more diverse. The gang contained two factions: one comprised of youths employed at Worrall's dye-works in Ordsall Lane, the other of lads living in and around the vice strip of Providence Street, the so-called She Battery. The gang was ethnically mixed too. Some of its members were Catholics of Irish descent, in keeping with the changing character of the district. The bulk of the gang, however, were English-born Protestants. They had no sectarian quarrel with the Hope Street scuttlers. However, the sheer proximity of the two gangs ensured a natural enmity. They lived either side of the Liverpool to Manchester railway line, which carved its way through South Salford, dividing 'Hope Street' and Ordsall into clearly distinguishable – and rival – neighbourhoods.

The leading figures in the Ordsall Lane gang were Peter Moffatt, Peter Nevin, and the brothers Ralph and Squire Taylor. Nevin lived with his brother's family in Providence Street and recruited a number of She Battery lads for the Ordsall Lane gang. He also worked as a dyer at Worrall's, which meant that he played a pivotal role in the gang, helping to bond its two factions. Ralph and Squire Taylor and their seven siblings were raised by Dennis Taylor, a labourer, and his wife Ellen in Granville Street, just across Regent Road from the She Battery.

Peter Moffatt was born in Ordsall in 1870. His parents, Hugh and Margaret, came from Newcastle-under-Lyme in Staffordshire. They moved to Salford in search of work and settled in Ordsall once Hugh Moffatt found employment as a dyer at Worrall's. Peter was their first child. They nursed him in a two-up, two-down terraced house in Crowther Street shared with two other families. It was home to five adults and seven children and the Moffatts rented a single room. By the time their daughter, Maggie, was born in December 1871, they had moved a short distance to Alpha Buildings, off Regent Street. At the age of eleven, Peter Moffatt was convicted of theft and sent to an industrial school. At fifteen, he was brought back before the Salford magistrates on another charge of theft. On this occasion he was merely fined. The following month, he was back on a similar charge. He was now sentenced to twenty-one days' imprisonment, to be followed by three years on the *Akbar*, a reformatory ship for Protestant boys moored on the River Mersey at Birkenhead. With three convictions for theft at the age of fifteen Moffatt was deemed by Salford's magistrates to be an incorrigible offender even though his third conviction, in May 1885, was for stealing Eccles cakes.

Perhaps not surprisingly, Moffatt deeply resented his treatment by the judicial authorities. He was no model prisoner. Quite the reverse: in September 1887, he led a mutiny on the *Akbar*. The ship's captain was absent on leave and a group of the older inmates on board, including Moffatt, broke into his cabin to look for anything worth stealing. They took a number of pieces of jewellery and several ornaments. The break-in was later discovered by one of the other officers. Knowing that retribution would be severe, the culprits incited a mutiny. On the afternoon of Sunday, September 24, they disrupted a reading by the assistant schoolmaster. The chief officer, in charge of the *Akbar* in the captain's absence, managed to bring the boys under control and warned them of the consequences of any further breach of discipline. His strictures were ignored. They renewed the disturbance, despite pleas from the ship's chaplain. The chief officer sent for the police and an inspector and four constables from Rock Ferry, near Birkenhead, boarded the vessel. Their arrival triggered uproar. The boys began running all over the ship, shouting abuse and hurling everything they could get their hands on at the police. Having smashed all of the ship's lights, they began to wreck the furniture and fittings.

The chief officer had only four other officers and two schoolmasters on board when the disturbance broke out and, even with five policemen to assist them, they could not restore order among 150 boys. From nine o'clock in the evening until after midnight, the boys effectively took possession of the ship. All efforts to quell the disturbance seemed only to spur them on as they went about smashing up the vessel. The police were bombarded with pieces of wood and the chief officer eventually urged them to withdraw, recognising that the presence of the police was only inflaming the boys' anger.

The boys then lowered a boat. Seventeen of them rowed ashore, landing in the Dingle, a tough, dockland district on the Liverpool bank of the Mersey. They were pursued by some of the officers in another boat, but the boys got ashore first and scattered. Nine of them were recaptured overnight and brought before the Liverpool stipendiary magistrate the following morning. The ringleaders, charged with breaking into the captain's cabin and stealing the jewellery and other items as well as absconding, were Peter Moffatt and James Wilcox. All nine prisoners were remanded for a week. When they made their next appearance in court, they were joined in the dock by another five of the absconders. The magistrate asked the lads if they had anything to say for themselves. Moffatt replied, 'There are three officers in the ship who are trying to do all they can against me.' The other boys began to levy accusations against each other, arguing over who had stolen what. Moffatt, by contrast, cut a composed figure, keen to assert his right to fair treatment.

Ten of the group were committed for trial at the Liverpool Assizes, where they appeared before Mr Justice Day. They all pleaded guilty to the charge of mutiny. Justice Day caused a furore when he declined to impose any further punishment, declaring that, 'The discipline of the *Akbar* is defective, the staff of officers inadequate, and the whole matter characterises a want of firmness and determination on the part of the staff which, if exhibited at the right time, might easily have quelled the whole disturbance.' The lads were returned to the *Akbar*, where they were subjected to corporal punishment by the ship's officers: eighteen strokes of the birch rod, followed by solitary confinement in darkened cells with diets of ship's biscuit and water. A government inquiry bore out Justice Day's condemnation of the regime on the *Akbar*. Echoing the judge's blunt assessment of the collapse of discipline among the boys, HM Inspector Colonel Inglis concluded, 'The cause may readily be traced to a want of firmness and energy in dealing with a mere handful of vicious and depraved youths who would have at once succumbed to a resolute and determined effort to bring them to their senses.'

The most 'vicious and depraved' of them all, Peter Moffatt, returned to Salford at the age of eighteen having spent the bulk of the past seven years in penal confinement. His years in an industrial school and his exploits on the *Akbar* had left him with a reckless disregard for authority and a readiness to avenge the slightest insult with his fists. He enlisted in the army, but soon found that military discipline was no more to his taste than the naval regime on the Akbar. He deserted, returning once more to Salford where he quickly assumed the leadership of the Ordsall Lane scuttlers, uniting the two wings of the gang into a formidable fighting mob. His sister Maggie, two years his junior, was courting another member of the gang, an iron foundry labourer named Robert Whittaker, and revelled in her brother's reputation. During the course of 1889, the Ordsall Lane scuttlers became a force to be reckoned with on the streets of Salford.

According to the Salford police, the Hope Street and Ordsall Lane gangs 'carried on a dangerous sort of guerrilla warfare' for a period of eighteen months from January 1889, during which the two gangs clashed once or twice a week with knives, belts, and a host of improvised weapons. On the night of Sunday, 2 June 1889, the forty-strong Ordsall Lane mob raided their rivals' territory at around ten o'clock. Their main target that night was Hope Street leader John Allmark. They soon found him, lounging at his gang's adopted corner of Hope Street and Oldfield Road. Ralph Taylor seized Allmark by the collar and swung him round, before plunging a knife into his shoulder. Allmark tried to run, but he was hit on the back of the head with the buckle end of a belt. He tumbled, picked himself up, and tried again to outrun his pursuers. He looked round as he ran, only to see Peter Moffatt gaining ground on him. Moffatt ran his knife into Allmark's thigh.

Four members of the Ordsall Lane gang were subsequently apprehended by the police. At trial, their only defence was that Allmark and his companions had used 'aggravating language' to them. A surgeon from Salford Royal Hospital testified that Allmark had suffered an inch long wound on the scalp, three additional stab wounds and severe bruising to his back. The jury found Taylor and Moffatt guilty of unlawfully wounding John Allmark and both were sent down for nine months.

Whilst Moffatt and Taylor languished in Strangeways, the feud between the gangs continued. The New Year saw an intensification of hostilities. The Ordsall Lane scuttlers launched another raid on the night of Monday 6 January, 1890. This time the Hope Street lads were well-prepared. They had armed themselves with knives, pokers, belts, and sticks. The Ordsall boys were ambushed the moment they turned into Hope Street and one of them, fifteen-year-old Paddy McDonough, was badly beaten. George Leonard buckled him on the head and Billy Rogers stabbed him in the side with a knife, to shouts of, 'Go on, lads, dose him!'

Six of the Hope Street scuttlers were arrested following inquiries by the Salford Borough Police. They were charged with unlawfully wounding Patrick McDonough and riot, and were tried before the new recorder, Joseph Maghull Yates, at the recently inaugurated Salford Borough Quarter Sessions on February 4. Taking the witness stand at the outset of the hearing, McDonough swore that he had gone for an innocent stroll through Hope Street with one of his friends when they were suddenly set upon without warning. A hospital surgeon provided medical testimony, telling the jurors that McDonough had been treated for a knife wound which had left his shirt saturated with blood.

Not surprisingly, the Hope Street scuttlers contested McDonough's version of events. They told the Recorder that McDonough, far from being an innocent victim, was a scuttler himself and had taken an active part in a fully-fledged ruckus between the two gangs. McDonough denied both allegations, and the Recorder did not ask him to explain why he had chosen Hope Street for his evening stroll. The families of the Hope Street scuttlers organised a series of witnesses, including neighbours, workmates and relatives, to provide alibis. The parents of four of the prisoners swore that their sons had been at home during the evening in question. However, their testimonies were severely undermined by the counsel for the defence, Mr Cottingham, who subsequently told the jurors that the lads were present at the scene of the affray only as onlookers. A local clogmaker admitted under cross-examination that he had been asked to provide alibis for two of the lads by the mother of one of the other defendants. This points to a wider conspiracy, in which parents were not only willing to give false testimonies themselves, but were determined to arrange for other witnesses to commit perjury on their sons' behalf.

Counsel for the defence appeared to be somewhat half-hearted in his pleading in court. This was ironic in the light of the efforts made to raise his fee. The lads' parents had organised a raffle to raise the required funds, capitalising on the fact that it was the Ordsall Lane gang who were the aggressors on this occasion. As their parents saw it, the Hope Street lads had acted only in self-defence. One Hope Street shopkeeper broke ranks and testified against the prisoners, telling the court that the lads had attacked the premises next to his own, believing a member of the opposing gang to be inside.

The jury found five of the six Hope Street scuttlers guilty of riot. The Recorder sentenced them to terms of imprisonment ranging from one to five months. Two other batches of scuttlers were convicted at the Quarter Sessions on February 4 in relation to separate incidents.[22] Joseph Maghull Yates, three months into the post of Recorder of Salford, was to become much more familiar with the deeds of the Hope Street and Ordsall Lane gangs in the coming months.

PETER MOFFATT was released from Strangeways at seven o'clock on the morning of 7 April 1890. It was a Bank Holiday Monday, usually an occasion for much drunken revelry in the factory districts. Moffatt had served nine months for unlawfully wounding rival gang captain John Allmark. Moffatt's lieutenant, Ralph Taylor, had also served nine months. That afternoon, the pair made their way to their gang's adopted beerhouse, the Sunnyside Inn on Ordsall Lane. They spent the Bank Holiday renewing acquaintances and, as the beer flowed, talk turned to the ongoing feud with Hope Street. Moffatt and Taylor were still angry that several of the Hope Street lads had testified against them. As they saw it, this was no way for a true scuttler to behave. As the day wore on, talk of revenge grew louder. Finally,

---

22   See Chapter 13.

Moffatt stood up and announced that payback would be immediate: they would raid the Hope Street lads' beerhouse, the Prince of Wales, that very night.

At 9 p.m., the Ordsall Lane gang marched up Oldfield Road towards Hope Street. Peter Moffatt, Ralph Taylor and Peter Nevin were at the head of a bloodthirsty mob nearly forty-strong, all of them armed with knives or belts. It took them less than ten minutes to reach the Prince of Wales. Their approach was undetected, despite the clatter of their clogs on the cobbles. The Hope Street lads were packed inside the beerhouse, but they were making the most of the day's holiday and enjoying 'a good sup'. Their festive mood was quickly shattered. The Ordsall Lane scutlers announced their arrival with an almighty crash by hurling bricks through the beerhouse windows. The wild-eyed Peter Moffatt stood in the pub doorway, his belt in one hand and a knife in the other.

'Come on you bleeders!' he called out. 'I've come out this morning from doing nine months and I want my revenge!'

Pandemonium. The Hope Street scuttlers, many of whom were themselves the worse for drink, spilled out into the street, flinging glass tumblers, bar stools and even spittoons at the Ordsall lads. Many of the Hope Street lads were armed with knives; others wielded chair legs as makeshift batons. The two gangs clashed in the street directly outside the Prince of Wales and fell on each other like hyenas. As shouts and screams rent the air and the brawling figures spilled across Oldfield Road, terrified passers-by ran into nearby shops to seek shelter. Shopkeepers ran outside to pull down shutters to protect their windows from the showers of bricks and stones flying back and forth across the street.

The Hope Street scuttlers forced the Ordsall boys to back off, chasing them into Hampson Street. But there 'the Lane' regrouped and stood their ground, and a pitched battle involving up to eighty lads now raged for ten minutes. For a scuttle, this was an eternity. Youths from both sides fell clutching wounds. Jimmy Heaton and Jacky Dyer, who fought at the front of Hope Street gang, were both cut severely on their hands. Dyer's fingers were almost severed, but his injuries paled in comparison to those suffered by Peter Moffatt. As the fighting intensified, several of the Hope Street lads targeted Moffatt as the leader of the Lane mob. A blow from the buckle end of a belt eventually felled him, and as he lay prostrate in Hampson Street he was stabbed seven times in the back. When they saw Peter Moffatt tumble to the ground, the rest of his gang fled. The Ordsall Lane scuttlers were routed, leaving Moffatt crying out, 'Where's my lads?'

Having woken up that morning in Strangeways Prison, Moffatt ended the day in Salford Royal Hospital. On arrival he was 'faint from loss of blood', his shirt soaked red from seven incised wounds in his back. The house surgeon judged one of the wounds to be serious on account of the amount of bleeding. Moffatt also had a scalp wound, a cut lip, and extensive bruising on his chest, hip and thigh.

News of the bloody scuttle travelled fast around the beer-houses of south Salford. The following morning, knots of lads gathered on street corners and in factories and workshops across the borough, passing on the tale of how the Hope Street scuttlers had 'dosed' Peter Moffatt. And no-one had been arrested; the entire affray had taken place without police intervention. Any beat constables in the vicinity of Oldfield Road had wisely made themselves scarce as the fight raged. After all, what could one or two constables do when faced by eighty lads, all of them wielding weapons, determined to pursue their alcohol-fuelled vendetta in the streets of Salford? Police inquiries began in the aftermath of the fight, as cowed passers-by emerged from the shops on Oldfield Road and shopkeepers began the task of clearing debris from their store fronts. Detectives soon obtained the names of a number of youths from the immediate neighbourhood who, it was alleged, had taken part in the fighting, and Detective Constable Ernest Dillon arrested two members of the Hope Street gang at around midnight. This marked the beginning of a major operation against the gang by the Salford Borough Police.

The intensity of the police activity reflected the timing of the affray as much as its ferocity. The widely publicized condemnation of Salford's scuttling gangs by the recorder Joseph Yates had heightened interest among the local press and increased pressure upon the police to deal with the gangs. Ten members of the Hope Street gang were arrested between April 7 and May 1, and after a series of hearings before the magistrates, they were committed for trial at the Quarter Sessions to face charges of unlawful wounding and riot.

The Hope Street gang were surprised by the detectives' perseverance. For all its ferocity, the scuttle was hardly unusual, and while Moffatt's wounds were serious, they were not life-threatening. In any event, the Hope Street lads decided that, if they were to face the full force of the law, so would their adversaries. Jimmy Heaton, by now effectively the Hope Street leader, handed over a list of names of prominent members of the Ordsall Lane gang during a hearing at the Salford Police Court on April 23. He requested that warrants should be issued for their arrest. As the Hope Street lads saw it, the fight had been started by the Ordsall mob – why should they remain at liberty, whilst the Hope Street lads were rounded up one-by-one? Stipendiary Joseph Makinson agreed. Warrants were issued and seven of the Ordsall Lane scuttlers, including the recovering Moffatt, were in turn taken into custody and charged with riot and unlawful wounding.

In their sworn witness statements, taken in preparation for the trials to be held at the Salford Borough Quarter Sessions in June, members of the two gangs gave conflicting accounts of what happened on the night of April 7. Peter Moffatt was asked to testify against eight of the Hope Street lads: John Allmark, Fred Bagley, Tommy Brown, John Dunn, Jimmy Heaton, James Johnson, William McGrath, and Billy Shaw. In reply to a series of questions posed by Mr Makinson, Moffatt stated:

I live at 11 Prescott Street, Salford. I am a labourer. On the 7th April I was on the fair ground all the afternoon. I was told some men were looking for me so I went up Ordsall Lane. About 9 p.m. I went to the Prince of Wales beerhouse in Hope Street. I didn't go in. About 30 men came outside including all the prisoners but Bagley.

They all had weapons. They had cartshafts, table legs about 3 feet long and belts. I saw 5 of them with knives, Brown, Johnson, Dunn, Allmark and one not in custody.

I ran away and they all ran after me.

When they overtook me I saw Shaw. He said, 'I'll give you what you have given others.'

He caught hold of my scarf. He had a stick in his hand and he hit me on the head with it. A man not in custody had the piece of iron [shown to the court]. He made a clout at me and missed me.

Brown was in the crowd with a knife. He came round me and stabbed me in the back.

I saw Johnson, Allmark and Dunn with knives in their hands. Then I felt the knives going in my back. I think I had 4 cuts. I fell down and all the rest surrounded me and kicked me all over the body. I saw each of the prisoners except Bagley kick me. Others kicked me, I can't tell who.

Dyer, the man not in custody, came out of the beerhouse with the two spittoons [produced in court] and another one. He threw 2 at me which struck me in the stomach, with the third he struck me in the mouth. Then he ran in the beerhouse and brought out the piece of iron which they use for a fender, that was the commencement, before I was struck with the knives.

Dyer threw the things at me before I began to run.

I know Bagley. When I got up after being kicked I saw him running away with a thick stick in his hand.

After I was assaulted there was a cry of 'Police!' and they all ran away. I went home with great difficulty. I was bleeding, the blood was running down my legs. I could hardly walk. I was taken to the [police] station and then to the hospital where I remained till the 16th April.

I was wearing the same coat that I am now. All the cuts in it were produced by the knives that night.

Three of the Hope Street scuttlers identified by Moffatt as having wielded knives – John Allmark, James Johnson and John

Dunn – had given evidence at the Quarter Sessions in July 1889, when Moffatt had been sent down for nine months.

Throughout the hearings, the members of the Ordsall Lane gang followed a coherent strategy. Moffatt insisted time and again that he had gone to Hope Street on his own that night, presenting himself as the lone victim of an unprovoked assault. The rest of the Ordsall Lane lads denied that they had been present, with the exception of Jim Smith, who claimed to have witnessed the events entirely by chance. Smith told how he had decided to take a walk and happened to be passing by when he witnessed the assault on Moffatt. The Ordsall Lane scuttlers had devised a story, rehearsed their lines, and stuck to them well.

Not surprisingly, Hope Street had a very different tale to tell. Jimmy Heaton told the court that the attack on the Prince of Wales was led by Moffatt, Taylor and Nevin. 'I saw a knife fastened to Moffatt's arm,' testified Heaton. 'It was about a foot long, like a dagger.' Jacky Dyer, the first of the Hope Street lads out of the beer-house, was stabbed as soon as he went through the door. According to Heaton, the rest of the group then ran out into the street:

> I saw Moffatt and Walter Adams. As well as those two, I saw Ralph Taylor, Squire Taylor, Peter Nevin, Paddy McDonough and Hickey McDonnell, and a lot more, 30 or 40. They all ran into Hampson Street and our lot followed them.
>
> They turned round in Hampson Street and we fought.
>
> I got cut in 3 places on my right hand in trying to take the knife off Moffatt. We fought for 10 minutes and we ran away leaving Moffatt on the ground. Dyer had a cut on the back of his hand and we two went to the Dispensary.
>
> I saw Hickman throw a brick in the fight. It missed me and hit McGrath's foot.
>
> They had a lot of sticks which they fired at us. We picked them up and fired them back, that's how we got our sticks. We had none when we came out.

Unlike Moffatt, Heaton admitted that he had taken part in a fully-fledged scuttle. In Heaton's account, however, it was clear that Ordsall Lane were the aggressors. When the fighting began, Moffatt shouted out, 'Shoot them!' This was the signal for Ordsall Lane to hurl a volley of sticks as Hope Street emerged from the beerhouse.

Seventeen lads from the two gangs appeared before Joseph Yates at the Salford Borough Quarter Sessions on June 6. At the outset of the proceedings, Mr Foard, counsel for Jacky Dyer of the Hope Street gang, gave a damning portrait of Peter Moffatt. Mr Foard claimed that Moffatt was 'origin and foundation of all the mischief'. He had been on a reformatory ship, he was a deserter from the army, had served nine months for scuttling and had only come out of prison on the day of the fight. Three women from the Hope Street district testified against the Ordsall Lane scuttlers, describing in turn how Moffatt had stabbed Jacky Dyer. In response, Moffatt alleged that the women had conspired to commit perjury. Moreover, he pointed out to the court, not unreasonably, that one of the women was Jacky Dyer's aunt. Three lads from the Hope Street neighbourhood also appeared as witnesses. They too presented a highly coherent and apparently co-ordinated account, again highlighting the use of weapons by the Ordsall Lane scuttlers. However, their testimony was also fiercely disputed from the dock by Moffatt, who alleged that two of the witnesses, including Joseph Allmark, had taken part in the affray themselves. The jury found twelve of the seventeen scuttlers before them guilty of unlawful wounding and riot. Six of those convicted were from Hope Street, six from Ordsall Lane. The recorder jailed all twelve. The sentences ranged from three to twelve months with hard labour, with the longest sentence reserved for Peter Moffatt.

The affray had received blanket coverage in the local press. By the time of the trials on June 6, headline writers for the Salford newspapers were at fever pitch. 'Bank Holiday Butchery in Salford: Demoniac Conduct of Scuttlers,' proclaimed the *County Telephone*, while the *Salford Reporter* labelled the raid on the Prince of Wales 'A Carnival of Knives and Belts'. Editorial commentaries dwelled at length on the vicious character of the scuttler and the reign of terror wrought by the gangs. The case of Peter Moffatt was widely used to illustrate the apparent futility of imprisonment as a deterrent. The *Salford Chronicle* led calls for the flogging of scuttlers, pleading, 'Let them taste the pain they mete out to their victims.'

The police operation against the gangs was generally judged to have been a success, but the sentences imposed by Joseph Yates received a mixed verdict. The *Manchester Examiner and Times* applauded their severity, but in Salford, commentaries were much more critical. The *Chronicle* and the *Reporter* both claimed that the terms were too lenient. Many of the newspapers profoundly misrepresented the nature of the Bank Holiday disturbance. Although the fight had involved members of two gangs, the *Chronicle* preferred to emphasise instead the menace posed to more law-abiding citizens. 'Gangs of youths and young men assemble in the public streets and, for no earthly reason beyond that of wanton mischief, attack any peaceably inclined citizen who may happen to be passing,' it complained. 'They freely use knives, belts, and sticks to whoever may have the misfortune to fall in their way ... It is unsafe to walk abroad.' The fact that, on this occasion, scuttlers were only fighting among themselves was deliberately obscured. Gang violence was presented as random and indiscriminate, and thus as more terrifying.

THE FULL fury of the Salford press was only aroused in the weeks following the trial, when the Ordsall Lane gang unleashed a further torrent of violence. One of their principal targets was a beat constable, P.C. William Chapman, who bore the brunt of the gang's resentment at their treatment by the Salford Borough Police. Barely a week after the trial concluded, P.C. Chapman was making a Saturday night patrol of Ordsall Lane when two youths came running towards him. When Chapman stopped them, the youths stated that they were being chased by a group of lads who had challenged them to fight. Moments later, in what appears to have been a carefully staged ambush, around fifteen scuttlers emerged from the Sunnyside Inn beerhouse and rushed at the constable. Chapman grabbed one of the scuttlers and clung to his prisoner for all he was worth as the rest of the gang set about him. Chapman was knocked down, kicked and beaten unconscious. The arrival of two more constables sparked a frenzied free-for-all, with the beleaguered officers desperately appealing to passers-by to come to their aid. By the time police reinforcements arrived, two of the scuttlers had been apprehended but the rest of the mob had disappeared.

P.C. Chapman was taken to Salford Royal Hospital with extensive bruising and severe internal injuries. Detective Constable Ernest Dillon began to round up members of the Ordsall Lane gang in the early hours of Sunday morning. In total, eight scuttlers – five lads and three girls – were arrested and charged with assaulting a police officer and riotous assembly. The prisoners included some of the gang's key figures – Peter Nevin, aged eighteen, Paddy McDonough, sixteen, and Tommy McDonald, eighteen – as well as Annie Tucker, seventeen, Maggie Moffatt, eighteen, Hannah Wright, sixteen, Robert Whittaker, eighteen, and Ernie Bamber, twenty. Court reporters noted that all eight of the prisoners, including the girls, wore their hair in the customary scuttler style 'with a fringe falling over the forehead'.

A passer-by who had witnessed the assault, an iron moulder named William Jones, told how he saw the gang strike the officer Chapman, adding that if they had not been stopped they would have killed him. 'The girls were the chief cause of the disturbance,' he recalled. 'They acted like Amazons, and were very active in the fray.' In Jones's view, only the arrival at the scene of two other police officers and the assistance of a handful of passers-by saved the constable from being killed. He effectively blamed the three girls for the ferocity of the assault.

The eight scuttlers were remanded without bail amid fears that the case would eventually be one of murder. When the prisoners were brought back before the magistrates, Detective Constable Dillon told a hushed courtroom that when he visited P.C. Chapman the previous night, 'He was very bad, and could not turn round in bed for the pains in his stomach.' The Chief

Constable confirmed that Chapman's condition was still 'dangerous'. As the magistrates discussed the possibility of granting bail to the three female prisoners, D.C. Dillon interjected: 'I am just told, your worships, that Constable Chapman has had a very bad night, and is worse this morning.' The prisoners were remanded in custody for a further four days. With the prospect of a murder charge looming over them, the three girls were led back to the cells in tears.

The scuttlers spent an uncomfortable weekend awaiting further news. When they made their next appearance at the Police Court on June 23, they were surprised, and mightily relieved, to see P.C. Chapman helped into a specially erected seat in the witness box. Against all expectations, he had recovered sufficiently to testify. Chapman now gave his own version of events. He told the Salford Police Court how he had initially arrested Robert Whittaker during the disturbance outside the Sunnyside Inn. Maggie Moffatt and Annie Tucker shouted, 'Don't let him take you,' before grabbing Chapman and striking him about the body. Maggie Moffatt was the sister of Peter, the volatile leader of the Ordsall Lane gang, who had been sentenced the previous week to twelve months. According to Chapman, her intervention prompted an assault by the entire gang in which he was knocked to the ground, struck on the head, kicked repeatedly all over his body and bitten. Four passers-by corroborated Chapman's account, with one testifying that he saw Tucker strike Chapman several blows with a clog, whilst Moffatt hit him with her boot.

From the bench, Joseph Makinson declared that, with the exception of sixteen-year-old Hannah Wright, the prisoners were 'equally guilty'. Nonetheless, he sentenced only the five male defendants to the maximum sentence for assaulting a police officer: six months' hard labour. Tucker and Moffatt, both of whom were known to the police, were sentenced to only three months despite Makinson's assertion that they were as guilty as the lads. The evidence against Wright was less substantial and she was given fourteen days, with Makinson commenting that he hoped she would keep better company when she came out.

With all of its leaders now in Strangeways, the Ordsall Lane

Jerome Caminada, legendary Manchester detective and the scourge of publicans, prize-fighters and scuttlers alike.

The ugly façade of the People's Concert Hall, popularly known as the Cass and frequented by bands of scuttlers from across Manchester and Salford. The Cass could seat up to 3,000 people.

The deadliest spot in Manchester: Bengal Street, Ancoats, at its junction with Hood Street. The death-rate in this hotbed of tuberculosis appalled investigators during the 1880s. Eleven pubs and fourteen beerhouses stood within 300 yards of the White Swan.

Blossom Street, off Bengal Street, where Joe Brady grew up. The surrounding slum streets and courtyards formed the recruiting ground for the Bengal Tigers.

ALLEGED MURDER IN MANCHESTER — THE HOUSE

The killing of the Bengal Tiger Joe Brady by the Meadow Lads in February 1887, as depicted in the national press. The Meadow Lads were aged in their late teens and early twenties, but appear much older in this sketch.

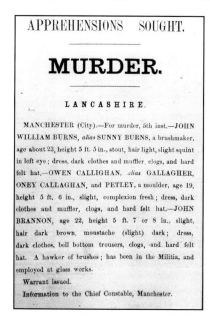

A *Police Gazette* wanted notice for three members of the gang suspected of Brady's murder, detailing their distinctive, dark uniforms. Owen Callaghan was found guilty of manslaughter and jailed for twenty years.

MICH^lC KING

Mick King, the volatile leader of the Brown Street scuttlers from Salford, stabbed a Deansgate rival named Henry Swift in a gang fight on Chapel Street in September 1896. He was sentenced to penal servitude for six years and this mug-shot was taken upon his arrival at H.M. Prison Stafford.

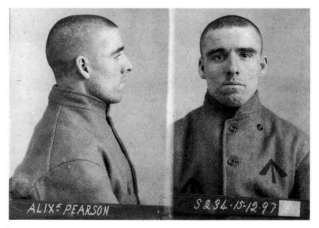

ALIX^r PEARSON   S 234·15·12·97

The formidable Ancoats scuttler Alexander Pearson was jailed for five years following a fight with the Meadow Lads in June 1892. He was released early on licence, but quickly re-offended and by December 1897 found himself behind bars once again.

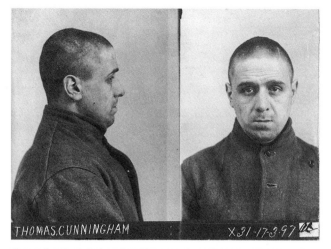

THOMAS.CUNNINGHAM   X.31-17-3·97

Tommy Cunningham from Angel Meadow was jailed following a clash with the Bengal Tigers in 1888. He rose to become one of the leaders of the Meadow Lads by the mid-1890s. By the time he was sentenced to three years' penal servitude for scuttling in 1897, he had a string of convictions for crimes of violence.

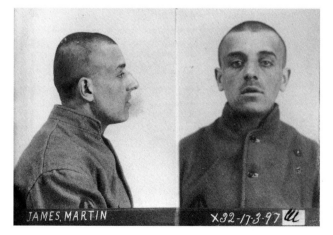

JAMES.MARTIN   X.32-17-3·97

Jimmy Martin, one of Cunningham's followers, was sent down for three years for stabbing John Durkin of the Deansgate mob in a frenzied gang brawl on Christmas night, 1896.

A group of flower sellers, photographed around 1905. Although Manchester's gang conflicts had by now largely faded, traces of scuttler style can be seen in some of the lads' neckerchiefs, fringes and tilted caps.

An Adelphi Lads' Club summer camp during the 1900s. The lads' club movement offered healthy pursuits for the youth of the slums and was seen as a major factor in the decline of scuttling as the nineteenth century drew to a close.

gang had effectively been wiped out as a fighting force – for the time being. Peter Moffatt, Ralph Taylor and Peter Nevin would later re-emerge as criminal figureheads of some repute, but in the meantime other gangs came to the fore – with fatal consequences.

CHAPTER 15

Death in Ancoats

THE CONSERVATIVE HOME Secretary, Henry Matthews, was troubled by the gangs of Manchester for a second time during the spring of 1892. On this occasion, the city's scuttlers came to the attention of the national press following the murder of a youth in Ancoats. The fatality arose out of a feud between the Bradford Street scuttlers from Ancoats and the Lime Street Boys from Miles Platting. The Bradford Street lads accused Peter Kennedy of the Lime Street gang of 'banging', or hitting, some girls. Warnings, threats and insults were exchanged between members of the two gangs, leading to minor skirmishes and culminating in a full-scale scuttle on Sunday, April 17. In the week that followed, younger members of the two gangs embarked on a series of tit-for-tat reprisals.

Peter Kennedy was sixteen years old. He lived with his parents, two brothers and two sisters in Addington Street, New Cross. His parents, Thomas and Mary, worked as hawkers, pounding the streets off the lower end of Rochdale Road selling bruised fruit and vegetables to those too poor, or too busy, to shop at the nearby Smithfield market. With five children to feed, they depended on the wages brought home by Peter and his elder brother to get by. Peter was persuaded to join the Lime Street scuttlers by a group of his workmates at Crabtree's dye-works in Ancoats. His association with the Lime Street gang had a price: each day after work, he had to walk home through the dense slums packed between the Rochdale and Ashton canals – the territory of the Bradford Street mob.

On Thursday, April 21, Kennedy was heading home at around half-past five when he was accosted by a group of Bradford Street lads in Alum Street. William Willan, a sixteen-year-old cooper, demanded, 'What of this scuttling?' Kennedy replied cockily, 'We will talk about scuttling when I have put two or three in the Infirmary.' The Bradford Street lads let Kennedy go, but Willan was seething; Kennedy had humiliated him. He vowed to wait for Kennedy on his way home from work the following evening. On the Friday, Willan gathered three companions – Jimmy Hands, Teddy Fleming and Charlie Davidson – in an entry off St Thomas Street. Willan had told them to 'Get some pop bottles and have a smack at Kennedy.' Wary of further trouble, Kennedy rushed home that night, hurrying past St Thomas Street before Willan and his accomplices had time to respond.

The Bradford Street lads resolved to wait for him again the following day. This time, Willan declared, he was going to 'dose', or stab, Peter Kennedy. Willan gathered together a dozen boys on the corner of Great Ancoats Street at half-past twelve on the Saturday afternoon. Kennedy was due to finish his half-day shift at the dye-works at one o'clock. Kennedy knew by now that he had been singled out for reprisal. Wary of the walk home through Ancoats, he arranged for four lads to meet him at the end of his shift. James Meehan, John Carr, Ned Armstrong and Paddy Mannion all turned up at the dye-works gates at one o'clock, as promised. As they set off for Rochdale Road, they were joined by one of Kennedy's workmates, nineteen-year-old Jimmy Cowan. The presence of Cowan ought to have guaranteed them safe passage through Ancoats: Cowan was one of the infamous Bengal Tigers.

The Bradford Street gang spotted Kennedy with his escort in Mill Street at around half past one. As Kennedy and Cowan turned into Great Ancoats Street, they were surrounded. Kennedy asked William Willan, 'What is it to be?' This was one of the standard preludes to a scuttle. In effect, Kennedy was accepting Willan's challenge, but he wanted to know the terms: how many lads were going to take part in the fight and what weapons were to be used? Willan, who was holding an open clasp-knife, replied, 'Anything you like.' Then the Bradford Street lads attacked. Charlie Davidson struck at James Meehan with a belt. Kennedy tried to run away, but Willan quickly caught up with him and plunged his knife into Kennedy's side from behind. As Kennedy cried out, Willan fled. He turned and ran down Alum Street, leaving his victim writhing on the ground.

Shortly afterwards, Willan met Jimmy Hands near the public baths in New Islington in Ancoats. Hands, a sixteen-year-old dyer, had been recruited by Willan for the planned ambush of Peter Kennedy. Their conversation was remarkably matter-of-fact.

'I have dosed him,' said Willan.

'Who have you dosed?' asked Hands.

'Kennedy.'

'Have you stabbed him in the head?'

'No, in the ribs.'

Willan offered his weekly wage packet to Hands, before asking, 'Will you take my knife?' Hands agreed. Willan wiped blood off the blade before passing it over with the instruction, 'If you get copped, don't round [tell] on me.'

Kennedy was taken to Manchester Royal Infirmary in a state of collapse. He 'complained very much' of a pain in his left side, where the doctors found a wound bleeding freely. On close examination, they discovered a second wound which appeared to have been caused by the withdrawal of the knife after the initial stabbing. This wound was two inches deep. Thomas Kennedy visited his stricken son at the Royal Infirmary that evening. Word of the seriousness of Kennedy's injuries began to circulate in the streets and pubs of Ancoats and Angel Meadow. By Sunday morning, most of the youthful population of the city knew that a scuttler's life was hanging in the balance. At three o'clock that afternoon, Jimmy Hands walked into Cannel Street police station in Ancoats and handed in a clasp-knife, telling the desk sergeant that the weapon had been used by William Willan to stab Peter Kennedy.

Willan was arrested at dawn on the Monday morning. Detectives called at his family home, a one-up, one-down in Lower Canal Street. Here, Willan lived with his father, mother and his five younger siblings. His father, George, was a thirty-four-year-old engineer. As a 'journeyman', or skilled craftsman, he belonged to the elite ranks of Manchester's industrial work-force, but a lengthy bout of unemployment had left George Willan and his family crammed into a hovel in one of the poorest streets in Ancoats.

Willan claimed that he had been given the knife by Teddy Fleming, and Fleming in turn was taken into custody shortly afterwards. Kennedy's condition worsened during the course of Monday morning, and one of the resident surgeons at the Royal Infirmary took the decision to operate that afternoon. Detectives arranged for Kennedy to give a deposition before the operation commenced, fearing that these might be his last words. With a trial for murder looking ever more likely, the police arranged for Willan to be brought to the Infirmary so that he might cross-examine Kennedy once the deposition had been taken. Kennedy swore that he had been stabbed from behind, but claimed that he did not see who did it. He told how he was chased by 'some lads with belts', and named one of them as Teddy Fleming. According to Kennedy, Fleming had a stick – not a knife – in his hand during the chase. Kennedy then told how, after he had been stabbed, he had said to William Willan, 'What do you mean?' Willan and his companions then ran away. Kennedy insisted that he had never had a quarrel with Willan, and he saw nothing in Willan's hands during the row in Great Ancoats Street.

Peter Kennedy rallied after the operation. He lay in the Royal Infirmary for a fortnight, but then his condition suddenly worsened on Sunday, May 8. He died at eight o'clock that evening. The cause of death was an internal haemorrhage from a knife wound between two of his ribs.

Three of the Bradford Street scuttlers were indicted for wilful murder: Willan, Fleming and Charlie Davidson. The evidence against Willan was damning, not least as several members of his own gang had testified against him. Davidson gave a lengthy statement to the police in which he told how Willan had boasted of dosing Kennedy. Jimmy Hands had already made a similar statement when he handed the murder weapon over to the police. Two other lads who admitted that they were with Willan during the 'bother' in Great Ancoats Street similarly testified to seeing him stab Kennedy. Willan's fellow scuttlers were no doubt under intense pressure from the police; in any event, they were unwilling to share responsibility for his actions.

Willan, Fleming and Davidson were tried before Mr Justice Collins at the Manchester Assizes on May 20. The shadow of the gallows loomed over all three of them. The case for the prosecution was led by Henry West, Q.C., the Recorder of Manchester, who told the jury that, 'The case arose out of what was known as scuttling, which was so great a reproach to this city.' He insisted that there was nothing heroic about the fight in Great Ancoats Street on the afternoon of April 23. Quite the reverse: 'Kennedy was stabbed by Willan in the back, and did not even see his assailant, which rendered the act still more cowardly and dastardly.' The prosecution called members of three different gangs, all of whom testified against Willan. The witnesses included Jimmy Hands, of the Bradford Street scuttlers; James Meehan, of the Lime Street Boys; and Jimmy Cowan, of the Bengal Tigers. This was highly unusual. When members of rival gangs were called to give evidence at the Assizes, their testimonies were generally wildly at odds. In this instance, the scuttling fraternity closed ranks against one of their own. Even in their eyes, William Willan had gone too far.

Counsel for the defence, Mr McKeand, told the jury that by their verdict they had to say whether 'those three little fellows now in the dock were to live or to die'. His rhetoric did not visibly move the jury as much as the prisoners, all three of whom burst into tears and sobbed through the remainder of their counsel's speech. His voice rising above the wails of the boys in the dock, McKeand continued his address to the jury. Were they going, he asked, to send the prisoners to the scaffold to die like dogs, or were they going to take the more charitable and more merciful consideration of the facts, and stop short of the terrible result they were asked by the crown to take? McKeand pressed hard for the charges against Fleming and Davidson to be dropped altogether since there was no evidence to show that either of them knew Willan intended to stab Kennedy. Mr McKeand did concede that there had been a conspiracy to 'dose' Kennedy, but he nonetheless insisted that there was no evidence of 'murderous intent'. Even Willan therefore ought only to be convicted of manslaughter.

Summing up, Mr Justice Collins was adamant that it was Willan who had struck the fatal blow. Moreover, the judge indicated, it was not clear that the other prisoners knew of his intention to use the knife. The jury's principal task therefore was to gauge Willan's intent: what was in his mind at the time the fatal blow was struck? Did he intend to kill Kennedy? To do him grievous bodily harm? Or merely to give him a thrashing? The jury took one hour and fifteen minutes to consider their verdict. When they returned to the courtroom, the foreman announced, 'We find William Willan guilty of wilful murder, but we strongly recommend him to mercy on account of his youth. Fleming and Davidson we find not guilty.'

The agitation in court was palpable as Justice Collins donned the black cap to pass the sentence of death by hanging. The terrified Willan repeatedly interrupted the proceedings, shouting, 'Oh master, don't, I'm only sixteen.' He became so frantic that two policemen in the dock had to seize him, pinning his arms to his side until Justice Collins had finished proclaiming the sentence. Chaos broke out in the gallery, where a number of women, including Willan's mother, began screaming. The gallery was immediately cleared. Amid bedlam, Justice Collins quietly informed the rapidly emptying courtroom that he would ensure that the jury's recommendation to mercy was forwarded 'to the proper quarter'.

THE SENTENCE of death imposed on William Willan prompted lengthy editorial commentaries in the Manchester press. To the *Manchester Courier*, the evidence relayed at the

Assizes showed that scuttling was a 'barbarous' form of crime. Yet, as the *Courier* pointed out, this tribal warfare had been carried on 'almost unchecked' for years:

> Although a revolting condition of savage life was revealed at the trial yesterday, Manchester citizens were not unfamiliar with the depravity, the wickedness, and the cruelty of these desperadoes, who organise bands for offence and defence, for onslaught and protection, as if they were living in the wildest part of an uncivilised country where police law is unknown. They are eternally at war with one another. Each member of a gang is as well known to an enemy by a common name as are the Red Indians known by their tribes. Apparently there are no two gangs allied, and each are ready to declare war against another, the grievance of one member being a sufficient justification for a battle.

In fact, whilst there were no formal alliances, rival gangs from districts such as Ancoats would periodically suspend hostilities to repel incursions by bands of scuttlers from further afield. In the face of war parties from Salford, for example, local grievances would be momentarily set aside.

The *Courier* was appalled by the scuttlers' calculated use of weapons. Broken bottles were collected prior to affrays because, as one witness at the Assizes had put it, 'bottles like that hurt more'. Moreover, according to the scuttler's fighting code, it was the 'understood thing' to seek to injure an enemy on the head. As Jimmy Hands admitted under cross-examination at the Assizes, he was surprised that Willan had stabbed Kennedy in the ribs. The *Courier* acknowledged that scuttling was generally restricted to lads; however, it had continued 'for generation after generation'. Police interference was frequently impossible. Outbreaks of scuttling were too sudden, and were generally over before the police were alerted. The *Courier* hoped that the sentence of death imposed at the Assizes might effect a 'salutary warning', but noted that clemency would no doubt be granted to Willan on account of his youth. As the *Courier* noted, 'In size and appearance the condemned boy looks to be less than sixteen years of age.'

The *Manchester Guardian* saw the conviction for murder as entirely justified. If the perpetrator were a grown man, said the *Guardian*, 'he would certainly be hung'. However, the *Guardian*, like the *Courier*, was in no doubt that Willan's sentence would be commuted to one of penal servitude for life. In practice, he would serve no more than twenty years. The *Guardian*'s interpretation of the case was otherwise very different from the *Courier*'s. The *Guardian* saw the trial as a warning, but not just to the gangs: 'the sordid and hideous details of this juvenile conspiracy to murder' ought to shame every citizen of Manchester. As the *Guardian* put it, 'the community at large must bear a certain responsibility for these sordid horrors so long as the only playground such boys have is the street, while their only exercise is fighting with one another.' Manchester's lads' club movement, still in its infancy in 1892, offered at least glimmers of progress; the clubs' provision of uplifting recreation for the youth of the slums drew enthusiastic support from newspapers such as the *Guardian*.

The *Manchester Evening News* described the death of Peter Kennedy as the terrible but inevitable culmination of the city's gang conflicts. Like the *Courier*, the *Evening News* put the case into historical perspective: 'These scuttling encounters are surely the oldest development of which modern civilisation knows anything. They are, it is only fair to say, not new. Middle-aged men will be able to remember that thirty years ago very much the same sort of thing was going on in very much the same way.' The newspaper's own columns had carried extensive reports of scuttling for twenty years. Yet however entrenched scuttling appeared to be on Manchester's meaner streets, still the *Evening News* could find no rational explanation for the conduct of these 'young roughs': 'The whole thing seems to have its origin in sheer unmitigated brutality and blood-thirstiness. The one object before both sets of combatants is to maim, and, if possible, to kill their opponents. All that decent citizens know with certainty is that wide areas are from time to time made so dangerous as to be almost uninhabitable by the ravages of these hordes of young savages whose cowardly achievements would put an untamed Red Indian to the blush.' Stern lectures from the magistrates and terms of imprisonment had done nothing to subdue their ardour and, at last, 'the inevitable has happened'.[23]

To the *Evening News*, scuttling was the antithesis of everything manly, and everything English. 'Indeed the essence of this scuttling is its intense cowardice,' it claimed. 'All traditions that we like to call English in the way of fighting fair are disregarded. To hit below the belt, to hit or kick a man when he is down, to fight with knives rather than fists, are amongst the first principles of the scuttlers' art. If he can so marshall his forces as to overwhelm a single opponent by fighting three or four to one so much the better for him.'

Scuttling was itself by now so deeply rooted as to be a neighbourhood tradition throughout the low districts of Manchester and Salford – yet still the *Evening News* clung to an idealized notion of 'fair play' as the defining characteristic of the Englishman. Finally, according to the *Evening News*, the terror shown by Willan, Fleming and Davidson in the dock proved that if scuttlers were afraid of nothing else, at least they feared the hangman. All lesser punishments had failed to cure the scuttler, but here at last was a deterrent, for, 'Like his comrade the garrotter the scuttler is at heart an arrant coward. If he really can be made to understand that his neck is in danger he may possibly mend his ways.'

WILLIAM WILLAN was to be executed at Strangeways, where the distraught scuttler was held in the condemned cell. The local press was convinced that Home Secretary Henry Matthews would show leniency on account of Willan's age but the condemned youth's relatives were taking nothing for granted.

---

23 Although apparently determined to place the case in its historical context, the *Evening News* curiously failed to mention the deaths of Christopher Sheffield in 1885 and Joe Brady in 1887.

On Monday, May 23, the first working day after the trial, they instructed a solicitor to prepare a petition pleading for mercy which might be circulated in Ancoats and the surrounding districts. The petition stressed the prisoner's youth, but also questioned whether Willan had actually used the fatal knife. After all, other lads had taken part in the attack. Reverend Father Timony, the priest in charge of St Alban's Catholic Church in Ancoats, had visited Willan in his cell before the trial. He now offered to lead prayers for Willan's reprieve. The petition stated that Willan was 'a highly respectable boy' up to within a short time of the fatal affray; his companions had led him astray. Viewed in this light, Willan and Kennedy might both be numbered among the victims of the Ancoats scuttling gangs. Five copies of the petition were circulated in Ancoats and the adjacent slum districts either side of Rochdale Road and Oldham Road. Thousands signed on Willan's behalf.

An additional appeal was made to the famous Manchester detective, Jerome Caminada. At Willan's request, the Governor of Strangeways, Major Preston, sent a note to Caminada, stating that the condemned youth wished to see him. Caminada was puzzled; he had not been involved in the case, but Willan's request pricked his curiosity. He went to Strangeways immediately. The experience shook him:

> Though I had been visiting the prison for over 20 years, it was the first time that I was ever inside a condemned cell, and I hope it will be the last. The poor lad put his arms through the bars which separated us, and, with tears streaming down his cheeks, implored me to save him. I was much affected, and promised that I would do all in my power towards this end.

Willan's mother Hannah, a thirty-five-year-old French polisher, was maintaining a vigil at the prison gates. She accosted Caminada as he left:

> At the door of the prison I was met by a poor woman with a shawl over her head, who was his mother; she seized me by the

hand, and, after ascertaining that I had seen her son, prayed of me to use what influence I might have in saving him from the gallows.

Caminada quickly went to work on Willan's behalf, meeting with Charles Lister and Robert Armitage, two prominent Manchester magistrates who had taken up Willan's case. Lister had led the campaign for the flogging of scuttlers less than two years previously. Together with Armitage, he now rallied support for Willan among his fellow magistrates and the city's legal community, whilst Willan's friends and relatives gathered support from those of more humble means in Ancoats and Angel Meadow.

Willan's case quickly became a cause célèbre in Manchester. By the following weekend, it was claimed that 25,000 signatures had been gathered on his behalf. On May 29, the Willans' solicitor received a telegram from the Home Secretary requesting that the petition be dispatched to London forthwith. He did not delay. Having only one of the five petitions in his possession, he bundled that up with an accompanying letter and posted it immediately:

To the Home Secretary.

I have this day forwarded to you per parcels post a petition asking for the commutation of the death sentence passed upon William Willan for the murder of a lad named Peter Kennedy. The petition contains over 4,000 signatures, including those of justices of the peace, barristers, solicitors, &c. The signatures which have been obtained by myself have been got without canvassing, and no one under sixteen years of age was allowed to sign. A few of the signatures have been obtained by the prisoner's mother. Many people here have expressed the hope that you will take into consideration the prisoner's extreme youth.

The Home Secretary's decision was announced by Major Preston at Strangeways Prison the following morning. He informed local journalists that, on the instruction of the Home Secretary, Willan was to be reprieved. Henry Matthews had decreed that, 'after careful consideration of all the circumstances and consultation with the learned judge, he felt justified in advising Her Majesty to commute the capital sentence passed upon the prisoner Willan to one of life penal servitude'.

THIS LURID story of gang warfare, reprisal and murder was given extra spice by the sudden introduction of sex. In the days between Willan being sentenced to death and his reprieve, it emerged that he had a moll who was herself an eager participant in the scuttlers' battles for supremacy. Hannah Robbin was arrested following a series of disturbances in the vicinity of the music halls and beerhouses dotted around Lower Mosley Street in Manchester city centre. Gangs of scuttlers from across the Manchester conurbation congregated here on weekend evenings, and running fights and mass brawls were commonplace. In the wake of the sentence of death passed at the Assizes, feelings among the scuttling fraternity were running high and even the prospect of the gallows looming over Willan did nothing to quieten the city's streets.

Hannah Robbin and three girlfriends were spotted at around 11 p.m. on Friday, May 27, in the midst of a scuttle at the corner of Chepstow Street and Oxford Road. According to P.C. Willburn of the Manchester City Police, the girls were taking a 'lively' part in the fight. Willburn and a fellow constable tried to arrest them but the girls got away. Despite the knowledge that the police would be looking out for them, they stayed in the city centre into the early hours of Saturday morning. They were eventually apprehended at 1.30 a.m.

Robbin and her friends appeared at the Manchester City Police Court the following morning, charged with disorderly conduct. Inspector Drysdale told the court that Robbin was drunk when she was taken into custody. She was also found to be armed with a formidable-looking belt with the usual heavy buckle at the end. Tattooed on the right arm were the words 'In loving remembrance of William Willan'. She had already resigned herself to the imminent execution of her beloved. Inspector Drysdale said that the four girls were of loose character. He added that the neighbourhood of Chepstow Street and Lower Mosley Street was infested by bands of scuttlers, actively supported by girls like the prisoners. Hardly a night passed without a fight taking place.

Robbin's relationship with the now-infamous Willan aroused great interest in court. Inspector Drysdale informed the court that Robbin had been an inmate of St Elizabeth's, an industrial school for Catholic girls in Liverpool, to the age of sixteen. Another officer added that the police had received many complaints on account of the girls' behaviour in the public streets. Robbin and her three companions were each sentenced to one month's hard labour. These were exceptionally harsh sentences for 'disorderly conduct' and it is likely that the bench was swayed as much by Robbin's association with Willan, whose trial had generated enormous outrage in the local press, as by the police account of events on the night of May 27. The *Manchester Evening News* reported with grim satisfaction, 'The severity of the sentence evidently astonished the four, who were removed from the dock crying loudly.' The news that her sweetheart would not be hanged must have been some consolation at least to Hannah Robbin.

WILLAN'S TRIAL reopened the debate on the desirability of flogging for scuttlers. A correspondent to the *Manchester Courier*, writing under the pseudonym 'Flagellant', argued that Willan, Fleming and Davidson ought all to have been convicted of manslaughter rather than murder. Willan might then have been sentenced at the outset to penal servitude for life; Fleming and Davidson might have joined him for five years. Flagellant insisted that the Home Secretary should introduce a bill to empower judges to have 'these young scoundrels' flogged: eighteen or twenty-four lashes of the cat as soon as they were sentenced, and a second ration on the day prior to their release.

Flagellant claimed to have personally witnessed the effect of flogging upon prisoners: 'I have never known them require a second "dose", they seem to have become quite altered characters.' 'Justice', a correspondent to the *Manchester Guardian*, made a similar case albeit in more guarded terms. Justice was equally convinced that only corporal punishment would put a stop to scuttling; just as the late Lord Bramwell's resort to flogging had put a stop to garrotting. In fact, the deterrent effects of flogging during the 1860s were by no means clear-cut. In Manchester, however, few among the correspondents to the local press held any qualms. Moreover, even if the cat failed to deter, it would surely satisfy the lust for retribution voiced by many of those appalled by Willan's deed.

'J.A.C.', a correspondent to the *Courier*, claimed to have lived for some years in the midst of scuttlers, and to have dealt with both the gangs and their victims in the way of duty (presumably either as a police officer or a medical practitioner). J.A.C. was adamant that it would be a gross mistake to assume that the neighbourhoods afflicted by scuttling contained only a few 'youths of the Willan type'. On the contrary, these localities were bristling with such characters. On this basis, J.A.C. argued that Willan ought to pay the extreme penalty of the law. Not one of Manchester's scuttlers had ever been hanged. If Willan were now to be granted clemency, what would be the effect on the scores of other young miscreants willing and able to emulate him? As J.A.C. put it, 'A remedy is surely somewhere ... To-day justice has one such [scuttler] in her grip.'

Having ordered Willan's reprieve, Home Secretary Matthews instructed his under-secretary to write to the Mayor of Manchester demanding that steps be taken to put a stop to the practice of scuttling. The Home Secretary had been aghast to learn that both Willan and Kennedy were 'little more than boys', and that the latter's death arose from a 'completely senseless' feud with 'no cause or provocation'. Matthews acknowledged that the Manchester authorities were alive to the evil, and he recognised the difficulties inherent in dealing with such young offenders in the courts. Since public feeling would not stand for the hanging of mere boys, scuttlers such as Willan were unlikely to ever suffer the full punishment authorised by law.

Henry Matthews had another idea. He proposed that local employers should join together in concerted action alongside the police 'by making it a fixed rule of their establishments that any youth, whether boy or girl, discovered to belong to a scuttling gang will be immediately dismissed'. The Home Secretary was not sure whether such a scheme was practicable but urged the Mayor to pursue it nonetheless. The proposal was quite draconian and, as the Home Secretary knew full well, there was no legal basis for it.

At the end of June, recorder Henry West wrote a private letter to the Home Secretary in which he suggested an alternative remedy. Pointing out that he had recently dealt with 'a very bad case indeed' at the Quarter Sessions, West observed that scuttling appeared to be on the increase 'at a time when all other crime is diminishing'. He added that, so far as he was aware, scuttling was confined to 'a not very extended area in the city'. In that light, he suggested that 'extra police should be employed in this area specially charged to watch the gangs of scuttlers and to control them'. The Home Secretary promptly dictated another letter to the Mayor of Manchester, relaying West's suggestion as though it was his own.

The Mayor, Thomas Bosdin-Leech, replied that the two proposals had been fully considered by the Watch Committee of Manchester City Council. The proposal that the police should liaise with local employers so that scuttlers might be dismissed was deemed to be too fraught with difficulty. The Mayor was too polite to say so, but the members of the committee must have wondered how young people barred from legitimate work could possibly have supported themselves without turning to crime. The Mayor suggested that the police presence in the areas afflicted by scuttling would be increased instead.

In the wake of this correspondence, E. Leigh-Pemberton, Under Secretary of State at the Home Office, interviewed the Chief Constable of Manchester, Charles Malcolm Wood, and the chairman of the Watch Committee – the former Mayor,

Alderman John Mark – on July 16. Twelve days later, Alderman Mark wrote to the Under Secretary to clarify the committee's stance on scuttling. As Mark pointed out, the members of the committee had no desire to 'interfere between the scuttler and his employer'. Mark insisted that in every case in which an injury was inflicted, the scuttler was apprehended and brought before the magistrates. However, when he went on to address the stationing of extra police in the districts affected by scuttling, Mark pleaded: 'I beg to point out that this has already been done, but the circumstances attending a Scuttling Affray are so peculiar that even a large body of extra Police are comparatively useless in stopping it.' This remarkably frank admission under-mined entirely his previous claim that scuttlers were invariably arrested and charged if they inflicted an injury during an affray.

Alderman Mark claimed that the area of Manchester in which scuttling took place covered roughly one and a half square miles. This was a gross under-estimate. Moreover, no mention was made of the spread of scuttling across the Manchester conur-bation, from Whit Lane, Pendleton, in the west to Openshaw in the east, a distance of five miles. Mark acknowledged that the gangs monitored police patrols, staging their fights so as to mini-mise the risk of police interference. Moreover, as he pointed out, the timing of affrays was 'very uncertain' and the police generally received no advance warning.

Mark referred to the killing of Peter Kennedy, noting that even the sentence of penal servitude for life imposed on William Willan appeared to have had no deterrent effect. The Watch Committee, he added, had deliberated on the subject of scut-tling many times. They were unanimously of the view that 'the only plan of stopping these outrages is to whip the delinquents when caught'. As Charles Lister had argued in 1890, there was nothing to be gained by sentencing scuttlers to long periods of imprisonment and thus 'turning them into criminals'. The committee could only urge the Home Secretary to reconsider the proposal put to him by the deputation from Manchester and Salford in December 1890. The law, they remained convinced, must be changed for the express purpose of dealing with scuttlers. Once again, however, Henry Matthews was unconvinced; the Government was unwilling to frame national legislation to deal with Manchester's problems.

THE PERSISTENCE of scuttling was all the more puzzling to the civic authorities since it bucked the wider trend in the criminal statistics. An apparent diminution in crime was noted by many legal commentators during the 1880s and 1890s. Trials for indictable, or serious, offences in England and Wales declined from a peak annual rate of 288 per 100,000 of population in the early 1860s to 187 per 100,000 by the early 1890s. Manchester shared in this general trend, prompting recorder Henry West to declare in October 1888, 'It must be gratifying to all people here to feel that Manchester, once known as a great criminal city, should have gained a very different character. There has been a general improvement in the morals of its citizens.' How frustrating, therefore, that scuttlers continued to stain the city's reputation.

As Alderman Mark pointed out to the Under Secretary of State, another fearful 'scuttling outrage' took place within three days of William Willan's reprieve. At around 9.15 p.m. on Thursday, June 2, a group of Meadow Lads – the fearsome Angel Meadow scuttlers – were stood talking in Ludgate Street when they spotted a gang from Ancoats emerging from a side street. The Ancoats mob recognised the captain of the Meadow Lads, Joe Wood, and began shouting, 'Claim him! Cut him up!' Heavily outnumbered, the Meadow Lads sprinted for their lives. Wood was caught by John Kelly, who felled him with a poker. The howling pack gathered around Wood and swiped at him with knives and wooden batons. One of the other Meadow Lads, Michael Hignett, tried to run into a nearby police station, only to find that some more Ancoats lads were waiting outside. Wood lay in Manchester Royal Infirmary for five days while doctors attended to a knife wound on his scalp.

Alexander Pearson, a lantern-jawed, beetle-browed, bullet-headed labourer from Ancoats, stood trial at the Manchester Quarter Sessions on June 19, charged with unlawfully wounding and inflicting grievous bodily harm upon Joseph Wood. Pearson gave his age as nineteen. Alongside him in the dock were John Kelly, twenty-three, a labourer; and John Dean, twenty-eight, a galvaniser. Dean was the oldest scuttler to appear in the court-rooms of Manchester since the onset of the Rochdale Road War in 1870. Under cross-examination, Wood admitted that he knew the prisoners but insisted that he had no quarrel with them. This was an unlikely story, since, by Wood's own admis-sion, Pearson had chased him into a grocer's shop with a knife a month earlier. Wood protested that he was not himself a scut-tler. He did admit to having been in prison, but again, he insisted, this was 'not for scuttling'. Henry Leathby, one of the other Meadow Lads chased by the Ancoats scuttlers on the night of June 2, described the weapon carried by John Dean as 'a short staff'. As Leathby pointed out, it looked suspiciously like 'one of those carried by the police'. Leathby added that, in a previous incident at the end of May, Dean had been present when another scuttler 'had his head cut down to the ear'. Michael Hignett, the third Meadow Lad to testify at the trial, told the jury that the Ancoats scuttlers had completely filled one end of Ludgate Street during the disturbance.

Counsel for the defence told the court that there was evidently bad blood between the two gangs. He urged the jury to disregard the testimony of the Meadow Lads, dismissing it as a 'trumped up' story. John Dean called two witnesses who swore that he had been in a pub with them from nine o'clock to half past ten on the night in question. One of the witnesses, a pave-ment artist, told the court that he had heard Joe Wood threaten to 'swing for Pearson'. Under cross-examination, however, the witness admitted that he bore a grudge against Wood, who had once stolen money from him.

In his summing up for the jury, Henry West declared that it was the most serious case he had dealt with at the sessions for some time, especially considering how rife scuttling was in Manchester. He found it remarkable that while all other crime had decreased, scuttling was on the increase, and now even armed men were joining in. The jury found all three prisoners guilty. West then stunned the court: he sentenced each of them to five years' penal servitude. He added that, along with the Recorder of Salford, he had hoped that the sentence of death imposed on William Willan might have put a stop to this 'wild warfare'. Only Willan's youth had saved him, 'Yet here they had grown men armed in this way to go out and make attacks of which death and the death penalty might have been the result.'

Alexander Pearson was unrepentant. As he was led down to the cells, he shouted, 'Five stretches for nothing. Wait till I come out!'[24]

WILLIAM WILLAN served eight years in prison for the murder of Peter Kennedy. Following his liberation in 1900, he returned to Manchester. He resumed his former occupation as a cooper and set up house on his own in Harpurhey, several miles from his former stomping ground in Ancoats. In an astonishing post-script, he married Florence Caminada – daughter of the legendary detective Jerome Caminada, who had campaigned for Willan's reprieve in 1892. Their first child was born in 1905. Florence Willan taught for many years at a school in Angel Meadow, whilst William ended up working in a foundry. They are buried together at Philips Park Cemetery. A branch of the Willan family still lives nearby in Ancoats and their story of the killing of Peter Kennedy, handed down over three generations, casts new light on the role of 'Billy' Willan. The Bradford Street scuttlers did indeed nurse a grievance against Kennedy. The gang's younger members were instructed to draw lots to deter-mine who was to carry out the 'dosing'. Billy Willan drew the short straw. No mention of this was made by any of the witnesses at the trial lest it was used to prove premeditation.

---

24 Like many scuttlers brought to trial, Pearson routinely lied about his age. Re-arrested soon after his release, he was sentenced to a second term of penal servitude. The Stafford gaol register recorded his age in 1897 as nineteen – the same age he had given five years previously.

CHAPTER 16

Girl Rippers

HANNAH ROBBIN MAY have become the most famous female scuttler by virtue of her relationship with William Willan, but she was not alone. In his landmark survey of scuttling for the *Manchester Guardian*, Alexander Devine defined a scuttler as a male between the ages of fourteen and nineteen. Charles Russell, another prominent commentator on the city's gangs, similarly defined the scuttler as a 'Manchester boy'. Even so, young women were afforded a central place in Russell's account of scuttling – not as combatants, but as providing the pretext for fights between gangs of lads. As Russell put it: 'If, for instance, a lady previously regarded as the sweetheart of a member of, say, the "Forty Row" gang were seen in the company of a "Bengal Tiger", the assumed insult had to be avenged and provided an excellent occasion for an outburst of blackguardism.' In 1898, the *Guardian* went so far as to claim that girls actively incited conflicts between the gangs and were thus responsible for the majority of scuttling affrays. To the *Guardian*, this was a natural female role, since, 'Everyone likes to feel herself a Helen of Troy.'

Girls were also portrayed as forming an audience for the lads' displays of fighting prowess. As J. H. P. Leresche, stipendiary magistrate at the County Police Court, explained to the Home Secretary in December 1890, 'The girls, who harry on the respective gangs, also produce a great deal of mischief. The notion that the gangs must acquit themselves well before their women has had a great deal to do with aggravating the violence.'

Within these accounts, girls were depicted in conventional feminine roles: as handmaidens, bringing up rounds of bricks and bottles for the lads to throw, or as nurses, ready to tend to the lads' wounds. Young women played an additional supporting role in the courtroom where, it was believed, they habitually perjured themselves on behalf of scuttlers. Salford magistrate Joseph Makinson complained upon sentencing one scuttler in 1894, 'Lads like the prisoner were the greatest curse they had in Salford, but rough fellows could always find equally disorderly young women to come forward and give false evidence on their behalf.' Like their male counterparts, the young women who associated with scuttling gangs were acutely fashion conscious. They wore clothing that set them apart as scuttler's 'molls', and informed observers could tell which gang a girl belonged to by the pattern of her skirt. In Salford, for example, a skirt with vertical stripes denoted that a young woman was actively associated with the Hope Street mob.

Victorian social commentators defined women as by nature gentle, submissive and morally pure. Women of all social classes were expected to adhere to higher standards of decorum than their menfolk, and female criminals were doubly damned, as 'unnatural' women as well as law-breakers. Yet in practice the majority of women were anything but passive in their everyday lives. In the Manchester conurbation, most young, working-class women took on paid employment, at least prior to marriage, and older women tended to dominate the street life of the densely populated slum districts. Married women would occasionally fight in the streets to avenge insults, or solve disputes, whilst in private, many stood up to violent and domineering husbands.

Young, single women spent much of their time socialising in the streets: promenading around their own neighbourhoods with groups of friends, frequently exchanging banter and flirting with the knots of lads congregated on the street corners. Middle-class visitors to Manchester were appalled by the brazenness of the young women, and so were the local magistrates. In their view, the only respectable place for a female was in the home. Those mill girls and seamstresses who paraded the streets in their cheap finery betrayed their 'boldness'. To Victorian moralists, this was evidence enough that they lacked the essential feminine virtue of chastity. Disorderly conduct on the public streets, after all, was the hallmark of the prostitutes who paraded on Market Street or hung around the barracks at Ardwick Green or Regent Road in Ordsall.

When young women fell out, they were not averse to fighting one-on-one in the street. Such fights quickly drew crowds of enthusiastic spectators, who formed rings around the combatants, just as they did during 'fair fights' between lads. In June 1869 two correspondents to the *Sphinx*, one of Manchester's satirical magazines, witnessed 'a very savage affair' in Greengate in Salford:

> The combatants were two young women, apparently factory operatives, who, having finished their duties as minders, piecers, or what not, showed they could do in the noble art of self-defence. Their mode of fighting was what we believe would be considered unscientific by 'the fancy', but it appeared to us to be sufficiently punishing, and caused strong excitement among the spectators. During the encounter between the women, one of whom was an Irish girl called Biddy, and the other a Lancashire Lass, Mary Ann, the partisans of each were very demonstrative. Mary Ann generally succeeded in throwing Biddy, whose head appeared to rival in hardness the stone pavement against which it came in contact. A tall, decently-dressed wench, in the inner ring, kept encouraging her champion most vigorously, shouting 'Go into her, Mary Ann,' with infinite gusto. Both girls would have benefited much by having false chignons, and would have saved that mode of punishment which consists in tearing out handfuls of hair by the roots.

Such set-tos were far less common than brawls between lads, but their relative infrequency only added to their appeal as entertainment.

When respectable passers-by were confronted by the sights of two women fighting, they were appalled. In April 1875, a Salford councillor named Daniel Hall attempted to break up another street skirmish between two young women in Greengate. David Sudlow, a local dyer, was enraged by the councillor's interference and promptly floored him. Sudlow was arrested and charged with assault. Councillor Hall told the Salford Police Court how:

... about eleven o'clock on Saturday night he was passing down King Street, when he saw two young women fighting. They were surrounded by a number of roughs, of whom the prisoner was one, and a ring was made in order to allow the women to fight. He (Councillor Hall) remonstrated with the men for allowing such disgraceful conduct, for it was the most disgraceful scene he ever witnessed, when he was knocked down by the prisoner and those who were with him, and received a severe blow on the back of the head.

Sudlow was sent down for three months.

Brawls between young women were a recurring theme at the Salford Police Court. In July 1875, Lizzie Johnson and Annie Ashton were arrested following a riot in Greengate. The court heard that around thirty scuttlers – male and female – had gathered in Greengate at pub closing time and proceeded to stone passers-by. One young woman targeted by the scuttlers ran away in a flood of tears and complained to two beat constables. With some difficulty, the officers managed to take Johnson and Ashton into custody. When the two girls appeared before the magistrates, they were asked to give their occupations as well as their addresses. Johnson stated that she worked in a mill and lived in Birtles Square, Greengate. Ashton said she lived in Style Street in Angel Meadow and worked as a French polisher. Detective Inspector Hargreaves pointed out that Johnson had previously been convicted of wilful damage. The inspector added that he had to send four or five plain-clothes constables to Greengate every night to suppress these bouts of stone-throwing. The magistrate's response was to declare that he would give the two girls another chance. He warned them as to their future conduct, and discharged them.

In June 1876, eight scuttlers were arrested for stone-throwing in Brown Street, off Chapel Street. Seven came from Greengate, four of them women. The eighth hailed from Ordsall, and appears to have been a member of a rival band of scuttlers. The prisoners were tried together before two of Salford's lay magistrates, Henry Lee and Edward Walmsley, who took a chivalrous view of the episode. They regarded three of the lads as the ringleaders and fined them five shillings each. The fines were halved for the four girls.

In addition to repelling raids by marauding bands of scuttlers, the young toughs of Greengate specialised in harassing passers-by. The more refined inhabitants of Lower Broughton were obliged to make their way through Greengate if they wished to walk the short distance home from Manchester city centre. This frequently meant running the gauntlet of the Greengate scuttlers. During June 1876, Chief Constable Torrens received a string of letters from irate pedestrians complaining that they had been molested in New Bridge Street. The local scuttlers were subjecting passers-by to streams of 'the most filthy language', and assaulting anyone that dared to protest. Captain Torrens formed a squad of plain-clothes constables with instructions to clamp down on the offenders. Police Constables Tatton and Ormrod were detailed to patrol Greengate on the night of Friday, June 16. As they turned into New Bridge Street on one of their circuits of the locality, they immediately noticed the scuttlers at work: more than twenty lads and girls were waylaying pedestrians, molesting men and women alike. When the scuttlers spotted the two constables they fled, but three of them were caught and charged with riotous and disorderly conduct. They were brought before Sir John Iles Mantell the following morning. Two were mill girls: Jemima Barrow and Maggie O'Donnell. Both were fined.

The following month a group of long-suffering Greengate residents organised a petition protesting about 'the outrages of roughs who nightly collect in the streets'. The petition was sent to the Chief Constable, Captain Torrens, with the demand that steps be taken to protect the law-abiding people of the neighbourhood. Beat constables were ordered to clamp down on the most minor infringements of public order. So when two constables patrolling Greengate spotted a group of young people jostling adult passers-by and forcing them off the pavement, they arrested four sixteen-year-olds. Once again, two of them were girls: Annie Dooley and Eliza Carr. They were all tried for disorderly conduct before W. Goulden at the Salford Police Court the following morning. Detective Inspector Hargreaves testified to the problems faced by the police, telling the court that, 'Greengate seemed to be the meeting place for all the young roughs residing within a radius of a mile of Manchester and Salford.' Mr Goulden was not overly impressed by the inspector's hyperbole; he fined each of the four prisoners two and a half shillings, with the option of three days' imprisonment.

On an October Saturday in 1876, Mrs Ellen Lee, of Broughton Street in Greengate, was walking home through nearby Wheathill Street with her husband when they were accosted by a gang of scuttlers. The youths surrounded Mr Lee and assaulted him. Mrs Lee attempted to defend her husband, only to be knocked down herself. Her shawl was stolen, along with her purse which contained five shillings. The couple immediately complained to the police, and Detective Howard arrested four local factory girls the following week. Ann Jane Callaghan, Betsy Gorman, Mary Davies and Mary Jane Kearns were charged with assault and robbery. All four hailed from Greengate: Callaghan and Gorman from the dreaded Birtles Square and Kearns from Paradise, the most inappropriately named street in Salford.

Detective Inspector Hargreaves told the stipendiary, Sir John Iles Mantell, that the prisoners were known 'to belong to a gang of scuttlers, who were the terror of the neighbourhoods they infested'. Callaghan had only just come out of prison for her part in a previous scuttling affray, whilst Kearns had previously served a term of one month for scuttling. Sir John was not amused. He jailed Callaghan and Kearns for three months. Gorman and

Davies each got one month. Having passed sentence, Sir John told the court that he should have sent the prisoners for trial at the Assizes, only he did not think the judges knew the full extent of wickedness and depravity among the scuttlers.

Sir John noted that the police had been unable to verify the prisoners' ages. Had it been confirmed that they were under sixteen years of age, he would have preferred to send them to an industrial school. As Sir John told the court, he did not believe in the reforming effects of prisons. In his view, most inmates came out worse than they went in. Nonetheless, as he saw it, the respectable people of Greengate should at least enjoy some respite from harassment by the prisoners.

Betsy Gorman, the youngest of the group, was aged just thirteen. She hailed from a well-known Greengate family. Her mother, Ann, was a hawker with a fondness for drink and a legendary temper; she had eight convictions for drunkenness and disorderly conduct and had herself spent several months in Strangeways, courtesy of Sir John. Betsy's brother, Michael – a 'rough-looking young fellow' of twenty-one – had just been convicted of indecently assaulting a young woman and sent down for six months. He had nine previous convictions for assault and disorderly conduct. Ann Gorman had attended her son Michael's hearing at Salford Police Court and accosted his victim on the way out, threatening her with violence for 'going against' her son. Mrs Gorman was arrested immediately and brought before Sir John, who bound her over to keep the peace for six months, adding that 'he was quite strong enough to deal with Greengate roughs'. For all his bluster, Sir John had failed to reform Ann Gorman. Now thirteen-year-old Betsy seemed destined to follow in her mother's footsteps.

AT AROUND midnight on Saturday, 18 January 1890, a twenty-five-year-old collier named John Cunliffe was making his way home through the Whit Lane district of Pendleton after an evening's drinking. At the corner of Gill Street, he noticed the local scuttlers: Buffalo Bill's gang. Ignoring a stream of insults from the assembled youths, Cunliffe turned into the street.

Moments later, he heard footsteps on the pavement. He turned round to find Jimmy Foley and Joe Allen facing him, their belts wrapped around their wrists. Before Cunliffe could run, Foley lashed out, swinging his buckle repeatedly. By the time the blows stopped, Cunliffe was lying in the road, his face and forehead covered with bruises and cuts. But rather than stop there, Foley gave a whistle to summon the rest of the gang, and they began to kick the crumpled figure on the ground. Cunliffe momentarily blacked out. By the time he came round, the scuttlers were nowhere to be seen. He limped the final hundred yards home, where he told his two brothers what had happened. Joe Cunliffe was twenty-nine years old, Charlie twenty-two. They both worked alongside John at the Pendleton pit. They were not men to be pushed around. The three of them set out in search of Foley and Allen. The search did not take long; the scuttlers had re-assembled at the corner of Gill Street.

Joe Cunliffe showed no fear as he walked up to the knot of youths gathered on the street corner. He approached Foley and asked, 'Are you one of them?' Foley, who was aged seventeen, knew that he would be no match for the older man in a fair fight – but he had no intention of fighting fairly. 'Yes, I'm one,' he replied. 'What of it?' Before Joe Cunliffe could respond, the gang's female members made a sudden charge at the three brothers and began to strike at them with their clogs. Only the unexpected appearance of a pair of beat constables saved the Cunliffe brothers from a beating. The brothers reported both the initial assault upon John and the subsequent barrage by the female scuttlers. Ten minutes later, a constable took John Cunliffe to Foley's house and the bruised and battered collier identified both Foley and Allen after peering in through a window.

Foley and Allen also worked at the Pendleton pit and it appears that the pair were unwilling to face the wrath of their fellow colliers on the following Monday. At half past six that morning, rather than turning up as usual at the colliery gates, the two lads surrendered themselves at Pendleton police station. The Buffalo Bill gang's female members were equally well-known to the police, and on the morning of January 25, Sergeant Anderson went to a Pendleton mill and asked for Amelia Higginbottom and Agnes Garforth. The two girls gave false addresses, so the sergeant let them return to their work only to arrest them at the mill gates shortly after midday. The girls had toiled long hours for their weekly wage of four shillings and ten pence; now they risked swapping the incessant heat and thunderous clatter of the card-room for the gloom and solitude of Strangeways.

The four prisoners, aged from fifteen to eighteen, appeared together at Salford Police Court. P.C. Malin identified all four as members of a scuttling gang which assembled nightly in Whit Lane. He described how the scuttlers rallied reinforcements at the first sign of any bother: 'The boys had a whistle, and the girls a whoop, or scream. When those signals were given a number of roughs assembled.' Questioned by stipendiary magistrate Joseph Makinson, P.C. Malin insisted that he had heard these signals given, and then watched the gang assemble. Sergeant Anderson told the court that the gang was forty-strong, adding that only a week earlier he had had to use his stick to get away from them. When the police pointed out that Foley had also already served two months in Strangeways for a similar offence, the magistrate was livid. He committed all four prisoners for trial.

At the Quarter Sessions a week later, John Cunliffe told how he was initially assaulted by the male prisoners, who rushed at him as he was making his way home along Gill Street. Foley, he said, struck him on the forehead and face four times with a belt, cutting his hat and face and blackening his eyes. When he was on the floor, Allen kicked him, after which he passed out. He had also heard Foley give a peculiar kind of whistle, and a lot of lads and girls came from all directions. The kicks made him sore all over and he had to lie in bed all the next day.

All four prisoners, described by court reporters as 'of unkempt appearance', were convicted of unlawful wounding. The two male prisoners protested that Cunliffe had provoked the row by making insulting remarks to one of their female associates. The Recorder of Salford, Joseph Yates, was unmoved. He sentenced Foley and Allen to six months. The two girls, who appear to have played a less ferocious part in the assault upon the Cunliffe brothers, got three months.

In total, thirteen scuttlers faced charges of assault, unlawful wounding or riot at the sessions that day. With the exception of Amelia Higginbottom and Agnes Garforth, all of the prisoners were male. The editor of the *Salford Chronicle* did not hesitate to demand that the lads should be flogged. He was more circumspect when it came to the young women, but on reflection, he advocated equal treatment for them: 'According to what the police say, these viragoes are no less cruel than the lads for whom we advocate flogging, and, therefore, perhaps, some arrangement might be made by the prison matron for a similar bestowal of the principal mark of disapproval of their vixenish behaviour.'

SARAH ANN Crook was born in Salford in 1868. She was one of eight children to William Crook, a bleacher, and his wife Rachel. The family lived in Hankinson Street, the road which gave its name to the surrounding district: Hanky Park. Sarah Ann moved out of the family home during her teens following the death of her mother, finding cheap lodgings in Black Ditch in Pendleton. Rooms here were cheap on account of the legendary rowdiness of the inhabitants, many of whom made regular appearances before the magistrates. Fights between the women of Black Ditch ranged from bouts of window-smashing to free-for-alls with sticks, stones and belts.

When the police had cause to enter the area, they often meted out violence of their own. In May 1895, residents complained that during one Saturday night revel in the street, two beat constables pursued Ellen Walsh into her own home and 'ill-treated' her children when they went to their mother's aid. Walsh was charged with being drunk and disorderly. She admitted 'having had a little drink' but insisted that she had been singing in her own house when the constables barged in and dragged her outside. Nevertheless, she was sent down for a month.

Six months later, John and Ellen McLaughlin of Black Ditch

were charged with neglecting their two children 'in a manner likely to injure their health'. The prosecution had been brought by local officers of the National Society for the Prevention of Cruelty to Children. P.C. Shore, called as a witness, told the court that he had found the children at their own door around midnight. Their mother came to the window upstairs but refused to allow him entry. The children's clothing was thin, dirty and ragged. The mother, the constable added, was a drunken and violent woman. Another police officer corroborated the story, informing the magistrate that twelve months previously Mrs McLaughlin kept a small pig in the house and had to be 'threatened' before she would remove it. On one occasion, the constable added, he found one of her children in an ash-pit. Two inspectors from the NSPCC told the court of the filthy condition of the house and the habits of the prisoners. One said 'he had seen the woman drunk and dancing with the pig in her arms'. Joseph Makinson was appalled. He jailed Mrs McLaughlin for a month, telling her, 'There was no excuse for filth.' John McLaughlin was discharged, but only after Makinson warned him that 'if a wife did not do the work of the house, the husband should do it'.

Sarah Ann Crook fitted into Black Ditch only too well. During her late teens and early twenties she amassed convictions for disorderly conduct, drunkenness, vagrancy and theft. In 1889, she was arrested three times. She was jailed for fourteen days in March after she was convicted of using obscene and profane language in Regent Road. In October, she spent another two weeks in prison for shouting obscenities in Chapel Street. When she emerged from Strangeways she hired a barrel organ and took up a lucrative pitch on the fringes of the Salford fairground, adjacent to the Flat Iron market. The market itself was an embarrassment to Salford's municipal leaders. The second-hand clothes dealers, operating on the open ground around Trinity Church at the gateway to Manchester, were too visible a reminder of the poverty for which the borough was renowned. Yet most Salfordians loved the Flat Iron. The auctioneers delighted the crowds with their patter: 'by turns wheedling the people with a honeyed tongue, or with winks and sideways glances setting the women giggling and the men roaring,' as the *Manchester Guardian* put it. The fairground attached to the market contained roundabouts, shooting galleries, boxing booths and a cheap theatre.

For three weeks Sarah Ann Crook flourished there, attracting rowdy but good-natured crowds of young people, many of them scuttlers, who staged impromptu outdoor dances on the pavement flags of Chapel Street. Her prosperity was short-lived. On the night of Saturday, November 23, she fell foul of P.C. Milne of the Salford Borough Police. According to the constable, Crook had attracted a throng of lads and girls whose dances spilled into the street, repeatedly holding up the horse-drawn traffic. Three times in as many hours, P.C. Milne ordered Crook to move on or face arrest; the dancers would disperse only to re-assemble as soon as the constable departed.

By half-past nine, Sarah Ann Crook's limited patience was wearing thin. When P.C. Milne moved her on for the fourth time that night, she threw herself onto the ground in protest and began hurling threats and abuse at the constable. He promptly arrested her, only to find that as he tried to pull her up he was assaulted by one of the dancers. His assailant, Sarah Ann Hickson, was a Hanky Park girl, just like Crook, and she was known to the police as one of the Chaney Street scuttlers. She lashed out at the startled officer, who blew his whistle for assistance. With the help of a fellow constable, P.C. Milne eventually managed to take the two furious young women into custody.

Crook and Hickson appeared in court on the Monday morning. The magistrates were informed that Crook had five previous convictions, the last as recent as November 1. They promptly jailed her for a month. Hickson was only fifteen, and had no criminal record. She was fined twenty shillings, with the alternative of a month's imprisonment.

Hickson was soon brought back before the magistrates. In March 1890, sensational headlines in the Salford press proclaimed the discovery of 'A GANG OF FEMALE SCUTTLERS'. The gang was by all accounts exercising a reign of terror in Hanky

Park. The headlines were prompted by the arrest of three girls in their mid-teens, charged with violently assaulting Mrs Mary Allen, of Pimlot Street. They were identified in court as Sarah Ellen Fitzgerald, aged fifteen; Susannah Hickson, fifteen; and Sarah Ann Hickson, now aged sixteen. A detective told the magistrates that all three girls belonged to an organised gang of female scuttlers. He said that Mrs Allen's daughter had also belonged to the gang, but in order to break her from such company, her parents sent her from the town. 'Prisoners went to Mrs Allen's house and demanded to know her daughter's whereabouts, and on being refused the information savagely attacked her, after which they ran off, Fitzgerald taking her shawl.' The detective added that Pendleton on Saturday nights was 'a small pandemonium' because of the conduct of these girls.

The reaction of stipendiary Makinson was intriguing. His usual response when faced with a batch of scuttlers was to issue fines or prison sentences, committing the more serious offenders for trial at the next Quarter Sessions. On this occasion, he remanded the three prisoners on their parents' recognizances, requesting that the parents thrash them. Confronted by a group of female scuttlers, the magistrate was eager to devise his own system of summary justice. The girls' parents agreed to the request. When Sarah Fitzgerald next appeared in court, her father stated that 'in accordance with the expressed wish of the bench', he had soundly thrashed his daughter, who in any case denied that she had been party to the assault, alleging that she got the shawl from her companions. Fitzgerald was bound over to be of good behaviour in future and was then discharged. The Hickson sisters were likewise thrashed by their father. Susannah was in turn bound over and released. Like Fitzgerald, she had no previous convictions.

Sarah Ann Hickson, the oldest of the three 'scutteresses', was singled out for stiffer punishment. Her conviction alongside Sarah Ann Crook four months earlier weighed heavily on the mind of Joseph Makinson, who was clearly determined that she should be removed from the corrupting streets of Salford. Makinson gave Sarah Ann Hickson a stark choice: she could go to work as a domestic servant in a 'respectable home', or she could go to Strangeways for a month with hard labour. By offering domestic service as an alternative to imprisonment, the stipendiary magistrate was acting entirely outside of his legal powers. In any event, Hickson was distinctly unimpressed. She chose prison. She was willing to sacrifice her liberty altogether for one month rather than endure years of poorly paid drudgery as a 'slavey', or household servant.

Although the police had identified the Hickson sisters and Fitzgerald as part of an organised gang of female scuttlers, they in fact belonged to the Chaney Street mob from Hanky Park. Eight months later, in November 1890, following a clash between Chaney Street and Hope Street, witnesses described how 'about a hundred girls and lads' took part. On New Year's Day in 1892, Sarah Ann Hickson was arrested yet again. She was charged with assaulting a policeman and attempting to rescue a prisoner from custody. When Hickson was brought before the Salford magistrates, the police stated she still 'belonged to a gang of scuttlers', but on this occasion made no reference to the sex of her associates. Hickson was jailed for six weeks.

Like Hickson, Sarah Ann Crook was entirely undaunted by prison. In March 1890, she was arrested at her barrel organ pitch at the Salford fairground for the second time in four months. She was charged with obstructing the footway 'by dancing with others thereon' and fined twenty shillings. Two months later she was accused of stealing a pair of trousers from a shop, but the evidence against her was inconclusive and she was discharged. Within two weeks, however, she was arrested once more and fined ten shillings for being drunk and disorderly in Chapel Street. She was unable to pay the fine, so she served seven days in Strangeways instead.

Three months later, in September 1890, Crook was jailed for fourteen days for again being drunk and disorderly in Chapel Street. On the night of her release, two beat constables discovered her sleeping rough in Gravel Lane, close to her former pitch at the fairground. The constables took her into custody and charged her with 'lodging in the open air and having no visible means of subsistence'. The magistrates took a dim view and jailed her for another month. This time she celebrated her release with her old associates in the pubs of Chapel Street, but the revelries got out of hand and she was arrested before the night was out. A fine of five shillings was imposed the following morning. This time her friends rallied round and the fine was paid. Crook managed to stay out of prison for nearly two months, but she still saw in the New Year in Strangeways, having been given fourteen days for using obscene language in Chapel Street on December 29. Yet again, she re-offended within a week of her release. Beat constables arrested her for 'disorderly conduct with others by shouting and using obscene language in Chapel Street' and the Salford magistrates obliged by sending her back to prison for another fourteen days.

Sarah Ann Crook eventually turned to prostitution. She was regularly brought before the Salford magistrates throughout the remainder of the decade. When she was charged with soliciting and drunkenness in October 1897, it took three constables to restrain her in the dock. She maintained a running commentary of abusive epithets as P.C. Lewis gave evidence against her and could plainly be heard issuing threats to the police in general, and certain constables in particular, as she was jailed yet again.

FEMALE MEMBERS of the Ordsall Lane gang were involved in the systematic intimidation of witnesses. George White, one of the gang's former members, was a key witness to the attack on police constable William Chapman (see Chapter 14). White suffered persistent harassment to deter him from testifying. On the night of 16 June 1890, he was pursued through the streets of Ordsall to his family's house in Walmer Street by a chasing pack headed by a gang of girls, some of them allegedly waving knives. As White cowered inside the house, the mob assembled at the front door shouting, 'Come out, Totty White, and we'll rip you open.' 'Totty' was a Victorian slang term for a girl – or a prostitute. One of White's neighbours ran to the Regent Road police station and two detectives rushed to Walmer Street, only to find that the mob had departed. The officers made their way into Ordsall Lane, where they found scenes of chaos: between 2,000 and 3,000 people had gathered, with the gang of girls in their midst 'yelling and dancing about among the throng'. When the girls spotted the detectives, they turned and ran. A desperate chase ensued in which a woman and her four children were knocked down before the officers caught up with the scuttler-esses on Woden Street bridge.

The detectives apprehended three fifteen-year-old girls known to be connected with the Ordsall Lane scuttlers. They appeared before Joseph Makinson the following morning, charged with breaching the peace and using threats of violence against George White to prevent him giving evidence. White confirmed that the prisoners had threatened to 'rip him up with a knife' if he gave evidence.

The prisoners vigorously protested their innocence. One, Elizabeth McGregor, claimed that she had been to a shop in Regent Road for some wool and was returning home by way of Ordsall Lane with the other girls, whom she had met on the way, when a woman told them the police were following them and they ran away. McGregor had a ball of wool, a stocking, and four knitting needles in her possession when she was taken into police custody. None of the prisoners was found to have a knife. Makinson addressed the prisoners exhaustively on the state of depravity into which they had fallen, telling them if they had not been so young he would have sent them to prison for a long period. Instead, he bound them over to keep the peace for six months.

Makinson was in turn severely admonished by the local press. The *Salford Chronicle* protested that magisterial pronounce-ments were worthless if a mob of knife-wielding girls could escape imprisonment, ignoring the fact that none of the girls had been found with a knife. Elizabeth McGregor and her friends Matilda McStay and Alice McEwen were described as 'female roughs' and 'disorderly females' by the press, while the *County Telephone* labelled the trio 'GIRL RIPPERS'. Less than two years after the Whitechapel murders attributed to the so-called Jack the Ripper, Salford appeared to be in the grip of a fearsome band of knife-wielding scuttleresses.

IN NOVEMBER 1890, Joseph Makinson was again confronted by the perplexing sight of a group of female scuttlers in the dock. On this occasion, they were members of a gang from the Adelphi. Alice Cullen, Mary Ann Cullen, Mary Ann Meagan and Lizzie Dugan were aged between fifteen and twenty-one. They were charged with assaulting Sarah Ann Gordon, one of the gang's former members. They were angry because Gordon had left the gang following an ultimatum from her mother. On the night of Saturday, November 15, the gang's female members gathered at the front door of the Gordon family's house in Arlington Street and began yelling that they would 'dose' Sarah Ann as soon as they got her outside. In the event, Gordon was punched, rather than stabbed, when her former companions caught up with her the following Monday evening.

Meagan, Dugan and Alice Cullen all had previous convictions and Mr Makinson initially jailed them for fourteen days. Mary Ann Cullen, with no prior record, was bound over to be of good behaviour. Having imposed prison sentences on three of the prisoners, however, Makinson suddenly relented. He ordered that they should be remanded in custody for one night. They were brought back to court the following morning, when he made them promise not to go near Gordon's house again and to stop loitering in the streets. Joseph Makinson was clearly unwilling to treat female scuttlers with the same severity as their male counterparts. The three scuttleresses agreed to the stipendiary magistrate's terms and were duly bound over and released. This was scant consolation to Sarah Ann Gordon. Her persecutors lived nearby in Cannon Court, and few of those present believed they had any intention of keeping their promises to the stipendiary.

Makinson's decision to remonstrate with the prisoners rather than to impose custodial sentences was surprising since two of the girls had been convicted at the same court in the previous two months. Seventeen-year-old Dugan had been fined for being drunk and disorderly, while Alice Cullen, aged sixteen, had been fined for an assault on a young woman named Harriet Scarborough. When she was arrested for her part in the assault on Sarah Ann Gordon, Alice Cullen attempted to disguise her identity from the police by giving her name as 'Kate' and her place of birth, rather sarcastically, as 'America'. At twenty-one, Mary Ann Meagan, alias Scott, was an old offender. She had appeared before Makinson twice that September, first when she was convicted of being drunk and disorderly and assaulting a police officer, and second for drunken and disorderly behaviour.

Joseph Makinson appears to have been more concerned to deter the girls from loitering in the streets than to punish them for the assault upon Sarah Ann Gordon. His efforts were in vain. Alice Cullen renewed her acquaintance with Makinson six weeks later, after she was arrested for being drunk and disorderly outside the Gordon family's house in Arlington Street during the early hours of Christmas morning. She was apprehended at quarter past two, spent the night in the cells to sober up and appeared in court on December 27 to be fined ten shillings, with the alternative of seven days' imprisonment. When she told Makinson that she was unable to pay the fine, he offered her the chance to go into service in a 'respectable home' rather than to Strangeways. Like Sarah Ann Hickson before her, Alice Cullen chose prison.

In the case of the scuttleresses of the Adelphi, there were clear echoes of the assault upon Mary Allen by the Chaney Street gang in Pendleton in March 1890. In both cases, mothers were determined to keep their daughters from associating with the local scuttlers. In both instances, the mothers' efforts met with reprisal. The assault upon Sarah Ann Gordon may well have been an act of punishment after she broke an oath of allegiance to her former comrades. The following year, fifteen-year-old Frederick Hopwood took revenge upon Annie Topping after she left Salford's Bury Street gang. On the night of the assault, Topping had attended a Church Mission room with a friend. Hopwood ran up to her from behind and stabbed her in the shoulder with a penknife.

THE MOST persistent scourge of the Salford magistrates was Susan Wilson. Born in 1847, she married in her twenties and settled in Ordsall with her husband and three children. Her husband was a heavy drinker and prone to fits of temper. He repeatedly walked out on his family, returning to subject Susan to torrents of violence and abuse. By the time Susan reached her thirties, she too had turned to drink. Over a period of twenty-five years, she spent her time between Strangeways Prison, the Salford Union workhouse, and her home in Heap's Court, off Regent Road. She was arrested more than 200 times by the Salford Borough Police. The officers generally found her drunk and abusive, but they also took her into custody for her own protection when they saw her lying drunk in the road.

Her relationship with the stipendiary magistrate, Joseph Makinson, was laced with a mixture of resignation, humour, and threats on both sides. Their early exchanges frequently ended with moralising sermons on his part and fierce retorts on hers. As often as not, she hurled one of her boots at the stipendiary as he pronounced sentence. The cricket-loving magistrate was an accomplished batsman and his agility served him well, prompting a local journalist to remark that he had more than once seen a duck's beak, but this was the first time he'd seen the 'beak' duck.

Making her first court appearance of 1896, Wilson greeted Mr Makinson with a hearty 'Happy New Year, sir.' The court heard that she had been apprehended in East Market Street, shouting and singing. Makinson asked if she wanted another spell in Strangeways: 'I suppose you want another month's lodgings?'

'Good lad,' she replied. 'I will live to come out again.'

She left the dock singing 'Ireland's the Gem of the Sea'.

CHAPTER 17

King of the Scuttlers

THE GANG LEADERS of late Victorian Manchester were castigated in the courtrooms and demonised in the pages of the local press. On the streets, however, they were viewed differently. The captains of scuttling gangs were feared and admired in equal measure, but their notoriety brought problems as well as prestige. The police were constantly watching over them and members of rival gangs sought them out during affrays. To youths with reputations of their own to forge, the scalp of a rival captain was a valuable prize. When two captains came into conflict, neither could afford to back down.

Fighting prowess was much valued in the poorer districts of Manchester and Salford. Skill and courage were greatly admired, but a willingness to fight – to stand your ground – was essential if a youth was to be accepted into the life of the streets. Boys were taught to stand up for themselves from an early age and to fight back if they were provoked. For older men, teaching sons to be 'manly' was all-important. Billy Doyle, who was born in Greengate in 1882, remembered how his father tried to prevent him helping his mother with the housework: 'A lad hadn't to do anything. We had flag [paved] floors and we mustn't clean the floor. "They're not going to make a girl of my lad." That was his idea.' His father even punished him for losing in a fight. 'If I got a good hiding outside [my father] would give me another one for getting a good hiding.' Peer-group pressure only added to the need to be prepared to fight. Joe Toole, born in Ordsall in 1887, recalled, 'You had to fight to survive in my early days in Salford. If you were not fighting for a living [as a boxer], you had to periodically defend your skin, which included your honour; if you declined a challenge to fight, you took a back seat at all games; and if you didn't swear vigorously, nobody believed what you said.'

Fights were one of the great spectacles of the slums. The ritual of the 'fair' or 'stand-up' fight saw two men strip to the waist and shake hands before fighting with their fists. This was the accepted means for two working men to resolve their differences. Police officers rarely interfered unless the crowd gathered at the scene became unruly. Breaches of the fighting code, such as pulling out a weapon, or kicking a man when he was down, were resented and might well lead to a court summons for assault. Fights outside public houses at closing time at weekends were eagerly anticipated by local children. William Bowen, who grew up in Greengate during the 1880s, recalled: 'I can remember as a boy one Sunday afternoon, after closing time, a glorious summer afternoon, a crowd came out of a public house with two men stripped to their naked waists who began to fight and they fought until their naked bodies were streaming with blood. I thought, when I am a man I would like to be able to fight like that.' Men earned enormous respect both for displays of fighting prowess and for their capacity to withstand pain. To young boys, such men were nothing less than heroes, to be both admired and emulated.

Lads aged in their teens were frequently required to prove their mettle in the workplace as well as on the streets. Challenges to fight could not be shirked if a new lad was to be accepted by his co-workers. In the workshops of Ancoats, any boy who refused a fair fight would be bullied relentlessly. Fights between lads who worked together were almost nightly affairs, often prompted by the most trivial disputes, and bouts between youths, as between men, were highly public. They were arranged for dinner hours or the end of the working day and onlookers gathered in large crowds, heaping praise on those who acquitted themselves well.

In May 1889, sixteen-year-old John Rowlands challenged any lad of his own size in Derbyshire's glassworks in Oldfield Road, Salford, to fight him. Arthur Jones took up the challenge and the two lads went to a plot of vacant land opposite the works, where they took off their coats in front of a crowd of their workmates. Rowlands struck Jones several blows to the head and body, knocking him to the ground. Jones appeared to have some sort of fit and died shortly afterwards. When apprehended, Rowlands told the police, 'I will give myself up; but it was a fair fight. We shook hands before we fought.' Rowlands stood trial for manslaughter at Liverpool Assizes. The jury found him guilty after hearing the testimony of the house surgeon at Salford Royal Hospital. In the surgeon's view, Jones 'died from shock, as the result of a blow to the left side of the body'. The judge sentenced Rowlands to just one day's imprisonment after accepting witnesses' accounts of Jones's death as an unfortunate accident.

As youths began to frequent pubs and beerhouses in their mid to late teens, their displays of bravado were frequently fuelled by drink. The resulting violence often appeared to be as random as it was fierce. Jimmy Rook, a twenty-one-year-old labourer, was one of a gang of youths from Ordsall who rampaged through Chapel Street, Salford's main thoroughfare, at closing time one Saturday night in January 1889. Rook ran down the middle of the road shouting that he 'could beat any man in Salford' as he struck out wildly at passers-by. He was arrested by two beat constables. When Rook was brought before the magistrates the following Monday morning, the constables reported that his behaviour was 'more like a madman than anything else'. Similar scenes were witnessed in the streets of Salford every Saturday night as police officers wrestled with powerfully built men such as Sam McGowan, 'the Salford fighting man', William Fowler, 'the champion bruiser of Greengate', and John Crawley, a labourer from Hanky Park who bragged in court in 1887 that 'there was not many others could lick him about Ellor Street at fighting'.

JOHN JOSEPH Hillier was born in Fermoy, a market town in County Cork, Ireland, in 1874. His mother, Bridget, was widowed shortly afterwards and moved to England in search of work to support herself and her child. She settled in Salford, where she found employment as a mill-worker and cheap lodgings in Providence Street, Ordsall – the She Battery. The street housed a number of prostitutes, drawn by the proximity of a nearby barracks. Bridget and her son occupied a single room in a sublet four-roomed house which they shared with a foundry labourer, his wife and stepson, and another married couple. The Hilliers then moved to lodgings in Gold Street in Hanky Park, before returning to Ordsall when Bridget married for the second time. Her new husband was a furnaceman, ten years her senior, and the family moved to a small terraced house in Woden Street, off Ordsall Lane. Woden Street was much quieter than the She Battery – and far too quiet for John Joseph Hillier.

His first conviction for scuttling was in June 1889, at the age of fifteen. He was arrested in Quay Street, close to the bridge over the River Irwell, during a ruck between a young Salford gang and a raiding party from Manchester. Hillier was convicted of disorderly conduct by throwing stones. He was fined ten shillings by the Salford magistrates, with the alternative of seven days' imprisonment. His mother agreed to pay the fine in instalments. Five months later, Hillier was arrested for the second time. On this occasion, around thirty Salford lads had gathered on Chapel Street to wait for a Manchester mob. The cry went up, 'Here is Manchester coming!' and the two gangs surged into each other, knives and belts flailing. Beat constables arrived on the scene as the fight spilled into North George Street, and the scuttlers fled in all directions. Hillier had played a prominent part in the fight, but at some cost: he was struck hard with belts by some of the Manchester lads during the affray, and was arrested at the scene by police officers who adopted their customary tactic of apprehending the walking wounded in the aftermath of a scuttle. They caught Hillier easily. He was bleeding profusely, having been gashed by several buckles. He was also found to be in possession of a butcher's knife, which he had concealed in his trousers as the police approached.

Hillier appeared before Joseph Makinson at Salford Police Court on a charge of unlawful and riotous assembly. If convicted, he was almost certain to be sent down. Makinson asked what he had been planning to do with the knife, to which Hillier replied, 'Nowt, I found it.' Police witnesses depicted scenes of violence and chaos in North George Street, whilst Superintendent Hallam informed the court that there had been frequent complaints of scuttles between lads from Manchester and Salford around Chapel Street in recent months. Mr Makinson, who had heard many such tales in recent years, was not unduly perturbed, noting that there was no proof that Hillier had actually used the knife found on him. Nonetheless, he was satisfied that Hillier had been present at the scene of the affray for an 'unlawful purpose'. He passed sentence of fourteen days' imprisonment and Hillier spent that night, the first of many, in Strangeways.

Prison only hardened him. On his release Hillier plunged straight back into the fray. On 8 January 1890, he appeared at the Manchester Police Court charged with assault and was jailed for one month. On March 28, he was brought back before the Manchester magistrates on another assault charge. This time he got two months. Hillier's repeated spells in Strangeways made it increasingly difficult for him to find legitimate employment and by the autumn of 1890 he had turned to burglary as an alternative means of making a living. However, his drift into property crime soon brought him back before the courts. Along with a lad named Stephen Byrne, who court reporters noted was deaf and dumb, he came up for trial at the Quarter Sessions charged with breaking into a dwelling in Cumberland Street, Deansgate, and stealing an array of household items: two coats, one clock, one pair of blankets, one counterpane, one chemise, one shirt, two aprons, one pair of drawers, one rug, one skirt, one pawn ticket and one piece of paper. Between them, the lads had cleared the house of most of its saleable, or pawnable, contents. After hearing the evidence, the jury acquitted Byrne but found Hillier guilty of breaking and entering and larceny. The recorder sentenced him to two months' hard labour.

When he emerged from Strangeways, Hillier joined a gang of scuttlers from Hardman Street in Deansgate. Although the dens of Deansgate had been partially cleared during the construction of

Central Station, Hardman Street was one of a cluster of slum streets and courts which remained. It contained a number of sleazy lodging-houses, and many young working lads took fourpenny beds there when they fell out with their parents. It seems likely that Hillier did so after making the acquaintance of Deansgate lads in Strangeways. The Deansgate mob were involved in frequent skirmishes with bands of scuttlers from nearby districts in Salford, making raids into Chapel Street and beyond to the slums of Greengate.

By the time he was seventeen, Hillier was well known to the members of scuttling gangs across Manchester and Salford. With his fellow Deansgate lads, he regularly attended the People's Concert Hall, a popular music hall in Lower Mosley Street better known as the 'Casino', or 'Cass'. This was the largest music hall in Manchester, a squat, ugly, utilitarian building that catered for a low class – some said 'no class' – audience. The Cass, which opened in 1853, held up to 3,000 people and drew lively crowds every Saturday night. Admission to the gallery cost threepence. The atmosphere was raucous to say the least: the audience made nearly as much noise as the performers, maintaining an unceasing chatter and pausing only to smoke 'tabs' and sip beer. Joe Toole, who was born in 1887, was a regular at the Cass from the age of six. 'The audience were very rough,' he recalled, 'and always ready for a disturbance.'

The *Manchester City News* characterised a typical Manchester music hall programme:

Comic man with three songs, all glorifying drink, disorder, and someone else's wife; young lady with two songs, one on 'pals' who were always tippling together, the other with a chorus in which a well-emphasised phrase had a double-meaning; a 'classic' dance, by a lady who seemed to be clothed mainly in limelight; sensational trapeze tricks; performing animals going through their work with depressing mechanical accuracy to the crack of a whip; more 'comic' songs, one of a man who repeatedly went to gaol for drunkenness and engaged in cheerful conversation with the magistrates, the other song on lodgers and mothers-in-law; song and dance by a young lady dressed as a man, who told of the delights of sitting in the sunshine with a negro Lady-love.

The *City News* regarded the low music halls as 'vicious in tone and effect', deploring their celebration of drunkenness, their mocking of the institution of marriage and the police, and the 'evil thoughts' aroused by the semi-clad female 'classic' dancers. The audiences had few such misgivings.

The Cass was well known as the haunt of scuttlers. On Saturday, 2 May 1891, Hillier was confronted inside the hall by Tommy Callaghan, the 'king' of the Bungall Boys, a fearsome band of scuttlers from the slum streets and courtyards off Fairfield Street and London Road. Close by Piccadilly, this was one of the toughest districts in Manchester. With thirty lads massed behind him, Callaghan tried to provoke Hillier with a series of threats and taunts. Sly blows were exchanged inside the hall, but the two gangs held back from a mass brawl in the gallery, preferring to settle matters later, in the street.

As Hillier and his followers emerged from the Cass, their adversaries stood waiting outside the Concert Inn, a nearby beer-house. Jim Southern stepped out of the ranks of the Bungall Boys to challenge Hillier's friend, John Kennedy.

'What's to do?' asked Kennedy.

'We want bother,' exclaimed Southern.

The Bungall Boy waved a belt tied around his wrist and then felled Kennedy with one blow to the head from the heavy brass buckle. Kennedy picked himself up and tried to run, but Southern quickly caught him and stabbed him in the side of his chest. Kennedy was surrounded by around a dozen Bungall Boys, who beat him with their belts and kicked him as he lay on the ground. In the thick of the action, the two rival leaders came together. Tommy Callaghan whacked John Joseph Hillier over the head with an iron bar and knocked him to the ground, where he too was kicked repeatedly by a gaggle of Bungall Boys.

Kennedy was taken to Manchester Royal Infirmary, where he was treated for a large gash on his right temple. In the surgeon's view, the blow 'must have been given with considerable force'. More serious by far were the two stab wounds on the right side of Kennedy's chest. Both had punctured the scuttler's right lung. The injuries were so serious that doctors feared for Kennedy's life for four days. A magistrate was summoned to the hospital to take a statement in which he identified Jim Southern as the youth who had struck him with a belt and stabbed him. Hillier had been carried to his mother's house in Woden Street in Ordsall after the affray. However, his injuries were so serious that his mother called the police on the following Monday morning, and Hillier was taken to Salford Royal Hospital, where he spent two weeks recovering.

Three Bungall Boys subsequently appeared before the recorder, Henry West. Tommy Callaghan and John Wolstenholme, both aged seventeen, and Jim Southern, nineteen, were charged with inflicting grievous bodily harm upon John Kennedy. Callaghan was further charged with violently assaulting Hillier, but swore, 'I was not there. I did not see any of them.' Southern, for his part, claimed that he had acted only in self-defence and made counter-allegations against Kennedy and Hillier from the dock, depicting them as eager participants in the scuttle. Southern alleged that Kennedy had tried to strike the first blow, swiping at him with a dagger. Counsel for the defence duly pointed to Kennedy's own previous convictions for scuttling, forcing him to admit that he had been jailed for twelve months in June 1889. Kennedy insisted, however, that he 'had had nothing to do with scuttling' since. Hillier likewise portrayed himself as an innocent victim on this occasion, claiming that he had not done any scuttling for nine months.

Counsel for the prosecution pointed out that nearly all of those involved in the proceedings – whether as perpetrators, victims, or witnesses – had previous convictions for scuttling, and speculated that revenge was the motive for the grave assault upon Kennedy since 'a good deal of resentment generally lurked in the minds of those who had had the worst of a scuttling affray'. The judge jailed Thomas Callaghan and James Southern for nine months.

Two and a half months later, John Joseph Hillier was involved in another Saturday night affray at the Cass. On Saturday, August 22, the Grey Mare Boys from Bradford turned up and made their way to seats in the gallery. The Bradford lads were making a statement of considerable daring. Simply by entering the gallery, they were effectively throwing down the gauntlet to Hillier and his associates. One of the Deansgate scuttlers singled out a Grey Mare Boy named Mick Conroy and challenged him to fight there and then. Conroy refused, but was immediately set upon and struck with belts. The gallery was instantly in uproar, with the scuttlers' threats and curses momentarily drowned out by screams and shouts from other members of the audience. Conroy tried to clamber into the next row of seats to get away but he was pulled back. Hillier lunged forward with his butcher's knife and stabbed Conroy just below the shoulder. The Bradford scuttlers were quickly routed. Ironically, however, their standing in the eyes of rival gangs was probably increased. By seeking out Hillier at his well-known haunt of the Cass, the Grey Mare Boys had certainly shown their mettle and among the scuttling fraternity, audacity was admired almost as much as fighting prowess.

The following night, Hillier was hanging around in Hardman Street, off Deansgate, with a group of his fellow scuttlers when they began arguing among themselves. The reason for the sudden dispute is unknown, but Hillier came to blows with Billy Newall, a fifteen-year-old carter. The younger lad was swiftly dealt with; Hillier, who was enraged by this unexpected challenge to his authority, stabbed Newall on the shoulder three times. He was too canny to inflict a more serious wound. He must have known that there would be a warrant for his arrest following the stabbing in the Cass on Saturday night. The brawl in the gallery at the Cass had been too public, and too dangerous, for the police to ignore. The manager of the music hall had tolerated Hillier's gang for several months, doubtless in the knowledge that the scuttlers and their hangers-on had, if anything, added to the glamour of the venue. But a fight in the gallery was potentially disastrous. If other members of the audience nearby had panicked, if the rush to escape the scuttlers' knives and belts had turned into a stampede, then the dreadful crush at the Ben Lang's music hall in 1868 (see Chapter 2) might have been repeated.

The police came for Hillier three nights later and he was charged with the stabbings of both Conroy and Newall the following morning. Hillier admitted to stabbing Conroy, but pleaded self-defence and was remanded in custody. At a second hearing, Hillier was convicted on both charges and sentenced to four months' imprisonment. His involvement in previous outbreaks of scuttling at the Casino was noted in court and aroused the curiosity of the press. The *Manchester Guardian*, for example, noted the seriousness of the wounds Hillier had sustained at the hands of Tommy Callaghan in May. Hillier had clearly not been deterred by his injuries. Quite the reverse: he was ready to battle with all comers. Rival gangs held no terror for him, and neither did prison. Yet John Joseph Hillier would be a marked man when he emerged from Strangeways in the New Year.

In May 1892, Hillier appeared once more at the Manchester City Police Court before the stipendiary magistrate, Francis Headlam. On this occasion, however, he was not the accused but the prosecutor. His adversary was a Salford youth, Billy Wood, who lived in Oliver Square, off Ordsall Lane. The facts of the case were impossible to ascertain, such was the tangled web of accusation and counter-accusation levelled between Hillier and Wood in the courtroom. According to Hillier, he had attended a Sunday evening religious service at St Anne's Ragged School in Deansgate. When the service ended, he went for a walk with some friends. They had only gone a few yards from the school when they met Wood, who called over to them. When Hillier crossed the road, Wood stabbed him in the side of his chest without saying another word. Hillier managed to walk to the infirmary where his wound, which was not serious, was stitched.

Wood's version of events was entirely different. Questioned by Mr Headlam, he claimed that it was not an unprovoked assault at all; when he met Hillier and his companions, Hillier menaced him with a big butcher's knife and a brass-buckled belt. Hillier then attacked him with the knife, which caught his shoulder, piercing the cloth of his coat. Wood only then pulled out his own knife and stuck Hillier with it in self-defence. Wood added that, but for the intervention of some women, he would have been 'mangled'. His claim that he had initially been set upon by Hillier's crew was corroborated by two witnesses, although reporters noted that one was Wood's sister. There were no police witnesses to the fight, but an officer of 'A' Division told the court that gangs of scuttlers infested this neighbourhood every Sunday. Mr Headlam was persuaded of Wood's guilt and jailed him for one month.

Hillier's previous experience of the courtroom had taught him some lessons in how to depict incidents to his own advantage. In the streets, he was a terror to his opponents. His weapon of choice, a butcher's knife, was by now notorious and struck fear into his opponents. His preferred method of attack was to stab opponents in the shoulders. That way he could wound them but avoid risking more serious injury or disfigurement, either of which might lead magistrates, judges and juries alike to come down too hard on him. And, of course, he was unlikely to kill them that way and risk the gallows. In court, Hillier was always willing to portray himself as the innocent victim of rival scuttlers, set upon for no reason and without warning. On this occasion, he turned his very presence in the streets of Deansgate to his advantage. Police testimony confirmed that the district was plagued by gangs each Sunday night, but by his own account, Hillier had just attended an evening service held for the 'ragged poor'. What better evidence of Hillier's reformed character could the magistrate require? In this guise, he was no fearsome scuttler but merely a destitute slum youth who had turned to the church for salvation.

Manchester's stipendiary might have been persuaded of Hillier's conversion but his adversaries knew better and so did the police. His reign continued unabated, although Hillier managed to avoid arrest for more than twelve months following his knife fight with Wood. The following summer, his luck ran out. On 6 June 1893, a Tuesday night, Hillier and his companions ventured into Greengate. Armed with belts and sticks, they terrorised passers-by before confronting a gang of local scuttlers led by the tough-looking Bill Brooks. As the two forces spread out and squared up to each other, P.C. Chapman of the Salford Borough Police ran between them. Chapman had been savagely beaten by the Ordsall Lane scuttlers three years earlier, but he was undaunted. He told the youths to disperse; they responded with a volley of abuse. Identifying Hillier as the ringleader of the disturbance, Chapman tried to arrest him. He called out for help to a group of older men who were walking by and, with their aid, Hillier was nabbed. As P.C. Chapman began to escort him to the station, however, the two gangs joined forces to 'rush the bobby'. Bill Brooks led the charge. P.C. Chapman drew his truncheon but relaxed his grip on Hillier, who promptly drew a 'knobstick', or heavy wooden baton, from up his sleeve and belaboured the constable with it. With the help of the passers-by, Chapman managed to take both Hillier and Brooks into custody. When the two lads appeared at the Salford Police Court the following morning Joseph Makinson asked what weapons they had used against the constable. Brooks's belt was held up before the court. P.C. Chapman then dramatically produced the knobstick which, he said, he had taken from Hillier.

Two local people bravely attended court as witnesses for the prosecution. A young woman testified that she saw the gang of youths charge at P.C. Chapman. Moreover, she recognised the stick that Hillier had used in the subsequent brawl. Mr Makinson asked her if she was familiar with the scuttlers. 'Yes,' she replied, 'everybody is afraid of them. They came and threatened my father what they would do if he appeared here today.' The second witness was a broker from Gravel Lane. He told the court that he had gone to Chapman's assistance when requested to do so. He had since been threatened by four or five different lads.

In the face of such respectable witnesses, the two scuttlers had no chance. Hillier was sentenced to two months' hard labour and Brooks to one. Makinson noted that Brooks ought to have known better, given the number of times he had appeared in court before. Nonetheless, admitted Makinson, 'You are not quite so bad as the other one.'

Brooks was the same age as Hillier. He had grown up in Durham Street in Greengate and in his mid-teens worked as a brickmaker. However, he became better known as the leader of a rising mob of scuttlers and petty thieves. His first conviction, in June 1889, at the age of sixteen, was for playing pitch and toss. Shortly afterwards, he was arrested with four other lads in Great Clowes Street. A pair of beat constables noticed that the youths were carrying a large quantity of apples. When stopped, they could give no satisfactory account of themselves. It transpired that they had been systematically stripping the orchards of well-to-do residents of Higher Broughton. All five were fined. The pugnacious Brooks, a short, stocky youth with a broad face and the battered nose of a street fighter, subsequently embarked on regular thieving expeditions with John Wallace, alias McInerney, a precocious thief with dreamy grey eyes and a choirboy look. In July 1890, Wallace was one of a group of seven boys, all aged between ten and twelve, convicted of breaking into a cabin on the Lancashire and Yorkshire railway near Bedlam Bridge and stealing twenty-seven fog signals. Six of the boys, including Wallace, were sentenced to six strokes with the birch rod.

Brooks and Wallace began to travel to the mill towns around Manchester, where they were less well-known to the police. In March 1894, they were arrested along with James Brown, who had a distinctive limp, in Rochdale. The three lads were convicted of stealing a single shawl from a clothes line. Wallace was jailed for one month, Brooks for fourteen days and Brown for one week. By the time Wallace was released from Strangeways, Brooks had been arrested again. He was committed for trial at the Manchester Assizes, where he was convicted of burglary and jailed for nine months. Upon his release, he quickly re-assumed the leadership of the Greengate scuttlers, leading the mob into fresh battles in Deansgate and tit-for-tat raids on the Adelphi.

JOHN JOSEPH HILLIER emerged from Strangeways in August 1893, aged nineteen. Three months later, his reputation as the leading scuttler of his generation was sealed. On November 10, Hillier ambushed Philip McLoughlin in New Bridge Street, Salford. McLoughlin was wearing the scuttler's customary uniform, including bell-bottomed trousers cut like a sailor's. Hillier accosted him with the words, 'Hallo, sailor! What do you say if I cut you in pieces?' Without waiting for a reply, he drew a dagger and stabbed McLoughlin on the left shoulder. McLoughlin went straight to Salford Royal Hospital to have the wound dressed. Hillier was found by the police later that night and told the arresting officer, 'McLoughlin thinks he is the champion scuttler in Salford, and he has got to see there is someone who can —— take him down.' When charged with unlawful wounding, Hillier simply replied, 'Yes, I did it.' He resorted to his alias, John Joseph Elliott, in an attempt to hide evidence of his string of previous convictions. However, he was too familiar to the police. As Superintendent Hallam pointed out when Hillier was brought before the magistrates, 'the prisoner was a well-known scuttler'.

Standing in the dock, Hillier faced his old courtroom nemesis, stipendiary magistrate Joseph Makinson. This time, Makinson committed him for trial at the Salford Quarter Sessions. There, in January 1894, the story of Hillier's ambush of Philip McLoughlin was relayed once more. Hillier pleaded guilty to unlawful wounding but, in mitigation, claimed that he had merely acted in self-defence. Recorder Joseph Yates was not swayed. He jailed Hillier for six months.

Hillier's assault on McLoughlin was the talk of the scuttling fraternity across Manchester and Salford. It was not just the assault itself that cemented his notoriety. The reporting of it in the local press played into Hillier's hands. When the case first reached the magistrates, the *Salford Reporter* deployed an unusually sarcastic headline: 'A CANDIDATE FOR THE SALFORD SCUTTLING CHAMPIONSHIP: GRAND FORM.' Following Hillier's trial, the *Reporter* drew on the prosecuting counsel's account of the enmity between Hillier and McLoughlin: 'There seemed to have been some rivalry between the two as to which was the most brilliant person in the heroic calling which they were adopting.' The lawyer's ironic tag, 'AN HEROIC CALLING', formed the *Reporter*'s latest headline. The irony ran deeper, perhaps, than either the lawyers or the journalists realised, for scuttlers like

Hillier and McLoughlin were indeed heroes, not just among the ranks of active scuttlers but among the thousands of other young people across Manchester and Salford who followed their exploits from the sidelines. Moreover, the most notorious scuttlers, like the prize-fighters of earlier decades, guarded their reputations with a desperate ferocity. The *Reporter* could not have done more to burnish Hillier's reputation. Faced with his longest stretch in Strangeways so far, six months, Hillier ensured that the lasting impression in court was of his own defiance. As the Recorder of Salford pronounced sentence, Hillier shouted, 'I will swing for it when I come out.' To his associates, packed into the public gallery, he was indeed a heroic figure. Even the hangman's noose, it appeared, did not scare him.

While Hillier served his sentence, the skirmishing between the Deansgate scuttlers and the Salford gangs continued apace. Late one night in February, the Deansgate lads were milling around in Chapel Street on the look-out for their Salford counterparts when they spotted a gang of scuttlers from nearby Barrow Street. Tommy Darlington walked up to Harry Swain, the leader of the Barrow Street gang, and issued the standard challenge: 'Are you called sailor?' Mindful no doubt of the Deansgate lads' reputation, Swain replied, 'No.' This was a humiliating response, but it did nothing to assuage the Deansgate mob. Billy Leather punched Swain, and another lad struck Swain's companion, George Hutton. The force of the blow knocked Hutton through the doorway of a beerhouse, leaving him sprawled at the feet of the surprised drinkers. The rest of the Deansgate scuttlers immediately began to lash out with their weapons. The Barrow Street lads fled, running through the throng of pedestrians making their away home from the Flat Iron market. They were quickly caught and a desperate, full-scale scuttle ensued. Darlington wrapped his belt tightly around his wrist for the fight and he struck Swain a fierce blow on the head. The buckle split open Swain's head. His face streaming with blood, Swain was carried to Salford Royal Hospital where he was found to have a fractured skull. Tommy Darlington was eventually sent down for two months for the attack and Billy Leather for one month. Both were aged eighteen, while Swain was two years older.

When the Barrow Street scuttlers took their revenge later that year, they claimed a bigger scalp than Darlington's. On the night of Friday, July 13, John Joseph Hillier once more led the Deansgate scuttlers on a raid into Salford. He had been released from Strangeways only a week earlier, having served his six month sentence for wounding. The Deansgate lads marched along Irwell Street with Hillier – who had adopted the alias of Elliott as his street name – at their head. Now a hardened lag, with his boys behind him and his reputation as the most famous scuttler of the day secure, he felt invincible.

Yet it was the inevitable fate of the King of the Scuttlers that, no matter how fierce the reputation he carved out on the streets, someone would emerge to take him down. At the corner of Stanley Street, the Deansgate mob were taken by surprise. Barrow Street captain Harry Swain leaped out from behind a wall, followed by a crowd of seventy youths.

'Come on lads,' Swain shouted, 'here's Elliott. Now we've got him.'

Leading from the front, Swain grabbed hold of Hillier and stabbed him repeatedly, inflicting wounds to his shoulder and body. He called to Robert Melville to follow suit, shouting, 'Give him another, Bob.' Hillier collapsed. He was taken to Salford Royal Hospital with a dangerous-looking, four-inch wound on his chest.

Harry Swain was arrested and duly appeared before Joseph Makinson at the Salford Police Court. It soon became apparent that Hillier had wasted no time at all before renewing old battles on his release from Strangeways. Swain told the court that Hillier had struck one of the girls associated with the Barrow Street gang the previous night, adding to the ill-feeling that had been building up between the two gangs since the New Year. Swain was committed to the Quarter Sessions along with Robert Melville, also of Barrow Street, Salford. They appeared at the sessions on August 29, charged with wounding Hillier.

Giving evidence, Hillier (describing himself in court as John

Joseph Elliott) told how 'at a quarter past nine at night [I] was walking down Stanley Street with half-a-dozen others, and at the bottom of the street [we] were met by a gang of about fifty others. Swain exclaimed, "Lads, here's Elliott," with which he stabbed me on the chest and twice on the shoulder. I fainted from loss of blood, and was an inpatient at the Salford Royal Hospital in consequence of my injuries.' The jury acquitted Melville but found Swain guilty. Passing sentence, Joseph Yates said that, 'he had not the slightest doubt Swain was the person who stabbed Elliott out of revenge for attacking a girl the night before. He appeared to be one of a rough lot.' Swain had already been in custody for one month. The recorder sentenced him to a further five months in Strangeways.

At the age of twenty, Harry Swain had already been convicted at the Salford Police Court on seven previous occasions: twice for drunkenness and five times for theft. His hauls included both everyday items such as clothes, boots and sacks of coal, and copious amounts of whiskey, which fuelled a succession of uproarious weekends in Barrow Street. Neither corporal punishment, at the age of twelve, nor three years' confinement at an industrial school for Catholic boys had reformed him. As a petty thief, his brushes with the law were predictable. Prison did not bother him. An outcast in the eyes of the law, Swain nonetheless enjoyed considerable prestige among his peers on the streets of Salford due to his prowess as a scuttler.

Hillier's henchmen, Tommy Darlington and Billy Wagstaff, were in turn brought before Joseph Yates at the Quarter Sessions on November 21. They were charged with wounding George Massey during a scuttle in Salford on the night of October 30. The jury found Darlington not guilty but convicted Wagstaff, who went down for nine months. Like Harry Swain, Wagstaff was a product of the industrial school system. At the age of ten he had been sent to the training ship *Formidable*, moored at Portishead, Bristol. The *Formidable* was an eighty-gun battleship converted to accommodate up to 350 boys under the terms of the Industrial Schools Acts of 1857–61. Wagstaff returned to his family home in Thompson Street, Deansgate, in 1890, at the age of sixteen. His subsequent criminal record included no fewer than sixteen summary convictions for offences such as drunkenness, and five convictions for theft and assault. Tommy Darlington, who had been sent down following the clash between the Deansgate scuttlers and the Barrow Street lads in February 1894, had served another two-month sentence imposed in June, when he was convicted of assaulting a young woman.

John Joseph Hillier resumed his leadership of the Deansgate scuttlers as soon as he had recovered from the stabbing by Harry Swain. At around ten o'clock on the night of 16 December 1894, he was involved in an affray outside a theatre on Deansgate in which he struck a Salford collier on the forehead with a belt and knocked him to the ground before stabbing him three times in the back. The collier's wounds were treated at Manchester Royal Infirmary. Hillier was apprehended later that night. He told the arresting officers that he 'might as well tell them that he had done it'. He then took a knife from his pocket and handed it over, saying that it was the weapon he had used. Tommy Darlington, who had been a central figure in the feud between Deansgate and Barrow Street, was committed to stand trial alongside him.

This incorrigible pair appeared at Manchester Assizes in February 1895, before Mr Justice Lawrance. They both faced charges of inflicting grievous bodily harm and attempted murder. Asked to account for his actions, Hillier claimed, 'He had a knife, and I did it in self-defence. They keep following me from all nations. I could only go in one part of Manchester. Certain people were not satisfied until they had got me in prison again.' The jury found both lads guilty of inflicting grievous bodily harm but acquitted them of the more serious charge. Before pronouncing sentence, Judge Lawrance reflected at some length on the phenomenon of scuttling. He told the court that the term was new to him, but noted that it was evidently well known in Manchester. He continued:

It was a monstrous thing that people could not walk about the streets without being interfered with by roughs like the prisoners ... It was quite time, as far as punishment would do it, that he should put a stop to a state of things like that. It was a disgrace to the city. The sentence would keep them out of mischief for a considerable time, and would be a warning to their companions, who might be inclined to follow in their footsteps.

He then sentenced Hillier to five years' penal servitude and Darlington to three years'. The sentences provoked uproar among the ranks of scuttlers gathered at the back of the court.

By removing the now legendary Hillier from the streets for five years, Mr Justice Lawrance should have put an end to his career as a scuttler. Hillier was already aged nineteen. Most scuttlers left the gangs by their early twenties, acknowledging the widely held view that scuttling was a pastime for lads, not men. Hillier would be twenty-three or twenty-four by the time of his release.

WITH HILLIER confined in penal servitude, the feud between the Deansgate mob and Salford continued. Michael Charles King, leader of the Brown Street gang, quickly replaced Harry Swain as the Deansgate lads' principal target. Mick King was born in the inappropriately named Garden Street in Salford in 1872. He assumed the leadership of the Brown Street lads by the time he was seventeen, and rapidly acquired a lengthy series of convictions for using obscene language, drunkenness, riotous and disorderly conduct, assault by stabbing, and scuttling with belts. King exuded an air of menace. A confident, commanding figure with a cold, hard stare, he acknowledged no authority but his own. Like Bill Brooks, he turned to petty theft following one of his stretches in Strangeways and took to roaming the streets of Salford, grabbing whatever he could from the pavement displays of unsuspecting shopkeepers. This crude method served him well enough until Salford detectives caught up with him in February 1890. Joseph Makinson sent him to Strangeways for six months.

King was still renowned as one of the terrors of Chapel Street six years later. At around 11.30 p.m. on Friday, 5 September 1896, King's mob clashed with the Deansgate scuttlers at the junction of Brown Street and Chapel Street, on the Salford side of the river. King lunged at a Deansgate lad named Henry Swift with a knife. A sickened passer-by witnessed a thrust so fierce that Swift's bowels were ripped open. Two beat constables were also watching from the opposite side of Chapel Street. When the cry went up – 'He's stabbed him!' – they charged into the crowd. King turned to his followers.

'I have done it, boys,' he hissed. 'Here, take the knife.'

After a brief struggle, King gave himself up to P.C. Patterson, a tough bobby with plenty of experience of scuttlers. King allegedly told the constable: 'I have done it. It is a — good case for you.' Swift had to be carried to Salford Royal Hospital.

King was brought before Joseph Makinson on Monday morning, charged with wounding. Inspector Lyogue confirmed that King had been before the court on no fewer than seventeen previous occasions. Asked what he had to say for himself, King replied, 'I was drunk. I do not know anything about it.' Makinson was livid. 'Drunk? You will get seven or ten years this time.' King was taken to Henry Swift's bedside at the hospital, where a deposition was taken as Swift was not expected to recover.

With King in custody, the Deansgate lads wasted no time in seeking revenge. They marched into Salford on the Sunday night, fighting a series of skirmishes in the streets off Chapel Street. The following Saturday, with Billy Wagstaff at their head, they marched to Chapel Street once more. A sizeable Salford contingent was waiting for them. Recognising Cornelius Parkinson as one of King's henchmen, Wagstaff shouted, 'There's Parkinson. Let's go for him.' The Deansgate mob charged. Parkinson was quickly overwhelmed, going down under a hail of belts.

Parkinson gave the names of three of his assailants to Salford detectives later that night. Wagstaff was arrested along with two of his followers at a lodging-house in Deansgate at 2 a.m. He bluntly told the detectives that he was determined to 'rip Parkinson up'. When charged at Salford Town Hall, Wagstaff was warned that he was facing a lengthy term of penal servitude. He was still unrepentant: 'If I do get fifteen years I will do for Parky the first chance I get,' he vowed. 'I will take the rope for it.' In the event, Joseph Makinson jailed Wagstaff for two months.

King was held on remand for more than five months while Henry Swift lay injured in Salford Royal Hospital. By the time of his tenth remand hearing, on November 16, his patience was running thin. 'I have been on remand a long time,' he protested to Joseph Makinson. 'Manchester Assizes are over, the Liverpool Assizes are just about coming on, and the Salford Borough Sessions began on Thursday. Will you grant me bail?' Makinson refused, prompting King to threaten to 'write to the Home Secretary'.

Mick King was finally tried before Mr Justice Collins at Manchester Assizes the following February. More articulate in the dock than most other scuttlers, King conducted his own defence having obtained copies of the depositions from the clerk to the Salford magistrates. Before cross-examining Henry Swift, he told the jury that 'past relations between us have resulted in a lot of bitterness. Animosity and malice have a good deal to do with the present case.' Once the prosecution witnesses had testified, King read a carefully prepared statement of his own for nearly three quarters of an hour. Court reporters noted that 'he detailed matters altogether foreign to the present charge, and contended that he was the victim of a plot'.

Justice Collins was unmoved. He was equally unimpressed by the testimony of the victim, Swift, who was dismissed as 'more than likely one of a gang of roughs himself'. The judge advised the jury to rely on the evidence of P.C. Patterson, who had told the court that he saw the prisoner 'strike a downward blow' with a knife on the night in question. The jury concurred, finding King guilty of inflicting grievous bodily harm. Addressing the prisoner, Justice Collins declared that the state of society in the area of the fight seemed to be 'deplorable' and handed down the exemplary sentence of six years. King exploded. He hurled his documents to the floor, but quickly regained his composure. As he was led from the dock, he paused, took a large white handkerchief out of his pocket, and waved it at some young women in the gallery, 'whose sobs were distinctly audible'. As King was led down, he called to them, 'Never mind, I'll be out in 1903.'

Vengeance was exacted on King's behalf eight months after the trial. One of his associates, William McDonald, stabbed the now recovered but badly scarred Henry Swift in the shoulder during a scuttle outside the Finney Arms in Greengate. The unfortunate Swift also suffered five more cuts to his face. He told the Salford Borough Sessions that McDonald struck him without provocation, shouting, 'You got Mick King six years and I'll do twenty for you.' McDonald called several witnesses to confirm that there had been a 'free fight' outside the pub and that Swift had struck him first. McDonald was jailed for nine months.

JOHN JOSEPH HILLIER'S final recorded episode as a scuttler took place on Tuesday, 25 July 1899. He was now aged twenty-four, a ripe old age for a scuttler, and he was only out of prison on a ticket-of-leave (an early form of parole). At four o'clock that afternoon, Hillier, accompanied by eighteen-year-old Samuel Royle, set out for the Prince of Wales' Feathers public house. The pub stood near Windsor Bridge, which crossed the Manchester–Bolton railway line. Five scuttlers from nearby Hanky Park were waiting for them. As they approached the pub Hillier carried a belt in one hand and a knife in the other. Royle's belt was wrapped around his wrist, in fighting style. The Hanky Park lads spilled out of the pub to meet them, belts at the ready. Three of their molls were close by, one with an axe under her shawl. They knew Hillier's reputation and were taking no chances.

Hillier charged at the Hanky Park lads, swinging his belt round and yelling, 'You'll die, you'll die!' He and Royle lashed out with their belts, but they had the worst of the ensuing fight, which lasted for several minutes. Hillier in particular was badly mauled by his younger opponents. He ran from the scene with blood pouring from a head wound, only to be chased along the Crescent, where, according to one witness, 'he was lifted bodily off his feet' and thrown down on the tram lines. As he lay on the ground, the Hanky Park scuttlers formed a circle around him and kicked him like a football.

Hillier and Royle were arrested, whilst their adversaries made their escape. Hillier was brought once more before Joseph Makinson at the Salford Police Court on August 2, where he was described as 'the King of the Scuttlers'. His head swathed in heavily blood-stained bandages, Hillier appeared anything but a champion scuttler. He was charged along with Royle with being drunk and disorderly and scuttling. A police constable told the court that both prisoners were drunk when he took them into custody. In reply to a query from Makinson, Hillier named two of his adversaries as McCauley and McKenna. Chief Detective Inspector Lyogue informed the court that inquiries had been made after the two youths named, but without success. Inquiries had also been made after a girl named Taylor, said to be living in Rossall Street, Pendleton, but 'the only girl of that name was under fifteen years of age and was stated to have been at home when the fight took place'.

Makinson asked Hillier, 'Would you like the other men to be brought here?' Hillier's reply brought the house down. He told Makinson, 'If you will give us a chance, we will say no more about it.'

Inspector Lyogue read out a list of Hillier's convictions for scuttling, pointing out that the last of these, four years previously, had resulted in penal servitude. Lyogue further reminded the court that Hillier was currently out of prison on a ticket-of-leave. Makinson, however, appeared almost to sympathise with Hillier. He told him that he would not deal with the charge of scuttling unless 'anything further turned up'. He fined Hillier ten shillings and Royle five for being drunk and disorderly. Hillier must have seemed an anomalous figure in court. He was too old to be a scuttler in any case, but he appeared all the older when it transpired that one of the girls in the Hanky Park group was aged just fourteen.

Hillier's reputation was such that he was recalled, by his alias of Elliott, by elderly Salfordians many decades later. Arthur Collier, who was born in the Hanky Park district in 1885, described the scuttlers when he was asked to talk about the 'rough' districts in the Salford of his childhood. In an interview which took place in February 1970, Collier declared, 'Oh, they were terrible. They always wore belts you know, scuttler's belts with brass buckles on.' Asked whether he knew any scuttlers personally, he replied, 'Oh yes, I knew a lot of them. There was Red Elliott ... he was one of the leaders ... He wore a jersey which said "Red Elliott" on it and "King of the Scuttlers" ... He stabbed a fellow on Hope Street bridge ... where the Prince of Wales [public-house] is.' According to Arthur Collier, the stabbing occurred as Red Elliott fought against the Hanky Park scuttlers in a 'row over girls'. Thus Collier recalled an incident which had taken place over seventy years earlier, adding in four details that were missing from newspaper reports of Hillier's exploits at the time.

If that long-remembered account is accurate, it appears that Hillier wounded at least one of his adversaries before he was worsted in the fight outside the Prince of Wales' Feathers. This might in part explain the ferocity of the beating to which he was subsequently subjected. Secondly, Collier recalled Hillier's 'street' name in full: to his peers, John Joseph Hillier became 'Red Elliott'. 'Red' was a common nickname for youths with ginger hair. Thirdly, Collier's account of Hillier's clothing gives us a glimpse of the extent to which John Joseph Hillier celebrated his notoriety. He was first identified as the 'champion' or 'King' of the scuttlers in 1893. The label was still used by the police and local journalists to describe Hillier six years later. Yet a label originally devised by a journalist was eagerly adopted by Hillier himself, for whom the title must have formed an ironic, yet welcome, mark of his status. Finally, Arthur Collier insisted that Hillier was not a physically-imposing figure: 'There was nothing about him in build. He was a thin, thinnish chap, summat like me, not very tall. He was a fellow that wouldn't tackle anybody on his own. Got to have three or four of them together ... He just used a knife.'

CHAPTER 18

War in the City

TOMMY CALLAGHAN, THE king of the Bungall Boys, was as notorious a figure in the slums of London Road and Ancoats as Hillier was in Deansgate and Salford. Callaghan's reputation was sealed in June 1891 when he was sent down for nine months for bludgeoning Hillier with an iron bar. Like Hillier, Callaghan saw imprisonment as no deterrent. By the spring of 1892, out of prison and full of fight, he was leading the Bungall Boys on a series of raids into hostile territory.

On May 24, a Tuesday night, the Bungall Boys headed west. Keeping to side streets to avoid the police, they moved quietly in twos and threes, skirting the rougher beerhouses and ignoring the knots of women sat 'neighbouring' on their doorsteps. As they entered Chorlton-on-Medlock they spotted the Mount Street scuttlers stood on the corner of Higher Temple Street. Callaghan stepped into the middle of the road and shouted his challenges: did they want 'bother'? Was their best lad willing to fight him one-on-one? To the Bungall Boys' surprise, the leader of the Mount Street mob accepted Callaghan's challenge. The rival scuttlers quickly formed a ring around the two combatants. All of those present were armed, some with belts, others with both belts and knives, but this was to be a fair fight: man-to-man, without weapons. No sooner were the first blows struck, when the police arrived. P.C. Bloomfield, of 'D' Division, ran into the middle of the crowd, his staff raised, ignoring shouts of 'Let's dose the copper.' He managed to collar Callaghan and used his staff to keep the rest of the Bungall Boys at bay. Had Bloomfield known more about Callaghan's reputation, he might well have thought twice before interfering.

Callaghan was brought before the Manchester magistrates on June 23. In court, police officers dwelled at length on his reputation as a 'king' among the scuttlers. Callaghan admitted that he had been fighting, but claimed that he had acted only in self-defence. He was fined £2, the equivalent of more than two weeks' wages for an ordinary working man, with the alternative of a month in Strangeways.

The following summer, Callaghan led his gang on a Friday night rampage through Ancoats. Two of the mob were in full soldier's uniform at the time, but they showed no sign of military discipline as they roamed the streets picking out victims at random. P.C. Singleton of 'C' Division encountered the gang in Lower Canal Street, where Callaghan was threatening to dose anyone who came near him. At the head of a sizeable group of his followers, Callaghan must have presented a formidable sight. Singleton was unintimidated and arrested him. Callaghan was brought yet again before the Manchester magistrates, where he was once more introduced as 'the King of the Scuttlers'. He was convicted of assault. Three of the gang's victims had given statements to the police: a railway detective who had been making his way home at the end of his shift, a scavenger (another term for a 'night soil man' employed to empty outdoor privies), and a girl. Callaghan was sentenced to six months' imprisonment. Apparently unperturbed, he shouted that he would 'do it again' when he came out.

By 1895, Callaghan and his gang had found a new Saturday night haunt: St James's Theatre, in Oxford Street in Manchester city centre. They did not take kindly to members of rival gangs attending, so when the Meadow Lads arrived thirty- to forty-strong to take up seats in the gallery on a Saturday night that March, trouble was inevitable. The Bungall Boys bided their time until the interval. When the rival scuttlers tried to return to their seats, they were confronted by Callaghan, who set on William Southern with a shout of, 'This is one.' He promptly stabbed Southern in the head and kicked him. Callaghan then threw another youth, eighteen-year-old Paddy Mannion, down the gallery steps, before fencing with John Bake and Tom Wrexall, both of whom were armed with knives. Bake was stabbed in the shoulder during the ensuing mêlée, while Southern had to be carried half-conscious and bleeding to the Royal Infirmary.

Callaghan stood trial at the Manchester Quarter Sessions before the new Recorder of Manchester, Joseph Leese, Queen's Counsel and Member of Parliament, on April 3. Callaghan was now aged twenty-one and gave his occupation as labourer. He was charged with wounding Southern and Bake. Another of his opponents, Paddy Mannion, appeared in the dock alongside him, charged with wounding John Quinn during the same row. Mannion pleaded guilty but Callaghan denied the charges, claiming that he had acted in self-defence after Southern had rushed at him and stabbed him in the thigh. The jurors gasped when a dagger was produced in evidence. The blade was fifteen inches long. Southern claimed that the weapon was Callaghan's. Maria Brassington, who had witnessed the whole disturbance, described the chaos as rival gangs charged up and down the gallery, waving knives and bottles. 'There was a great deal of blood about,' she told the court, 'and a woman and four boys were taken to the Infirmary.' The jury found Callaghan guilty and Recorder Leese sentenced him to five years' penal servitude. Mannion got three years.

Callaghan's criminal record suggested that he was indeed a terror on the streets of Manchester. He had no fewer than eighteen previous convictions: six for assault and twelve for assorted public order offences such as breaching the peace and being drunk and disorderly. He had been jailed at least four times, spending a total of eighteen months in prison. Mannion, by contrast, had no previous convictions and three years was a hefty sentence for a first offender, even allowing for his alleged use of a knife. One crucial fact relating to Mannion was not mentioned in court: three years earlier, he had been part of William Willan's escort on the afternoon that Willan was fatally stabbed in Ancoats. Mannion knew the risks he was taking when he followed the life of a scuttler. Neither life-threatening injury nor the prospect of a long stretch had deterred him.

THE GAYTHORN district took its name from Gaythorn Street, which lay between the southern end of Deansgate and Oxford Road station. During the 1860s, Gaythorn, along with Charter Street and Deansgate, was widely recognised as one of the hotbeds of 'Criminal Manchester'. However, repeated police raids during the early 1870s cleared Gaythorn of most of its dens of thieves. By the middle of the decade, the remaining population was judged to be 'rough and turbulent truly, but honest as far as their lives are known'. According to the *Manchester Evening News* in 1874:

> They are as completely poverty stricken as any of the poorest amongst us, and their abodes are as a rule without comfort or any of the little home luxuries that the hard-working classes can sometimes afford to indulge in. They are a quarrelsome race, too, and yet so clannish that when a street row takes place the police have always a difficult task to restore peace, much less to arrest the leading spirits. It would scarcely be an exaggeration to say that more assaults upon men in uniform are reported from the Gaythorn streets than any other single quarter. It is like putting one's hand into a bag of snakes to draw out an eel, for a constable to take into custody the leader of one of the drunken broils that are of so frequent occurrence here.

The district's most notorious figures during the late 1860s and early 1870s were 'Aunty Mary', who kept a brothel in Abraham's Court, and 'Fat Helen', whose lodging-house on Gaythorn Street was a veritable thieves' headquarters until Helen herself was sent to prison.

During the 1890s, Gaythorn became renowned for its scuttlers, and their 'king' was Paddy Hughes. However, with both Tommy Callaghan and John Joseph Hillier banged up for lengthy terms by the spring of 1895 it seemed that scuttler royalty was being carefully targeted by the judicial authorities. On Saturday, 2 February 1895, Hughes and the Gaythorn Scuttlers attended the Cass music hall. They were spotted inside by the Adelphi scuttlers from Salford. The Adelphi had arrived mob-handed and paraded up and down the 'pit' before the performance began, scanning the audience for members of rival gangs. Their leader, Dick Beattie, shouted orders as they effectively sought to take control of the Cass for the night.

The Adelphi lads thought that they had spotted a Gaythorn scuttler by the name of Murray. In fact, the youth's name was John Fallon, but the Salford gang had nonetheless found their prey. Fallon was struck by Dick Beattie and the punch was the signal for a free-for-all with knives and belts in which the Adelphi lads targeted Fallon and Paddy Hughes. Beattie stabbed Fallon on the back of the head and Robert Brassell struck him with a belt. The row had begun inside the music hall but quickly spilled out into the street, where Fallon found himself surrounded. Billy Norris struck him with a belt and then stabbed him on the arm. Hughes, seeing that his friend Fallon was in grave danger, cried out that the attack by superior numbers was 'shameful'. In effect, he was accusing the Adelphi scuttlers of bullying in a desperate attempt to save Fallon. Dick Beattie turned to Hughes and shouted, 'We will shame you, too, Hughes.' He then lunged at Hughes with a knife. Hughes dodged the blow and turned to run. He was immediately pursed by the Adelphi scuttlers, one of whom yelled, 'Let's chiv him.'

The king of Gaythorn was caught, surrounded and kicked until he fell to the ground. The Adelphi lads rained blows on him with their belts. As he tried to get to his feet, Beattie stabbed him in the head. Billy Norris, eager to prove his own mettle, followed suit. Then Joe Hewitt, another of the Adelphi scuttlers, stabbed Hughes in the chest. Hewitt then stood over him, triumphantly flourishing his blood-stained knife, and called out, 'Shall I run it into him again?'

The onslaught only ceased when two passing gentlemen came to Hughes's rescue and struck out at the Adelphi lads with their walking sticks. Beattie and his gang, who knew that the courts would mete out severe punishment to any youth convicted of assaulting passers-by of such superior social standing, walked away. They left Paddy Hughes unconscious in the street. He had fared far worse than Fallon. He had two cuts on the head and severe bruising caused by blows from Adelphi belts. More seriously, he had suffered a knife wound to his chest. He was carried to the Manchester Royal Infirmary, where doctors discovered that the knife had punctured his left lung. For several days, his life hung in the balance.

Six of the Adelphi scuttlers were subsequently rounded up by Warrant Officer William Ashton of 'A' Division. Ashton had twelve years' experience of dealing with such lads and he had no qualms about tracking them down. The accused all denied using belts or knives in the scuttle, but did admit to having struck Hughes and Fallon with their fists. Mindful that the charge against the Adelphi gang might eventually be one of murder, police continued gathering evidence on the details of the fight and the likely motives of those involved. As it became clear towards the end of February that Hughes would live, a charge of inflicting grievous bodily harm was prepared against the Adelphi lads. Dick Beattie, their leader, was committed for trial at the Manchester Assizes along with Robert Brassell, Joe Hewitt, John Green, Christopher Matthews and Billy Norris. Beattie was the oldest at twenty-one; Brassell and Matthews were the youngest at seventeen. Five of the six were labourers while Green, a native of Belfast, was a tailor. Their trial was scheduled for March 1. The stakes were high. John Joseph Hillier and Tommy Darlington had appeared at the same assize the previous week, when Mr Justice Lawrance had sentenced them to five and three years' penal servitude. Lawrance was scheduled to try the Adelphi scuttlers too.

Counsel for the prosecution, Mr McKeand, depicted the Adelphi lads as a disgrace to Manchester, dwelling on their threat to 'chiv' Paddy Hughes. As McKeand pointed out, that was a scuttler's phrase for 'stab', and was 'popularly used among young men who indulged in the amusement of scuttling'. Hughes had recovered sufficiently to give evidence against his assailants. He told the court that Beattie had led the initial attack on Fallon, shouting, 'Come on, lads, let's cut him up.' Hughes then told how the Adelphi scuttlers had turned on him. He described how Beattie, Hewitt and Norris all stabbed him. One of them shouted, 'I will murder you.' According to Hughes, had it not been for the intervention by the gentlemen passers-by, the Adelphi lads would indeed have murdered him.

Hughes was cross-examined by Beattie himself. As the leader of the Adelphi scuttlers, Beattie acted as the gang's spokesman in court. He alleged that Hughes had been part of the initial quarrel in the Cass. According to Beattie, Hughes had issued the first challenge by shouting, 'We will either have beer or blood!' In their defence, the Adelphi scuttlers claimed either to have taken no part in the disturbance or to have fought only with their fists. Joe Hewitt claimed that he had been drunk on the night in question and knew nothing about the disturbance. John Green insisted that he had taken no part in the row. The jury found Green not guilty, and he was discharged. His five fellow gang members were found guilty. Detective Inspector Yates of the Salford Borough Police was asked by Mr Justice Lawrance to provide some background information on them. Yates was only too keen. He described the prisoners as 'members of a gang of scuttlers who infest the neighbourhood of the Adelphi. They are a terror to the neighbourhood. Beattie is the leader of the gang. I already wanted Brassell for a felony.'

Judge Lawrance was as stern in his handling of the Adelphi scuttlers as he had been with Hillier and Darlington of the Deansgate gang. Addressing the court, he declared that the city of Manchester should no longer be disgraced by ruffians like the prisoners; packs of boys armed with knives 'must be put down with a strong hand'. He sentenced Beattie to five years' penal servitude, matching the sentence imposed on Hillier the previous week. Hewitt and Norris were sentenced to four years. Beattie, Hewitt and Norris in turn interrupted the judge, loudly protesting their innocence. Beattie repeatedly contradicted the judge, shouting 'No!' throughout Justice Lawrance's pronouncements on his part in the affray. Hewitt shouted, 'I never was at the Casino.' The judge brushed their objections aside. When Norris shouted, 'I was not in it,' Justice Lawrance simply drew the court's attention to Norris' criminal record, which included five years on the reformatory ship *Akbar*. As Lawrance pointed out, Norris had joined the Adelphi scuttlers the moment he returned to Salford. Brassell and Matthews were treated more leniently, partly on account of their youth. Nonetheless they were both sent down for eighteen months.

The Adelphi scuttlers ought to have been well aware of the sentences that Mr Justice Lawrance had passed on Hillier and Darlington the previous week. They must have known what was coming to them once the jury found them guilty. This might explain their anguished pleas as the judge addressed them. As in the case of Hillier and Darlington, the sentences caused a commotion in court. The *Manchester Guardian* dryly noted, 'The prisoners appeared much astonished at the severity of the sentences, and as they passed down the steps to the cells there were loud lamentations amongst their friends in the gallery.' Faced with the Adelphi scuttlers, Mr Justice Lawrance had issued his second pronouncement on scuttling within a week. He addressed the prisoners in the knowledge that his warning to the gangs of Manchester would be relayed across the entire conurbation by the local press.

Two months later, in June 1895, Paddy Hughes got into an altercation in a public house in Gaythorn. Accompanied by several other youths, he entered the Vulcan Inn on Albion Street late on a Monday afternoon. He was already the worse for drink. The landlady, Janet Lowry, refused to serve him, so Hughes picked up a bar stool and smashed one of the pub windows with it, before turning on her. Mrs Lowry was holding a three-month-old infant in her arms, but Hughes still punched her four times. Mr Lowry tried to intervene but Hughes leaped onto the counter and kicked him in the chest. The scuttlers departed, leaving the pub in chaos.

Hughes was arrested by William Ashton, the warrant officer who had previously rounded up the Adelphi scuttlers, and duly appeared at Manchester Police Court on a charge of assault. Ashton described Hughes as the 'king' or 'captain' of the Gaythorn scuttlers, adding that he was a dangerous character who had been known to the officers of 'A' Division for years. According to Ashton, whenever the Gaythorn scuttlers were involved in an affray, Hughes was at the forefront. Hughes denied assaulting Mrs Lowry. He claimed that he had only asked to be served when the landlord struck him without provocation. In Hughes's account, he struck the landlord twice in self-defence. With tears in his eyes, he pleaded that he had told the truth and begged the magistrates to show mercy. They didn't. Hughes was pronounced guilty and sent down for two months. Had either Mr or Mrs Lowry alleged that Hughes had wielded a knife that afternoon, he would almost certainly have joined the growing band of scuttlers serving lengthy sentences of penal servitude.

THE MEADOW Lads were the hardest gang of all to crack. Most of them lived in common lodging-houses, regularly flitting between the different establishments in the neighbourhood of Charter Street, and few held regular jobs. Many of the lads were known by several aliases and the more active thieves among them regularly absconded to Liverpool or Leeds for months at a time when things got 'hot' for them in Manchester. The new king of the Meadow Lads, Joe Wood, was a hawker. Badly mauled by a gang from Ancoats during the summer of 1892, he nevertheless quickly restored his reputation as leader of a pack of 'noted thieves and scuttlers, and the terror of the neighbourhood'. He was arrested along with two of his henchmen in March 1894 following an affray in Lever Street in the city centre. A police constable intervened to save a lad who was being beaten as he lay on the ground. Wood hit the officer over the head with the buckle end of his belt, and one of the other Meadow Lads tried to stab him. Wood was arrested at his lodgings later that night. At his trial, it transpired that the Meadow Lads had accepted payment 'to scuttle some men in Lever Street'.

Wood's most fearsome follower was Harry Burgess, 'one of

the worst characters in Manchester' according to the police. With convictions for manslaughter, burglaries and assaulting the police as well as scuttling, Burgess was a noted terror even by the standards of the Meadow. In July 1894, he was given six months for assaulting P.C. Curtis of the City of Manchester Police. Finding Burgess 'creating a scene' in Angel Street one Friday night, Curtis told him to go away. Burgess replied that the constable's days were numbered. He then disappeared, only to return moments later with a knife in one hand and a poker in the other. He told the officer, 'Your time has come. I am going to settle you.'

Curtis lashed out with his staff. Burgess replied with a blow with the poker, and then made off. Curtis sought reinforcements before tracking his tormentor down and bludgeoning him in the street. Magistrate Robert Armitage did not hesitate to support the constable's resort to violence, telling Burgess that the lawless characters of Angel Meadow would find their punishments both heavy and swift. Burgess was sentenced to another six months' hard labour.

In March 1895, Joe Wood was arrested following a Saturday night fracas in an Angel Street lodging-house. The row had begun at around half-past ten when a Meadow Lad named Riley got into an argument with James Doherty, a fellow lodger. Doherty ran off and stayed in a nearby beerhouse until closing-time before returning to Angel Street. Riley was waiting with Wood and Tommy Cunningham. Another Meadow Lad of long standing, Cunningham had been jailed in 1888 after a fight with the Bengal Tigers in Smithfield Market. The three scuttlers had been drinking heavily. Riley shouted, 'Let's cut Doherty up,' only for Doherty to floor him with a single punch. Cunningham, a roguish young man with a shifty look, took off his coat and vest, and dared anyone in the lodging-house to fight him. The manager asked the Meadow Lads to leave, only for the scuttlers to turn their ire on him: Cunningham stabbed him in the forehead, Wood kicked him and Riley stabbed him in the back of the head. Cunningham threw a lit paraffin lamp at him for good measure. When the manager's brother tried to step in, Wood lunged at him with a knife. A police constable arrived to find Cunningham stood over the manager, knife in hand. The officer knocked Cunningham down with his staff. 'It's lucky you have come,' Cunningham told him. 'I might have done some more.'

The three Meadow Lads were committed to the Liverpool Assizes, where one witness told the jury that the manager's face had been covered in so much blood that he 'looked like a Red Indian'. The Lord Chief Justice, Lord Russell, presided at the Assizes. With no little understatement, he told the jurors that the prisoners were 'a very bad sample of the young men of Manchester'. His sentences, however, were remarkably lenient: Cunningham got eighteen months and Riley fifteen. Wood got just nine.

At quarter past nine on Christmas night, 1896, the Meadow Lads arrived mob-handed in Deansgate. They were searching for a lad named John Durkin. They found him ensconced with the rest of the Deansgate mob in a pub in Gregson Street, where Jimmy Martin challenged Durkin to a 'fair fight'. Durkin accepted, and the two lads went outside and took off their coats. The two gangs followed them out into the street, but instead of forming a ring they launched into a frenzied free-for-all. Martin stabbed Durkin in the fray. The Deansgate youth lay in the Royal Infirmary for eleven days before he recovered sufficiently to be treated as an out-patient. The Recorder of Manchester, Joseph Leese, sentenced Martin to three years' penal servitude at the Quarter Sessions. Joe Wood got eighteen months for his part in the affray.

Three more Meadow Lads appeared at the same sitting of the sessions. They included Tommy Cunningham, not long released from Strangeways following his assault upon a lodging-house manager in March 1895. On the night of Saturday, 9 January 1897, the Meadow Lads had set out for a pre-arranged scuttle with a gang from Ancoats. With Joe Wood in police custody, Cunningham led the mob through the packed streets around Smithfield market. The rival gang were spotted in Back Hanover Street. As the Ancoats mob walked slowly forward, Cunningham screamed, 'Go for them!' With the ferocious Harry Burgess at his side, Cunningham ran headlong into the fray. As the gangs collided, he stabbed a hawker named Joe Metcalfe twice in the shoulder. Metcalfe collapsed, and Cunningham and two other Meadow Lads stabbed him repeatedly as he lay on the ground. This time Cunningham paid a heavy price for his blood-lust. Recorder Leese sentenced him to three years' penal servitude.

Tommy Cunningham's career as a scuttler had spanned more than ten years. By the time he joined Jimmy Martin in penal servitude at Stafford gaol in March 1897, he was twenty-three years old. Martin was a year younger. Both lads were Catholics; their occupations were recorded as labourer and painter respectively. The Salford scuttler Mick King arrived at the gaol the following week. On 24 November 1897, Cunningham and Martin were transferred to Parkhurst Convict Prison on the Isle of Wight. The timing of their removal was highly fortuitous. Three weeks later their long-standing enemy, the formidable Ancoats scuttler Alexander Pearson, arrived at Stafford. It was better for all concerned that Cunningham and Pearson were kept apart.

NO DOUBT mindful of the lengthy jail terms imposed on their rivals, the Greengate scuttlers began to quieten their operations during the mid-1890s. Fewer raids were launched into the Adelphi or Ancoats, but the young toughs of Greengate still jealously guarded their territory and maintained a close watch over the romantic attachments of the girls of the district. When sexual jealousy was combined with territorial infringements the consequences could be dire. Late one Saturday night in January, 1897, James Tynan and Peter Fleming from Chorlton-on-Medlock in Manchester offered to walk Kathleen Whitham and Catherine Chambinzetti home to Salford after a night at the Cass music hall. The two girls lived in Greengate. Tynan and Whitham had been 'walking out' together for the last month, but their arrival in Greengate at around twenty past eleven that night provoked a furious reaction among the lads gathered on the corner of Queen Street. In an instant Tynan and Fleming were surrounded by a dozen local youths, one of whom shouted, 'This lot is out of

Manchester.' The Salford lads began to lash out at Tynan and Fleming with the buckle ends of their belts. Sixteen-year-old Billy Hopwood shouted, 'If you come round this way, we will rip your bleeding hearts out.' He then plunged a knife into Tynan's chest, puncturing his lung.

Hopwood, it transpired, was 'keeping company' with Catherine Chambinzetti. The sight of his sweetheart with the two Manchester lads was enough to drive him almost to murder. Fleming helped to carry Tynan to Manchester Royal Infirmary, while the two girls were told that they too would be severely dealt with if they 'brought any more Manchester lads to Queen Street'. Tynan lay in hospital for eighteen days. For the first week he was in a constant fever; the doctors fearing that each day would be his last. Four Greengate lads were arrested and committed for trial at the Manchester Assizes, where were they were charged with unlawful wounding and assault. 'Do you like fighting?' the prosecuting counsel asked Tynan. 'I like taking my own part,' he replied. Counsel for the defence protested that the affair should not be classified as a scuttling affray: it was merely 'a row over a girl', in which a jealous young lover had acted in 'a moment of irritation'. Hopwood was convicted of wounding and sentenced to twelve months' hard labour. Three of his mates were jailed for assaulting Peter Fleming with their belts. Tynan and Fleming appear to have assumed that they could walk unmolested into Queen Street, the traditional headquarters of the 'Greengate roughs'. They could not have been more wrong. Retribution was instant and, in Tynan's case, near-fatal.

BY 1897, with scuttlers languishing in increasing numbers behind bars, the judiciary had dealt a severe blow to many of the most feared gangs in Manchester. The leaders of the Deansgate mob, the Bungall Boys and the Adelphi were still only halfway through five-year stretches. More than a dozen other notable terrors had joined them. Rival kings could hardly fail to take note. Yet far heavier sentences had been imposed during the previous decade to little apparent deterrent effect. By the 1890s, however, judicial severity was no longer viewed as the only means of combating the gangs. A brave new social experiment was underway in the slums of Manchester and Salford that, it was hoped, might at last change the behaviour of the city's young incorrigibles for the better.

CHAPTER 19

The Vanishing Scuttler

JOHN JOSEPH HILLIER was the last King of the Scuttlers. No-one seemed to want to claim his crown. The gang conflicts which had terrorised Manchester and Salford for almost thirty years finally diminished between the late 1890s and the outbreak of the First World War. There is no simple explanation for the demise of scuttling. But the wider society was changing around the turn of the century, and life in the slums of Manchester was slowly beginning to change, too. By the middle of the first decade of the new century, local commentators were beginning to speak of scuttling in the past tense. Confident that the scuttler was at last disappearing from the city's streets, they even began to reminisce on the subject of his 'nobler' qualities.

Attitudes towards the slums changed significantly during the South African War of 1899–1902. In all of Britain's great cities, young men rushed in droves to enlist to fight the Boers. To the dismay of the nation, huge numbers were rejected as unfit for military service. No fewer than 12,000 Manchester men volunteered to fight: 8,000 were rejected outright and only one in ten was accepted as 'completely fit'. A series of calamitous defeats for British forces in the early phase of the war heightened the national sense of shock. The tide of the conflict turned the following year and by the summer of 1900 victory was assured. At home, attention had turned to the problems of the industrial conurbations. In Manchester and Salford, as elsewhere, working-class lads were increasingly viewed in a new light: as victims of a degraded environment. To the nation's political and religious leaders, and to

334

scores of columnists in the press, nothing less than the 'physical deterioration' of the British race seemed to be at stake.

Concern with conditions in the slums had grown during the 1880s and had begun to figure in press debates on scuttling following the killing of Bengal Tiger Joe Brady in 1887. Against the backdrop of the South African war, anxieties surrounding urban degeneration became more urgent and more compelling. If the national interest was to be served, the rising generation in the slums could not be written off as vicious and depraved. The youth of 'Outcast Manchester', 'Blackest Birmingham' and 'Squalid Liverpool' had to be redeemed. In Manchester and Salford, the local press began to look afresh at the slums themselves. The physical environment in districts such as Ancoats had changed little since the 1880s. Manchester City Council had established an Unhealthy Dwellings Committee in 1885 to identify the worst pockets of slum housing and prepare for their demolition. One of the first schemes centred on Bengal Street, where 239 houses were demolished during the early 1890s, displacing 1,250 people. Victoria Square was built on the site, a five-storey block containing nearly 300 flats. This was Manchester City Council's first municipal housing scheme, but elsewhere in the slums progress was painfully slow. The moral climate remained the cause of grave concern, too. Understanding of the causes of Britain's urban crisis, however, was beginning to shift. The *Salford Reporter* published a survey of 'Life in the Adelphi' in October 1901, introducing the district as 'the plague spot of the borough'. As the *Reporter* pointed out, the Adelphi had long been known for 'its high death-rate, its scamps and scuttlers, its wife beaters, its ruffianism, and rowdyism'. The landscape remained that of 'gehenna' – hell on earth. The Broughton Copper Works had belched nitric acid fumes over the entire district for decades. Moreover, according to the *Reporter*'s correspondent, environmental degradation had combined to deadly effect with its human equivalent: the Adelphi was a place where 'drink, dirt, disease and death are in constant collaboration'.

Weather permitting, most of the family life of the Adelphi took place in the streets. People ate and drank on their doorsteps and in summer they slept outside, driven from their beds by plagues of bugs that no amount of scouring could shift. The *Reporter* was shocked by how much of people's lives was on display: 'doors were wide open, women squatted on the steps, children romped about.' There was not a single blade of grass in the district, yet the Adelphi was anything but drab: the streets teemed with children and at weekends the pub vaults were crammed with drunks. Those who drank themselves into a stupor were carried outside and laid on the pavement to sleep it off. The *Reporter* pleaded for the erection of a bandstand and a public reading room, so that the people of the Adelphi might be 'lifted and not lowered'.

There was, the *Reporter* noted, still a widely held notion elsewhere in Salford that the Adelphi 'is what the dwellers have made it'. The newspaper, however, demurred: 'Two factors have contributed largely to the degeneration of the people – overcrowding, and an abnormal number of liquor shops.' Responsibility lay firmly with the municipal authority, Salford Corporation: 'They are to blame, not the people.' The *Reporter*'s correspondent gave a graphic example of overcrowding: 'The house has one room up and one down. Father, mother, and six children live in it. The bedroom contains two beds; that old bassinette in the corner is the baby's crib. There is a fire-place, and one window, which will not open. I leave readers to imagine the life.' Desperate to escape such surroundings, young couples married early to set up homes of their own, only to find that their lives soon mirrored those of their parents.

The only sign of progress that the *Reporter* could find in the Adelphi was a marked change in the behaviour of the district's young people. During the mid-1890s the Adelphi scuttlers, led by Dick Beattie, had been the scourge of the neighbourhood. By the turn of the century, although the young men of the district were still renowned for their toughness they were no longer so inclined to parade the streets in armed gangs. 'Bad as the Adelphi is it would be considerably worse but for the Lads' Club and its staff of self-sacrificing workers,' observed the *Reporter*. 'The club has caught much of the rough life of the district, and has turned it from aimlessness to purpose. Here is a young man about to checkmate an opponent at chess – he might have been leading a band of scuttlers.'

THE ESTABLISHMENT of working lads' clubs was one of the most profound changes taking place in the slum districts of Manchester and Salford at the close of the nineteenth century. The first clubs were formed in response to the reported escalation of scuttling in the late 1880s. The Adelphi Lads' Club, which grew out of the local 'ragged school', was the first in Salford.[25] The Adelphi Ragged School had been established under the auspices of the Richmond Congregational Chapel in 1867. Funded by charitable donations, it offered free lessons for the children of 'this unsavoury part of the borough'. The opening of a Protestant school in an area of heavy Irish-Catholic settlement initially met with fierce local opposition, some of it violent. The school's promoters persevered, however, and by 1881 demand for places had increased sufficiently to warrant a move to bigger premises in the form of a disused mill in Pine Street. In 1888, one of the teachers, twenty-three-year-old Walter Southern, decided to open a lads' club as an extension of the school's work. His aim was: 'To direct these lads' energies into channels more elevating than congregating in gangs at street corners.' The new club drew between seventy and eighty lads a night to the school-rooms in Pine Street in its early months, but Southern knew that more spacious accommodation was required if the Adelphi Lads' Club was to grow.

Southern worked tirelessly to gather support from local employers, politicians and clergy. The foundation stone of the club's new, purpose-built premises in Hall Street was laid in November 1889. Stephen Ashburner, one of the Adelphi Ragged School's longest-serving teachers, told the gathering that their object was to help the lads of the Adelphi to lead good and useful

---

25 'Ragged schools' were intended for the children of the very poor – those who could not, or would not, attend day schools run by the various churches. There were more than 350 such schools in Britain by the time of the 1870 Education Act. Most were subsequently absorbed by the new Board Schools.

lives by imparting useful lessons. The club would be non-sectarian, with Catholics as free to join as any other denomination. To much laughter, Ashburner impishly added, 'I look forward to the time when, as a result of the establishment of lads' clubs, the Gorton scuttler shall lie down with the Salford lamb and the Manchester rough should make a pleasing trio of law-abiding citizens.'

Here the impulse behind the early development of lads' clubs in Manchester and Salford was laid bare. The clubs were intended to turn the youth of the slums into good Christians and diligent workers but, more urgently, they were to put down scuttling. By April 1892, Walter Southern was able to announce that there were 576 names on the club's register. The typical nightly attendance was between 180 and 190. In Southern's own account, the club workers 'tried by constant contact with them, to teach the lads lessons in order, obedience, and Christian feeling one towards another, and it was hoped they might be made better able, both physically and morally, to go through their daily work of life'.

The lads' club movement gained impressive momentum in Manchester during the late 1880s under the energetic leadership of Alexander Devine. His earlier stint as police court news reporter for the *Manchester Guardian* had exposed Devine to horrific tales of the brutality of the city's scuttlers and convinced him of the need to establish recreational clubs for the youth of the slums. Much as he abhorred the scuttlers, Devine passionately believed that their violence might have been prevented. He established Hulme and Chorlton-on-Medlock Lads' Club in Mulberry Street, Hulme, in January 1887. Within three months, the club's average nightly attendance was 700. The following year, with assistance from staff and pupils at Manchester Grammar School, he founded Hugh Oldham Lads' Club in Livesey Street, Ancoats. Devine was a relentless publicist and was not shy of asking favours of the wealthy and powerful. His perseverance paid off: the opening ceremony at Livesey Street was attended by Albert Victor, Prince of Wales; the Mayor of Manchester, Sir J. Harwood; the Bishop of Manchester; the Earl of Derby; Lord Egerton of Tatton; C. P. Scott, editor of the *Manchester Guardian*; and G. A. Atkinson, editor of the *Boy's Own Paper*.[26]

Inspired by Devine, no fewer than four separate clubs were established in Ancoats alone between 1888 and 1890. Additional clubs were formed in Openshaw, and in Pendleton as well as in the Adelphi in Salford. All of the clubs were founded and initially run by middle-class philanthropists, whose motives combined a sense of civic duty with a Christian compassion for the youth of the slums. As in the Adelphi, however, the primary purpose of the clubs was in each case to curb the activities of the local scuttling gangs. The clubs were brought together under the umbrella of the Manchester Working Lads' Association, with Devine at the centre.

In his vision, once working lads had been taken off the streets their characters could then be remoulded according to the ideal of 'Christian manliness'.[27] The clubs would bring religion into the lives of lads otherwise untouched by the churches. Ultimately, the lads of the slums were to become 'manly, plucky fellows, following Christ'. Devine envisaged that lads' clubs would provide reading rooms and instruction in crafts such as woodwork in addition to lectures, concerts, lantern-slide shows and opportunities to play sport. In practice, it was the latter which ensured that the clubs took root. Clubs across Manchester and Salford quickly established football, rugby and cricket teams, and actively promoted gymnastics, athletics and swimming. They found hundreds of willing takers. The Manchester Working Lads' Association organised its own cup competitions from 1891 onwards and many stayed loyal to the clubs solely to ensure that they could take advantage of the sports facilities on offer. The clubs' other great draw was the Whit-week camps held in the Derbyshire countryside or on the North Wales coast. Few families in the slums could afford to take holidays

---

26 The club was named after the former Bishop of Manchester and founder of Manchester Grammar School.
27 Proponents of 'Christian manliness' sought to reinvigorate Christianity by combining godliness with the traditional manly virtues of physical courage, hardiness, chivalry and patriotism.

so the camps organised by the clubs were much prized. The Adelphi club's first camp, at Great Hucklow, near Buxton, in 1892, proved immensely popular: nightly attendances notably increased when the camp was announced.

Devine spotted another opportunity for work with lads following the introduction of the First Offenders Act in 1887. This granted magistrates the authority to release young offenders brought before them for the first time into the care of a 'responsible guardian', thus avoiding the stigma of imprisonment. Devine put himself forward as a guardian for lads coming before the magistrates at the Manchester City Police Court. Thus he secured a new post as Police Court Missionary, bringing him into closer personal contact with juvenile offenders. The following year he established the Gordon Boys' Home, named after General Gordon, the hero of Khartoum, to provide temporary accommodation for boys released into his care under the terms of the 1887 Act. No fewer than 255 lads passed through the home during its first year. Devine used his extensive contacts in Manchester's commercial and philanthropic circles to place them in work.

Alexander Devine's leadership was inspirational, but his book-keeping was shambolic. He was obliged to resign from the Manchester Working Lads' Association during 1890 following the discovery that he had been passing cheques payable to the various clubs through his own bank account. Stung by insinuations of embezzlement, Devine protested that he had sunk a good deal of his own money into the clubs, but to no avail. In November that year, he was forced to relinquish control of the Gordon Home following an investigation into its management chaired by the Recorder of Manchester, Henry West. Alexander Devine left Manchester for London in 1892. His legacy was a burgeoning association of lads' clubs, whose growth survived Devine's haphazard accounting. Clubs were by now firmly established in many of the areas afflicted by scuttling. The gangs still plagued districts such as Ancoats, as the killing of Peter Kennedy in April 1892 demonstrated only too well, but the attempt to rehabilitate the youth of Manchester's slums had begun in earnest.

The momentum generated by Alexander Devine was sustained by a new generation of volunteers, most notably Charles Russell. Born in Accrington in 1866 and educated at Dulwich College, Russell worked for the London and North Western Railway. He transferred to the company's Manchester office towards the end of 1892, whereupon he volunteered his services at the Heyrod Street Lads' Club in Ancoats. The club was short-staffed, so the offer was eagerly accepted. Russell spent every night at the club and quickly became a popular figure among the boys. However, he attracted criticism from his fellow workers, who noticed that Russell tended to befriend the more reckless lads, whilst having much less time for the 'steady, reliable type'. The Heyrod Street Lads' Club, they agreed, was rapidly becoming a 'rough-house'.

During the summer of 1893, one of Russell's fellow workers at the club persuaded him to divert some of his energies into the Boys' Brigade. The brigade's object – 'The advancement of Christ's Kingdom among Boys' – was entirely in keeping with that of the Heyrod Street Lads' Club, but its methods were much more disciplined. The 5th Manchester Company of the Boys' Brigade was formed in September of that year, with Russell as captain. Once again, he threw himself wholeheartedly into the venture. He formed an officers' council to oversee the work of the boys' brigade throughout Manchester, with himself as secretary. Within eighteen months, under Russell's leadership, the number of Boys' Brigade companies in the city had increased from twelve to twenty and membership of the Manchester battalion had grown to 1,000. The brigade's emphasis on discipline had as much effect on Russell as upon any of the boys under his command. His work at the Heyrod Street Lads' Club was transformed, bringing a new emphasis on order, and with many of 'his lads' subscribing to both institutions, the Boys' Brigade drills began to unite the street-based factions which had co-existed at times uneasily within the lads' club.

Like Alexander Devine before him, Russell began to devote more and more of his energies to the welfare of the youth of Manchester's slums. From his office at the Heyrod Street Lads' Club, he worked with juvenile offenders, street hawkers, racecourse touts and 'out of works'. He was especially concerned with the welfare of lads living in the city's common lodging-houses, or dosshouses. When Russell moved to Manchester in 1892, he took lodgings in the leafy suburb of Altrincham, eight miles south of the city. In 1894, at the age of twenty-eight, he moved to a 'mean street' in Ardwick only a few minutes' walk from Heyrod Street. Here, he lived and dressed as a 'working lad', refusing to wear an overcoat and making one suit and a pair of heavy workman's boots last for years at a time. From eleven o'clock each night he toured the dosshouses of Ancoats, Angel Meadow and Red Bank, playing board games with groups of youths, engaging them in conversation and attempting to befriend them. Russell was determined to understand the lodging-house lads and their lives, but his intrusions were not always welcome: he was stabbed on two occasions and showered with spit whilst 'speaking of Christ to men in a lodging-house in Angel Meadow'.[28]

WHEREAS FORMAL schooling offered little prospect of advancement to working-class lads, most of whom still entered full-time work aged twelve or thirteen, the clubs offered a bois-terous camaraderie, a host of organised activities and, crucially, a sense of belonging that extended beyond the confines of the street or workplace. The opening of lads' clubs initially had little impact on existing gangs of scuttlers, some of whom – in the Adelphi, for example – invaded the clubs' early meetings, mocking and picking fights with those in attendance. However, as the clubs became more established over the course of the 1890s, they contributed to the development of more peaceable pastimes among the rising generation of youths. Russell was adamant that lads' clubs made a significant impact on the districts in which they were established, echoing the *Salford*

---

28 Russell's endeavours were extraordinary, but he was not alone. By the 1890s, increasing numbers of young middle-class men and women went 'slumming' in the belief that social problems could only be solved by those who had seen for themselves how the poor of the great cities lived.

Reporter's assessment of the Adelphi Lads' Club in October 1901. Writing for the *Guardian* in 1905, Russell claimed that, 'during the last few years there has been an appreciable change for the better. The rough noisy horse-play and disorder of the artizan quarters has greatly decreased.'

Russell was nonetheless guarded in the claims he made for the impact of the clubs. He acknowledged that only a relatively small number of lads ever joined. He also pointed out that, whilst the clubs were formed with the aim of civilising 'the very roughest or very lowest lads of a district', such lads were precisely those hardest to attract. In its early years, a club might well manage to draw in the rough lads of the locality. However, as the club consolidated its work, it inevitably became more respectable in tone, thus 'frightening away prospective new members of the primitive type'. In that sense, the clubs were victims of their own success. Russell's own club in Heyrod Street in Ancoats was a good example: by 1908, the most common occupations among the club's active members were warehouseman and clerk; labourers were scarce in proportion to their numbers in the local population.

It is possible, however, that the indirect influence of the lads' club movement was more important than even Russell recognised. Participation in sport and gymnastics rose significantly in Manchester during the 1890s. Association football, especially, grew massively in popularity. The lads' clubs played an important part in football's growth, as did the rise of Manchester's two professional teams: Newton Heath and Ardwick – soon to become Manchester United and Manchester City. Lads flocked in their thousands to Bank Street, Clayton, to see Newton Heath and to Hyde Road in Ardwick to watch City.

Football's most spectacular growth, however, was in the streets. Groups of youths in districts across Manchester and Salford began to form teams of their own, quickly taking control of the sport out of the hands of the lads' club workers. 'In the artisan quarters of the city, boys attempt to play the game in the heat of summer with small balls of tightly rolled-up bundles of paper; and few indeed are the lads who do not make an effort to play football during the winter,' noted Russell. 'Towards the middle of August, the youths of almost any street in the poorer quarters of the town gather together with their chums of the immediate neighbourhood to form a Football Club.' Groups of boys as young as ten or twelve would beg, steal or borrow a football and rudimentary kit. Then they would adopt a name for themselves – Russell picked out Albion Red Star from Ancoats as an example – and set about finding rival teams to play. Older lads, aged in their mid- or late teens, formed teams of their own. Matches were held on crofts across the poorer districts of the Manchester conurbation. No quarter was expected or given. 'The game is generally played with considerable vigour,' Russell noted, 'and where the boys are not under proper control the language and conduct of the players leave a very great deal to be desired.'

In previous years, however, gangs of scuttlers had fought a very different kind of battle for neighbourhood supremacy on the same crofts.

AGAINST THE backdrop of anxieties over 'physical deterioration' in British cities, Russell wrote a series of sketches of 'Manchester Boys' for the *Guardian*, whose editor, C. P. Scott, had been an early supporter of the Hugh Oldham Lads' Club. On the basis of his ceaseless work in Ancoats, Russell was better qualified to describe the lives of youths in the city's slums than any other commentator in the local press. Perhaps uniquely, his work encompassed dealings with 'respectable' lads – in the Boys' Brigade and the lads' clubs – and the 'rougher' types found in the lodging-houses, many of whom were routinely dragged before the magistrates at the police court in Minshull Street. Russell had worked tirelessly with all types for more than a decade.

Writing in November 1904, Russell declared that the scuttler 'has now almost disappeared from our midst'. He admitted that scuttling and 'kindred forms of ruffianism' had not ceased altogether but was adamant that they were not nearly as prevalent as they had been a few years previously. As secretary of Heyrod Street Lads' Club, Russell had a vested interest in downplaying the persistence of scuttling after 1900. After all, the reported waning of the city's gang conflicts provided the best possible vindication of the clubs and their work. Nonetheless, his account stands as a useful overview of the gangs of late-Victorian Manchester and Salford.

Russell reminded the *Guardian*'s readers that the scuttler been all-too-common a sight on the streets of districts such as Ancoats: 'Let us recall him for a moment. You knew him by his dress. A loose white scarf would adorn his throat; his hair was well plastered down upon his forehead; he wore a peaked cap rather over one eye; his trousers were of fustian, and cut – like a sailor's – with "bell bottoms".' Russell's use of the past tense was significant: by the middle of the first decade of the new century the scuttler was already largely a thing of the past.

In Russell's view, the causes of scuttling were not difficult to discern: the problem was emphatically not the lads themselves, but their environment. The scuttler had not been born evil. First and foremost, working-class lads had been driven to street fighting by 'the absence of any proper facilities for the outlet of the physical energies of youth'. Russell insisted that:

> The 'scuttler' of years gone by was the victim of his own high, animal spirit. He must find scope for his powers, and he had no legitimate field in which to exercise himself. When the day's work was done, his energy was not exhausted; how was he to amuse himself? He must have society, and he must have something to do. He loved romance. So he banded with his fellows and made a gang. Here, at any rate, was company. But what to do? War was his amusement and his avocation, and he must make war upon his neighbours of the next street. His gang must show its prowess by thrashing all other gangs.

Once unleashed, scuttlers had been driven by the seemingly endless quest for neighbourhood supremacy. The resulting violence had been inflamed, Russell insisted, by arguments over girls.

The scuttler's own 'high, animal spirits' had made him a force to reckon with on the streets. To make matters worse, his mind had all too often been poisoned by the bloodthirsty melodramas performed in the city's cheap theatres:

> Horrible murders and terrible tragedies were enacted before the footlights; boys became familiar with pictures of the most violent passions – hatred, revenge, malice. It is certainly a question whether the frequency with which they witnessed this kind of play was not partly responsible for the wretched condition of mind which in the past, led to so many instances of violence on the part of young men in the back streets of the city.

Manchester's youthful audiences certainly had an appetite for violence and crime. Popular productions such as *The Ticket-of-Leave Man* guaranteed full houses. The St James's Theatre in Oxford Street 'staged all the blood and thunder you could ask for', recalled elderly Salfordian Jack Lanigan approvingly. As a boy, he paid twopence to sit in the gods (gallery) or threepence for the pit (stalls) when he was feeling flush. The audiences were invariably rowdy, pelting the villains with faded tomatoes and oranges and raising the roof when scenes met with their approval. The Prince of Wales theatre in Hope Street, Salford, was better known locally as the 'Blood Tub'. Admission was costlier than at the St James's but the body-count nonetheless represented good value for money. As another Blood Tub regular, Joe Toole, recalled, its patrons 'could always depend on at least sixteen murders for fourpence'. Yet good always ultimately prevailed over evil in popular melodramas, a moral message somehow lost on the critics of the cheap theatre.

Russell was adamant that scuttling was 'very bad'. The authorities in Manchester had been gravely troubled by it; the police had struggled to put it down. However, the lads involved were not without their admirable qualities. 'The "scuttler" was not wholly bad; he would rather be a blackguard than a dullard,' insisted Russell. 'His real desires were natural and healthy. They were not controlled, and they were not directed to proper ends; but here at least was force, and something can be made of that.'

In the wake of the outright rejection of three-quarters of the Manchester volunteers for the South African war, Russell's implication was clear: improve his environment, subject him to discipline, and the Manchester boy would make the ideal soldier. Russell even claimed that the majority of scuttlers adhered to a code of honour. The 'rougher and more unscrupulous gangs' might assault unknown passers-by, but 'in justice to the Manchester lads who gloried in the name of "scuttler" it must be recorded that they were wont to declare that no *real* "scuttler" would ever commit such an act'. The record, unfortunately, did not bear this out.

THE GROWTH of working lads' clubs cannot offer a sole explanation for the decline of scuttling. Russell also commented that scuttling had been 'put down, not without trouble, by vigorous action on the part of the police'. He gave no details as to how the Manchester and Salford constabularies had finally managed to suppress the warring gangs of youths who had plagued the streets for so long. It is significant, however, that Russell attributed the diminution of scuttling to the actions of the police rather than the supposedly salutary sentences imposed by the courts.

Surviving police records give no account of this belated triumph over the gangs, but the unpublished memoirs of a former Manchester beat constable provide one tantalising clue. S. P. Ford, who served in the Manchester City Police from 1924 until his retirement in 1949, learned of the scuttlers through the folklore of the police canteen. When he arrived in Manchester the old hands of 'E' Division, who had worked under the leadership of Jerome Caminada during the 1890s, liked nothing better than to regale young probationary officers with tales of how they had 'subdued' the scuttlers. There is a hint here that the police resorted to strong-arm methods in driving the scuttlers off the streets. As Ford reflected, 'If some of the stories told were only half true, Manchester in the 1890s must have been a pretty lively place to live in.'

One case which lingered long in the memory was that of

Ford's namesake, John, an eighteen-year-old scuttler from Hulme. One of John Ford's mates in the Clopton Street mob decided to join the militia in August, 1889, and the gang organised a drinking spree as a send-off. The revelries lasted until one o'clock in the morning and the last half-dozen drinkers were stood talking on the corner of Chester Street when they were approached by P.C. Henry Yardley of 'D' Division:

'What do you want lounging about at this hour of the morning?'

'We are going home,' replied Ford.

P.C. Yardley promptly punched Ford in the face, and kicked him as he fell to the ground. When a second constable, John Moore, came round the corner, the rest of the lads ran off down the street. Moore also began to kick Ford. The stricken youth's plea – 'Oh, don't kick me' – woke a local woman, who leaned out of her bedroom window and shouted, 'Don't ill use the lad, lock him up.' The two constables marched John Ford to the corner of Poplar Street, where he lived, striking him repeatedly along the way. His face was badly swollen and he bled heavily from his nose and mouth. Ford felt so weak the following morning he stayed in bed rather than turn in for his work as a dyer. When he showed no sign of improvement, his mother sent for a doctor. However, pneumonia set in and John Ford died four days after the assault.

At the coroner's inquest, three of Ford's pals gave vivid descriptions of the blows inflicted by the constables. Their account was corroborated by residents of Chester Street. A sergeant from 'D' Division insinuated that the beating had been inflicted by Ford's father, but this was vehemently denied. When P.C. Yardley was called to give evidence, he stated that he had seen the lads on the night in question, but 'he had no disturbance with them. He did not strike any of them.' He did admit, however, that 'he had run the same gang many times from street corners for scuttling'. P.C. Moore flatly denied that he had seen the scuttlers at all that night. The doctor who attended Ford on the Saturday testified that the youth's face was marked, 'but there was nothing else the matter with him'. He did not think that the facial injuries had anything to do with the lad's death. The resident surgeon at Manchester Royal Infirmary, who had conducted the post-mortem examination, concurred. He told the inquest that Ford's death was caused by asphyxia from acute pneumonia. The jury took just a few minutes to return a verdict of death by natural causes.

A second investigation was launched by the Watch Committee of Manchester City Council the following week. P.C. Yardley was subsequently compelled to resign from the force, while P.C. Moore was admonished. The use of violence by the police only came to light due to Ford's death. Had the unfortunate youth recovered, no more would have been heard of it. In the light of the boasts by the detectives of 'E' division in later years, it seems more than likely that many other beatings of scuttlers went unreported over the course of the following decade.

The magistrates did their bit to combat the gangs during the 1890s, too. Denied the power to have scuttlers flogged, they worked hand-in-hand with the police to eradicate their meeting places. In the wake of the killing of Peter Kennedy in Ancoats in April 1892, they began to act against those pubs and beerhouses known as the haunts of scuttlers. Licences were refused at the Farriers' Arms on Ashton New Road in Bradford and two premises in Ancoats: the Shakespeare Inn on Every Street and the Mechanics' Arms, a tiny beerhouse on Beswick Street. The keeper of the Mechanics' had struggled to control her customers. If she refused to serve them, they smashed her crockery and furniture. According to the police, the beerhouse was 'in a very low neighbourhood, and was frequented by roughs who had been locked up times without number'. A constable testified that the Mechanics' was 'a resort of scuttlers. He had seen young men go in and come out and engage in a scuttling affray.' Police evidence likewise helped to close the Royal Oak on Silver Street in Hulme, another 'disorderly house' frequented by scuttlers and loose women.

None of these establishments was as disreputable as the Alma Inn – 'the Scuttlers' Den' – in Openshaw. No fewer than ten police officers testified to the preponderance of scuttlers among the Alma's clientele at a licensing appeal in October 1893. A solicitor acting for the publican protested that the word 'scuttler' was unfairly and improperly used by the police: 'They knew the magic of the word, and that any batch of magistrates in the country would be only too glad to protect the public from offenders of this class.' Customers vouched that while there were 'a few rough 'uns' in the vault now and then, 'the house was frequented chiefly by respectable working men from the Gorton Tank', the popular name for Gorton Locomotive Works, situated in Openshaw. The licence, however, was refused.

The clampdown was maintained for the next ten years. John Nield, keeper of the Napoleon III beerhouse in Miles Platting, lost his licence after Jerome Caminada led a raid on the premises in June 1896. Following a tip-off, Caminada and two fellow detectives found 300 people gathered to watch a prize-fight between John Pearson and Ike Cohen for £15 a side. The crowd was crammed into an upstairs room measuring just forty-five feet by twenty-five. Access was by a single narrow staircase in the back yard. As Caminada pointed out, had there been a fire the consequences would have eclipsed even the disaster at Lang's music hall three decades earlier. When the two fighters arrived at half-past eight, they were immediately arrested. They were subsequently charged with attempting to breach the peace and bound over in the sum of £20 each for twelve months.

When John Nield's licence came up for renewal two months later, the police objected. Caminada attended the Brewster Sessions and gave a graphic description of the raid on the prize-fight. 'All classes of people were gathered there,' he told the magistrates, 'business men, publicans and criminals.' According to Caminada, the Napoleon III was a demoralising influence on the neighbourhood. More than 500 people had gathered for the Pearson–Cohen fight. Two hundred were milling around outside the pub, and local urchins were squaring up to each other in the street, taking 'their first lessons in the art of fistiana'. Nield protested that Caminada's arrival had drawn the bulk of the crowd that night: 'It went round the neighbourhood like wildfire that the wonderful Caminada had come. People who had never been in the house before came in when they heard that Caminada was there.' The magistrates were more impressed by the additional police witnesses, who described the Napoleon III as a refuge of thieves and the meeting place of the infamous Holland Street scuttlers.

In the summer of 1901, the police targeted the Duke of Connaught beerhouse on Ludgate Hill, headquarters of the Meadow Lads. The licence of the Connaught had changed hands almost every year since 1869. The police insisted that it had been 'the resort of thieves and scuttlers and women of ill repute' for the past ten years. Caminada boasted that he had helped to 'put an end to' no fewer than 400 lawless pubs and beerhouses in a career as a detective spanning nearly thirty years.

As the century drew to an end, tough action against those publicans and beerhouse keepers who provided havens for gangs of scuttlers was accompanied by a determined drive to clear youths from the streets irrespective of their involvement with gangs. Beat constables were emboldened by the appointment of a new Chief Constable, Robert Peacock, in 1898. Peacock was the first head of the Manchester force with personal experience as a beat constable. He had joined the police in Bradford, Yorkshire, aged nineteen. In Manchester, he inherited a force demoralised by poor working conditions, low pay and recent revelations of widespread corruption in 'D' division. His first task as Chief Constable was to restore morale.[29]

Peacock was a bobby's bobby. He gave his men *carte blanche* to 'move on' any gathering of lads on street corners, however few in number, and however orderly their conduct. By 1903, confident that the scuttling menace had finally more or less subsided, the *Manchester Guardian* became concerned that the police were showing too much zeal in sweeping youths off the streets of districts such as Ancoats. The editor of the *Guardian*, C. P. Scott,

---

29 Morale had plummeted in 1897 following a public inquiry into the conduct of 'D' division, where Superintendent William Bannister had been conniving at the misdeeds of beerhouse and brothel keepers for fifteen years. Fourteen constables resigned in the wake of the inquiry and thirteen others were dismissed. The Chief Constable, Charles Malcolm Wood, took a six month leave of absence, never to return to his post.

used the paper's leader column to bemoan the use of the 1844 Police Act to arrest lads for 'obstruction' even though they were innocent of any real wrong-doing.[30] Scott's outburst was prompted by a letter from Charles Russell, who claimed that beat constables were arresting lads who were merely stood talking to their friends. They were brought before the magistrates, costing them a day's wages and, in some cases, their jobs.

Two Manchester magistrates wrote to the *Guardian* in support of Russell. Other correspondents pointed out that the police allowed men of commerce to congregate in their hundreds in the streets surrounding the Royal Exchange. William O'Hanlon, one of Russell's co-workers at the Heyrod Street lads' club, protested, 'It ought to be realised that under the law poor people have as much right as rich ones to the use of the streets, and neither class can legally be proceeded against if they do not obstruct the passage along the footway or annoy other inhabitants. There seems, however, to be one law for St Ann's Square and another for Ancoats or Hulme. Why should there be?'

The answer surely lay in the legacy of the scuttlers. For three decades, gangs of warring youths from Ancoats and Hulme had brought terror to Manchester's streets. Russell's stricture against heavy-handed policing provoked the ire of many influential figures in the city. Patrick Lynch, parish priest of St Wilfrid's in Hulme, described the criticism of the police as entirely unwarranted: 'These hobbledehoy corner-boys ruined our evening school here last winter. They broke our windows, and were it not for the kind protection of the police our life here would not be worth the living.' Joseph Nunn, rector of St Thomas's in Ardwick, agreed: 'A few weeks ago I witnessed a bad case of scuttling on Ardwick Green, which I attempted to stop. Two men were badly injured by kicking and by blows with a belt, and taken to the Infirmary.' Nunn demanded an increase in police numbers. A resident of Miles Platting complained that Sunday

---

30 The Borough Police Act of 1844 forbade the people of Manchester 'standing, loitering, or remaining together with other persons on any footway without reasonable cause'.

evenings had long been ruined by a gang of twenty youths, who congregated at a nearby street corner. 'Here they would play pitch-and-toss and other games, sing comic songs and dance, and use the most filthy and abominable language. It was impossible to read or write or even converse in the house.' Repeated complaints to the police prompted a constable to drive the lads off, but only after a number of 'quiet and respectable' families had left the street.

Chief Constable Peacock claimed that he had personally investigated many cases in which youths had been arrested for obstruction: 'in every instance', he insisted, 'the police had been perfectly justified'. Peacock revealed that he had challenged Russell to provide examples of cases in which innocent lads had been arrested. Russell, however, had failed to do so. In response to Peacock's demand, another lads' club worker sent a list of cases to the *Guardian*. It featured two Ancoats lads fined for waiting for friends at a street corner before going to a Sunday evening service at Ardwick Lads' Club. Peacock met with Russell at Manchester Town Hall to discuss the furore on 29 September. Russell conceded that he ought to have approached the Chief Constable before airing his complaint in the press. Peacock, in return, gave an assurance that any case of unfair treatment reported by the secretary of a lads' club would be promptly investigated: if the lads were in the right, no further action would be taken.

PERHAPS A combination of factors led to the steady erosion of scuttling from the late 1890s. Uncompromising policing and harsh sentences might have dealt blows to the established gangs at the very moment when lads' clubs were increasing their appeal among thirteen- and fourteen-year-olds – the very lads needed to replenish the ranks of the gangs. At the same time, the proliferation of street-based football teams offered a new basis for territorial rivalries, and gave working-class lads acceptable grounds to walk together through neighbouring districts which, a decade earlier, they would have entered only at their peril.

While football increased steadily in popularity during the

1890s and 1900s, another form of popular entertainment swept through the slums of Manchester and Salford with astonishing rapidity. Within a decade of its inception in 1896, the cinema had begun to eclipse the music hall in the affections of the youth of the slums. By 1914 Manchester had 111 cinemas; Salford had seventeen. The combined figure far exceeded that of every other provincial city. Moralists worried about the 'corrupting' influence of early silent films, but senior police officers were grateful to see so many lads and lasses spending as many as three or four evenings a week in picture houses rather than on the streets. Even some older men fell under the spell of the early silent films, prompting bitter complaints from slum publicans whose takings dropped spectacularly. Drunkenness began to decline and so did convictions for assault. Heavy drinking and domestic violence were still widespread in 1914, but cinema had already done more to reduce levels of both than any of the measures introduced by successive governments from the 1870s.

WHAT BECAME of the scuttlers themselves? Most settled down as they entered their twenties, acquiring a degree of respectability in later life that they had explicitly rejected during their teens. As the author Robert Roberts recalled of Salford's Hope Street gang, by the time of the First World War, 'most of them were married and worthy householders in the district'. Once they married and took on adult responsibilities as breadwinners they could ill afford to appear before the magistrates. To be jailed for scuttling could bring more than disgrace to the family – it could bring destitution. Few of those aged in their twenties were willing to pay that price.

Even 'Mr Carey', the father of one of Roberts's childhood friends, came to see himself as a model citizen. One of the leaders of the Hope Street mob in the early 1890s, in later years he boasted of how the gang had prevented Jewish refugees from settling in the district: 'A Jewish dealer, we heard, had opened a second-hand clothes shop in the district, only to see his goods pulled out on to the pavement and burned openly by scuttlers, while a policeman stood by to see fair play. "That kep' 'em out!

We got no more o' the buggers!" He felt he had performed a social service.' As Roberts recognised, the scuttlers' action accorded with the neighbourhood's prevailing anti-Semitism. On this occasion, it appeared, even the police chose not to see the lads as criminals.

For some former Hope Street scuttlers, however, the transition to adulthood was far from smooth. Fred Bagley, a fearsome street fighter during the gang's heyday in the early 1890s, remained one of the terrors of the district for the remainder of the decade. He acquired a string of convictions: for theft, as well as for drunkenness and assault. Shortly before Christmas in 1898, Bagley was convicted of assaulting his mother. She brought the prosecution herself, telling the magistrate that Fred had initially assaulted his sister. When his mother intervened, 'he struck her two blows in the face'. Fred Bagley was far from a dutiful son. According to his mother, 'He had only given her sixpence [for his keep] in two years.' He was well-known to Salford police. Chief Detective Inspector Lyogue told the court that Bagley had no regular work but 'occasionally got a job at public houses'. Bagley was sent down for two months. Unusually for a lad of his generation, he did not marry until he was forty years old.

Bagley's associate, Bobby Verney, was no more gallant. On the evening of 24 August 1894, he accosted Elizabeth Ann Newsome in Oldfield Road. According to Newsome, Verney asked her to go for a walk with him but she declined, whereupon he seized her, dragged her into an entry, threw her down and bit her lip. Police officers noted that 'the marks of his teeth were afterwards plainly visible'. The evidence bore all the hall-marks of attempted rape. In his defence, Verney claimed that Newsome had been following him around ever since he jilted her for another girl. Salford's stipendiary magistrate, Joseph Makinson, believed there was an element of truth in both stories: 'No doubt the prosecutrix, who ought to have had more sense, had followed him about, and no doubt, too, there had been quarrels, in which they had threatened one another.' Bobby Verney had been before the court on sixteen previous occasions. Still only twenty years old, he had already served numerous terms of imprisonment. Makinson jailed him for six months.

The Ordsall Lane gang – sworn enemies of the Hope Street scuttlers during the early 1890s – likewise splintered over the course of the decade. Like many of their counterparts in Hope Street, some of 'the Lane' mob settled down, exchanging infamy for obscurity and – they hoped – relative comfort once they married. The gang's leaders, however, found it difficult to stay out of the clutches of the Salford Borough Police. Peter Nevin and Ralph Taylor were notorious figures long after the Ordsall Lane scuttlers had gone their separate ways. Both now settled in Providence Street – the She Battery.

Nevin's new ploy was to assault and rob drunken men in Providence Street's numerous brothels. Few of his victims reported their losses: fearful of publicity should they appear at the Salford Police Court, they were no doubt equally scared of retribution from Nevin. To maintain his reputation as a brawler, Nevin took to boxing in the street. In May 1893, he was arrested by P.C. Moore of Salford Borough Police in Providence Street on a charge of being drunk and disorderly. The constable told Joseph Makinson that: 'It was a nightly occurrence amongst the young men of the neighbourhood, who arranged matches amongst themselves and fought them out with boxing gloves.' Nevin protested, 'I did not think we were doing any harm.' Mr Makinson responded, 'It is not the boxing; it is getting a crowd to collect. You cannot play games in the streets of Salford.' On reflection Mr Makinson acknowledged: 'Well, this offence is not so bad as scuttling.' He fined Peter Nevin five shillings.

Ralph Taylor worked in the She Battery as a bully, 'looking after' the street-walkers who spent their afternoons and evenings loitering on Regent Road. The barracks closed in 1896, but the opening of the Salford docks two years earlier and the consequent influx of seamen had vastly increased demand for the services of Salford's prostitutes. Taylor, like Nevin, was determined to cash in. In April 1898, a detachment of constables was sent to Providence Street after a 'gentleman' passer-by reported that 'a free fight was going on in The Battery'. The officers later reported,

'A dog, which was in the habit of seizing men's legs when there was a row, seized [George] Leonard's leg with its teeth.' The dog might well have been used to settle an old score: George Leonard was a former Hope Street scuttler. The constables were severely assaulted for their trouble. P.C. Kelly was struck and repeatedly kicked in the ruckus which followed their arrival in the She Battery.

Peter Moffatt served twelve months in Strangeways following the affray between the Ordsall Lane gang and the Hope Street scuttlers during the spring of 1890. His prospects of rehabilitation following his release were nil. He was back in Strangeways within a month, convicted of assaulting the police. On this occasion, Moffatt was part of a crowd of young men who stopped a 'coloured' man named John McPherson in Gore Street, near Chapel Street, to ask for money. McPherson told the lads that he had none. One of the youths struck him with a belt. Another lad pulled out a knife, but two beat constables appeared at the scene before he could use it. The lads ran off, but the officers gave chase and arrested John Moore and Geoff Hughes. The constables were bombarded with missiles as they took the lads to the police station at Salford Town Hall. Peter Moffatt, who was wielding a knife, shouted: 'It won't be a sessions job this time!' He then threw a brick at the constables. A warrant was issued against Moffatt and he was arrested the following day. He was jailed for one month by the Salford magistrates.

Over the course of the 1890s Peter Moffatt turned increasingly to petty theft – just as he had done during his childhood. He was repeatedly jailed. Between 1897 and 1903 he served nine separate stretches. As a habitual offender he faced draconian punishment: three months' hard labour for stealing a pair of leggings in May 1898; six months for stealing a rug in May 1899; twelve months for stealing a rug in December 1901 and another twelve for stealing another rug when he got out. Repeated convictions for stealing single items such as rugs and overcoats suggest that Moffatt was living in Salford's common lodging-houses throughout his twenties and thirties. He was a prisoner in Strangeways at the time of the 1901 census. His old adversary Bobby Verney, from Hope Street, was serving a stretch alongside him.

As Moffatt's case demonstrates, the leading figures in scuttling gangs were difficult to rehabilitate. Veterans of violence, they were veterans of Strangeways, too, and prison did nothing to deter them. Their lengthy criminal records made it difficult for them to find legitimate employment even if they wanted to. They no longer marched proudly through the streets at the head of bands of armed lads. By the late 1890s, however, a number of once-notorious scuttlers lurked in the murky underworld of 'Criminal Manchester'.

One such figure was Billy Wagstaff, John Joseph Hillier's successor as 'captain' of the Deansgate mob in the spring of 1895. Wagstaff was sent down for twelve months at the Manchester Quarter Sessions in July 1902. Along with a known bully named Edwin Stephens, Wagstaff, now aged twenty-four, was convicted of picking the pocket of Frederick Duckett on 15 May. Their haul was one watch plus two shillings and sixpence in coins. Wagstaff, who had been sent to the industrial training ship *Formidable* from the age of ten to sixteen, served four stretches in Strangeways for scuttling. By the late 1890s, picking pockets was Wagstaff's specialism. The conviction in the summer of 1902 was his third for such an offence. He now had thirty-four convictions in total: for theft, drunkenness, assault, assaulting the police and unlawful wounding.

John Kennedy, one of Wagstaff's companions in the Deansgate mob of the mid-1890s, appeared at the same sitting of the Quarter Sessions in July 1902. Kennedy was now aged thirty-two. His wife, Mary Alice, appeared in the dock alongside him. They were both charged with breaking and entering: their haul from the shop of Arthur Steinberg allegedly comprised one brooch, one buckle, one gold ring and two ivory figures. John Kennedy was found guilty and sentenced to twelve months' hard labour. Mary Alice was discharged. John Kennedy's last conviction for scuttling had been in 1889, though he had nearly died following a fight with the Bungall Boys two years later. He had subsequently served a term of penal servitude for stealing thirty shillings, only to be arrested once more shortly after release on licence. His record contained fewer convictions than Wagstaff's – sixteen in total – but only because Kennedy had spent most of his twenties behind bars. Detectives from 'E' Division of the City of Manchester Police kept John Kennedy under close surveillance whenever he was at liberty. As a habitual offender, they had the power to arrest him for merely acting 'suspiciously' even if he had not committed a crime.[31]

ONLY ISOLATED outbreaks of scuttling were reported during the 1900s. Even in Ancoats, once the domain of the Bengal Tigers, the rising generation of lads seemed to be unwilling to continue the old territorial battles with the regularity or ferocity seen ten years earlier. Scuttling now persisted only in much milder form: gangs of school-children from one street still gathered to wage war upon neighbouring streets, but their battles rarely extended beyond bouts of stone throwing. The days of gangs of older lads armed with knives and belts marching several miles across Manchester and Salford to seek out their opponents were over.

The legends of the gangs, however, lived on well into the twentieth century. Stories of the scuttlers and their exploits were many and varied; some bore little relation to Victorian reports of the gangs' activities. In 1958, when Manchester was gripped by fear of 'Teddy Boys', the Lord Mayor, Alderman James Fitzsimons, told the press that 'he would like to see the birch brought back as punishment for certain violent attacks on old, defenceless

---

31 Under the terms of the Habitual Criminals Act (1869) and the Prevention of Crimes Act (1871), police officers could arrest those with two or more convictions for indictable (i.e. serious) offences 'on suspicion'. The accused had to satisfy the magistrates that they had not been about to commit a crime nor waiting for the opportunity to do so. Failure to do so was punishable by twelve months' imprisonment with hard labour. Paddy Mannion, a former Meadow Lad, also appeared at the Manchester Quarter Sessions in July 1902. He was sentenced to seven months' hard labour for the theft of twenty shillings. Mannion by now had thirteen previous convictions for theft; he too had served repeated stretches in Strangeways.

people'. An elderly resident of Whalley Range wrote to the *Evening News* pointing out that the solution had been identified by the great Victorian detective Jerome Caminada more than fifty years earlier. In Caminada's words: 'One touch of the lash would do far more good than years of imprisonment.' The letter-writer added, 'Round about 1890 Mr Caminada had a lot to do with breaking up the gangs of scuttlers. I personally lived in a "hot" part of Manchester and I know that the rough element spoke with awe of "Caminada". I am sure that his efforts had a lasting effect and I feel confident that anyone born after about 1896 has never heard the word scuttler.' The *Evening News* published the letter under the heading: 'BIRCH THUGS – IT WORKED ONCE!' Yet corporal punishment had never been inflicted on scuttlers, as the newspaper's own archives amply testified.

Such myths doubtless provided comfort to many of the *Evening News*'s readers. The stories reinforced the popular belief during the 1950s that if only policing and punishment were made more stringent then order would prevail on the streets. The myth that scuttling was cured by the 'lash' seeped into popular memory, as shown in the following account provided by Gladys Chorley in 1995:

> I am eighty-nine years of age, born and bred in Salford. My father was born in 1879 and he often talked of the scuttlers, in particular an event when he along with his brother and a friend walking home one night became aware that they were being followed by a gang of scuttlers. My father and his brother were fast runners and could easily have outstripped the scuttlers, but their friend was a poor runner. They ran as fast as they could dragging their friend along with them. They were getting close to home but knew the scuttlers would be on them before they reached the house. In desperation my father whistled his dog. On hearing the whistle the dog jumped a five foot stone wall which surrounded the house, and bounded towards them. The scuttlers seeing and hearing the dog did an about turn.

In those days the policemen walked the streets in pairs; when a scuttler was caught he did not receive a prison sentence but a number of lashes from the cat o' nine tails. This punishment was carried out over a period of time and when complete the man was sent home. The punishment appears to have been effective since scuttling gradually died out.

Yet again the cat was invoked as the solution to the problem of violence among Manchester's young people.

Scuttling gangs took various forms in twentieth-century lore – some of them very different to Victorian accounts of the gangs and their activities. Harry Beesley was born in Ordsall in 1928. His mother had grown up in the district during the 1890s and she too had plenty of tales of scuttling to tell her children. In her account, they appeared as muggers:

My mother told me that one night, [her family] were all sat there [in the front room of their house], and there was an almighty bang on the door, not a knocking, a banging, a thumping. Whoever got up and opened the door and a young man ran in, naked, and the mother of the house – my grandmother – she slammed the door. And as she slammed the door, the panel was smashed in by a brick. And that was the scuttlers. They'd waylaid this young man, stripped him of everything he had, whatever they wanted to do with him then, I really don't know, and he found refuge in my grandparents' house, and they smashed the panel of the door in.

Victorian police officers seldom accused scuttlers of robbing their victims. Had gang members been convicted of robbery with violence they would indeed have been flogged under the terms of the Security from Violence Act of 1863 – as were the High Rippers of Liverpool (albeit without the deterrent effect that later writers were fond of describing).

George Whitworth was born in Salford in 1897, seven years after the feud between the Hope Street and Ordsall Lane gangs was interrupted by the trial of seventeen lads at the Salford

Borough Quarter Sessions. Nonetheless, he had grown up listening to tales of the scuttlers. In an interview conducted in 1970 he was even able to compile a league table of gangs whose exploits had taken place before he was born. He insisted the worst gang was Ordsall Lane: 'They had all sorts. Buckles with belts on. They were the top scuttlers of Salford ... They'd come up and have a go at Pendleton. Meet 'em on Broad Street.' By the 1970s, softened by the passage of time, such stories were often told with a chuckle.

During the early decades of the century, parents had used the legend of the scuttlers to keep children from straying too far from home. Mrs Tierney was born in the Adelphi in Salford in 1902. To outsiders, the Adelphi remained a district to be entered only with caution. Yet Mrs Tierney's mother used tales of the scuttlers to warn her against crossing Blackfriars Road into Greengate. 'Don't go into Greengate,' she would say, 'because of the scuttlers.' These cautionary tales were still being invoked by parents a generation after scuttling had disappeared. Mrs Phillips, who grew up in the respectable Salford suburb of Seedley during the 1920s, recalled her own mother's warnings quite vividly: 'Don't go down Hanky Park,' her mother used to say. 'The scuttlers will get you.'

Acknowledgements

This book has been long in the making. An early phase of the research (1994–6) was funded by the Economic and Social Research Council as part of a research programme on 'Crime and Social Order', award no. L210252006. Geoff Pearson and the late Ian Taylor provided fantastic support.

The bulk of the research was undertaken in Manchester Central Library and Salford Local History Library, and I am much indebted to the staff of both for their assistance. I am especially grateful to David Taylor and Tim Ashworth for sharing their expertise and enthusiasm with me over many years. I am grateful, too, for the assistance of staff at the British Library Newspaper Library, Greater Manchester Record Office, Lancashire Record Office, the National Archives, the Qualidata Archive at the University of Essex, Salford City Archives, Staffordshire Record Office and Tameside Local Studies and Archives Centre.

John Davies of Salford Magistrates' Court granted access to the nineteenth-century registers of Salford Police Court, and Claire Langhamer made a meticulous job of entering a sample of the records into a database. My thanks to them both. Duncan Broady of the Greater Manchester Police Museum has provided a good deal of practical assistance, and took time out to show me what a billycock hat looks like. Leslie Holmes of Salford Lads' Club likewise provided much help and support.

Sandra Mather of the University of Liverpool drew the map of scuttling gangs in the early 1890s, whilst Ian Qualtrough helped in the preparation of the illustrations. I am deeply grateful to them both.

I have discussed the scuttlers many times with my fellow historians of crime over the years and owe a lot to their constructive engagement. Special thanks go to John Archer, who has generously swapped references and ideas for more than a decade. David Moore and Philip Gooderson shared findings of their own research on the gangs of Manchester, and Bill Williams kindly passed on references to scuttling in Bradford and pointed me to the cartoon in *Spy*. Helen Archer and Carol Baker both read sections of the book in draft. I am grateful for their feedback.

Mike Duff and Robert Brady guided me on the geography of north and east Manchester respectively. Mike's encouragement at a difficult stage in the writing meant more than he realised. This book is dedicated to him, with thanks.

I am grateful to all the people who have shared their family stories of the scuttlers with me. Particular thanks are due to Harry Beesley, Gladys Chorley, the late Gilbert Owen and Mrs E. Phillips. Brenda White kindly allowed me to read the unpublished memoirs of S. P. Ford.

I am especially grateful to the Willan family of Ancoats for supplying me with the postscript to Chapter 15. It has been a pleasure to meet Mrs Bertha Towey (*née* Willan), Billy Willan's niece.

Peter Walsh has been a model editor in matters of both substance and style.

My nephews, Sam and Josh, have been the source of much welcome distraction. And thanks to my mates, not least for all the nights in the King's Arms and the Lamp Oil. You kept me going – cheers.

Most of all, I want to thank Selina Todd. Her support – emotional, intellectual, and practical – has been immense.

Notes

Most of the material in this book was gathered from the extensive reports on scuttling in local newspapers. Heavy use has been made of the *Manchester City News*, *Manchester Courier*, *Manchester Evening News*, *Manchester Guardian*, *Manchester Weekly Times*, *Salford Chronicle*, *Salford County Telephone*, *Salford Reporter*, *Salford Weekly News* and *Gorton Reporter*. I have also drawn upon a number of satirical magazines published in Manchester between the 1860s and 1890s, notably the *City Jackdaw*, *City Lantern*, *Free Lance*, *Shadow* and *Spy*. Details of cases tried at the Quarter Sessions or Assizes have been checked against calendars and depositions held at the National Archives in London, Manchester City Archives and Salford City Archives. Further information was gleaned from the registers of the Salford Police Court (held at Salford Magistrates' Court), H. M. Prison Manchester, Strangeways (now held at Manchester City Archives) and H. M. Prison Stafford (held at Staffordshire Record Office).

The following notes identify key sources of background information. Full titles of books and essays are given in the bibliography.

Chapter 1

Angus Reach's account of 'smoky, dingy' Manchester is taken from *Manchester and the Textile Districts*, p. 3. For the well-heeled lady's visitor's description of Ancoats, see the *Manchester City News*, 3 November 1888. 'Hard labour' in nineteenth-century gaols is described by Philip Priestley, *Victorian Prison Lives*, chapter 6; for the use of the treadwheel at Stafford, see pp. 127-8. Alexander

Devine's account of scuttling was originally published in the *Manchester Guardian*, 5 September 1890. It was reprinted shortly afterwards as a pamphlet entitled *Scuttlers and Scuttling: Their Prevention and Cure*. My account of Devine's work with young people in Manchester is drawn from Frank Whitbourn, *Lex*. On the building of the Police and Sessions Courts in Minshull Street, see Parkinson-Bailey, *Manchester*, pp. 115-16. The description of 'penny dreadfuls' is taken from John Springhall, *Coming of Age*, pp. 128-9. The interview with four Ancoats scuttlers by the 'Wanderer in the Slums' was published in the *Manchester Guardian*, 5 February 1898. On the scuttler's notoriety and the staging of fights 'by appointment', see Robert Roberts, *The Classic Slum*, pp. 123-4.

Chapter 2

De Tocqueville's assessment of Manchester is taken from Kidd, *Manchester*, p. 38. The phrase 'shock city' was used by Briggs, *Victorian Cities*, p. 96. On pollution and noise, see Mosley, *Chimney of the World*, pp. 4, 18, 23-8, 29-31, 78-83; Lanigan, 'Thy Kingdom Did Come', pp. 96-8. For Engels' account of drunkenness in the city, see *Condition of the Working Class in England*, p. 157. Statistical information on licensed premises during the 1840s is provided by Kidd, *Manchester*, p. 52. Reach's descriptions of weekends in the city are taken from *Manchester and the Textile Districts*, pp. 57-8, 61-2. Extensive use is made in this chapter of the Manchester and Salford Temperance Society's *Statistical Report of Sunday Public Tippling in Manchester*, pp. 1-8. Engels' description of 'Little Ireland' appears in *Condition of the Working Class in England*, p. 93. On Gaythorn, see *Criminal Manchester*, pp. 15-17. On licensed premises and arrests for drunkenness in 1873 see the first report of the *Select Committee on Intemperance* (1877), p. 335. For an illustration of 'the shortest way out of Manchester', see Roberts, *Classic Slum*, p. 98. The description of a visit to a Deansgate den appeared in the *Free Lance*, 17 April 1869. On the precocious independence of Manchester youth, see Shone, 'The Ancoats Rough', and Weinberger, 'Policing juveniles'. The Lang's music hall disaster was reported by the *Manchester Courier*, 1 August 1868. On Shudehill, see Davies, 'Saturday night markets'.

For accounts of the promenades on Stretford Road and Oldham Street, see the *Free Lance*, 6 November 1869, 6 August 1870 and the *City Lantern*, 6 August 1875. 'Bonneting' is discussed by Archer, 'Men behaving badly', p. 48. Jewish settlement in Red Bank is described in Williams, *Making of Manchester Jewry*, chapter 11. The hostile response in the local press is examined in Williams, 'Anti-Semitism of tolerance'. For a report on the 'Jersey Street Outrage' and the subsequent trial at the South Lancashire Assizes, see the *Manchester Guardian*, 8 December 1866.

Chapter 3
For Reach's account of Angel Meadow, see *Manchester and the Textile Districts*, pp. 53-7. The descriptions of Angel Meadow in the 1850s and 1860s are taken from the *Manchester Guardian*, 20 April 1865, *Manchester Weekly Times*, 24 November 1866, and Redfern, 'Journey from Withy Grove to Newtown', pp. 122-36. Redfern described the fight between 'Bacup Billy' and 'Stumpy'. On Fenianism, the 'Manchester Martyrs' and the wider culture of anti-Irishness in Victorian society, see MacRaild, *Irish Migrants in Modern Britain*, pp. 138-42, 155-84. For the Manchester detective's account of Angel Meadow in 1869, see the *Sphinx*, 30 October 1869. The exchange between Superintendent Godby of the City of Manchester Police and magistrate Charles Rickards on the subject of scuttling was reported in the *Manchester City News*, 28 October 1871. The *Free Lance*'s commentary on the 'Rochdale Road War' was also published on 28 October 1871. For the annual report on Belle Vue gaol, see the *Manchester Weekly Times*, 6 January 1872. My account of the Manchester press is taken from Kidd, *Manchester*, p. 137. Charles Rickards' outburst on the propensity for violence among Manchester's Irish population was reported in the *Manchester Courier*, 3 July 1872. The Irish tradition of 'faction fighting' is analysed by Conley, 'Agreeable recreation of fighting', p. 60. Henri Misson's remark on the Englishman's love of fighting is discussed by Langford, *Englishness Identified*, p. 137. The interview with Gilbert Owen was conducted by the author. Bob Heald described his career as a prize-fighter in an interview with the *Salford Reporter*, 20 June

1896. For a report of his fight with Bill Preston, see the *Preston Chronicle*, 15 June 1839. The police action against prize-fighting at Throstle Nest is noted in the Salford Watch Committee minutes, 12 October 1863. Jerome Caminada described prize-fighting in Manchester in *Twenty-five years of Detective Life*, p. 17. James Bury's history of scuttling was published in the *Manchester City News*, 13 December 1879. On the etymology of the term, see Rowley, 'Glossarial notes', p. 48. For Charles Gordon's comment on the 'poor scuttlers', see Gordon, *Letters*, pp. 22-3.

Chapter 4
For Engels' account of the slums of Salford, see *Condition of the Working Class in England*, pp. 95-6. Wood's description of Queen Street is taken from his *History of Salford*, p. 7. The description of pugilistic encounters in Greengate and Broughton Road appeared in the *Sphinx*, 19 June 1869.

Chapter 5
On garrotting, see Pearson, *Hooligan*, pp. 128-46; and Emsley, *Hard Men*, pp. 15-17. For the Manchester convict's account of a flogging, see *Criminal Manchester*, pp. 17-19. The lessons from the Leeds assizes of 1863 were discussed more than thirty years later in the *Glasgow Herald*, 21 August 1906. On the 'Tithebarn Street Outrage' of 1874, see MacIlwee, *Gangs of Liverpool*, chapter 1. The murder of P.C. Lines in Birmingham the following year and subsequent trial were reported by *The Times*, 10-13 July 1875. The epidemic of brutality in Manchester was decried by the *Manchester City News*, 19 September 1874. The inquiry established by Disraeli's government the following month led to the publication of a volume of *Reports to the Secretary of State for the Home Department on the State of the Law Relating to Brutal Assaults, & c.* (London, 1875). The findings are discussed in Woods' essay on 'Community violence'. On the development of Gorton and Openshaw, see Kidd, *Manchester*, pp. 111, 122. Sam Kirkham's reminiscences of Gorton in the 1870s were published in the *Gorton and Openshaw Reporter*, 12 December 1931. British responses to the 'Bulgarian Atrocities' are analysed by Cunningham,

Challenge of Democracy, p. 115-16. William Housman Higgin was profiled by Parry, *What the Judge Saw*, chapter 6.

Chapter 6
The indictment of 'Rowdy Salford' appeared in the *City Jackdaw*, 25 August 1876. For profiles of Sir John Iles Mantell, see the memorial notice in the *Manchester Guardian*, 19 July 1893 and the *Manchester City News*, 16 January 1926. On the case of Henry Bennett, see the *Free Lance*, 14 January 1876. The tirade against indecency on the Crescent was published by the *Manchester Courier*, 7 October 1869. On juvenile reformatories and industrial schools, see Radzinowicz and Hood, *History of English Criminal Law, vol. 5*, chapter 7, and Jolly, 'Origins of the Manchester and Salford Reformatory'.

Chapter 7
The label 'Professor of Riot and Disorder' was coined by the *Free Lance*, 27 April 1877.

Chapter 8
On the relative strength of the police forces of Manchester and Salford, see Hewitt, *History of Policing in Manchester*, p. 86 and Wood, *History of Salford*, p. 16. For Caminada's account of Deansgate around 1870, see his *Twenty-five Years of Detective Life*, p. 16. For the account of a Saturday night in Goulden Street police station, see the *Manchester City News*, 14 November 1885. The attack on a police station in Ancoats during the 1840s is described by Storch, 'Plague of the blue locusts', pp. 73-4. For Caminada's recollections of his own tangles with scuttlers, see *Twenty-five Years of Detective Life, vol. 2*, pp. 404-6. Clock Alley was the subject of a feature in the *Manchester Guardian*, 29 May 1891. The description of 'pitch and toss' is taken from Bean, *Sheffield Gang Wars*, p. 7. On the trial of James Farrer, see *The Times*, 5 December 1873.

Chapter 9
On economic downturn of the mid-1880s, see Pelling, *Modern Britain*, pp. 12-14. Events in London in February 1886 and the pervasive sense of urban crisis are discussed by Stedman Jones,

Outcast London, and Mayne, *Imagined Slum*. Charitable endeavours in Manchester are described by Kidd, *Manchester*, pp. 150-53. Scott's findings were published as 'The condition and occupations of the people of Manchester and Salford'. Housing conditions in Bengal Street and the surrounding districts of Ancoats are described in Hewitt, *Emergence of Stability in the Industrial City*, p. 63; Ransome, 'Where consumption is bred', pp. 88-90; and Roberts, 'Residential development of Ancoats', pp. 19-20. The Medical Officer of Health's report for 1884 was cited by Ransome. On the building of the Assize Courts, see Parkinson-Bailey, *Manchester*, pp. 100-102. Justices Day and Wills are both profiled in the *New Dictionary of National Biography*. For a fuller portrait of 'Judgement' Day, see the biography by his son, *John C. F. S. Day*.

Chapter 10

On housing conditions in 'Outcast Salford' and municipal responses in 1889, see the *County Telephone*, 11 May, 2 November and 23 November 1889. Statistical data on infant mortality and population density are taken from Greenall, *Making of Victorian Salford*, pp. 171-2, 366. On prostitution, see Mercer, 'Conditions of life in Angel Meadow', pp. 172-3. A short biographical sketch of Joseph Makinson was published in the *Manchester Courier*, 25 January 1911. A more detailed, unattributed portrait depicting his relationship with Susan Wilson is held in the collection of biographical cuttings in Manchester Central Library.

Chapter 11

For a profile of Henry West, see Parry, *What the Judge Saw*, chapter 6. On the 'High Rippers' of Liverpool, see Sindall, *Street Violence in the Nineteenth Century*, pp. 66-71; and MacIlwee, *Gangs of Liverpool*, chapters 12-15. My account of the rampage through the streets off Scotland Road is based on the report in the *Liverpool Daily Post*, 21 May 1887.

Chapter 12

Superintendent James Bent described the struggle to subdue the scuttlers of the eastern townships in *Criminal Life*, pp. 223-6.

Chapter 13

For a survey of contemporary debates on corporal punishment, see Radzinowicz and Hood, *History of English Criminal Law, vol. 5*, chapter 21. On the pubs of Hanky Park, see Richardson and Flynn, *Salford's Pubs, vol. 1*. On 'Buffalo Bill's Wild West' show, see Rydell and Kroes, *Buffalo Bill in Bologna*. The visit to Salford is described on the BBC Manchester website: http://www.bbc.co.uk/manchester. The description of the Pendleton pit is taken from Eddie Little, 'James Connolly in Salford', http://www.wcml.org.uk/people/jamesc1.htm. The appointment of Joseph Maghull Yates as the first Recorder of Salford was reported by the *Manchester Guardian*, 30 August 1889. For the Manchester Art Museum, see Harrison, 'Art and philanthropy'. On Hulme, see Reach, *Manchester and the Textile Districts*, pp. 3-4; Kidd, *Manchester*, p. 40, 128; Russell, *Social Problems of the North*, p. 9. Thomas Thornhill Shann's description of the district was reported in the Manchester magazine *Faces and Places*, 16 (1905), p. 281. The recollections of William Luby were published in Burnett, *Useful Toil*, pp. 89-99. On prize-fighting and the advent of Queensberry Rules, see Russel Gray, 'For whom the bell tolled'. For a portrait of Charles Lister, see the memorial notice published in the *Manchester Guardian*, 6 November 1894. The meeting between the Home Secretary, Henry Matthews, and the civic deputation from Manchester and Salford was reported in *The Times*, 13 December 1890. Matthews is profiled in the *New Dictionary of National Biography*. On Francis Headlam, see the *Free Lance*, 14 January 1876; and *Spy*, 1 April 1893.

Chapter 14

The Hope Street district is vividly brought to life in Robert Roberts' books *The Classic Slum* and *A Ragged Schooling*. For Engels' description of the district in the 1840s, see Engels, *Condition of the Working Class in England*, pp. 95-6. On the Ordsall district, see Wood, *History of Salford*, pp. 19-23 and Toole, *Fighting through Life*. The state of Providence Street – the 'She Battery' – was described by the *County Telephone*, 4 January 1890. The mutiny on the *Akbar* was reported in *The Times*, 27 September; 4 October 1887.

Chapter 15
For Jerome Caminada's recollections of his dealings with the Willans, see *Twenty-five Years of Detective Life, vol. 2*, pp. 338-9. On trends in criminal statistics, see Gatrell, 'Decline of theft and violence', pp. 281-3. Henry West's comments on the diminution of crime in Manchester were reported in the *Manchester City News*, 13 October 1888. The postscript to this chapter was kindly supplied by Terry Towey.

Chapter 16
For a fuller discussion of the themes covered in this chapter, see Davies, 'These viragoes are no less cruel than the lads'. The fight between two girls in Greengate was described in the *Sphinx*, 19 June 1869.

Chapter 17
The 'career' of John Joseph Hillier is analysed in Davies, 'Youth gangs, masculinity and violence'. He was recalled by his alias 'Red Elliott' by Arthur Collier in an interview for a project on 'Family Life and Work Experience' headed by Professor Paul Thompson. The transcript is held in the Qualidata archive at the University of Essex (tape no. 90). I am grateful to David Moore for alerting me to this reference, and to Professor Thompson for his permission to consult the tape. 'Collier' is a pseudonym. On the Casino music hall, see Kidd, *Manchester*, p. 129; and Toole, *Fighting through Life*, p. 2. The description of a typical music hall programme is taken from the *Manchester City News*, 31 October 1908. For a report on the industrial training ship *Formidable*, see *The Times*, 15 March 1890.

Chapter 18
On Gaythorn, see *Criminal Manchester*.

Chapter 19
On local responses to the rejection of Manchester volunteers to fight in the South African ('Boer') War, see Heggie, 'Lies, damn lies, and Manchester's recruiting statistics.' The course of the

conflict is described by Cunningham, *Challenge of Democracy*, p. 143. On slum clearance in Bengal Street, see Roberts, 'Residential development of Ancoats', pp. 24-5. The survey of 'Life in the Adelphi' was published in the *Salford Reporter*, 12 October 1901. On the origins and growth of the Adelphi Lads' Club, see Hill, *Story of Adelphi*. The growth of the lads' club movement in Manchester and Salford is described in Russell and Rigby, *Working Lads' Clubs*. On the contribution of Alexander Devine, see Whitbourn, *Lex*. 'Manly, plucky fellows, following Christ' is taken from *The Chronicle: A Monthly Record of the Hulme and Chorlton-on-Medlock Lads' Club and Gymnasium*, no. 1 (November 1887), p. 1. On nineteenth-century conceptions of manliness, including 'muscular Christianity', see Mangan and Walvin (eds), *Manliness and Morality*. On the life and work of Charles Russell, see Gibbon, 'C. E. B. Russell'. For a broader discussion of 'slumming' in late-Victorian England, see Koven, *Slumming*. Russell's articles for the *Manchester Guardian* were published in one volume in 1905 as *Manchester Boys*. For his account of scuttling, see pp. 51-55; on football, see pp. 61-5; on the evils of popular melodrama, see p. 94. His article on 'The scuttler and the ike' was originally published in the *Guardian* on 16 November 1904. For recollections of the St James's Theatre and the Prince of Wales (the 'Blood Tub'), see Lanigan, 'Thy Kingdom Did Come', pp. 14-15; Roberts, *Classic Slum*, p. 116; Toole, *Fighting through Life*, p. 35. The unpublished memoirs of S. P. Ford are entitled 'Night and Day'. For the case of John Ford, see the *Manchester Weekly Times*, 17, 24 August 1889. On the raid at the Napoleon III beerhouse in Miles Platting, see the *Manchester Courier*, 24 June 1896, and the *Manchester Guardian*, 11 September 1896. Caminada's boast that he had helped to close 400 low pubs and beerhouses was made in *Twenty-five Years of Detective Life*, p. 17. For his own account of raid on the Napoleon III, see *Twenty-five Years of Detective Life, vol. 2*, pp. 321-4. For the career of Robert Peacock and the scandal on 'D' Division in 1897, see Hewitt, *History of Policing in Manchester*, pp. 96-101, 104-5. Charles Russell's allegation that the policing of lads in districts such as Ancoats had become over-zealous was published by the *Manchester Guardian*,

16 September 1903. For the growth of the cinema in Manchester and Salford, see Davies, *Leisure, Gender and Poverty*. For Robert Roberts' accounts of the Hope Street scuttlers, see *Classic Slum*, p. 123; *Ragged Schooling*, p. 102. Gladys Chorley wrote to the author in response to a feature on scuttling gangs in the Salford 'Talking News for the Blind'. Mrs Tierney was interviewed by a researcher from the Manchester Studies unit at the former Manchester Polytechnic (now Manchester Metropolitan University). The interview is held in the Manchester Studies Tape Collection, housed at Tameside Local Studies and Archives Centre (tape no. 816). 'Tierney' is a pseudonym. The interviews with Harry Beesley and Mrs E. Phillips were conducted by the author.

Bibliography

Printed works

John Archer, '"Men behaving badly"? Masculinity and the uses of violence, 1850–1900' in Shani D'Cruze (ed.), *Everyday Violence in Britain, 1850–1950* (Longman, 2000).

Peter Bailey, *Leisure and Class in Victorian England: Rational Recreation and the Contest for Control, 1830–1885* (Routledge & Kegan Paul, 1978).

J. P. Bean [pseud.], *The Sheffield Gang Wars* (D & D Publications, 1981).

James Bent, *Criminal Life: Reminiscences of Forty-two Years as a Police Officer* (John Heywood, 1891).

Michael R. Booth, *English Melodrama* (Herbert Jenkins, 1965).

Asa Briggs, *Victorian Cities* (Penguin, 1968).

Duncan Broady and Dave Tetlow, *Law and Order in Manchester* (Tempus, 2005).

John Burnett (ed.), *Destiny Obscure: Autobiographies of Childhood, Education and Family from the 1820s to the 1920s* (Allen Lane, 1982).

John Burnett (ed.), *Useful Toil: Autobiographies of Working People from the 1820s to the 1920s* (Penguin, 1984).

W. Burnett-Tracy and W. T. Pike, *Manchester and Salford at the Close of the Nineteenth Century: Contemporary Biographies* (W. T. Pike & Co., 1901).

Jerome Caminada, *Twenty-five Years of Detective Life* (John Heywood, 1895)

Jerome Caminada, *Twenty-five Years of Detective Life, vol. 2* (Jerome Caminada, 1901)

Carolyn Conley, 'The agreeable recreation of fighting', *Journal of Social History*, 33, 1 (1999).

Criminal Manchester (G. Renshaw, 1874). [Reprinted from the *Manchester Evening News*.]

Hugh Cunningham, *The Challenge of Democracy: Britain, 1832–1918* (Longman, 2001).

Andrew Davies, *Leisure, Gender and Poverty: Working-class Culture in Salford and Manchester, 1900–1939* (Open University Press, 1992).

Andrew Davies, 'Saturday night markets in Manchester and Salford, 1840–1939', *Manchester Region History Review*, 1, 2 (1987).

Andrew Davies, '"These viragoes are no less cruel than the lads": young women, gangs and violence in late Victorian Manchester and Salford', *British Journal of Criminology*, 39, 1 (1999).

Andrew Davies, 'Youth gangs, masculinity and violence in late Victorian Manchester and Salford', *Journal of Social History*, 32, 2 (1998).

A. F. Day, *John C. F. S. Day: His Forbears and Himself: A Biographical Study by One of His Sons* (Heath, Cranton, 1916).

Richard Dennis, *English Industrial Cities of the Nineteenth Century: A Social Geography* (Cambridge University Press, 1986).

Alexander Devine, *Scuttlers and Scuttling: Their Prevention and Cure* (*Manchester Guardian*, 1890).

Clive Emsley, *Crime and Society in England, 1750–1900* (Pearson Longman, 2005).

Clive Emsley, *Hard Men: Violence in England Since 1750* (Hambledon and London, 2005).

Frederick Engels, *The Condition of the Working Class in England* (Panther, 1969). [First published in 1845.]

Steven Fielding, *Class and Ethnicity: Irish Catholics in England, 1880–1939* (Open University Press, 1993).

William James Forsythe, *The Reform of Prisoners, 1830–1900* (Croom Helm, 1987).

V. A. C. Gatrell, 'The decline of theft and violence in Victorian and Edwardian England' in V. A. C. Gatrell, Bruce Lenman and Geoffrey Parker (eds), *Crime and The Law: The Social History of Crime in Western Europe Since 1500* (Europa, 1980).

F. P. Gibbon, 'C. E. B. Russell, 1866–1917' in R. S. Forman (ed.), *Great Christians* (Ivor Nicholson and Watson, 1933).

Philip Gooderson, 'Terror on the streets of late-Victorian Salford and Manchester', *Manchester Region History Review*, 11 (1997).

R. L. Greenall, *The Making of Victorian Salford* (Carnegie, 2000).

M. Harrison, 'Art and philanthropy: T. C. Horsfall and the Manchester Art Museum' in A. J. Kidd and K. W. Roberts (eds), *City, Class and Culture: Studies of Cultural Production and Social Policy in Victorian Manchester* (Manchester University Press, 1985).

Dave Haslam, *Manchester, England: The Story of the Pop Cult City* (Fourth Estate, 2000).

Vanessa Heggie, 'Lies, damn lies, and Manchester's recruiting statistics: degeneration as an "urban legend" in Victorian and Edwardian Britain', *Journal of the History of Medicine*, 63, 2 (2008).

Eric J. Hewitt, *A History of Policing in Manchester* (E. J. Morton, 1979).

Martin Hewitt, *The Emergence of Stability in the Industrial City: Manchester, 1832–67* (Scolar Press, 1996).

Henry Hill, *The Story of Adelphi: Sixty Years History of the Adelphi Lads' Club, 1888–1948* (Adelphi Lads' Club, 1949).

Stephen Humphries, *Hooligans or Rebels? An Oral History of Working-class Childhood and Youth, 1889–1939* (Basil Blackwell, 1981).

Steve Humphries, *A Secret World of Sex. Forbidden Fruit: The British Experience, 1900–1950* (Sidgwick & Jackson, 1988).

Sandra Jolly, 'The origins of the Manchester and Salford Reformatory for Juvenile Criminals, 1853–1860', *Manchester Region History Review*, 15 (2001).

David Jones, *Crime, Protest, Community and Police in Nineteenth-century Britain* (Routledge & Kegan Paul, 1982).

Alan Kidd, *Manchester* (Ryburn, 1993).

A. J. Kidd and K. W. Roberts (eds), *City, Class and Culture: Studies of Cultural Production and Social Policy in Victorian Manchester* (Manchester University Press, 1985).

Seth Koven, *Slumming: Sexual and Social Politics in Victorian London* (Princeton University Press, 2004).

Paul Langford, *Englishness Identified: Manners and Character, 1650–1850* (Oxford University Press, 2000).

Michael MacIlwee, *The Gangs of Liverpool* (Milo, 2006).

Donald M. MacRaild, *Irish Migrants in Modern Britain, 1750–1922* (Macmillan, 1999).

Manchester and Salford Temperance Society, *Statistical Report of Sunday Tippling in Manchester* (Manchester and Salford Temperance Society, n.d. [William Tweedie, 1854]).

J. A. Mangan and James Walvin (eds), *Manliness and Morality: Middle-class Masculinity in Britain and America, 1800–1940* (Manchester University Press, 1987).

Alan Mayne, *The Imagined Slum: Newspaper Representation in Three Cities, 1870–1914* (Leicester University Press, 1993).

Rev. J. E. Mercer, 'The conditions of life in Angel Meadow', *Transactions of the Manchester Statistical Society* (1896–7).

Gary S. Messinger, *Manchester in the Victorian Age: The Half-known City* (Manchester University Press, 1985).

Stephen Mosley, *The Chimney of the World: A History of Smoke Pollution in Victorian and Edwardian Manchester* (White Horse Press, 2001).

John J. Parkinson-Bailey, *Manchester: An Architectural History* (Manchester University Press, 2000).

Edward Abbott Parry, *What The Judge Saw: Being Twenty-five Years in Manchester by One Who Has Done It* (Smith, Elder & Co., 1912).

Geoffrey Pearson, *Hooligan: A History of Respectable Fears* (Macmillan, 1983).

Henry Pelling, *Modern Britain, 1855–1955* (Cardinal, 1974).

Philip Priestley, *Victorian Prison Lives: English Prison Biography, 1830–1914* (Pimlico, 1999).

Sir Leon Radzinowicz and Roger Hood, *A History of English*

Criminal Law and its Administration from 1750, vol. 5: The Emergence of Penal Policy (Stevens, 1986).

Arthur Ransome, 'Where consumption is bred in Manchester and Salford', *The Health Journal: A Medium for the Popular Treatment of Sanitary and Other Social Topics*, 5, 5 (1887).

Angus Bethune Reach, *Manchester and the Textile Districts in 1849* (Helmshore Local History Society, 1972). [Edited by C. Aspin. Reports first published in the *Morning Chronicle* in 1849.]

B. A. Redfern, 'A journey from Withy Grove to Newtown' in George Milner (ed.), *Selections from 'Odds and Ends': A Manuscript Magazine Issued by the St Paul's Literary and Educational Society, vol. 1* (St Paul's Literary and Educational Society, 1875).

Neil Richardson, *The Old Pubs of Ancoats* (Neil Richardson, 1987).

Neil Richardson and Tony Flynn, *Salford's Pubs, vol. 1* (Neil Richardson and Tony Flynn, 1978).

Jacqueline Roberts, 'The residential development of Ancoats', *Manchester Region History Review*, 7 (1993).

Robert Roberts, *The Classic Slum: Salford Life in the First Quarter of the Century* (Manchester, 1971).

Robert Roberts, *A Ragged Schooling: Growing Up in the Classic Slum* (Manchester, 1976).

C. Rowley, 'Glossarial notes on the slang of boyhood' in George Milner (ed.), *Selections from 'Odds and Ends': A Manuscript Magazine Issued by the St Paul's Literary and Educational Society, vol. 1* (St Paul's Literary and Educational Society, 1875).

W. Russel Gray, 'For whom the bell tolled: the decline of British prize fighting in the Victorian era', *Journal of Popular Culture*, 21, 2 (1987).

Charles E. B. Russell, *Manchester Boys: Sketches of Manchester Lads at Work and Play* (Manchester University Press, 1905).

Charles E. B. Russell, *Social Problems of the North* (Mowbray, 1914).

Charles E. B. Russell and Lilian M. Rigby, *Working Lads' Clubs* (Macmillan, 1908).

Robert W. Rydell and Rob Kroes, *Buffalo Bill in Bologna: The Americanization of the World, 1869–1922* (University of Chicago Press, 2005).

Fred Scott, 'The condition and occupations of the people of Manchester and Salford', *Transactions of the Manchester Statistical Society* (1888–9).

Rob Sindall, *Street Violence in the Nineteenth Century: Media Panic or Real Danger?* (Leicester University Press, 1990).

John Springhall, *Coming of Age: Adolescence in Britain, 1860–1960* (Gill and Macmillan, 1986).

Gareth Stedman Jones, *Outcast London: A Study in the Relationship Between Classes in Victorian Society* (Penguin, 1984).

Robert D. Storch, 'The plague of the blue locusts: police reform and popular resistance in Northern England, 1840–1857', *International Review of Social History*, 20 (1975).

Joe Toole, *Fighting through Life* (Rich & Cowan, 1935).

Barbara Weinberger, 'Policing juveniles: delinquency in late nineteenth and early twentieth century Manchester', *Criminal Justice History*, 14 (1993).

Frank Whitbourn, *Lex: Being the Biography of Alexander Devine, Founder of Clayesmore School* (Longmans, Green & Co., 1937).

Bill Williams, 'The anti-Semitism of tolerance: middle-class Manchester and the Jews 1870–1900' in A. J. Kidd and K. W. Roberts (eds), *City, Class and Culture: Studies of Cultural Production and Social Policy in Victorian Manchester* (Manchester University Press, 1985).

Bill Williams, *The Making of Manchester Jewry, 1840–1875* (Manchester, 1976).

W. H. Wood, *The History of Salford* (W. H. Wood, 1890).

David Woods, 'Community violence' in John Benson (ed.), *The Working Class in England, 1875–1914* (Croom Helm, 1985).

Manuscripts

S. P. Ford, 'Night and Day' (n.d.), unpublished memoir in the possession of Mrs Brenda White, Glasgow.

Jack Lanigan, 'Thy Kingdom Did Come' (n.d.), unpublished memoir held at Brunel University Library.

BIBLIOGRAPHY

Geoffrey Shone, 'The Ancoats Rough', 'Odds and Ends', manuscript magazine of the St Paul's Literary and Educational
Society, Bennett Street Sunday School, Manchester (1882),
held at Manchester City Archives.

Index of Gangs

Index of Names

Dwyer, Thomas, 79
Dyer, Jacky, 248, 251-3

Edwards, Esther, 112
Egerton, Lord, 339
Elliott, Alf, 158-9
Elliott, John, 200
Elvidge, Arthur, Constable,
    Manchester City Police,
    198
Engels, Friedrich, 26-7, 29,
    58-9, 235
Evans, George, 163

Fallon, John, 324-6
Farrer, James, 133-6
Finch, Alf, 148
Finn, Charles, 76
Fisher, Bobby, 147, 154-6
Fitzgerald, Sarah Ellen, 289-90
Fitzpatrick, Joe, 178-9
Fitzsimons, James, Lord
    Mayor of Manchester, 359
Flanagan, Annie, 154, 156
Flanagan, Maggie, 198
Flattely, John, 200
Fleming, Peter, 331-2
Fleming, Teddy, 259, 261-3,
    266, 270
Fletcher, Mary, 239
Flowers, Edwin, Sergeant,
    Manchester City Police,
    148-50

Flynn, Catherine, 97
Foley, Jimmy, 221, 284-5
Folkes, Frederick Hyde, 172
Foard, James, 253
Ford, John, Harpurhey
    scuttler, 11
Ford, John, Hulme scuttler,
    348
Ford, S. P., Constable,
    Manchester City Police,
    347-8
Forrest, John, 86-7
Fowler, William, 298
Fulton, John, 209

Gaffney, William, 213
Gallagher, Jimmy, 214
Garforth, Agnes, 221, 285-6
Garner, Henry, Chief
    Inspector, Manchester
    City Police, 47
Gerrard, Jimmy, 76-7
Gibbons, John, 202
Gibson, James, 110
Gilbert, John, 206, 208
Gilbert, Samuel, Constable,
    Manchester City Police,
    82
Gilmore, Joseph, Constable,
    Salford Borough Police,
    138-9
Glass, Theresa, 166-7, 172
Gleaves, John, 87